TESTED
NEWSPAPER PROMOTION

Frank W. Rucker

Associate Professor of Journalism at the University
of Missouri and Former Co-publisher of the
Independence, Mo., **Examiner**

Bert Stolpe

Publisher of the Glendora, Calif., **Press** and Azusa,
Calif., **Herald,** and Former Promotion Manager of
the Des Moines, Iowa, **Register** and **Tribune**

The Iowa State University Press, *Ames,* Iowa, U.S.A.

070.3
R82t

63999

December, 1968

Library of Congress Catalog Card Number 59-12368

Tested Newspaper Promotion

In this same series:

Newspaper Organization and Management
FRANK W. RUCKER and HERBERT LEE WILLIAMS

Newspaper Circulation; What, Where and How
FRANK W. RUCKER

Dedicated

to

SHARRIE STOLPE,
Daughter of Junior Author

DIANE BUNYAR
Granddaughter of Senior Author

and
aspiring young journalists
throughout the entire free world

Foreword

by
GARDNER COWLES

President, Des Moines, Iowa, *Register* and *Tribune* Company, Cowles Magazines, Inc., and Ft. Pierce, Fla., *News-Tribune;* Chairman, Cowles Broadcasting Company

A good newspaper is far more than a communications medium. It is a community's conscience, its pulse, and its heart.

But a newspaper can fulfill all of its functions most successfully only if the newspaper is itself successful — and for that reason, newspaper promotion in all its phases is a vital subject. This is particularly true today when a strong press and an informed populace are more important than ever before.

Strength enables a newspaper to spend as much as is necessary for superior editorial coverage. Strength enables a newspaper to exercise the kind of leadership every community needs. And strength enables a newspaper to invest in the kind of research that will help increase its usefulness to both readers and advertisers.

Yet strength is an attribute that doesn't come automatically to any medium of communication or to any company. Skillful promotion is required to build a newspaper to its full circulation and advertising potential, and the promotion must be particularly skillful in our present-day economy when competition — both for the readers' time and the advertisers' dollar — is at an all-time high.

Perhaps there was a time when a newspaper could win success simply by being a good newspaper, but certainly that is far from true now. In fact, there are many excellent newspapers today that are far from successful, and even the most successful newspaper publishers know that they have to run very fast all of the time just to stand still. Virtually every newspaper publisher therefore automatically accepts the idea of promotion for his paper.

But with the acceptance of the idea comes a multitude of questions. How much should he spend? What's the best kind of promotion for him? Should he have one centralized promotion department,

or separate staffs promoting editorial, advertising and circulation?
How can he best promote his news coverage, his feature stories, his
sports articles, the women's page, and so on? What avenues can he
explore to increase advertising linage? How can he increase the prestige of his newspaper?

There are, of course, no pat answers to any of these questions.
The right answer depends on city size, on the extent of competition,
and numerous other factors.

But in this book you will find concrete information on how various newspapers — from very small ones to very big ones — have successfully solved assorted promotion problems and capitalized on promotional opportunities.

In assembling this valuable information, the authors (both of whom
are experienced newspaper men themselves) have drawn on the knowledge and experience of more than 100 newspaper publishers and promotion executives — and the ground they cover has almost no limits.

Anyone interested in any phase of newspaper promotion will find
in this book a treasury of information. It can be a "silent partner"
in successful operations. For, in addition to material on general circulation activities, anyone interested in promoting increased circulation also will find "case histories" on specific circulation-building
efforts that have paid off for various newspapers. These efforts run
the gamut from successful get-acquainted offers by mail to successful
selling through carriers or salesmen.

From the standpoint of advertising promotion, here are "100
Tested Ways To Increase Linage," as well as specific information on
increasing general advertising, retail advertising, classified advertising, and advertising in special editions.

In addition, you — as a practicing newspaperman — will find in
this book valuable "thought starters" on promoting a newspaper's personality; on building community good will; and on developing greater
prestige. You also will find ideas for making a newspaper the focal
point for community activity and community progress.

In short, "Tested Newspaper Promotion" is a book of tremendous
value to newspaper publishers, advertising managers, circulation managers, and promotion directors, and also to anyone contemplating a
career on the business side of newspaper publishing. For the teaching of newspaper promotion, an important part of realistic, comprehensive journalism instruction, here is certainly an excellent basic text.

Preface

Promotion should be as much a part of a newspaper's program as covering the news, providing interesting features, serving advertisers and selling subscriptions. It is, indeed, the activity that gives life and service to all other activities and makes secure a newspaper's position with relation to competing media.

Edward L. Bernays, noted public relations consultant, believes that the newspaper of today faces a challenge for the future. "If it is to fulfill its important function to our society," he says, "it must adjust to public need, let the public know its values, and persuade the public."

When the situation is analyzed carefully only one conclusion is forthcoming: A newspaper's responsibility to society as well as to itself is to promote its services *continuously* and *effectively* and to *guard well* its public relations. It must succeed if it is to serve well. It must promote well its services if it is to succeed. This circle of responsibility must be complete if the community is to benefit and the newspaper is to maintain a stable existence.

Recognizing the important part that promotion may play in successful newspaper publishing, the authors of this book point out the avenues through which promotion may be applied in the making of better newspapers and in widening their influence. Discussed herein are the organization and personnel required, effective methods to be employed, and benefits to be derived.

In assembling this material, they acknowledge with deep gratitude the cooperation of more than 100 promotion-minded publishers and newspaper promotion managers. Appreciation is expressed also for leads to valuable material provided by *Editor & Publisher, Publication Management, Publishers' Auxiliary, American Press, National*

Journalist, Quill, Journalism Quarterly, Printer's Ink, Sales Manage-ment, Advertising Age, Mediascope, Western Advertising and *Tide,* and for information supplied by the National Newspaper Promotion Association, International Circulation Managers Association, National Association of Newspaper Representatives, American Newspaper Pub-lishers Association and its Bureau of Advertising, Inland Daily Press Association, Southern Newspaper Publishers Association and other area organizations of newspapermen.

The association brought about through this project, together with the encouragement and assistance received from so many sources, has made it highly pleasant and challenging. We are sincerely appreci-ative for all the valuable aid given.

FRANK W. RUCKER
BERT STOLPE

July, 1960

Contents

PART IV — PROMOTING THE NEWSPAPER'S CIRCULATION

PART V — PROMOTION THROUGH PUBLIC RELATIONS

Illustrations

PART I

Aims and Organization

"Newspapers everywhere,
more than ever before,
recognize the need
of a productive
promotion department
as prices rise
and competition
stiffens."

—WALTER ARONOFF,
Circulation Manager,
Detroit, Mich.,
Times

CHAPTER 1

Promotion

A Major Requirement

THE MAN WHO MAKES a better mouse trap, writes a better book or *publishes a better newspaper* has learned that, amidst the intensive competition of today, it takes more than product quality to have the world beat a path to his door.

Information concerning a product's merits and the general character of the firm which produces it must be disseminated widely, consistently and effectively. Proper contacts must be made with the public to gain and to hold good will. The general obligation of any and all industries is to "tell, tell, tell" and "sell, sell, sell." To do this every modern, alert business has its promotion or public relations department — a division of its organization that gives reputation to the work done in all other departments. At the same time it develops employee morale and gains public endorsement for the institution, its services and products by every ethical and businesslike means.

The newspaper is no exception in this respect. Responsibility rests heavily upon newspapers to promote their services and to maintain right relations with the public mainly for four reasons:

1. Newspapers primarily have an obligation to inform.
2. Newspapers have important services to sell.
3. Newspapers have strong competition to meet.
4. Newspapers must keep themselves financially sound in order to be ethically sound.

Primary Duty Is To Inform

The chief responsibility of newspapers is to give the public accurate and complete information concerning what is going on in the world that directly affects their interests and their general welfare. It does not restrict the information it imparts to any one group, cause or interest. Through its news and advertising columns it keeps families informed of events, situations, products and services.

If the newspaper is short anywhere in its program of disseminating information, it is in the field of giving out facts concerning itself — its organizational setup, its personnel, its policies, its services and its accomplishments for the common good. There is no excuse for such deficiency. There is no reasonable call for modesty in this respect by any newspaper. Any organization that has close contact with the community is obligated to reveal its purposes, operations and accomplishments.

"Promotion is tremendously important even to the smallest weekly," says Paul S. Gauthier, publisher of the Corning, Iowa, *Adams County Free Press* (circulation 3,200, population 2,104). "This is especially true in this age of fast-moving events and constantly changing methods of merchandising, public relations and advertising."

In 1931 representatives of several outstanding American newspapers decided that some concerted effort should be made through a common organization to make promotion a more important part of newspaper operation. They met in Chicago at the call of George Bennayan of the New York *World* and formed the National Newspaper Promotion Association. Bennayan was elected its first president and provided all the funds needed for the organization's first year. The association grew in membership and in influence. Today it is one of the major organizations of newspapermen, composed mainly of promotion managers of the larger newspapers but welcoming always into membership the representatives of smaller newspapers. It has been a great factor in the making of better newspapers and in acquainting the public with their broad program of service.

A newspaper carries power, prestige and inspiration and has many opportunities to give practical and effective service. No other business gives greater satisfaction to those whom it serves and to those who serve it. And since practical rewards always follow swiftly on the heels of practical service, no other business offers such remarkable possibilities for leadership and progress. This is a story the public should never be allowed to forget.

It Has Services To Sell

The fact that a newspaper offers services that so directly affect individual and public welfare makes still more imperative a well-organized and thorough promotion and public relations program.

Government could not well carry on in a civilized nation without newspapers. It needs facilities for quick contact with its people, and the public needs a medium of reliable information concerning affairs at the city hall, county courthouse, state house and national Capitol.

Business would face difficulties without newspapers to carry advertising to an eager, money-spending public.

Community progress would be thwarted without newspapers to carry news of organization plans and activities. And society in general would have a dull time without news of weddings, births, anniversaries, festivals and parties.

Moral standards would drop and religion would be less forceful without newspapers to expose crime and criminal intent and to encourage churches, schools and social agencies in their community uplift movements.

The newspaper thus helps to raise living standards and to bring employment and business to higher levels. And in addition to these many services, it provides entertainment that makes life more pleasant and information that makes the world more intelligible.

The American press today is infinitely superior to the press of any other era or any other country. It is increasingly less biased and more informative, and never have editors worked so constructively for community betterment. John S. Knight, president of Knight Newspapers, emphasized this characteristic when he said at the 54th Anniversary Convention of the Southern Newspaper Publishers Association:

"Newspapers throughout the country are helping to build better towns and cities by their advocacy of progressive policies. Newspapers can prod a public official into action. They can and do 'audit' government. They can and do 'investigate everything.'" And to this he added:

"Newspapers, and newspapers alone, can perform these public services. Unfettered by government licensing, they are under no restraint except that imposed by the bounds of good taste and responsible journalism."

A newspaper's services are so closely linked with family ties, economic development, community progress, national welfare and world relations that they automatically become the basis of a sound and effective promotion program. There is great opportunity for strong emphasis and convincing presentation. To neglect such an opportunity would be a failure in duty difficult to explain by the standards of sound journalism and public responsibility.

It Has Competition To Meet

The newspaper, like every institution that serves the public, has competition to meet, and it is a competition constantly increasing. For this reason, as well as for those already outlined, it needs effective, scientific promotion and sound public relations.

Any business institution that stands at the top in its field of service constantly draws attack and competition. By its success it challenges others to excel it.

Horse-drawn vehicles for centuries were the common mode of travel, and manufacturers of chariots, wagons, buggies and surreys did a thriving business. Later the steam engine put trains on rails to carry people more rapidly from place to place across the continent. This, however, was followed by the automobile when inventive minds developed the gasoline engine and applied it to transportation. The wagon-makers and the railways had vital competition to contend with and yielded in part to the motor industry, which today has found a rival in air travel. The atomic age has brought travel in space and we may soon be making trips to planets far from the earth. Scientific study and invention constantly are bringing improvements to replace old modes and customs and to enable men to reach far out into new realms of discovery and progress.

Newspapers in the field of communication, just as wagons in the field of transportation, through the years have had their competition to meet. Fortunately, however, they have held their place with better success and thus far have been unsurpassed by rival media.

The period since 1920 has seen the birth of radio, facsimile, television, the news and picture magazines and countless other publications. But in spite of these entrants to the field of communication, the circulation of American newspapers has more than doubled. Today 29,000,000 more newspapers are bought every day than in 1920 — a growth far faster than the national gain in population.

More than 61,000,000 copies of daily newspapers are sold in America every 24 hours — over 57,500,000 in the United States and over 3,500,000 in Canada. Winter and summer these figures stand up, with very few signs of the hot weather slump that hits so many businesses.

The newspaper is a basic medium in the field of advertising. It has continuously held its place at the top of the list of favored media. Today newspapers receive from all advertisers more than 30 per cent of all United States advertising dollars. According to *Printer's Ink*, they carried in 1958 the largest single segment of the advertising dollar:

Newspapers	$3,120,000,000
Magazines	770,000,000
Business Papers	540,000,000
Farm Publications (regional)	34,000,000
Television	1,360,000,000
Radio	616,000,000
Direct Mail	1,560,000,000
Outdoor	191,100,000
Miscellaneous	1,996,900,000[1]

[1]*Printer's Ink*, Feb. 6, 1959, p. 9.

This is a tribute to the indispensable service given by newspapers. It is evidence of the alertness and efficiency of publishers in meeting competition as it has developed. It is testimony to the effectiveness of sound newspaper promotion and public relations.

Although publishers have spent close to $1,000,000,000 since World War II to produce more and better newspapers and better advertising, their work in the field of newspaper promotion is just beginning. Claims being made for radio, outdoor and direct mail advertising captivate many national advertisers. Television, primarily an entertainment vehicle, is a new medium with a fresh story. For this reason, it easily obtains a hearing. Newspapers have a long record of service and it is an old story. It must be told again and again in different ways and through different media. It must be told honestly, constructively and convincingly.

It Must Keep Financially Sound

A reason above all others for promoting the newspaper in every acceptable way is to attract maximum business in order to keep it financially sound. A newspaper must keep itself independent of all alliances, particularly those that may deeply involve it financially. Its moral obligations to readers and advertisers are too great for it to be tempted in any way to lower its standards or lessen its services.

Nothing can replace the newspaper in the daily life of the average American. Just any newspaper will not do. Only the local newspaper with its inimitable reporting of the news and events concerning family, friends and neighbors and its attractive and convincing presentation of offerings at local stores can fill the bill. The newspaper has become an integral part of the daily lives of people everywhere almost to the same degree as the home they live in, the food they eat, the clothes they wear. It is depended upon for guidance in community affairs and for honesty in news and advertising.

A newspaper's worth to its community never is more clearly demonstrated or more firmly realized than when a strike ties up its plant, depriving its readers of their usual source of news and advertising for several days.

The first week of the shutdown of all papers in New York during December, 1958, due to a strike instituted by the Newspaper and Mail Deliverers Union, imposed a great inconvenience on readers and a deprivation of holiday business on New York stores that was little short of disaster. Charged against it were $25,000,000 of advertising and circulation revenue that was lost to newspapers, $5,000,000 in wages lost to newspaper employees, $10,000,000 in retail sales lost to merchants because consumers were deprived of information concerning holiday offerings and $10,000,000 lost to other businesses which depended upon newspaper advertising.

When a strike prevented Detroit newspapers for a time from printing and reaching the homes of subscribers, Detroit newsstands were loaded with papers from Windsor, Toronto, Chicago, Cleveland and New York. Radio and television canceled all network shows to serve communication needs of the area, but on every hand was heard the plaintive cry, "When are we going to get *our* newspaper back?" No other medium has this kind of emotional demand.

The modern publisher is profit-minded not because he wants to be but because he has to be in order to stay in business. He must be free to say what should be said through his newspaper and to do what is best for his community. He should never be in a financial condition where a "squeeze" may be put on him to withhold information or exaggerate or to refrain from attacking crooks in office or evil in any form. As a publisher once remarked, "the penniless newspaper, like a penniless young lady, is more susceptible to an immoral proposition than one well heeled." To be assured of ethical soundness a newspaper should be financially sound.

Constructive promotion and scientific public relations are strong factors in maintaining a safe balance between income and expenditures. This has always been true, but more so today. These are practices that will provide security and yield returns for newspapers of all sizes — from the small weekly in its limited field to the large daily with nationwide distribution.

CHAPTER 2

Areas of Newspaper Promotion

NEWSPAPER PROMOTION mainly is in five areas:

1. Promotion of the press as a power for good in the world.
2. Promotion of the newspaper's services, including advertising, giving the news and delivering the publication promptly and in good condition.
3. Promotion of the newspaper's features.
4. Promotion of good will within the community.
5. Promotion of pleasant and effective working relations within the newspaper organization.

Every aggressive publisher engages in all five types of promotion. He upholds his profession by calling attention to the wide influence of the press and unites his efforts with those of other publishers in promoting better understanding of state, national and world problems. He throws his influence behind movements for safety, educational advancement, better government, general progress, national security and world peace. But a publisher places more emphasis, of course, upon the services he offers those in the newspaper's immediate territory. To them he explains the newspaper's organization, its departments and personnel, its policies and program, its news and features, its service to advertisers. This contributes to reader interest and community good will. He comprehends also the necessity of pleasant working relations within his newspaper plant and promotes in every way possible a spirit of interest, enterprise and cooperation.

Influence of the Press Is Far Reaching

Over the fireplace in the home of Daniel Burnham, noted Chicago architect, was inscribed this credo:

> Make no little plans; they have no magic to stir men's blood and probably themselves will not be realized. Make big plans; aim high in hope and work, remembering that a noble logical diagram once recorded will never die, but long after we are gone will be a living thing, asserting itself with ever-growing insistency. Remember that our sons and grandsons are going to do things that would stagger us.

Progressive publishers, realizing the public's reliance upon their ability to gather facts from all areas of information, aim high in their efforts to inform, guide and promote. They are sensitive to the thoughts of those in high places and keep themselves in touch with national and world movements as well as with movements within their state and local community. They "aim high in hope and work" and take part in big plans as well as small ones. The success of many plans for the security of the nation and the peace of the world has been due largely to the promotion given such movements by the newspapers of the nation and by persons in every town and township who have been stirred into action by editors through news, advertising and editorial expression. What they have thus recorded will be "a living thing, long after they are gone, asserting itself with ever-growing insistency."

Newspapers have had great influence in time of war by supporting government projects. The vigorous promotion given scrap metal drives, war bond sales, food rationing, health and morale building campaigns and other movements launched by the national government and carried on through newspapers brought instant and generous response.

National organizations contributing to better living readily receive the support of newspapers. The National Safety Council, the Better Business Bureau, the movements for curbing various diseases and building better health, and similar projects are promoted extensively through a press anxious to make its contribution to human welfare.

Newspapers, too, are leaders in the movement against suppression of information by public agencies. They staunchly defend freedom of the press not only in order that they may give the news freely but that they may also promote true democracy. Promotion of this kind is recognized as a professional responsibility. It is being practiced and applauded more than at any time in press history.

"Newspapers need a soul," said Felix McKnight in addressing promotion managers at a convention of the National Newspaper Promotion Association. "If you have one, search it and see where you stand. If you haven't a soul readily recognizable to your readers, you had better get yourself one. It doesn't cost a cent — just mix character, spirit and fervor and stir generously." At the same convention, Jenkin Lloyd Jones, editor of the Tulsa, Okla., *Tribune* (circulation 75,732, population 182,740), said: "A newspaper must have eyes that shine, fists that strike, arms that comfort and a voice that can be heard."

In other words, every newspaper should have a promotion department that will lend its influence far and wide with telling force, even beyond the local community, into the distant realms of state, national and world activity. Then from those remote sources may flow back to the newspaper's area indirect benefits that give strength to benefits directly derived from the newspaper's promotion efforts in its local field.

The Newspaper Serves Its Local Community

While it is important for a publisher to promote the power and influence of the press in general and to devote space to important national movements, it is from promotion of his newspaper's services to his local community that he will derive greatest benefit.

Merchants need to know well the power of advertising to bring trade to their doors. Residents of the community must know what the newspaper offers them in general news and other important information. Everything in the newspaper — from the small social item to the top story out of Washington, from the three-line classified to the full-page advertisement — is of interest to somebody.

Despite the many opportunities for effective promotion, many newspapers talk too little about themselves. They advocate publicity, advertising and promotion for others, but set a poor example themselves. They give little evidence of believing strongly in what promotion may do for them.

"If our newspaper is the most honored newspaper in the state from the community service angle," says Jack Lough, publisher of the Albion, Nebr., *News* (circulation 2,872, population 2,132), "we can see no reason why we should hide the fact any more than we would refuse to report the outstanding community assets in any other line of endeavor. It certainly makes sense that the promotion of a newspaper will pay off just like promotion of beans, bangles and bacon ...and he who thinks otherwise is a fraud to sell advertisers something he doesn't believe in himself."

Features Provide Recreation and Entertainment

The features that a newspaper offers may be the basis of striking promotion. The comics provide entertainment for all, the crossword puzzle provides relaxation, the sports page draws the attention of

Dad and the food pages interest Mother. Unusual fiction, special recipes, patterns, fashions and other subjects that interest women all rate advance publicity. Efforts to interest youth in newspaper reading are extremely important in this day when television is driving hard for time and attention.

What other manufactured product holds such a diversity of interest for so many types of people? Someone has said "the daily newspaper is luxury and necessity, plaything and utility, pastime and time-saver, basic need and shining toy all rolled up into one. People get too much fun out of their daily paper, too much pleasure, service and recreation ever to want to forego these benefits." It contributes to the health, convenience, pleasure and plain practical everyday earning power of millions of people. What a promotion story it has to tell!

Good Will Through Community Service

Tradition seems to dictate that newspapers take the lead, or at least lend support to economic, educational, cultural or entertainment programs. Many newspapers promote such affairs as music festivals, sports and home shows, medical clinics, science fairs, soil conservation programs and charity events designed to make the community a better place in which to work and live.

Successful public events promoted to help a charity reflect well upon a publication and bring to it an abundance of public gratitude and good will. Most newspapers lend financial assistance and publicity to such projects and often take an active part in their organization, development and management. This is where a good promotion department may give valuable service.

May Improve Morale Within the Plant

A publisher cannot expect maximum efficiency from his employees unless he puts forth some special efforts to build and maintain a high morale within his organization. Close cooperation between departments is essential to successful publishing. This is not realized until newspaper workers, naturally absorbed in the work of their individual departments, are able to visualize at the same time the complete newspaper operation and their relation to it. Here is where the promotion department may be extremely helpful. It can work with the heads and members of all departments to develop the cooperation that is needed. It can also help employees to build up a close contact with the public they serve. From within-the-plant promotion a newspaper draws benefits that are instantly evident and that will increase as the newspaper continues to promote.

"Get yourself something to say and say it," said S. R. Bernstein, editor of *Advertising Age,* in an address before the Advertising Managers Association of Wisconsin. "Say it, week after week, year after year, as often and as forcefully as you know how. Don't say the same thing each time, but one thing this week, something else next month, and still a third thing next year. And don't say the same thing every newspaper says. Your problem is to build up the things that make *your* newspaper *different* from every other newspaper — to build up, if you will, a personality for your publication which belongs to you and to no one else — and then keep on hammering on this theme forever."

This is sound promotion advice for any publisher or newspaper promotion manager.

CHAPTER 3

Standards for
Newspaper Promotion

—P. H. BATTE,
General Manager,
Charlotte, N.C.,
Observer

THE NEWSPAPER, itself a medium of advertising and promotion, must maintain high standards in its own promotion program. Newspaper promotion, in order to produce maximum results, must be:

1. More than propaganda.
2. More than press agentry or showmanship.
3. More than publicity.
4. Aimed at service.
5. Backed with truth through research.
6. Psychologically correct in its approach.

Propaganda Is Not Favored

Propaganda is neither a popular term nor a favored practice with newspaper publishers. Frank E. Lumley says that propaganda is "promotion which is veiled in one way or another as to its origin and sources, the interests involved, the methods employed, the content spread and the results accruing."[1] William Albig says social psychologists define propaganda as "any attempt to influence minds and opinions" but that "to the common man, it implies devious manipulation in which he is not left free to 'draw his own conclusions' and is the object of systematic, deliberate manipulations."[2]

On the other hand William Hummel and Keith Huntress attack the idea that propaganda is always harmful, always false; they con-

---

[1] Harwood L. Childs, *An Introduction to Public Opinion,* John Wiley and Sons, Inc., New York.
[2] William Albig, *Modern Public Opinion,* McGraw-Hill, New York, 1956, pp. 302–03.

tend it can be used for a good cause as well as for a bad cause.[3] Edward Bernays also looks upon it as "a consistent, enduring effort to create and shape events to influence the relations of the public to an enterprise, idea or group."[4]

Obviously, propaganda is evil when based on erroneous information, when the source is concealed, or when used with intentional viciousness.

There should be no question about the truth of any facts a newspaper puts out concerning itself or about the sincerity of its motives. Its standing as a fact-giving agency and as a guide in community activities may be quickly lowered by the use of any form of publicity with veiled intentions.

Press Agentry Is Taboo

Press agentry, another form of obtaining publicity by means that are not ethical, cannot be employed by newspapers. This is looked upon by publishers as an attempt to obtain favorable mention in the news columns that should appear in the advertising columns. It is called press agentry because the material for such publicity is generally put out by an agent who makes a business of "gouging" newspapers for free space. If it is to promote a movie, a theatrical performance or a sports event, usually a pair of tickets or an invitation to a dinner or cocktail party accompanies the press release as a bait to the editor or publisher. The value of the token seldom equals the value of the space provided by the newspaper. This practice of obtaining free promotion is often focused on other media as well as on newspapers.

A publisher who resents strongly such attempts to deal with him could not conscientiously bend to such practice. It would have to be on the basis of fair exchange, of giving value for value, instead of attempting to get something for nothing from another medium.

Some newspapers have made satisfactory arrangements with television stations, radio stations and movie theaters whereby they have exchanged advertising services on the basis of established prices. A theater might agree to contract for $1,000 worth of advertising in a newspaper if the publisher would agree to carry the same amount of advertising on the movie screen. A newspaper might take advertising on television at the television station's established rate in exchange for a listing of television programs at the newspaper's established advertising rate. Such an arrangement is not in the category of press agentry. It is advertising on a purely ethical and business-like basis.

---

[3] William C. Hummel and Keith G. Huntress, *The Analysis of Propaganda*, Henry Holt and Co., New York, 1949, p. 2.

[4] Edward L. Bernays, *Propaganda*, Liveright Publishing Corp., New York.

It Is More Than Publicity

Most public relations companies list publicity as their foremost function. "Ours is the business of communicating with people to create a favorable climate of thought in which to sell a product, a company or an idea," says one such company. "We do this by creating a believable image and by presenting that image to the correct 'publics' on a continuing basis." The first plank in its service platform is to "stimulate sales through *publicity*."

According to Harlow and Black, publicity is the most talked of and the least understood of all phases of public relations.[5] They contend that if a poll were taken of the millions of persons in the United States who know something of public relations, it could be expected that 99 per cent of them would think of publicity when the term "public relations" is used in their presence. Perhaps public relations workers themselves are mainly responsible for this confusion of terms. Their emphasis on it as a major factor causes clients to expect spectacular publicity results.

Publicity, of course, is a part of good newspaper promotion, but it is not all. It may be used to increase circulation and advertising linage. It may be used to reflect a newspaper's highest ideals and to portray it as an important social instrument. It may be used to acquaint readers with features and services the newspaper offers. It may be used to remind citizens of the advantages of living in the community and also to remind advertisers of various improvements in the area — changes which contribute to better trade. It may be used to promote the community and the newspaper in various ways. But advertising likewise is an effective instrument of promotion. And when it comes to improving community life, building genuine good will and strengthening inter-departmental relations, the newspaper must do more than publicize and advertise. Its publisher and staff must roll up their sleeves and take an active part in such projects.

For a newspaper, promotion consists of advertising, selling, marketing, merchandising and public relations — serving the public in every effective and available way to bring good will to the newspaper and to make of it a sustaining force in the community.

Service Must Be Its Aim

While most institutions plan their promotion generally with the profit motive uppermost in mind, a newspaper in developing its promotion must consider the service it may give as well as the profit it may derive. Indeed, a newspaper must often promote various projects for community betterment without any expectation of direct

---

[5] Rex F. Harlow and Marvin M. Black, *Practical Public Relations,* Harper and Brothers, New York, 1952, p. 283.

profit. A broad attitude toward the welfare of others enters strongly into a newspaper's success. It plays a leading role in community development. This spirit of helpfulness must enter into a newspaper's promotion as well as into its giving of the news, circulation building and advertising services.

A newspaper's promotion, in order to be effective, must be respected. A newspaper's promotion department should have the high regard of its personnel, of the newspaper's administrative department and of all on the newspaper's staff. Promotion must have a good footing in the newspaper plant before it can go far on the outside.

"I cannot imagine any grander way of making a living than this business of helping others to make a living by promoting and selling products of the world to people who will benefit by using these products and services in their daily lives," remarked a newspaper promotion manager to a group of his fellows. And then he added this word of caution: "Let's make certain that we become specialists in newspaper promotion rather than in self-promotion. By all means, make sure our stuff is legal and that it is honest."

Service should be the moving factor in newspaper promotion.

Backed With Truth Through Research

Another required quality of newspaper promotion is credibility. To have impact, it must be believable. Every statement should be supported with evidence.

A newspaper cannot afford to say that its advertising service brought a million dollars worth of additional patronage to home town stores without having actual figures to prove it. Consequently, the modern and efficient promotion department conducts surveys and engages in research to obtain important data.

It is the responsibility of the promotion department to keep a close check on all the newspaper's services. Is circulation holding up in all areas? Are all features in the newspaper still popular? Are advertisements drawing the desired readership? Is the newspaper giving national advertisers and advertising agencies all the facts they want about the newspaper's market and its circulation within the market? Some careful research and well-conducted surveys will provide the answers.

Concrete and specific facts are convincing while generalities are a waste of time and effort. A good promotion piece is devoid of exaggeration and double talk. It sparkles with truth and dependability.

Must Have Right Approach

The newspaper has many "publics" to deal with. It has readers and non-readers, advertisers and non-advertisers, and each of these groups contains individuals with different attitudes and interests. It is important that the promotion department be psychologically correct in its approach.

Persons of all ages, trades and professions read the newspaper. High school basketball scores may not interest grandmother but they receive first attention from young readers. The market quotations on eggs and butter have more interest for farmers than merchants. Women read the society page while men eagerly scan the sports pages. To what extent does the newspaper satisfy the interests of all members of the family and all groups in the community?

Represented in the newspaper's advertising columns are users of large space and those who use classifieds, and in the community are non-advertisers who should be convinced of the newspaper's ability to serve them.

What is the best way to approach these various elements of the community? This involves the ability to impart information and make convincing appeals but also to take criticism, admit faults and rectify shortcomings. Verne Burnett, long a successful public relations counsel in New York, says that the basic objective of promotion or public relations is "to know ourselves and those around us, to understand our relationships with our fellowmen and to guide our conduct so that those relationships may be more enjoyable and beneficial to ourselves and to others."[6]

A lot of applied psychology fits well into newspaper promotion.

A Promotion Decalogue

The chief essentials for success in newspaper promotion are summed up in the following "Ten Commandments of Good Newspaper Promotion":

1. Only one standard — build up to quality, never down to propaganda.
2. Only one kind of service — the best.
3. Only one method of operation — on a scientific, practical basis.
4. Only one code of ethics — fair dealing, but hard hitting, selling to all.
5. Only one philosophy — service before self.
6. Only one endeavor — constant improvement.
7. Only one ideal — completely satisfied customers.
8. Only one objective — get the order at a profit; keep every customer a friend.
9. Only one ambition — integrity before all else.
10. Only one hope — to be worthy of leadership.

---

[6] Verne Burnett, *You and Your Public,* Harper and Brothers, New York.

"We are looking for
people with creativeness
and salesmanship, but
if I had to make
a choice, it would be
the person with
salesmanship."

—LYNNWOOD ARMSTRONG,
Advertising Director,
Waco, Tex.,
News-Tribune

CHAPTER 4

Proper Organization for Effective Promotion

IN THE HEART of every conscientious publisher is a desire to improve his newspaper and the community it serves. He wants to increase reader interest, build circulation, develop advertising linage and strengthen inter-departmental relations within the newspaper plant. He wants to build good will for the newspaper from every source and uphold in every way the rights and purposes of a free press. He wants to build trade for local wholesalers and retailers· He desires also to do his part in bringing about a better understanding of state, national and world problems.

It is possible for any newspaper, even the smallest weekly, to accomplish something in all these categories of promotion and public relations. The extent of a newspaper's activities, however, will depend to a degree upon (1) size of the city in which it operates, (2) competition, (3) financial status, (4) management policies and (5) publisher's attitude. The larger the city and the more densely populated the newspaper's circulation area, the greater the opportunity it has for building business and developing good will. If another newspaper operates in the town and if one from a larger city encroaches upon the area, a newspaper is forced to promote its services and keep strong its community standing. Much depends upon the business vision and acumen of the publisher and the extent to which he will appropriate funds for promotion. Primarily, it is a matter of realizing and analyzing the need and of properly organizing and assigning responsibility.

TYPES OF PROMOTION HANDLING

Because of the different conditions under which newspapers operate, no pattern of organization for newspaper promotion can be pointed to as the most efficient and the most desirable. At least four ways of promoting a newspaper are in common use today:

1. A centralized well-staffed promotion department serving all departments of the newspaper — news-editorial, advertising and circulation — and giving attention to both newspaper and community development.
2. A promotion manager in each department — news, circulation and advertising — whose responsibility is to promote the business and the service of the special department to which he is assigned.
3. A one-man promotion department, wherein one person gives full time to promoting all departments of the newspaper and in making public contacts.
4. A part-time promotion manager, who carries other responsibilities demanding one-half or more of his time.

Centralized Operation

Most metropolitan newspapers have a centralized promotion department, headed by an experienced promotion man with a staff of capable assistants. The department then handles all phases of promotion for the newspaper. Its job is to explain its news and feature services, promote circulation and advertising, help build morale within the organization and build good will in the community. It lays out a carefully planned program for each year. This is formulated after conference with all department heads and the general manager.

With such a setup the entire personnel of the promotion department may be thrown into one major campaign or individual members may be given minor assignments. All members of the promotion staff are sufficiently trained to promote any phase of the newspaper's operation. At the same time, each member is somewhat of a specialist in some line of promotion. The promotion staff includes artists, copywriters, layout men, public service clerks and editors. Some of these, too, are proficient in public speaking and in planning group conferences, public meetings and exhibits.

Those who favor this type of promotion organization point out these advantages:

1. All departments of the newspaper are drawn together in the making of a better newspaper and a better community.
2. The promotion department, with its own well-organized staff, operates on a par of importance with other departments.
3. The centralized department promotes the newspaper as a whole but at the same time gives attention to the specific needs of each department.
4. The publisher or general manager has at all times a clear picture of what is being done in the way of promotion.

5. Promotion efforts are easily concentrated with full strength at vital points.
6. The expense of promotion may be carefully applied and easily controlled.
7. A general program of promotion may be quickly formulated, applied and completed.

Promotion in Each Department

While the centralized promotion department is the most popular system, some publishers believe that a better plan is for each department to have its own promotion manager and to do its own promoting.

Under this system each department formulates its own promotion program independent of what may be done in other departments. The advertising manager, together with his promotion manager, carries on the promotion needed for his department. The circulation manager has a promotion manager and together they keep circulation climbing or at least up to par. The news-editorial department also has a man to promote its features and services.

The declared advantages of this system are:

1. Each department has a promotion manager who is a specialist in the department's field.
2. The promotion problems of the department can be handled promptly and efficiently.
3. Definite study and attention are given constantly to the department's promotion needs.
4. The promotion man always is in close contact with the services and features he is employed to promote.

One-Man and Part-Time Operations

On smaller papers, where promotion is not so extensive, one person may plan, institute and direct all the promotion of the newspaper. He may have the help of the advertising department in preparing promotion copy and of the news department in preparing publicity material. But he is the promotion manager to whom the publisher looks for keeping the newspaper and its services sold to the public. He gives his full time and attention to promotion and draws on other office personnel when additional help is needed.

For a weekly or a small daily the work of promotion usually is carried on by the publisher himself or is assigned to a member of the staff who carries other important responsibilities. This person often is the advertising manager. However, it may be a member of the staff in the front office or a reporter who has a public relations personality and a flair for promotion writing.

Some economy advantages may be derived from carrying on promotion by such limited means, but there is great danger that the publisher will minimize the true worth of promotion and provide less promotion than should be provided in order to give the newspaper the benefits it needs and deserves.

HOW PROMOTION DEPARTMENT OPERATES

The manner in which newspapers of various sizes carry on their programs affords an interesting study. Beginning with the metropolitan press and coming on down to the small daily and weekly, one finds a wide range of operation.

On The Larger Newspapers

Newspapers with circulations of 50,000 or more carry on extensive promotion programs. For example, the promotion program of the Des Moines, Iowa, *Register* and *Tribune* (combined circulation 345,146, population 177,965) is divided into seven categories, as follows:

1. Editorial Promotion
   A. Strengthen readership of outstanding editorial features and build readership for worth-while, less-read features.
   B. Promote columnists, editorial writers, by-liners, news features, etc.
   C. Arrange for regular promotion space in the newspaper.
   D. Produce radio and television scripts.
   E. Help improve the newspaper as a vital product through readership studies and field contacts.
2. Advertising Promotion
   A. Create, develop and produce ideas and events for all advertising classifications that will result in additional linage and revenue.
   B. Prepare basic sales materials, presentations, selling tools and aids for all advertising departments. These include brochures, films, broadsides, etc.
   C. Plan and participate in sales meetings.
3. Circulation Promotion
   A. Suggest ideas and plans which will increase, retain and maintain circulation.
   B. Help reduce carrier turnover and increase parent interest.
   C. Improve delivery service.
   D. Produce plans, sales helps and selling aids.
   E. Produce carrier publications.
   F. Plan and participate in sales meetings.
4. Market Promotion
   A. Produce campaigns to bring greater prestige and awareness of market importance and coverage.
   B. Provide prospective advertisers and advertising agencies with full details concerning market for goods in newspaper's area.
5. Publicity
   A. Provide news department with stories concerning personnel, features and services.
   B. Produce and release publicity to trade papers, radio and television.

6. Public Relations
   A. Plan community events and services to convince readers that the newspaper is a vital civic factor.
   B. Conduct plant tours.
   C. Conduct promotions directed at future readers and subscribers.
   D. Produce school, civic and fraternal promotions.
7. Company-Employee Relations
   A. Produce internal publications.
   B. Produce information pamphlets and releases on company policies and activities.
   C. Plan and manage employee activities such as card tournaments, parties and athletic events.

REQUIRES LARGE STAFF

To carry out this program of promotion for the *Register* and *Tribune*, the promotion manager has a staff of eleven full-time assistants including an assistant promotion manager and some part-time help, varying according to size and type of projects sponsored. During the Iowa State Fair, he employs six extra women to handle the *Register* and *Tribune* information booth at the fair (see Fig. 4.1).

The production manager, in addition to supervising all production, okays all promotion space layouts before they are released to artists, promotes carrier service for the circulation department, handles window displays and exhibits and stands ready to take general assignments. The promotion manager's secretary figures and breaks down all bills and statements, sorts department mail and performs other secretarial duties. Another secretary, who serves the entire staff, types television and radio scripts, posts promotion ads on the Conference Room bulletin board, conducts tours of the plant and arranges film showings. She also assists in the State Fair booth when the fair is going on and takes general assignments when needed.

Two other members of the staff take care of general art work, and one of these prepares promotion ads on assignment. Two others take care of advertising promotion. One of these prepares promotion copy for retail, mail order and classified advertising and does other work on general assignment. The other promotes general advertising, the *World Affairs* school program, *Picture* magazine promotion and, in addition, some classified promotion, directs a Christmas party for children and assists with the 20-Year Club. He also takes general assignments.

Other work is divided among four remaining staff members. One of these takes care of space promotion for editorial features and circulation, okays all promotion copy before it is set, supervises space placement and helps with the 20-Year Club. Another handles circulation promotion on television, prepares trade paper publicity, provides copy for the Sunday round-up and sports promotion boxes, promotes *This Week Magazine* and the Cashword puzzle, receives general assignments and assists at the State Fair.

The two other members of the staff are equally busy. One handles promotion for the Farm and Home magazine section, prepares television slides, directs slide and film presentations, arranges exhibits and picture displays, helps at the State Fair and takes some general assignments. The main responsibility of the other member is *Spirit,* an employee magazine, but additional duties include circulation promotion on radio, promotion ads for the Women's Section, film showings, arranging for the Community Award public relations dinner and helping with tours and the State Fair.

The promotion department of the *Register* and *Tribune* does not handle research but assists in that area.

Other newspapers have different arrangements for their promotion departments. Some have fewer on their promotion staffs and some

DES MOINES REGISTER
and TRIBUNE

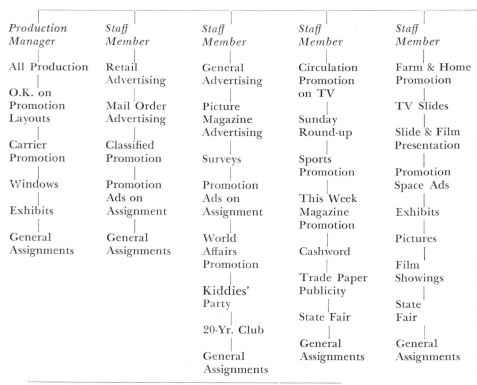

Production Manager	*Staff Member*	*Staff Member*	*Staff Member*	*Staff Member*
All Production	Retail Advertising	General Advertising	Circulation Promotion on TV	Farm & Home Promotion
O.K. on Promotion Layouts	Mail Order Advertising	Picture Magazine Advertising	Sunday Round-up	TV Slides
Carrier Promotion	Classified Promotion	Surveys	Sports Promotion	Slide & Film Presentation
Windows	Promotion Ads on Assignment	Promotion Ads on Assignment	This Week Magazine Promotion	Promotion Space Ads
Exhibits	General Assignments	World Affairs Promotion	Cashword	Exhibits
General Assignments		Kiddies' Party	Trade Paper Publicity	Pictures
		20-Yr. Club	State Fair	Film Showings
		General Assignments	General Assignments	State Fair
				General Assignments

FIG. 4.1 — Plan of operation for Promotion Department of Des Moines **Register** and **Tribune**.

more than the Des Moines newspapers. They also divide the work differently among staff members.

HAS A FORCE OF SEVENTEEN

The Washington, D.C., *Post* and *Times Herald* (circulation 390,104, population 802,178) has a promotion force of 17 persons (see Fig. 4.2).

The promotion manager is closely assisted by the assistant promotion manager, research supervisor, merchandiser and secretary. Other members of the staff are three artists and a production clerk, two copy writers, three research clerks, an order clerk, an assistant secretary and a plant tour guide.

The department takes care of all promotion, public relations and

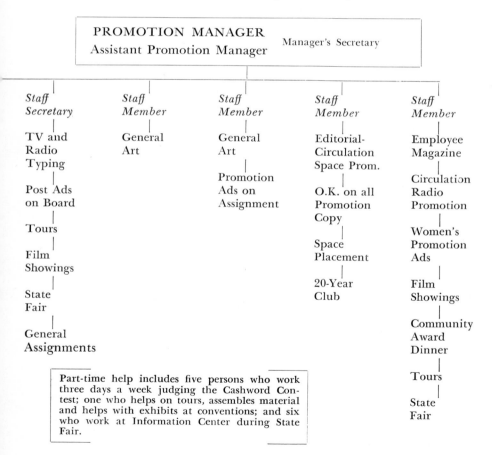

PROMOTION MANAGER
Assistant Promotion Manager   Manager's Secretary

Staff Secretary	*Staff Member*	*Staff Member*	*Staff Member*	*Staff Member*
TV and Radio Typing	General Art	General Art	Editorial-Circulation Space Prom.	Employee Magazine
Post Ads on Board		Promotion Ads on Assignment	O.K. on all Promotion Copy	Circulation Radio Promotion
Tours			Space Placement	Women's Promotion Ads
Film Showings			20-Year Club	Film Showings
State Fair				Community Award Dinner
General Assignments				Tours
				State Fair

Part-time help includes five persons who work three days a week judging the Cashword Contest; one who helps on tours, assembles material and helps with exhibits at conventions; and six who work at Information Center during State Fair.

THE WASHINGTON POST
AND
TIMES HERALD

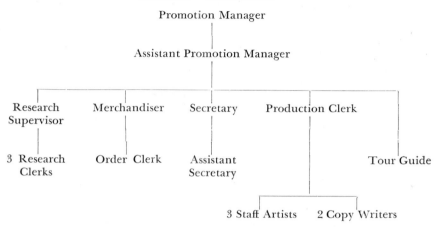

Promotion Manager

Assistant Promotion Manager

Research Supervisor — Merchandiser — Secretary — Production Clerk

3 Research Clerks — Order Clerk — Assistant Secretary — Tour Guide

3 Staff Artists — 2 Copy Writers

FIG. 4.2 — Plan of operation for Promotion Department of Washington, D. C., **Post** and **Times Herald.**

public events for the *Post* and *Times Herald.* This includes sales presentations and sales aids for retail, classified and national advertising; all sales aids for the circulation department and its sales force; all trade paper advertising and in-paper advertising promotion, and all direct mail advertising promotion. This department also does the rack cards, newsstand cards, flaps, radio and television copy and art for circulation and classified advertising promotion. All publicity in trade journals and other journals is gathered, written and assimilated by the promotion department.

This newspaper's promotion program also includes the sponsorship of a number of public events, including an annual football contest (30,000 entries per week), a Children's Book Fair (1957 attendance was 65,000), a Book and Author Luncheon, a Favorite Teachers Contest and a High School Christmas Painting project.

MANAGER FOR EACH DIVISION

The public relations director of the South Bend, Ind., *Tribune* (circulation 108,793, population 115,911) has arranged his promotion department in five divisions: Research, Editorial Promotion, Circulation Promotion, Advertising Promotion, Public Relations and Multigraph Department (see Fig. 4.3).

The research division conducts readership surveys, assembles and releases market data, conducts public opinion and other general surveys. Important features in editorial promotion are television and radio announcements, a high school page, an annual Voice Of The People dinner and various contests. Circulation promotion pertains mainly to carrier recruitment, outstanding newspaperboy program and good-will visits to smaller communities. The advertising promotion includes customer contacts, circulation breakdown, business conditions bulletin, trade paper advertising, sales presentations and classified promotion.

Principal public relations projects are plant tours, speeches before groups, direction of 4-H Club fair booth and other public events.

The newspaper public relations director also acts in this capacity for the newspaper's television and radio stations.

Less Emphasis by Small Dailies

Among newspapers with less than 50,000 circulation, promotion is not carried out so extensively. Here is where the one-man promotion department or the part-time promotion manager more often is found. Few small dailies fully comprehend the advantages to be derived from well-planned promotion. Some dailies with circulations between 25,000 and 50,000 have promotion departments, but not many with less than 25,000 employ a full-time promotion or public relations manager. Here the publisher, editor, advertising manager or some other member of the staff usually accepts promotion as a secondary responsibility. Too often the publisher feels that money spent on promotion and public relations could be better used to add a good reporter or advertising man to the staff. Few realize that promotion management is a specialized field capable of valuable service to readers and advertisers and of greater profits for the newspaper.

Among daily newspapers in the 15,000 to 25,000 circulation bracket, the Dothan, Ala., *Eagle* (circulation 22,714, population 21,584) does an effective promotion job. Its advertising director makes good use of the newspaper's advertising columns and direct mail to promote circulation and build advertising volume. He makes contacts with manufacturers' representatives and wholesalers and cultivates their friendship and good will. This is helpful in developing national advertising. His direct mail efforts are devoted to selling the market to advertisers and to building circulation. Crusades for community betterment are carefully planned and conducted by Wallace Miller, promotion manager.

The Pekin, Ill., *Times* (circulation 18,331, population 21,858) likewise is alert to the advantages of well-planned promotion. However, it does more promoting for circulation than for advertising. Each year it makes a special "introductory offer" to rural route patrons who are not subscribers. In the spring it conducts a contest among city carriers for new subscribers with attendance at a big league ball game as the reward. William D. McNaughton, the publisher, has stimulated reader interest in his paper by taking trips abroad and sending back stories about his experiences and the scenic and historic points he visits.

CALIFORNIA PAPER SETS PATTERN

The Alameda, Calif., *Times-Star* (circulation 8,414, population 64,430) has set before its staff members a "Handbook of General Policies" that might well be a pattern for other newspapers. It is particularly applicable to newspapers published in small communities where neighborliness and friendly concern prevail. Among the instructions offered are these:

"Be generous with praise for individuals and organizations doing good civic jobs. Public recognition of good work by a public servant encourages men of ability to run for public offices. We need that type if our kind of government is to work. The newspaper is in a better position to know who are deserving and to give this recognition than any other institution. Support churches, schools, Boy Scouts, Girl Scouts, Chambers of Commerce, veterans' groups and similar nonprofit organizations working for public welfare. Good schools well staffed are essential in any successful democracy and important in every aspect of life. To get and keep the best teacher personnel, encourage movements for adequate pay and community recognition.

"It should never be forgotten that a newspaper is a semi-public institution and as such occupies a position of trust in the community. There are steps which only a newspaper can take for righting wrongs and giving constructive leadership. Our obligations and opportunities in these matters of public service should always be kept in mind.

"A newspaper needs to have a heart. That should never be overlooked. It is easy for a newspaper by a few printed words to cause great embarrassment and anguish for a defenseless person and to cause life-long suffering. That is a stiff price for one person to pay for the momentary thrill or chuckle that thousands of other people may get from a hasty reading of something which they then proceed to forget.

"Although our community has long outgrown the village stage, our publication is still the 'home town paper' to the subscriber. If we hope to perpetuate that feeling, we must take a neighborly attitude and guard against a too highly developed impersonality in news evaluation."

Such counsel builds within a newspaper organization the spirit of promotion and forms the foundation for sound public relations.

PUBLISHER HANDLES PROMOTION

J. W. Stuff, publisher of the Cedartown, Ga., *Standard* (circulation 3,956, population 9,470), says that 10 per cent of the time he

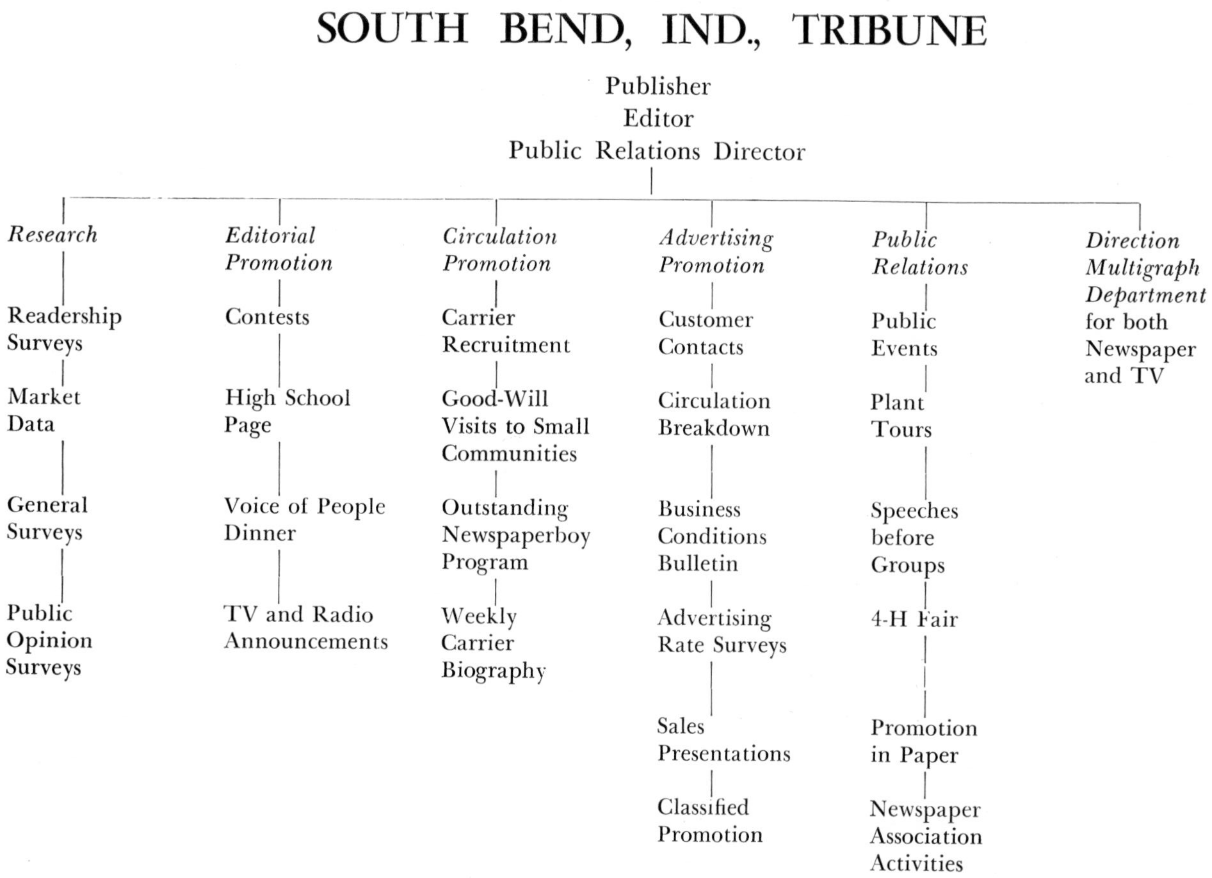

SOUTH BEND, IND., TRIBUNE

Publisher

Editor

Public Relations Director

Research	Editorial Promotion	Circulation Promotion	Advertising Promotion	Public Relations	Direction Multigraph Department for both Newspaper and TV
Readership Surveys	Contests	Carrier Recruitment	Customer Contacts	Public Events	
Market Data	High School Page	Good-Will Visits to Small Communities	Circulation Breakdown	Plant Tours	
General Surveys	Voice of People Dinner	Outstanding Newspaperboy Program	Business Conditions Bulletin	Speeches before Groups	
Public Opinion Surveys	TV and Radio Announcements	Weekly Carrier Biography	Advertising Rate Surveys	4-H Fair	
			Sales Presentations	Promotion in Paper	
			Classified Promotion	Newspaper Association Activities	

FIG. 4.3 — South Bend, Ind., **Tribune's** organizational setup for promotion and public relations.

spends in his newspaper office is devoted to promoting his newspaper. He senses its full importance and would like to do more.

Under his direction, carrier promotions, direct mail offers and premium announcements for subscriptions are developed in the circulation department. Brochures concerning the newspaper's service to advertisers are prepared for advertising agencies and the newspaper's special representative. Attractive features and service promotion ads also frequently appear in the newspaper.

A publisher's deep interest in community advancement is revealed in his generous allotment of space to local charities, the Chamber of Commerce and various improvement organizations.

Little additional help within the newspaper organization is required to carry on promotion programs such as those described. This, however, in no way lessens their importance. A single person giving liberal time or several giving portions of their time and efforts to promotion can do much toward developing a newspaper's prestige and increasing its profits.

A Part-Time Position on Weeklies

A weekly newspaper, of course, does not require as great an organization for promotion as a daily because it does not have the opportunities for elaborate or extensive programs of promotion. Whatever it does in this field is directed mainly to persons residing within its limited circulation area and to local merchants who are the chief advertisers. However, there is constant need for cultivating the national advertising field. Furthermore, every progressive publisher, no matter how small his newspaper, senses his obligation to elevate journalistic standards and to exert his efforts toward a better community.

Most weekly newspapers expect staff members to be able to perform in several capacities. Rarely is a person employed to give full time to promotion. Generally, whatever is done in the way of promotion is by the publisher, editor or persons who have other important responsibilities. Some examples will make clear the promotion methods most common to weekly newspapers.

ADVERTISING DEPARTMENT HELPS

Marlin S. Morgan, editor, and his advertising solicitors direct and carry out the promotion program for the Newton, N. J., *New Jersey Herald* (circulation 12,612, population 5,781), published weekly. Mr. Morgan makes occasional speeches before local organizations and extends greetings to advertisers on the occasions of store anniversaries and similar events. His advertising department prepares promotion material regarding circulation and advertising services to be run in the newspaper and conducts intensive solicitation for advertising from local merchants. He depends upon his special representative to promote his newspaper to national advertisers.

"Good public relations," says Morgan, "are established in the day-to-day contacts made by editor, reporters and advertising solicitors. If a newspaper's representatives are helpful, understanding, cheerful and cooperative, public support and appreciation invariably follow. By adhering to a policy of service to the community, our circulation has grown from 3,600 in 1945 to its present 12,612. Our news content has more than tripled and our advertising quadrupled."

MANY PROMOTION OPPORTUNITIES

The Patchogue, N. Y., *Advance* (circulation 6,560, population 7,361), another weekly, conducts an effective promotion program under the direction of Capt. John T. Tuthill, publisher. It promotes its various services to prospective readers and advertisers through its own news and advertising columns, direct mail messages, Welcome Wagon service, radio advertising, telephone solicitation and well-planned personal contacts. John T. Tuthill III, assistant publisher, and Mrs. Frances Johnson, society editor, frequently are asked to appear before luncheon clubs, women's clubs and other organizations. The publisher promotes civic progress through his editorial columns. Many groups of school children each year become acquainted with the newspaper's operations through tours of its plant, located in a $200,000 building, one of the finest in the country.

The Medina, Ohio, *Medina County Gazette* (circulation 7,052, population 5,097), published semi-weekly, has a full-time circulation manager, who takes care of promotion for his department, and three aggressive advertising salesmen who keep local merchants and prospective classified ad users well informed concerning the newspaper's advertising services. Martin H. and James E. Baldwin, co-editors, continually give thought to pictures and other features that will create interest and build good will for the newspaper.

PROMOTES GOOD WILL BETWEEN NATIONS

A weekly newspaper, as well as a metropolitan newspaper, may think also in terms of world welfare and exert strong influence toward better understanding between nations. Some excellent promotion along that line has been done by newspapers of small circulation.

Since 1954, the Ambler, Pa., *Gazette* (circulation 7,757, population 4,565) has issued annually a Freedom Edition, which has evoked nationwide interest and admiration. In 1956 this was an outstanding harbinger of international good will — a hefty 48-page edition, published as a salute to the city of Coburg, Germany, on its 900th anniversary. Published in both English and German, it symbolized the *Gazette*'s intention of telling people of this German town about life in an American community and how it prospers in a free society. On page 2, the Declaration of Independence was reproduced full page. The next page contained an editorial stating that "freedom is the keystone of our way of life." Other pages carried major German and English features — a German war bride, some of Ambler's outstanding citizens, young people's ideas about democracy, photographs of both Coburg and Ambler and many advertisements in both languages.

Sale of the edition was not limited to the newspaper's regular circulation area. Two thousand copies were rushed by air to Coburg's Burgermeister, accompanied by a Freedom Torch from Ambler's Burgess. The publisher of the *Coburger Tageblatt* put the copies on sale in newsstands throughout the city, which is only two miles from the Iron Curtain. All proceeds from these sales went to the German Red Cross.

The impact of the Freedom Edition was equally spectacular in the United States. Warm praise came from Secretary of State John Foster Dulles and German Ambassador Heinz Krekeler to William E. Strasburg, editor and publisher, and Carl K. Groth, advertising director. From the United States Information Agency, which works with private groups in promoting the "People-to-People" program, came its Certificate of Merit for the newspaper's "noteworthy contribution in furthering understanding of the United States and its people." Another recognition of the *Gazette*'s remarkable contribution to world friendship was the coveted George Washington Medal of Honor from the Freedoms Foundation at Valley Forge. The newspaper received also the Silver Anvil, the highest award of the American Public Relations Association.

In 1958 a similar exchange was affected with Goiania, Brazil, through the cooperation of that community's newspaper.

Here is promotion of a high order, demonstrating the extent to which a newspaper may go in developing good will not only in its home community but throughout the world.

QUALIFICATIONS FOR PROMOTION MANAGEMENT

Newspaper promotion has reached such a high stage of recognition that publishers require men of high caliber to direct their promotion programs. For this important work they select men with ideas, originality, personality and love of people. One, who through personal experience knows the qualifications required, says: "A promotion manager must have a genuine liking for working with people, managing people, meeting and dealing with people and studying people. He must realize how fascinating and stimulating a promotion job can be — to make things, sell things, manage things, write about things, organize and systematize. Promotion department personnel should have a liking and an eagerness for hard work and a sound educational background. They must be able to organize, supervise and deputize."

A study of promotion managers reveals that those who have been most successful have possessed four specific qualities and seven outstanding abilities.

The qualities are:

1. *Vision.* A complete understanding of the newspaper's opportunities for improvement in both contents and service; a knowledge of the area the newspaper serves.
2. *Initiative.* Courage to develop new ideas and institute new and better plans.
3. *Discrimination.* Judgment in directing appeals to the various groups in community life and in making personal contacts.
4. *Stick-to-itiveness.* The determination to carry through on every promotion that is planned and bring it to a satisfactory conclusion.

The abilities required are:

1. *Creative ability.* Ability to come up with something unique and interesting and to give a new twist to old ideas and methods.
2. *The ability to write clear, understandable copy.* One promotion manager says to his personnel: "Make it simple, factual and informative. Define your objectives. Select specific audiences, and shoot straight at them. Give one fact at a time — and don't exaggerate."
3. *The ability to make an attractive layout.* Ability to produce a layout that is pleasing enough to attract attention, interesting enough to hold the reader's attention and convincing enough to drive the reader to action.
4. *An understanding of production art.* Knowledge of typography and the effective use of photography and other illustrative material.
5. *A knowledge of distribution.* Familiarity with the various means of communication and transportation and a clear understanding of how they may be used advantageously.
6. *A technique for research.* Concern for authenticating promotion material by searching out facts and presenting them accurately.
7. *Ability to sell.* From start to finish, promotion is selling — selling by printed and spoken word and by personal contact.

Wise, therefore, is the publisher who carefully selects the person to direct his newspaper's promotion activities.

CHAPTER 5

Available

Promotion Media

T HE OPENED-MINDED, far-seeing, progressive publisher makes use of many media to tell widely and effectively the story of his newspaper — the news coverage it provides, the interesting features it contains, the delivery service, the pulling power of its advertising and its service to the community in which it circulates.

The rising appreciation for what promotion can do for newspapers is causing expansion of promotion programs into many areas of public contact. The average publisher of a small newspaper, always busy handling the general routine of his office and plant, generally limits his promotion efforts to the columns of his own newspaper and does too little of it there, but medium-sized newspapers with full-time promotion managers seek wide publicity and advertising through various avenues of communication. And the metropolitan newspaper, with its broad reach for additional advertising volume, increased circulation, better news services and greater community good will, will devote much of its space to promotion and also use a host of other media.

Some publishers are even using the columns of competing newspapers to propound the merits of their own papers. The *Wall Street Journal* (circulation 536,313, population 7,795,471) carries advertising from other newspapers, and uses this for promotion in *Editor & Publisher* (see Fig. 5.1). The New York *Times* (circulation 600,319, population 7,795,471) buys advertising space in the New York *World-Telegram* and *Sun* (circulation 454,224, population 7,795,471) to tell about its own "colorful, clear and complete" handling of the news. The St. Louis *Post-Dispatch* (circulation 380,495, population 856,796)

[34]

How 𝕿𝖍𝖊 𝕮𝖔𝖑𝖚𝖒𝖇𝖚𝖘 𝕯𝖎𝖘𝖕𝖆𝖙𝖈𝖍

SELLS SPACE THROUGH
THE WALL STREET JOURNAL

"Provides news people want," *says Mel E. Tharp*

We at the Columbus Dispatch have long admired, read and believed in The Wall Street Journal. We think other business people do the same.

We further believe The Wall Street Journal has done much to popularize business news to the average person as well as to the corporation president. The growth of The Wall Street Journal is proof enough it is providing the news about business that people want.

For the reasons stated above we at the Columbus Dispatch are carrying a consistent campaign in The Wall Street Journal for a second consecutive year.

Mel E. Tharp
Advertising Director
The Columbus Dispatch

"Sales messages seen...read...acted upon," *says Ralph G. Hemming*

The Wall Street Journal, edited crisp and fresh every morning with pertinent up-to-the-minute business news appeals to every alert business executive.

In these favorable surroundings we're certain our sales messages are seen, read and acted upon.

Ralph G. Hemming
Manager
General Advertising Dept.
The Columbus Dispatch

The Wall Street Journal is a medium's medium. Every business day it gets to the attention of those who authorize or influence decisions that affect advertising. They choose markets, okay appropriations, give the green light for tests. They choose plant sites, ride herd on community relations. And these busy men have a standing appointment with The Wall Street Journal—every business day!

Something really happens when you're in THE WALL STREET JOURNAL

published at:
**NEW YORK, 44 Broad St. and WASHINGTON, 1015 14th St., N. W. • CHICAGO, 711 W. Monroe St.
DALLAS, 911 Young St. • SAN FRANCISCO, 1540 Market St.**

Fig. 5.1 — An advertisement in **Editor & Publisher** explains that the **Wall Street Journal** sells space for other newspapers.

frequently advertises, in smaller papers of the state, the beginning of special features in its Sunday issues. The *Wall Street Journal* also advertises regularly in the large city papers of the country (see Fig. 5.2).

No longer is the line drawn anywhere by newspapers for the promotion of their services. The following media are used to a certain extent by newspapers, both large and small:

1. Their own news and advertising columns.
2. Local publications, association journals and the like.
3. Trade papers.
4. Radio and television.
5. Telephone and telegraph.
6. Direct mail.
7. Outdoor advertising.
8. Films, flannel boards and flip charts.
9. Theater screen.
10. Advertising novelties.
11. Bulletins.
12. House organs.

Own Columns Always Available

Most newspapers do more promoting through their own columns than anywhere. This is true mainly because it is a means of promotion always available and also because it is an effective medium. A newspaper must keep its regular patrons sold on the product and the services they buy. One promotion manager insists that no copy of a newspaper should leave the plant without containing promotion material concerning the paper's coverage of local news, coming features, its home delivery service or the interesting offerings of merchants through its advertising columns. Readers, of course, are acquainted with these services, but such services, continued from day to day, become common and forgotten, if not continually mentioned. Any daily newspaper of 12 pages or more per issue should average 150 column inches of promotion per week in its own columns, most promotion managers contend.

Regular readers must be made permanent readers. They should be made aware every day of what they will miss if they discontinue their subscriptions. Furthermore, regular readers are the newspaper's best salesmen, if plenty of good sales information is supplied to them. Attractive and convincing promotion ads in the newspaper concerning outstanding features, news content and delivery service make subscribers proud of the newspaper they read and furnish them with words they can use effectively in expounding the strong points of the paper to their neighbors.

The newspaper is well adapted to self-promotion. Through its own columns it may tell effectively about the following features and services:

1. **Coverage of Local News** — Readers do not comprehend the amount of space devoted to news unless some clear picture of it is given them. At least once a year a newspaper should report to its readers the number of column inches given to church organizations, Chamber of Commerce activities, service club programs, school improvements, youth groups, farm clubs and the like. Another fact seldom understood outside the newspaper office is the number of hours devoted each week to the gathering of news and the difficulties some-

---

I FOUND A NEW WORLD IN THE PAGES OF THE WALL STREET JOURNAL

By a Subscriber

The day I picked up my first copy of The Wall Street Journal I stepped into a new world. I saw right away that here was a newspaper that would help me get ahead. So I sent for a trial subscription.

I was not mistaken. Every day The Journal tells me about the far-reaching changes taking place in America. New inventions. New industries. New ways of doing business. New ways to earn money.

The Journal gives me quick warning of any business trend that may affect my pocketbook. Articles on food and clothing point out things to stock up on in order to save money. Reports on taxes guide me on what to do to keep my

taxes down. Since I started reading The Journal my income has increased $2,500.

This experience is not unusual. If you think The Journal is just for millionaires, you are wrong. The Journal helps salaried men earning $7,500 to $25,000. It is valuable to small business men. It can be of enormous benefit to ambitious young men who want to win advancement.

The Wall Street Journal is the complete business DAILY. Has largest staff of writers on business and finance. The only business paper served by all three big press associations. It costs $24 a year, but you can get a Trial Subscription for three months for $7. Just tear out this ad and attach check for $7 and mail. Or tell us to bill you. NYT 11-2

Address: The Wall Street Journal, 44 Broad St., New York 4, N.Y.

Fig. 5.2 — The **Wall Street Journal** ran this advertisement in a number of American newspapers. This one was clipped from the New York **Times**.

The Sun shines on the nation's capital!

It's not because Baltimore is such a close neighbor of Washington that we have long maintained one of the largest news bureaus in the nation's capital. It's because Washington is more than ever such a close neighbor of the rest of the world. Big news breaks constantly on every front—and it takes a big and experienced complement of correspondents to keep up with it, analyze it, report it. By practicing this first rule of good journalism—*be* where the news is and *get all* of it—the Sunpapers provide the kind of attentive readership which, in turn, results in overwhelming *advertising leadership*.

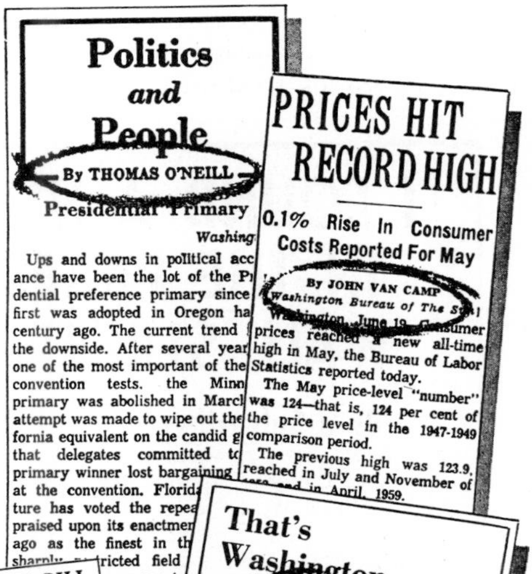

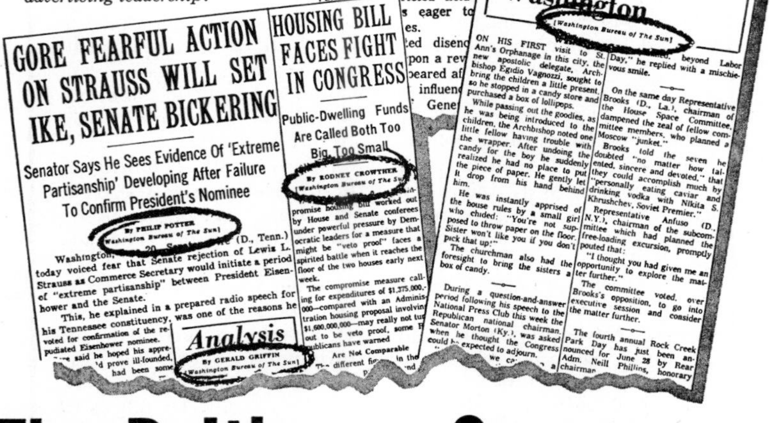

The Baltimore Sunpapers

ABC 3/31/59: Combined Morning and Evening 413,299 — Sunday 319,972

National Representatives: Cresmer & Woodward, Inc.—New York, San Francisco, Los Angeles
Scolaro, Meeker & Scott—Chicago, Detroit

Fig. 5.3 — The Baltimore Sunpapers use **Editor & Publisher** advertisements to promote the extensive coverage of national and international news provided by their Washington correspondents.

times faced by reporters. Hundreds of readers never come face to face with the men and women who constitute the news staff. Pictures of staff members with brief sketches of their training and experience draw the newspaper closer to its readers.

2. **Wire News Services** — The way in which news is gathered from all over the world and brought to readers of the home community completely and promptly each day is a thrilling story. The services of the Associated Press or United Press International should be explained. Particularly interesting is the way in which both news and pictures are brought into the local office on tape and plastic and quickly reproduced on the printed page.

3. **Washington Bureau** — Whatever is happening at the national capital is of vital interest in this age of scientific progress and international problems. Readers appreciate their newspaper more when they know it has its own experts on hand every day at the main source of national and international news. Promotional efforts to make them familiar with Washington correspondents and their activities are valuable in developing loyal readership (see Fig. 5.3).

4. **Special Writers and Columnists** — A newspaper's special writers, columnists and photographers distinguish it as a revealer of national thinking. These, along with Washington correspondents, may be promoted to good advantage in establishing the newspaper as an authority on politics, economics and science.

5. **All Types of Features** — The number and variety of features offered by a newspaper make an interesting promotion story. The extent to which they provide something of interest to all members of the family should be emphasized. Of special value to readers will be features that help solve human problems (see Fig. 5.4). Whenever a new feature, such as a new comic, cartoon, puzzle or magazine section is to appear it should be advertised not less than 10 days in advance and for a time after it is started. Even features that appear regularly from year to year should be given promotion space occasionally because an aggressive newspaper is constantly gaining new readers who need to become thoroughly acquainted with all the newspaper's offerings.

6. **Special Editions** — On certain important occasions the publisher will want to put out a special edition. In order to obtain appropriate and adequate material, considerable promotion will be required, and only by such means will enough supporting advertising and a sufficient number of copies be sold (see Fig. 5.5).

7. **Circulation** — Advertisers and subscribers both, more particularly the former, have a great interest in the extent of a newspaper's circulation. When such information is revealed through attractive promotion, merchants and manufacturers have a higher regard for

the paper in which they advertise (see Fig. 5.6). Readers, too, obtain satisfaction from knowing that the newspaper they read is the favorite of many.

8. Special Subscription Offers — By advertising special subscription offers and mailing sample copies of issues containing such announcements to prospective subscribers, a newspaper may increase circulation. Such promotion also helps regular readers to induce their neighbors to subscribe and it assists carrier-salesmen to increase the number of patrons on their routes.

9. Carrier Service and Recruitment — The morale of carrier-salesmen is lifted when their pictures, with stories about their good service to subscribers, appear in the newspaper. Such publicity also brings new blood into carrier ranks. Furthermore, it is helpful in obtaining the cooperation of parents and teachers so necessary in recruiting the best boys of the community for carrier service.

Fig. 5.4 — The Birmingham, Ala., **News** announces in its own columns a feature soon to appear.

There's an Extra Reason

Why Everybody

Who Plans to

Travel This Fall

Will Make a Date

To Read the Nov. 2

HERALD TRIBUNE

COMBINED

WORLD TRAVEL CONGRESS
FALL VACATION SECTION

There are two kinds of travelers:
those experienced and wise
enough to use the services of a
travel agent — and those who don't.

This year's HERALD TRIBUNE FALL
VACATION Travel Section will include
highlights of the coming World Travel
Congress — i.e., the ASTA Travel Agents'
own plans and ideas for the coming season.

Get the Travel Industry's own plans
— when you make yours — in the

Nov. 2nd Herald Tribune

FALL VACATION SECTION

Fig. 5.5 — To encourage advertisers to buy space in special editions, the New York **Herald Tribune** uses its own columns for advance promotion of the coming special.

10. Advertising Service — When special attention is drawn to the newspaper's advertising columns, it helps to stimulate sales at local stores and builds good will with advertisers. The service given by the advertising department in preparing copy and planning campaigns,

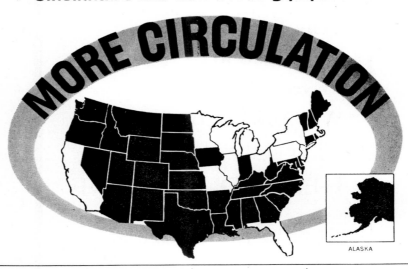

Cincinnati's BIG new evening paper has

ALABAMA	INDIANA	NEBRASKA	SOUTH CAROLINA
ALASKA	IOWA	NEVADA	SOUTH DAKOTA
ARIZONA	KANSAS	NEW HAMPSHIRE	TENNESSEE
ARKANSAS	KENTUCKY	NEW MEXICO	TEXAS
COLORADO	LOUISIANA	NORTH CAROLINA	UTAH
CONNECTICUT	MAINE	NORTH DAKOTA	VERMONT
DELAWARE	MARYLAND	OKLAHOMA	VIRGINIA
GEORGIA	MISSISSIPPI	OREGON	WASHINGTON
IDAHO	MONTANA	RHODE ISLAND	WEST VIRGINIA
			WYOMING

None of the 37 states listed above has a daily

newspaper—morning or evening—with a circulation as large as

The Cincinnati Post and TIMES-STAR

Total net paid daily circulation now 265,831

(ABC Pub. Stat. 9/30/58.)

SCRIPPS - HOWARD NEWSPAPERS

NEW YORK. *World-Telegram & The Sun*	COLUMBUS . . . . . . *Citizen*	DENVER . . . *Rocky Mountain News*	EVANSVILLE . . . . *Press*
CLEVELAND . . . . *Press*	CINCINNATI . . . *Post & Times-Star*	BIRMINGHAM . . . . *Post-Herald*	HOUSTON . . . . *Press*
PITTSBURGH . . . . *Press*	KENTUCKY . . . *Kentucky edition,*	MEMPHIS . . . . . *Press-Scimitar*	FORT WORTH . . . . *Press*
SAN FRANCISCO. . . . . *News*	*Cincinnati Post & Times-Star*	MEMPHIS . . . *Commercial Appeal*	ALBUQUERQUE . . . . . *Tribune*
INDIANAPOLIS. . . . . . . *Times*	KNOXVILLE . . . . *News-Sentinel*	WASHINGTON . . . . *News*	EL PASO . . . . . . *Herald-Post*

General Advertising Department, 230 Park Avenue, New York City

Chicago   San Francisco   Detroit   Cincinnati   Philadelphia   Dallas

Fig. 5.6 — The Cincinnati **Post and Times-Star** talks circulation to national advertisers through **Editor & Publisher.**

the results obtained by advertisers, the large number of homes that may be reached and the gains in advertising linage from month to month are all facts that may be featured effectively in promoting the newspaper's advertising service. The great variety of wants that may be answered on the classified pages, the number of replies received from certain ads and the reasonable cost of a few insertions are other points to be emphasized. For all this there is no better medium than the newspaper itself.

11. Market Data — Information concerning the area in which the newspaper is circulated is of interest to advertisers and readers alike. Market data, presented in attractive display, is effective promotion for advertising.

12. Research Findings — The results of surveys made to determine reader interest or advertising effectiveness are the basis of good promotion. Facts obtained by press associations, comparing newspapers of the state, frequently reveal good points concerning the local newspaper. A newspaper's winnings in editorial contests make interesting reading and at the same time stimulate pride in the newspaper's achievements.

13. Commercial Printing and Office Supplies — Newspapers that do commercial printing or sell office equipment and supplies as an auxiliary business have, in the newspaper, an advertising medium that gives it a great advantage over competing print shops and supply houses.

These are the chief ways in which a newspaper may be used to promote itself, but promotion should not be limited to a newspaper's own columns.

Local Publications Are Patronized

In its general promotion program a newspaper needs to explain its merits to more than those who are regular subscribers. It should constantly strive to obtain new readers and advertisers.

Newspapers often carry advertisements in publications that represent certain organizations and groups in the local area. High on this list are school papers, church bulletins, fraternal magazines and sports programs. Advertising in these usually is for the purpose of promoting circulation or for merely gaining the good will of the organizations publishing them.

Sometimes, to promote stories of special interest to persons of a certain city or town in the circulation area, a newspaper will use community papers serving those towns. This is done more often by metropolitan papers than by smaller ones. Occasionally, too, as already mentioned concerning the New York *Times,* a large metropolitan newspaper will insert promotion ads in another paper published in the same city.

Trade Papers Promote Advertising

To reach prospective national advertisers, trade papers are used with good effect. Advertising agencies, manufacturers and producers are interested in all the facts a newspaper may give them concerning its market and its service to advertisers.

Magazines read by advertisers in the national field are excellent media for a newspaper's advertising. Such papers also will accept news stories concerning any unusual services a newspaper may offer or exceptional sales results obtained by it for any product.

The advertising inserted in trade papers usually is of an institutional or market nature. It may pertain to the quality of the newspaper's contents and the type of readers it serves. Sometimes the medals or prizes the newspaper has won for excellence in reporting, editorial writing, advertising copy writing, typography or community service are mentioned. The newspaper's history may be another interesting item. On the other hand, copy may pertain more directly to the newspaper's coverage of the market the advertiser would like to reach, the general economic trends or the merchandising service that the newspaper provides.

The placing of well-prepared copy in carefully selected trade journals is an important part of a large newspaper's promotion program. Trade paper space is purchased also by smaller newspapers but usually on a cooperative basis by a group of papers serving a definite area.

Television and Radio Are Effective

A newspaper should take advantage of every available medium to the extent that appropriated funds will permit. Although television and radio compete with newspapers in the providing of news and general entertainment and cultural features, they may at the same time be of service to the newspaper in promoting its services and features.

Television and radio may be used in about every promotion way that the newspaper's own columns may be employed. The newspaper's editorial services, features, advertising service and carrier service may be presented with telling effect.

Special subscription and advertising offers, special editions, new departments and community activities sponsored by the newspaper may be described and emphasized.

Staff members may appear on television or radio to explain their part in producing the newspaper. Carrier-salesmen may be introduced to the television audience by the circulation manager, and the advertising manager may give a graphic presentation of the work done in his department.

Television and radio may be employed to good advantage in any general newspaper promotion campaign.

Telephone and Telegraph Are Used

Surprising, too, is the extent to which the telephone and the telegraph may be used in promoting a newspaper.

Circulation is built and advertising is sold by telephone. That is an ordinary procedure in every newspaper office. And the telephone often is the only instrument of communication used in an effective promotion campaign. Circulation departments have conducted many telephone solicitation campaigns with their carrier-salesmen. Special offers are quickly presented and deals closed by phone with remarkable success. Work concerning special features also may go by telephone to the heads of various groups who would be especially interested.

The telephone is so important an instrument in promotion and selling that special instruction pertaining to its use is given in many newspaper offices. A clear, pleasant, courteous voice at the switchboard to answer each call is an important part of a newspaper's promotion program.

Terse and pleasant messages by telegraph also are the basis of many successful promotion campaigns. They provide a quick, convenient and impressive way of putting the promotion idea across.

Direct Mail Is Another Means

Those who may not be reached by the newspaper, radio, television, telephone and telegraph may be contacted in a very personal way by mail. A letter with enclosure carries the promotion message direct from the newspaper to the person it wishes to reach.

This is the chief way for handling subscription renewals and a very effective way to present the merits of the newspaper to prospective new subscribers. A well-constructed business letter from the circulation manager to a list of prospects often results in substantial returns. An average return of 2 per cent or more is considered satisfactory.

Much classified advertising is sold by mail. Results obtained by classified users and the rates for classified ads may be featured in letter inserts. Letters and cards addressed to automobile dealers, realtors, supply companies and auctioneers are productive instruments in promoting classified advertising.

The service given by the newspaper in obtaining sales outlets and displays for merchandise advertised in its columns is outlined for manufacturers, jobbers and advertising agencies in attractive mailing pieces. Large sheets carrying circulation facts in color and folded to convenient size for mailing are sent to national advertisers.

Cooperative advertising pages often are sold through correspondence, and assents from local merchants for tie-ins with national ads are obtained in the same way.

Fig. 5.7 — National Newspaper Week was effectively promoted by the Columbus, Ga., **Ledger-Enquirer** with outdoor advertising.

A newspaper's success in direct mail promotion depends greatly upon the type of mailing material it produces. It should be colorful, attractive, easy to read, and convincing in its presentation.

Some Use Outdoor Advertising

Another means of promotion used by some newspapers, mainly those published in metropolitan areas, is outdoor advertising. Brief statements in bold type with attractive illustrations displayed on large bulletin boards, posters or panels catch the attention of passing throngs (see Fig. 5.7).

Most outdoor advertising promotes special pages and features, classified advertising, circulation growth, newspaper-sponsored events, exclusive advertising or the company slogan. The St. Louis *Globe-Democrat* (circulation 332,823, population 856,796), before the admission of Alaska to the Union, featured the Forty-ninth State. The Denver *Post* (circulation 253,410, population 415,786) promotes its Rocky Mountain Area, and the Chicago *Tribune* (circulation 868,455, population 3,620,962) presents its claim to world prestige.

A jury of art directors, agency and business executives chose a Chicago *Tribune* outdoor poster for First Grand Award in the 26th National Competition of Outdoor Advertising Art, sponsored by the Art Directors Club of Chicago. The poster, "More Ideas for Home Builders" was drawn by Ed Renfro, an artist on the staff of Foote, Cone & Belding.

Although outdoor boards are forbidden on some highways and main city streets, they are available in many areas.

Other Avenues of Promotion Used

Many other avenues of promotion are available for newspapers, varying in spectacular effect from advertising specialities to sky-signs.

Films of the newspaper office and personnel, the city and its various markets are used to promote the newspaper's service to merchants and manufacturers in developing new sales outlets and increasing sales volume. Slide or strip films generally are considered better for this kind of promotion than flip-over charts if the group is in excess of five persons. Flannel boards also are effective in making promotion presentations to small groups.

The use of the movie theater screen was popular before the advent of television and some smaller newspapers still use it to promote circulation and classified advertising. Usually, however, it is on an exchange arrangement with the theater for newspaper advertising. Larger newspapers seldom use the movie for advertising unless it can be done as a tie-up with the film that is being presented.

Hundreds of items in the field of specialty advertising, such as pencils, desk pads, calendars, blotters, whistles, sewing kits, desk sets and key rings, are distributed at Christmas and throughout the year to keep customers reminded of the newspaper's services. Newsstand cards also may convey Holiday Greetings (see Fig. 5.8).

Fig. 5.8 — Colorful newsstand card conveys Christmas greetings from the Columbus, Ga., **Ledger-Enquirer.**

Novelty advertising, such as sky-signs and balloons with trailing signs, is sometimes used to promote an event the newspaper is sponsoring or an unusual feature it is introducing.

Building Plant Morale Essential

In addition to advertising itself to the general public, a newspaper needs to keep itself sold to the working force that produces it. Much effective promotion may be done inside the newspaper plant to build morale and increase production efficiency.

House organs and bulletins acquaint the staff with the newspaper's history, policies, retirement plan, insurance benefits, sports and cultural activities, special sales events, discounts on advertising and other advantages provided the newspaper's employees. A house organ — even though mimeographed — is valuable in keeping employees loyal to the newspaper and interested in their work.

Style books are provided for those in the news room and advertising department in order that they may know the rules of copy preparation. Manuals are available also for carriers. These instruct the boys in selling, delivering and collecting for the paper.

For both inside and outside promotion many media are available. Every newspaper should use them to the extent that they give promise of economical and practical results.

CHAPTER 6

Costs of
Effective Promotion

PROMOTION should be considered not as an expense but as an investment. Only on that basis can sound consideration be given to promotion expenditures. When a publisher realizes that promotion can yield for him a definite return on the money he puts into it, he is ready to formulate a promotion plan and set aside money for that purpose.

Fortunate indeed is the paper whose publisher is promotion-minded. Then the promotion manager is not handicapped in formulating and putting through a promotion program. The necessary funds are readily available.

PROMOTION BUDGET PLANS VARY

The amount used for promotion varies according to conditions within the newspaper organization and within the newspaper's community. A newspaper that has a strong centralized promotion department with full supervision and control over the newspaper's promotion program likely will spend more for promotion than one not sufficiently organized to do an effective promotion job. The well-organized department is more capable of showing definite returns and, therefore, can more easily prove to management that promotion is a real investment — not an unnecessary expense. Furthermore, a newspaper with strong competition from radio and television or perhaps from another newspaper is certain to spend more for promotion than a newspaper that is the only effective means of communication within the community.

[49]

One of the nation's largest newspapers spends more than two million dollars a year for promotion and realizes a good return on every dollar thus invested. Two newspapers, each with a circulation less than 100,000, spend respectively $75,000 and $89,000 a year to promote themselves to advertisers and readers. One with a circulation of little more than 250,000 spends $350,000 a year, while another with 350,000 circulation spends more than $700,000 on its total promotion program. Some of the smaller newspapers also have found it profitable to be liberal with promotion expenditures. A newspaper of 35,000 circulation maintains an annual promotion budget of $33,000. Some papers with very small circulations and without regularly organized promotion departments have found it profitable to spend at least $5,000 a year for art work and materials to be used by the advertising department in preparing effective promotion copy.

Some newspapers set up an annual budget for promotion, others a monthly or quarterly budget and appropriate the amounts required. Still others simply make expenditures as promotion seems needed. The most common plans used are these:

1. Appropriate a certain percentage of the newspaper's annual gross income for the entire promotion program, and then set up a budget showing how the money is to be spent for the promotion of each department and the newspaper in general.

2. Appropriate for the promotion of each department a certain percentage of the current income the department produces — a percentage of circulation income to be used in promoting circulation, a percentage of advertising income for promoting advertising and a certain percentage of the newspaper's entire income for promoting its news and feature services. A budget then is set up for each department on the basis of the promotion fund available for its use.

3. Study in advance the promotion needs of each month and make a monthly promotion appropriation to take care of those needs.

4. Set up no definite annual or monthly budget and make no general appropriation but spend for promotion what may seem necessary from week to week.

Percentage of Income Basis Is Favored

There is a strong feeling among large daily newspapers that the publisher and the promotion manager should look upon the promotion department much as a furniture manufacturer and his advertising manager look upon the advertising agency that advertises and promotes the furniture company's products. The promotion department is the newspaper's advertising agency to sell to the public the newspaper's various services. To carry the comparison further, a certain percentage of the newspaper's income, they believe, should be expended for promotion just as a certain portion of the manufacturer's income from sale of goods is appropriated for advertising.

The actual percentage of total income customarily appropriated for promotion by newspapers that follow this plan ranges from approximately 1 per cent to 5 per cent.

The Cincinnati, Ohio, *Enquirer* (circulation 203,960, population 503,998) spends between 4 and 5 per cent of its gross income for all kinds of promotion. "This percentage probably is high," says Joel Irwin, promotion manager, "but we have been moving ahead under full steam. New people every year in agencies, among advertisers and in the community need to be told that 'Solid Cincinnati Reads the Cincinnati *Enquirer*.'" Irwin believes also that a newspaper's promotion policies should be consistent with its promotion preachments. "Our business depends on advertising," he adds. "If we don't believe in advertising ourselves, we don't have a right to ask others to believe in it."

Irwin S. Taubkin, promotion manager of the New York *Times* (circulation 600,319, population 7,795,471) believes that a good rule of thumb to follow in determining the amount to spend for promotion would be "somewhere between 2 and 3 per cent" of the newspaper's gross receipts.

Clarence W. Harding, director of public relations for the South Bend, Ind., *Tribune* (circulation 108,793, population 115,911) feels that for a paper of the *Tribune*'s size and with a similar market situation, 2 per cent of gross income is a fair appropriation for promotion.

Many papers, however, give no consideration to income in making up a promotion budget or in setting aside money to be used for that purpose. They base the expenditure entirely on need.

According to some surveys, radio and television stations are inclined to appropriate a higher percentage of their total income for promotion than are newspapers. A Master of Arts thesis written by James Aberle[1] in 1955 at the University of Missouri indicated that the percentage budgeted for promotion by individual television stations ranged at that time from one-half of one per cent to 11.5 per cent. On the average, the stations in the survey reported that 4.5 per cent of their annual gross was spent for promotion. A further breakdown showed that the average station spent 2.1 per cent for national show promotion and 2.4 per cent for local show promotion. Usually it is the aim of a television station to spend not more than 5 per cent of the amount of a contract in promoting the program specified in the contract. Generally, the greater the income of the station the

---

[1] James Aberle, *Television Audience Promotion,* Master of Arts thesis, University of Missouri, 1955.

greater the expenditure for promotion. Radio stations in recent years have cut down on promotion expenditure. It is less than that spent by television stations.

As with newspapers, the amount spent for promotion by television and radio stations varies greatly. With all of them, assistance in marketing becomes a troublesome part of promotion. The demands for marketing service always are great, and it is important for all advertising media to control the expense of it and at the same time bring satisfactory results to their advertisers.

General Budget for Some

Smaller papers, as well as large ones, have found a general budget for promotion to be advantageous in several ways. The chief benefit is that, once budgeted, expenditures need no further approval. The promotion manager has definite goals toward which he can work without delay and disturbance. Other reasons why a general annual budget is favored are:

1. Permits better planning.
2. Provides consistent promotion operation.
3. Enables setting up a balanced promotion program.
4. Provides better control and makes promotion expenditures more effective.
5. Enables the promotion manager to do a better job of administration.
6. Controls charges which other departments may wish to place against promotion.

It seems advisable, however, in most cases, to allow for some flexibility in the promotion budget. Some cushion money should be provided with which to take advantage of special promotion opportunities as they may arise.

While David A. Lindsey was promotion manager of the Appleton, Wis., *Post-Crescent* (circulation 36,302, population 34,010), he operated on what he called an "approximate budget." Lindsey explained that his promotion budget "was open at both ends because it was difficult to determine a year in advance what events or needs might arise which would cause the budget to become unrealistic."

Departmental Budgets for Others

Some newspapers, in addition to having a general promotion manager, have a circulation promotion manager and an advertising promotion manager. In such a situation, the promotion manager of each department makes a careful study of his requirements, estimates the amount of money needed for promotion of his department and then reports his findings to the general promotion manager. The general promotion manager, the department promotion managers and the publisher or business manager of the newspaper then set up a general promotion program and appropriate to each department an amount sufficient to cover costs of its part of the general program.

The appropriation for promotion in each department depends on the proportion of income it produces during the year and on the need for promotion in that field of newspaper operation. If the publisher wishes to push circulation, the circulation department is allowed a larger amount to spend for circulation promotion. If the advertising department feels that national advertising volume could be increased by a well-devised promotion plan, more money goes to that department.

All the items pertaining to promotion then are set up in a general program and budget to be supervised by the general promotion manager.

Short-Term Budget Seems More Practical

On account of possible fluctuating conditions throughout the year, some newspapers consider it almost impossible to set up an annual budget for promotion that can be adhered to. They agree that a definite sum should be appropriated and budgeted for promotion but that it had better be set up on a shorter-term basis.

"Operating on an exact annual allocation would hamper the flexibility of our promotions," says Jack Newman, promotion manager of the Battle Creek, Mich., *Enquirer-News* (circulation 37,170, population 48,666). "Our promotional budget is on a needed program. We attempt to analyze our objectives and plan the proper promotional programs to reach our goal, and we budget for a month or two months in advance rather than attempting to set up an annual budget. In that way we are able to meet the needs and requirements of current conditions."

In Cincinnati, where there are two aggressive newspapers, eight radio stations and three television stations, it is quite natural that a newspaper publisher would want to keep his promotion budget flexible. The Cincinnati *Enquirer* sets up a definite budget by months, quarters, etc., for anticipated expenses such as trade paper advertising, research, payroll and the like, but it also has a floating budget to "put out fires" or to "start them up." "When we 'set sail' to capture leadership in a particular classification or troublesome linage area we usually allocate a special emergency fund to this venture and plan it as a special advertising program," says Joel Irwin, promotion manager. "Similarly, circulation promotions are aimed at specifically weak areas and budgets are fitted to the necessary circumstances."

Would Promote Without Budget

Some newspapers that have a well-organized promotion department and spend liberally for promotion do not operate under a definite annual promotion budget. While in a general way they have in mind approximately the amount they will spend for promotion each year, they do not designate definite amounts to be spent by the departments or for certain promotion projects planned for the year.

"It is impractical to construct a budget in advance that adequately will fill our promotional needs," says Ed Templin, promotion manager of the Lexington, Ky., *Herald* and *Leader* (combined circulation 65,607, population 55,534). "Promotions are added or discontinued as conditions dictate. This, of course, does not mean that we spend money foolishly. Our promotion department is required to justify all expenditures. Each new promotional activity is surveyed to determine if it produced results equal to the effort and investment that went into it, and non-productive promotions seldom are repeated. It is difficult to construct a budget that can be adapted to rapidly changing conditions."

Rudy C. Marcus, advertising and promotion director of the Riverside, Calif., *Press* and *Enterprise* (combined circulation 46,429, population 46,764) has a similar feeling regarding promotion budgets. "Inasmuch as a newspaper promotion department must meet the needs of many other departments, as well as the needs of its own department, it would seem advisable to avoid fixed allocations," he says. "Most newspapers, we realize, do repeat on a majority of projects each year, but in a fast-growing city and with a rapidly increasing circulation, a promotion manager should have plenty of latitude to meet the day-by-day opportunities for promoting his newspaper."

Many daily newspapers use a "charge-back" system of promotion operation, which does not require the declaration of a specific overall budget the first of each fiscal year. Materials used in producing sales campaigns and presentations for revenue-producing departments are charged back to the department involved. For example, materials used in a circulation sales program, such as broadsides, brochures, point-of-sale displays, are charged back to circulation. The charge-back system also includes costs for engravings and other production materials. If overtime is required in a campaign, that too is charged at the rate of time-and-a-half to the department benefited.

Usually such expenses as salaries, office supplies and art work are not charged back to the department involved but are carried as general expenses. However, some newspapers charge back the art work at so much per hour.

Some publishers who believe strongly in promotion and carry on some very effective promotion campaigns do not even maintain a promotion department or set up a particular appropriation or budget for promotion. What is done is carried out by regular members of the staff, usually by those in the advertising department, with the publisher, the general manager or the advertising manager directing the campaigns.

The Marshall, Tex., *News Messenger* (circulation 11,582, population 22,327) allocates liberal funds to promote circulation contests, special sections and other phases of its newspaper operation as occasions arise, but it has no regularly organized promotion department or budget. Millard Cope, publisher, explains that promotion expenditures are not set up on any definite basis but are made as an investment toward attaining particular goals set up from time to time. "If we assume," he says, "that it is worth a certain number of dollars for us to produce additional circulation or some advertising promotion, we simply spend that much money. Often we do so, realizing that the return will be on a long-term basis or that a particular section may not pay off this year. However, we expect it to yield a return in the long run."

Many situations may arise within a year to alter any original budgeting for promotion. Among these are:

1. A decision of management to increase subscription rates immediately.
2. A decision to increase advertising rates.
3. A change in column widths and type faces for the classified advertising page.
4. Special retail events for which merchants want help from the newspaper in promoting.
5. Special events which the newspaper wishes to sponsor.
6. The development of some new editorial features that require immediate promotion.
7. Decision to issue an extra-large edition in commemoration of a special event.
8. A desire to increase classified advertising volume immediately.
9. Downward trends in advertising linage and circulation that need to be reversed quickly.
10. Sudden change in general business conditions.
11. Special research projects that need immediate support.
12. The abandonment of projects or services that proved unprofitable.
13. Special readership studies and public opinion polls that need supervision.
14. Expanded activities for the entertainment of youth.
15. Other definite plans for expansion and growth.

NOT EASY TO PLAN PROMOTION BUDGET

Perhaps one reason that many newspapers do not operate on a budget is because of the difficulty faced in compiling one. It is not a matter that can be worked out by the promotion manager alone. He must confer with department managers, each of whom is interested in obtaining a maximum of promotion for his department. The budget also must meet the approval of the publisher or the general manager and most likely the person who writes the checks for the company.

But regardless of the difficulties involved, more newspapers each year are going to the budget plan for their promotion departments. Those who operate on a budget see great benefits to be derived from meetings of their department managers with the general promotion manager to devise a constructive program and determine the financial means needed. It helps bring unity and cooperation into the working organization.

The Houston, Tex., *Chronicle* (circulation 192,062, population 596,163) determines its budget in October following conferences of the promotion manager, advertising director, general advertising manager and the business manager.

All budgets for the Cincinnati *Enquirer* are approved semi-annually, and the fiscal year ends on September 30. Although the promotion budget is checked carefully at the end of each six months, some parts of it may be revised monthly. The advertising promotion manager makes up a budget for his department, and the advertising director, after approving it, submits it to the general promotion manager. Usually the newspaper's special representative is conferred with in regard to what should be spent in trade papers to promote the sale of general advertising. The circulation promotion budget is submitted by the circulation director to the publisher and business manager for approval.

The Milwaukee *Journal* (circulation 361,856, population 637,392) makes up its budget in late November on the basis of recommendations from the promotion manager and evaluation of proposed allocations by departmental classifications.

The method used in making a promotion budget for the South Bend, Ind., *Tribune* is thus described by Clarence Harding, director of public relations: "Before beginning the fiscal year, we go over last year's budget and determine whether we will be doing this year all the things it covered. We then try to include all the things contemplated for this year that we did not do last year. We then eliminate the things we did last year that we will not repeat this year. The result is our budget."

At the New York *Times* the promotion department recommends and management determines the items and the amounts for the annual budget on the basis of present and anticipated need.

In compiling a promotion budget for the Rockford, Ill., *Star* and *Register-Republic* (combined circulation 83,973, population 92,927), the department heads are called into conference with the business manager. The program decided upon then is submitted to the publisher for approval.

When one considers the many items that must go into a promotion budget, the task of compiling becomes plain. Expenditures must be made for art work, engraving, printing, postage, express, telephone service, telegrams, souvenirs, favors, birthday gifts, entertainment, travel, organization dues and general supplies. Market information must be obtained through surveys and research. Bulletins, house organs and brochures must be planned and produced. The newspaper's advertising service, circulation, news and features must be promoted through the newspaper, trade publications, radio and television. Customer relations must be strengthened and good will built in the community through speaking engagements and entertainment features.

There is also the problem of dividing up the possible promotion expenditure between these items to the satisfaction of all the newspaper departments which must be represented. No pattern can be developed that would suit all newspapers, because each newspaper has an individual situation with respect to promotion. While one needs to spend heavily to promote advertising, another will want to place the emphasis on circulation. The one that has a well-organized promotion department will have to spend a greater portion of its allotment on payroll. Table 6.1 shows how the percentages of total promotion expenditure vary on principal items among several newspapers.

PROMOTION COSTS ARE JUSTIFIABLE

In whatever way one looks at promotion, the cost of it seems justifiable. For these days of intensive public relations, promotion is just as essential for newspapers as for any other business institution. It is just as much a part of the publishing business as selling advertising, building circulation or producing the daily or weekly issue. It should be treated as such by small and medium-sized newspapers just as it is by metropolitan newspapers.

Too many newspapers are afraid of promotion from the standpoint of costs and results. They think they are getting along well by letting someone with another important responsibility in their organization take care of promotion. By doing so, they believe they are holding down costs. But are they? By centralizing the promotion activities in a specially qualified person or in a department set up for that purpose, the time and efficiency of valuable people already carrying heavy loads can be saved for the particular work they are expected to do. At the same time, the efficiency of promotion campaigns is stepped up and the influence of the paper is widened.

What large papers can do, medium-sized and small dailies, and even weeklies, can do on a smaller but equally impressive scale. A little quick thinking and ingenious planning often is all that is needed. John B. Gordon, publisher of the Houma, La., *Courier* (circulation

TABLE 6.1
NEWSPAPER PROMOTION EXPENDITURES

Percentages of Total Budget Spent for Important Items
by Six American Daily Newspapers
Whose Circulations Range From 35,000 to 200,000

News-paper	Pay-roll	Travel	Telephone and Telegraph	Supplies	Print-ing	Classified and Retail Ad. Prom.	Gen. Ad. Prom.	Circ. Prom.	Edi-torial Prom.	Public Rela-tions
No. 1	15	2	1	1	3	4	23	24	6	21
No. 2	30	3	1	6	3	10	20	20	2	3
No. 3	73	4.2	1	1.6	.1	...	...	...	...	20.1
No. 4	24	5	1	10	3	...	...	57	...	...
No. 5	16	...	...	10	6	3	15	50	...	...
No. 6	9	...	...	21	...	4	9	30	...	27

Note: The widest range of expenditures is in the payroll department — from 9 to 73 per cent. This item will vary from year to year on any newspaper, depending upon the current promotion program, and from month to month, depending upon seasonal needs and local circumstances.

6,003, population 11,505), wanted to set aside a special fund for promotion and plant improvement. He opened a separate bank account, into which he placed all revenues from classified advertising and circulation, leaving the revenue from other advertising, commercial printing and other sources in the main bank account to take care of current expenses. Within two decades after starting the plan, he improved his plant to the amount of $175,000. The basic payment for this came from the special promotion account.

Promotion properly done creates added advertising linage, increases circulation, makes possible plant improvements, steps up reader interest and creates good will. These are all worth spending money for. Promotion is a wise investment.

PART II

Promoting News
and Editorial Services

Fig. 7.1 — Front for plant of the Mexico, Mo., **Ledger** is a replica of the newspaper's front page.

CHAPTER 7

Promoting the
Newspaper's Personality

A NEWSPAPER, like an individual, has a personality. It has a historical background, a style of dress, certain interests, ideals and
qualities that distinguish it. Persons who read it regularly or do business with it through its circulation, advertising and news departments
recognize these characteristics and appreciate them. They are points
of merit that may be as effectively promoted as any of the services the
newspaper offers. What it stands for, in fact, is a bracer for all it
attempts to do. Therefore, all the factors that contribute to a newspaper's personality should become major items in its promotion program. Among these factors are:

1. Its historical background.
2. Its established creed or policy.
3. Its complete, fair and objective coverage of news.
4. Its editorial page.
5. Its general support of journalistic ideals.
6. Its typographical makeup and appearance.

Should Promote Newspaper's History

A newspaper, the same as a person, is judged by its "upbringings."
Its past, if it is creditable, helps to make its present more glowing and
forceful. Consequently, a newspaper's history may be the basis of
interesting and effective promotion. This, in fact, seems to be the
appropriate starting point for most newspaper promotion.

In a handsome booklet of 43 pages, the Kansas City, Mo., *Star*
(circulation 334,518, population 456,622) goes back to 1880 when its

first small issue of four pages was scoffingly referred to by its rivals as the "Twilight Twinkler" and from there follows its record of growth through the years. It's a thrilling story of journalistic enterprise and community service — an ideal piece of promotion for one of America's great newspapers.

An important step in orienting a new staff member is to acquaint him with the history and policies of the newspaper. Facts that he should know about the newspaper's past record and its aims for the future usually are presented in an attractive company booklet. Thus he becomes acquainted at once with the organization he is to serve and represent.

If it is important for a staff member to understand the historic background of the newspaper he works for, it is equally important for readers to obtain the same facts concerning a newspaper upon which they are to depend for information and guidance. The modern promotion-minded publisher, therefore, takes advantage of every opportunity to reveal the history and the aims of his newspaper.

Anniversaries of a newspaper's founding are appropriate times to issue special editions containing an abundance of historical material concerning the newspaper and its community. Many newspapers within the past decade have observed their centennials in this way. A service record of 25, 50, 100 years, or more, readily becomes the basis of effective newspaper promotion. (See Chapter 24 for additional facts concerning special editions.)

Newspaper personalities — past and present — provide colorful material for newspaper promotion. In an interesting feature article the New Orleans, La., *Times-Picayune* (circulation 194,358, population 570,445) told about its own Pearl Rivers, who in 1876, took over the *Picayune* and became probably the first woman in the world to own a metropolitan newspaper. It was an interesting story for the newspaper's readers — one worthy of being preserved for future generations. So the *Times-Picayune* made it into a handsome two-color reprint illustrated with old photographs and drawings.

When Sam Gearhart, general manager of the Fayetteville, Ark., *Northwest Arkansas Times* (circulation 10,409, population 17,071) in 1953 completed 50 years in the newspaper business, the story of his rise from a paper carrier to publisher and manager was given in the bulletin of the Southern Newspaper Publishers Association, in his own paper and in various other publications. With Gearhart's climb up the ladder of newspaper responsibility, came improvements in his newspaper. His work for the progress of his city and state and for the advancement of journalism was emphasized. While a publisher thus received kudos, his newspaper also was promoted in an effective way.

A newspaper's early environment and progress may be presented in other interesting ways. When the Santa Barbara, Calif., *News-Press* (circulation 26,509, population 44,913) completed its new plant, Dick Smith, promotion manager, who had natural artistic skill, began painting murals on the walls leading from the lobby to the tower foyer. These murals depict the history of the newspaper and its community. Each day they speak out of the past to patrons and employees; continuing these fine traditions, the modern new building reveals the newspaper's high aims for the present and future.

A newspaper's face, just as a person's face, reveals personality. The front of the modern newspaper plant erected by the Mexico, Mo., *Ledger* (circulation 8,426, population 11,623) is a replica of the newspaper's front page (see Fig. 7.1). Consequently, the *Ledger's* bright face shines out to all who pass the building just as it does to subscribers as they receive the paper in their homes.

This newspaper's character and ideals again are revealed in the office lobby where, framed and hanging on the wall above the reception counter, are two highly important quotations. One is the First Amendment to the American Constitution: "Congress shall make no law respecting an establishment of religion, or prohibiting the free exercise thereof; or abridging the freedom of speech or of the press; or the right of the people peaceably to assemble, and to petition the government for a redress of grievances." The other statement is by Thomas Jefferson: "The basis of our government being the opinion of the people, the very first object should be to keep it right. Were it left to me to decide whether we should have a government without newspapers, or newspapers without government, I should not hesitate a moment to prefer the latter."

Policies Should Be Proclaimed

Closely connected with a newspaper's history is its creed or platform. Out of actual experience and by observing the successful operations of other newspapers, a publisher who takes seriously his responsibility to the public devises a policy for his newspaper. A published statement of a newspaper's ideals and goals helps it to obtain cooperation from readers in accomplishing the purposes it has in mind. Such a statement takes the public into confidence and honestly invites cooperation.

Great newspapers — both large and small — have obtained the reputations they hold by setting up and attaining certain journalistic goals and service aims. These form a creed that should be publicized. The public is entitled to know what sort of ideals and practices a newspaper upholds.

Following a consultation of executives and employees, the Yakima, Wash., *Republic* and *Herald* (combined circulation 33,498, population 38,486) a few years ago drew up a creed which has been an important factor in maintaining morale within the organization and in building good will within the community:

THE IDEALS OF THE
REPUBLIC PUBLISHING COMPANY

To apply the Golden Rule in our dealings with one another — "Do unto others as you would have them do unto you."

To remember never to take advantage of the fact that we publish the only daily newspaper in the Valley.

To use the facilities of our newspapers so that they will help to build a better Yakima Valley.

To guard jealously the quality of our newspapers and the products of the Republic Press.

To make no promises we can't fulfill, and to fulfill all promises we do make.

To remember that everything we produce is the result of many hands — that our continued success lies in teamwork.

To treat courteously all with whom we deal, both inside and outside the plant.

To be liberal with our commendations, generous with our patience and unsparing of understanding for the other fellow.

To make every effort to provide working conditions that will insure comfort and protect health.

To earn a profit which will return a fair share to investors and a fair wage to employees without setting prices so high that customers withhold their business.

To remember that, as members of one big team, we owe it to each other to conduct ourselves at all times so that we will be a credit to the organization we represent.

This well-composed statement of policy has been widely circulated. It presents a pattern for attractive promotion of a newspaper's good manners and warm heart.

"Three Commandments" guide the Des Moines, Iowa, *Register* and *Tribune* (combined circulation 345,146, population 177,965) in handling news and expressing opinions on issues of the day. Its code is brief and specific:

1. We believe in presenting ALL the news impartially and objectively in the news columns.

2. We believe in expressing our own opinions as persuasively and forcefully as possible but confining these expressions to the editorial page.

3. We believe in giving our readers the opinions of other writers representing ALL SIDES of important controversial issues in order that our readers may form their own judgments wisely.

Here again is effective promotion of a type that any newspaper may provide. The New York *Times* also believes that a declaration of policies is good business and produces an abundance of good will (see Fig. 7.2) .

For Reliability in the News

A newspaper's reliability, however, is best shown in its news columns. If it follows a policy of complete, fair and objective report-

"To give the news impartially, without fear or favor, regardless of any party, sect or interest involved"

Fig. 7.2 — In an **Editor & Publisher** advertisement, the New York **Times** features the newspaper's policy for handling news.

ing, it really has something to talk about, for it is those characteristics of news handling that make the newspaper dependable.

The Chicago *News* (circulation 547,796, population 3,620,962) made for itself some great promotion when in 1956 it trail-blazed a probe that pushed out into daylight one of the greatest frauds ever uncovered in state government — the misappropriation of $1,500,000 of public funds in the office of a state auditor. Hundreds of letters, praising the *News* for its exposé, came to its office from all sections of the nation. Newspapers and magazines applauded it in their editorial columns. Copies of these letters and editorials were reproduced in a flashy 2-color poster that was distributed widely.

"Probably the most useful purpose a newspaper can perform is to safeguard the public interest," said Publisher John S. Knight in reply to this great wave of public applause.

Emphasis on ways in which a newspaper protects its readers always is in good taste and is well received. Its everyday consideration for the public's needs and desires, as well as what it may do in a spectacular way in revealing crime and corruption, is something to be talked about.

The Detroit, Mich., *Times* (circulation 391,295, population 1,849,568) promotes itself as a "Family Newspaper," designed, edited and published with all members of the family in mind. It claims prudence, wisdom and discretion in selecting and preparing all copy that enters its columns. "We believe that reporting should furnish the desired information and yet remain within the realm of good taste for adult readers and youthful readers alike," it said in a full-page promotion advertisement over the signature of W. E. Anderson, publisher.

The Milwaukee, Wis., *Journal* (circulation 361,856, population 637,392) takes a firm stand for objective reporting. Each new man who joins its staff is given these instructions: "In our news columns we are to be as objective as is humanly possible. There is to be no coloring of the news, no playing up or playing down of legitimate news stories because the *Journal* is or is not supporting a measure, even though a statement or an event will knock into a cocked hat some measure which the *Journal* is supporting in its editorial columns. If it is legitimate news, it is to be written and published and given such display as its news value warrants. We must endeavor always to get both sides of every story and give every person who has a case the opportunity to state it. In our news columns we have but one purpose and that is to print all facts that can be ascertained."

Should Promote Editorial Comment

A newspaper's policy regarding current issues and movements generally is reflected in its editorials. Not all papers, however, have a strong and attractive editorial page. But those that do should promote it well.

A newspaper's editorials reveal its mind and heart, and the features that appear on its editorial page show also its scope of vision and understanding of movements that affect its readers. Here is where an editor may talk heart to heart with subscribers and they in turn may talk back to him through letters to the editor.

The Milwaukee *Journal* is as particular about keeping its editorial columns fair and reliable as it is about maintaining objectivity in its news columns.

"We try to make honesty, sincerity and common sense the guiding principles of our editorials," J. D. Ferguson, editor, told journalism educators at their annual convention in Madison, Wis., in 1950. "The *Journal* is interested only in principles. If a man who is running for public office espouses principles which common sense leads our editorial writers to believe to be right, that man's candidacy most likely will have the *Journal*'s support. Because we do follow principles and not political organizations, it has often been that in the same election the *Journal* has supported for various political offices a man who labeled himself a Republican and a man who labeled himself a Democrat and possibly a man who tagged himself a Socialist."

Such policies for the presentation of news and editorial comment provide excellent promotion material.

Each year in late December the Toledo, Ohio, *Blade* (circulation 183,143, population 303,616) reports to its readers, in a full-page announcement, the accomplishments of the past year and its aims for the year ahead. In one of these annual summaries it recounted a host of important movements it had instituted or supported. It had battled for a fair employment practices program for the city, state and nation; it had favored better schools, water and sewerage and, as usual, the St. Lawrence Seaway. It had always been against every kind of hypocrisy, bigotry and prejudice.

In other ways from time to time the *Blade* proclaims its policy of serving the public interest, "guided always by sound principles, high ideals and a free open mind."

That editorial comment is wanted by the reading public is shown by the number of editorial writers and commentators who are making a highly satisfactory living with their up-to-the-minute approaches to live issues and human experiences. Editors of small papers who write personal columns are continuously made conscious of wide readership. And the popularity of the editorial page has been further revealed in readership surveys.

In a page observation study of newspapers by Daniel Starch and staff in 1957, editorials rated fifth with men and seventh with women among all the pages offered by the Boston, Mass., *Traveler* (circulation 183,620, population 801,444), Houston, Tex., *Post* (circulation 198,636, population 596,163), Denver, Colo., *Post* (circulation 253,410, population 415,786), New York *Mirror* (circulation 880,500, population 7,795,471), Los Angeles *Herald and Express* (circulation 348,351, population 2,243,901) and Philadelphia, Pa., *Inquirer* (circulation 619,381, population 2,071,605). Seventy-seven per cent of the men interviewed and 67 per cent of the women said they read the editorial page and expressed appreciation for it. Men read the editorial page as closely as they read sports, and women read editorials with as great interest as they read comics.

Why then is not more attention given to editorials by publishers and why do not those who have editorial pages promote them more consistently?

One of the most interesting articles in "A Week in the Life of a Metropolitan Newspaper," an attractive promotion booklet put out by the Milwaukee *Journal,* is a description of this newspaper's daily editorial conference where the editorials to be written are planned and assigned.

Lindsay Hoben, chief editorial writer, explains that the six members of the editorial writing staff are comparatively young — no venerable graybeards among them. All have had news experience and write occasional news articles as by-products of their studies and travels. Each man is called upon to discuss timely subjects in his particular field. Sometimes there are questions that do not fall in any of the regular fields. Occasionally, in dealing with technical or complicated subjects, it becomes necessary to have an additional meeting in the afternoon.

The *Journal* tries to get a balance each day of national and international, state and local subjects. Nothing is too far away and — more important — nothing is too near for the paper to discuss editorially. Mr. Hoben explains that "if it is important to know what one is talking about on the subject of untouchability in India, it is 10 times more important to know exactly what he is talking about if he starts slugging it out with some of the building trades in a controversy over an unnecessarily restrictive local plumbing code."

Other details are given in the story to make editorial writers appear to readers for what they are — active, interesting men with alert minds rather than shabbily dressed individuals all wrapped up in themselves, the dictionary and encyclopedia. Such promotion helps to bring the editorial page more alive — a section of the newspaper to be sought and read consistently.

The Kansas City *Star* presented for its readers in a full-page advertisement a similar picture of its editorial writers. "The Eggheads and I" was the title given to this promotion, and topping the page was a picture of Dick Fowler, associate editor, and his corps of seven editorial writers.

"Some office observers, viewing the daily huddle of *Star* editorial writers pictured above, are unkind enough to suggest it resembles a brain wash," the copy continues. "Such a statement is miles wide of the mark. *Star* writers are traditionally tough-minded; they do not take readily to dictation. This discussion is wide open and all members of the editorial staff are expected to take part. From their lively give and take emerge the ideas for *Star* editorials."

Something then is said about the presiding genius of Fowler, his educational background and his aims for the editorial page. The promotion concludes with this statement: "Editorial opinions — and an editorial page would not be worth its salt without opinions — attract brickbats and bouquets. Dick Fowler wouldn't have it any other way. He's another reason why YOUR BIG READING BARGAIN BY FAR IS YOUR KANSAS CITY STAR."

The Des Moines *Register* and *Tribune* has an editorial staff meeting once or twice a week. Lauren Soth, editor of its editorial pages, believes the thoughts of competent writers not on the staff also should appear on the pages.

The editor of a good weekly or small daily who greets his readers regularly with thoughtful, friendly editorial comment could just as easily produce an interesting promotion for his editorial page by telling how he molded his thoughts while walking to the office each morning, or perhaps went to the office without breakfast before other staff members arrived in order to write his daily column or editorial undisturbed.

There are many ways to promote the editorial page. A résumé of subjects discussed in the course of a month or a year would be interesting information. Publishers frequently present a collection of their best editorials in booklet form.

Should Promote Journalistic Ideals

Closely connected with a newspaper's editorial policy is its devotion to and explanation of the general ideals and practices of journalism. When it promotes these, it not only helps to keep the public mindful of journalism's contribution to sound government and free enterprise but it makes for itself a warmer spot in the hearts of its readers.

The important part played by America's vigorous press in sustaining free government cannot be emphasized too strongly or too widely. There is still plenty of misunderstanding about freedom of the press, regardless of what it has meant to America and of what has been said so eloquently in support of it.

G. R. Closway, editor of the Winona, Minn., *News* (circulation 21,018, population 25,031) sent an "inquiring reporter" out to learn what the man in the street thinks about a free press and free speech. The reporter asked, "What, in your opinion, is freedom of the press?" Of 16 persons interviewed, nine tried to define it, four said they didn't know what it is, and three had no comment.

Publishers have come quickly to the defense of press freedom when it has been trampled upon by public officials, but they have been all too reticent about explaining that freedom of the press exists for the benefit of readers rather than for the protection of the newspaper. Freedom of the press never was intended to grant any special privilege to the publisher. It was intended to safeguard the reader's freedom to read anything that is being said on subjects that interest him.

Every newspaper has the opportunity to help sell the case for Freedom of Information to the American public, and at the same time lift its own prestige in the field of journalism and in the community it serves. And some are doing much about it.

The Des Moines *Register* and *Tribune* in 1947 published a series of articles prepared by Jack Wilson, Washington correspondent, dealing with specific cases of secrecy and suppression of news in the Federal Government. Wilson cited laws which bureaucrats use to hide information and explained how approximately 1,250 reporters for all media are not allowed to do a complete job because of an existing climate of secrecy in Washington. These articles appeared in full or condensed form also in the Chicago *News,* the Everett, Wash., *Herald* (circulation 28,435, population 33,849), the Indianapolis, Ind., *News* (circulation 170,490, population 427,173), Los Angeles *Mirror-News* (circulation 307,412, population 2,243,901), the Louisville, Ky., *Times* (circulation 175,579, population 369,129), the Nashville *Tennessean* (circulation 119,848, population 174,307), the Richmond, Va., *Times-Dispatch* (circulation 134,360, population 230,310), St. Petersburg, Fla., *Times* (circulation 90,014, population 96,738) and the Tampa, Fla., *Tribune* (circulation 128,927, population 124,681). In this united promotion project, a group of America's leading newspapers demonstrated their firm intention to protect the right of American citizens to know what is going on at the seat of government.

Press associations in all sections of the country are alert to restrictions on press freedom. At the annual convention of the National Editorial Association in 1907, Stanford Smith, assistant to the general manager of the American Newspaper Publishers Association, told publishers: "To whatever extent newspapers are able to dig out the facts by vigorous reportorial initiative and supply those facts to the public, to that extent important battles are won in the all-out war to protect the public's right to public information."

The publisher of a small weekly comes to the protection of this right as readily as the publisher of a large daily. When the City Council of Hamilton, Mo., passed an ordinance giving the mayor the privilege of holding secret meetings, Marion O. Ridings, publisher of the Hamilton, Mo., *Advocate-Hamiltonian* (circulation 2,130, population 1,728) protested and was escorted bodily from the council room. Ridings took the matter to the Attorney General who said that no city council or other governing body has a right to violate the principle of freedom of information — the people's right to know what their government is doing.

"When an office holder, who spends the people's money and uses the people's power, starts hiding public records, it's time to ask why," said the Mexico, Mo., *Ledger* in an editorial. "It's time to start digging. Since newspapers down through their history have done a fairly consistent job of serving well the people, people depend on them to do their asking-of-why, to do their digging. And in depending on newspapers, people act on what newspapers discover and reveal about suppressed information."

When publishers come forth quickly and boldly to defend this right so important to a free people, they help to elevate the profession of journalism and at the same time lift themselves a bit higher in the esteem of their patrons. Whatever a single newspaper can do to raise journalistic standards and to support the high ethics that prevail in the profession is a promotion of the press in general — and the good effect of it soon gets back to the paper's home community.

A strong point always to be emphasized is that a newspaper is a public record of events. The printed word is accepted in a court of law. Air waves cannot be introduced as evidence.

In 1958, when the School of Journalism of the University of Missouri, the first fully organized school of journalism in the world, celebrated its 50th anniversary, it sent to each newspaper in the world a copy of "The Journalist's Creed," written by Walter Williams, founder and first dean of the Missouri School of Journalism. Papers in many parts of the earth printed this creed (see page 74).

Thus the high standards to which all good journalists subscribe were proclaimed throughout the world — a concerted promotion effort reflecting credit on a free press everywhere.

Point Out Typographical Improvements

Along with a newspaper's history, policies, ideals and other things that make it distinctive is its general appearance. Thousands of dollars have been spent by publishers in recent years to make their papers easy to read and in every way attractive and serviceable. Sharp editing, more news-magazine style of writing, color printing, new type faces, better engraving, fewer column rules and more white space and the elimination of "jump" stories make the paper more appealing.

In many papers large promotion ads have appeared similar to one run in the Minneapolis *Star* and *Tribune* (combined circulation 502,252, population 521,718), announcing the use of a new type of special design.

THE JOURNALIST'S CREED

I believe in the profession of journalism.

I believe that the public journal is a public trust; that all connected with it are, to the full measure of their responsibility, trustees for the public; that acceptance of lesser service than the public service is betrayal of this trust.

I believe that clear thinking and clear statement, accuracy, and fairness, are fundamental to good journalism.

I believe that a journalist should write only what he holds in his heart to be true.

I believe that suppression of the news, for any consideration other than the welfare of society, is indefensible.

I believe that no one should write as a journalist what he would not say as a gentleman; that bribery by one's own pocket-book is as much to be avoided as bribery by the pocket-book of another; that individual responsibility may not be escaped by pleading another's instructions or another's dividends.

I believe that advertising, news, and editorial columns should alike serve the best interests of readers; that a single standard of helpful truth and cleanness should prevail for all; that the supreme test of good journalism is the measure of its public service.

I believe that the journalism which succeeds best — and best deserves success — fears God and honors man; is stoutly independent, unmoved by pride of opinion or greed of power, constructive, tolerant but never careless, self-controlled, patient, always respectful of its readers but always unafraid; is quickly indignant at injustice; is unswayed by the appeal of privilege or the clamor of the mob; seeks to give every man a chance, and, as far as law and honest wage and recognition of human brotherhood can make it so, an equal chance; is profoundly patriotic while sincerely promoting international good will and cementing world comradeship; is a journalism of humanity, of and for today's world.

— WALTER WILLIAMS

"This new type with taller, blacker letters," the ad said, "will result in sharp, clear printing and lead you from letter to letter and word to word with a minimum of eye effort. Reading will be easier, faster and smoother. It is another step in our continued effort to provide you with better newspapers."

The general advancement made by newspapers toward typographical excellence is revealed in the many typography contests held by press associations. More attractive and more functional headlines are employed in news columns, and better selection of type, better use of illustrations, borders and white space show up in advertisements. Progressive publishers are giving hours of research and hundreds of dollars to the general attractiveness and utility of their newspapers.

In announcing winners in the Inland Daily Press Association's 1958 Typographical Contest, Prof. Kenneth E. Olsen, chairman of the judging committee, said: "The only purpose of good typography and make-up is to make newspapers easy to read, attractive and interesting to subscribers, and it is pleasing to see how Inland papers have been improving in this respect since this competition started 19 years ago. Then many papers were still going to their readers 'dressed in overalls' — today most are going to subscribers in their best 'Sunday-go-to-meetin' clothes."

When a newspaper changes its dress and becomes more attractive and serviceable, it has something to promote — something to talk about.

"A solid promotion de-
partment can make
an editor look
amazingly good.
It can, if it wants to,
do a beautiful series
of promotion advertise-
ments on reporters
and editors."

— Frank A. Knight,
Former Managing Editor,
Charleston, W. Va.,
Gazette

CHAPTER 8

Promoting
the News

" A NEWSPAPER must function as a newspaper before it can function as an advertising medium," said the Philadelphia *Inquirer* (circulation 619,381, population 2,071,605) in an attractive full-page review of what it had given its readers during the preceding year. It said nothing about the newspaper's circulation growth or its increase in advertising volume, points more commonly dwelt upon in newspaper promotion. Instead, it called attention to a host of editorial and public service innovations it had pioneered during the year — a better way of letting the public know that something new and enlightening is always coming up in the *Inquirer* to make the paper of value to both readers and advertisers.

Evidence of fair and thorough handling of news is of more importance than the fact that a newspaper in the course of a year obtained more dollars of advertising than ever before or that its circulation was at an all-time high. When a publisher establishes the fact that his newspaper is doing a good job at giving the news he presents proof of its worth in all the other ways it may serve the public. Newspaper promotion, therefore, should place emphasis on:

1. The various types of news the paper presents.
2. The abundance of news and features to be found in a single issue.
3. The local and distant sources from which news is drawn.
4. The provisions made for interpreting the news.
5. The emphasis placed on human interest as well as factual news.
6. The efforts put forth to make its reporting accurate and timely.
7. The qualifications of those who gather and write the news.

Should Emphasize News Variety

Unless some sort of picture is drawn for them, few readers realize the great assortment of news offered to them in the average American newspaper: news of the world, nation, state and local community; news of happenings in the fields of government, politics, business, religion, education, agriculture, science, society and sports; news of special interest to adults, middle-aged and young; news that is serious and light, factual and entertaining; news that warrants big headlines and some that rates but a line or two of space — but all of it conveying information wanted by people within the newspaper's circulation area.

An issue of the Scottsbluff, Nebr., *Star-Herald* (circulation 13,906, population 12,858), casually selected for analysis, contained stories on its front page concerning politics, agriculture, banking, manufacturing, transportation, biology, nuclear science and meteorology. Then through its other pages, mingled with items about people of the local community, were stories pertaining to military matters, health and medicine, crime prevention, education, entertainment, retirement, religion, sports, labor, community progress, mining, social security, foreign aid, traffic, photography and marketing. Such a diversity of subject matter makes a newspaper a reliable text on the current happenings of the day in all the more important realms of thought and action.

Equally astonishing is the great variety of news that is offered in a progressive weekly newspaper. The Marshfield, Mo., *Mail* (circulation 3,030, population 1,925), which features only news from its local community, carried front page stories about high school activities, deaths of three prominent citizens, robbery of a mercantile establishment, the launching of a community fund drive, proceedings of the magistrate's court, livestock sales, the granting of a doctor's degree to a local man, road conditions, weather forecast, and "Jots from the Editor's Notebook," a personal column.

No better promotion advertisement for either of these two newspapers could be drawn than one explaining the different subjects of interest presented to readers in the course of a year. What a compendium of important material! It's a big package for the few dollars each reader spends to have it all delivered to his home fresh, bright and in convenient reading form.

Quantity of News Is Enormous

The volume of news is as striking as the great variety offered to readers by any newspaper of eight pages or more. A small weekly with an average of 12 pages in each issue presents during a year an astonishing stack of news, while the volume offered by a large daily is enormous.

Some of the smaller dailies have kept records on the space devoted to the various community interests or organizations in their news columns. This has provided effective promotion.

When it can be shown to the Ministerial Alliance and to church boards that the local newspaper carries from 40 to 50 pages of news about church activities each year, there can be little opportunity for criticism of the newspaper's attitude toward religion. When, at the bureau's annual dinner, officers of the County Farm Bureau can be shown newspaper clippings of Farm Bureau news that will string several times around the dining hall, it lets the farmers know in a graphic way that the newspaper is reporting the Farm Bureau's efforts. It also draws a lot of good will to the newspaper from an important element of the community.

Chambers of Commerce in many communities conduct what they call a Business-Industry-Education Day. This usually is held about a week before school opens in the fall, but sometimes it is held later. In that case, schools are dismissed for a day to allow public school teachers to become acquainted with the industries and business institutions which provide the majority of tax money that supports public education. The newspaper usually is one of the places visited and the publisher has a great opportunity to explain to teachers the way the newspaper operates for the benefit of the community.

One publisher, in advance of the teachers' visit, had a member of his staff make a careful check of all copy carried in his paper concerning the schools, and he told the teachers that during the preceding year his paper had carried 20,000 column inches of news pertaining to their work in the schools. This, he explained, was equivalent to 120 pages a year or 10 pages a month. He said further: "We are vitally interested in our schools. They are one of our chief sources of news and they receive our editorial support for their tax levies, school activities and educational aims."

The Kansas City, Mo., *Star* and *Times* (combined circulation 663,656, population 456,622) stresses in promotional material the great volume of news that appears daily in the morning and evening editions. The *Star* and *Times* carries 80,000 words of news daily, a volume equal to that of a full-length novel. To carry the illustration further, it gives to subscribers annually a quantity of reading material equivalent to what would be found in a library of 365 volumes.

News From Many Sources

Just as astonishing as the volume and variety of news to be found in the average newspaper is the great number of sources from which it comes. Publishers generally feel that in order to do right by their readers and inform them of events of greatest importance, they must tell much of what goes on abroad while at the same time giving ample coverage of events right at home.

The heart of the newspaper organization is the news room, where news of the world, nation, state and local community is assembled, written and edited. Fourteen wires bring to the news room of the Des Moines, Iowa, *Register* and *Tribune* (combined circulation 345,146, population 177,965) dispatches from all over the world, from the *Tribune*'s own Washington bureau and from many points within Iowa. These wires, maintained at a cost of more than $100,000 a year, are connected with automatic typewriters inside the news room which day and night hammer out the latest news developments from distant points. Here there are 122 persons employed, including editors, writers, photographers and artists. The newspaper's airplane, Good News XI, flies reporters and photographers to all sections of the country to cover stories rapidly and bring the news fresh to *Register* and *Tribune* readers. During the football season two or three additional planes are chartered for special game coverage.

It is doubtful if readers comprehend the wide scope of territory from which their home town newspaper draws the news it brings them. The date-lines on Associated Press stories in a single issue of the Scottsbluff, Nebr., *Star-Herald* revealed news from sixty distant cities, including London, England; Havana, Cuba; Seoul, Korea; Melbourne, Australia; Oslo, Norway; Damascus, Syria; and Ghana, Africa. This was not an unusual representation of world news for this newspaper. News from such distant sources is found in practically every issue.

Equally remarkable is the number of sources within the immediate territory from which a newspaper draws news. Some publishers of large papers are inclined to discredit the use by weekly newspapers of a multitude of items about the comings and goings of people living within the newspaper's circulation area. Correspondents perhaps should be encouraged to eliminate much of the chit-chat from their rural contributions and give greater attention to more significant news of their communities. Names, nevertheless, are a vital part of the news — and they promote the sale of the newspaper.

Mrs. Rose Thompson, co-publisher of the Rocky Ford, Colo., *Gazette* (circulation 2,231, population 4,087), told members of the Inland Daily Press Association: "Names make news, even if it is in the police court or divorce listing." She said that she had a goal of trying to get every reader's name in the paper at Thanksgiving and Christmas time. Before each holiday, her staff starts calling every person in Rocky Ford who has a telephone. The items thus collected at Thanksgiving time are listed under the heading, "Turkey Talk," and at Christmas under "Holiday Happenings."

Would anyone doubt that the 1,902 names, which appeared in an average 16-page issue of the Bethany, Mo., *Republican-Clipper* (circulation 4,685, population 2,714) helped to hold a thousand or more persons on the mailing list as paid-up, regular subscribers?

When a medium-sized daily like the Scottsbluff *Star-Herald* draws news from so many distant points of the world, it has something to talk about...material that may be used in promoting its coverage. Likewise, when a small newspaper like the Bethany *Republican-Clipper* or the Rocky Ford *Gazette* records for its readers happenings in the community that touch each subscriber's home and about 2,000 of his or her neighbors, it too has a wonderful selling point. Even the smallest newspaper may promote effectively its news service to the community and in that way accumulate for itself an abundance of good will.

Interpreting the News

A progressive newspaper does more than give the bare facts that compose the news. It interprets the news to its readers. It gives the background — what caused an event to happen or a condition to develop — and what may be the outcome. Columnists play an increasingly important role as interpreters of events, and the San Francisco *Chronicle* (circulation 225,429, population 775,357) uses an *Editor & Publisher* ad to stress its large staff of columnists (see Fig. 8.1).

In these days when science is delving into outer space, when the power of the atom is being measured and applied, when the governments of many nations are on the brink of change and peace of the whole world is dependent on so many factors that seem uncertain and unsure, newspapers are assuming with greater readiness than ever before the responsibility of explaining the significance of every important event that takes place. This is a costly but willing service and the public should understand the sincere efforts put forth by publishers to provide it. One of the important tasks of a newspaper's promotion department is to tell the public what the newspaper does to get at the truth and the responsibility its staff assumes to establish facts essential to an understanding of the news.

"One of the most difficult of journalistic tasks," says Erwin Canham, editor of the *Christian Science Monitor* (circulation 159,988), "is to make interesting that which is important. It is easy enough to get into the human mind with sensation, scandal, passion and disaster. It is infinitely more difficult to communicate to readers the things they ought to know and think about, but in which they think they have very little interest."

Mr. Canham told members of the Association for Education in Journalism that there should be more digging into old and suspicious angles and less emphasis on the sensational. He contrasted the coverage given the Girard trial in Japan with the lack of coverage of whether Japan is going to become a genuine democracy.

John Cowles, president of the Minneapolis *Star* and *Tribune* (combined circulation 502,252, population 521,718) said in an address to Sigma Delta Chi: "With a steadily rising educational level, readers

Fig. 8.1 — In announcing a new feature, the San Francisco, Calif., **Chronicle** calls attention to its entire staff of distinguished columnists.

will be more interested in news of science, medicine and education, more interested in the fine arts and more interested in the whole gamut of sociological problems. Top newspaper reporters will have to know as much in their respective fields as college instructors know in theirs."

No finer promotion can be put forth for a newspaper than a clear presentation of what it is doing to make the news understandable and to keep the public fully informed regarding the more important issues, their origin, their aims and their influence.

An effective promotion for two important American newspapers — the New York *Times* (circulation 600,319, population 7,795,471) and the Corpus Christi, Tex., *Times* (circulation 36,454, population 108,287) — was a page in *Editor & Publisher*, showing John Stallings, managing editor of the Corpus Christi *Times*, reading the New York *Times,* and beneath the picture this statement by Stallings: "Texas newspaper editors have been accused of being provincial. Perhaps some are. But I find reading the New York *Times* adds immeasurably to my knowledge and understanding of national and international affairs."

When News Is Breezy and Bright

While news must be understandable it must also be interesting, and some of it should be light and breezy. Whatever a publisher does to brighten the pages of his newspaper — to bring to them a burst of sunshine — is worthy of intensive promotion.

A well-written personal column by the editor or a staff member sometimes causes more comment from readers than anything else the newspaper contains. Especially is this true if it deals with the more human side — the hobbies of people, their favorite food, their most interesting experiences, the funny sayings of their children.

A sports writer with a human interest quirk to his writing sometimes, in addition to building up a great following of sportsmen, catches the attention of a host of readers not particularly interested in sports. This is true of Arthur Daley, sports writer for the New York *Times*. The promotion department of the *Times* used costly space in magazines and trade papers to promote Daley and his column, "Sports of The Times." A promotion ad in *Editor & Publisher,* showing Daley at his typewriter in the press box at a World Series game, had this to say:

" 'Sports of The Times' is an invitingly quiet and pleasant corner in this noisy world around us. In it Arthur Daley plays host to the personalities who make the sports news. Daley is a pleasant sort of guy. He loves sports and likes and respects its people. They return the compliment.

"The result is a daily sports column spiced with wit and salted with anecdote. It delights men and women everywhere. It so delighted the gentlemen who gave out the Pulitzer Prizes that in 1956 they gave Arthur Daley one. The Pulitzer is the highest award in U. S. journalism."

This was an ideal promotion story: A *Times* reporter a prizewinner and at the same time a favorite with *Times* readers because he gave a human touch to the news.

The Portland, Ore., *Oregon Journal* (circulation 182,956, population 373,628) considers it important to publicize its efforts towards producing a newspaper always fit for the home and of interest to youth (see Fig. 8.2).

In promoting its "commitment to the enlightenment and awakening of mankind," the *Christian Science Monitor* says: "A newspaper, like life itself, can be happy and joyous. The concerns of the home, the eager unfoldment of childhood, the development of hobbies and activities that make life rich and balanced are a part of necessary newspaper service."

The camera proves at times to be a valuable supplement to a news staff's ability to write crisply and clearly and in making the newspaper bright and cheerful. Photographic journalism is becoming more pronounced. The Chicago *Daily News* (circulation 547,796, population 3,620,962), distinguished for its camera reporting, frequently features its prize-winning photographers in effective promotion.

Readership studies reveal a high appreciation for a newspaper's efforts to present its news in attractive and interesting style. In a promotion booklet entitled "By Guess or By Guide?", the Utica, N. Y., *Observer-Dispatch* and *Press* (combined circulation 70,939, population 101,531) calls attention to the great job editors are doing to make newspapers more interesting and readable. It puts it this way:

"What a thrill it would be to make our papers so good, so attractive that our readers would be literally compelled to spend two hours with them! That would add up to 200 million reader hours. The effect upon world, national, state and city affairs would be atomic. It might spell the difference between peace and a Third World War. Isn't that worth trying?"

Accuracy Above All

Another quality greatly to be desired in a newspaper's coverage of the news is *accuracy*. If a newspaper is to stand in the good graces of its public, its handling of the news must be objective and dependable. Anything that may be done to show a newspaper's efforts in that direction is promotion par excellence.

Few people know the extent to which facts presented in a news story by a special correspondent are checked before the story is started

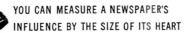

YOU CAN MEASURE A NEWSPAPER'S
INFLUENCE BY THE SIZE OF ITS HEART

JUNIOR GOLFERS

take on a new partner...
their home town newspaper

When a city newspaper takes time out from tight deadlines
and the daily flurry of details to "make" news fit to print — and,
better still, *good* to read, then that newspaper becomes more than just a
machine reporting the news. It becomes an individual, a respected member
of its community, a real leader.

So it is with the Oregon Journal. For half a century now, The Journal has
always made the time for the young citizens of its community. From Journal Junior
Department to specific events, The Journal lends a ready hand to help boys and girls
become juvenile assets instead of delinquents.

The Journal's Junior Golf School and Tournament is just one of the many events. It is a
home town activity planned by the home town newspaper. Scores of youngsters between
9 and 17 joined the Journal Golf School this past summer. They got professional pointers
from top-flight members of the Oregon section of the PGA. Portland's Bureau of Parks, known
as one of the finest in the country, enthusiastically co-supported the event.

Check your stance. Are you about to tee off on an advertising campaign?
Remember, when you are on the Oregon Journal fairway you get a long, beautiful drive
right into the richest market in Oregon. You'll like the results. Don't wait. Get all the details
you need right now. Call your nearest office of O'Mara and Ormsbee.

You can't sell Portland without...

The OREGON JOURNAL

EVENING AND SUNDAY
Home-Owned,
Controlled, Edited
Nationally represented by O'Mara &
Ormsbee, Inc., offices in New York, Chi-
cago, Detroit, San Francisco, Los Angeles

Fig. 8.2 — The **Oregon Journal**'s interest in youth is so widely recognized it is
featured in an **Editor & Publisher** promotion ad.

on its way to the news desk. The best reporters and correspondents are constantly reading books and magazines to keep fresh in their minds the latest information. Interviews with 13 Washington correspondents by Ronald W. May revealed that they read more books, magazines and newspapers than do Senators.[1] They turn their reading to subjects discussed in Congress in order that they may fully understand the background and present the news accurately.

Frank van der Linden, correspondent for the Nashville, Tenn., *Banner* (circulation 99,793, population 174,307), heard Senator Harry Byrd mention Thaddeus Stevens in a talk on the Senate floor. He immediately began looking into the life and character of Stevens and the national situation in his period and became fascinated. The Nashville newspaperman reads two or three books a week in addition to many newspapers and magazines. Efforts such as these, put forth by staff members to maintain accuracy and completeness in the news, may be made the basis of effective promotion.

An important annex to the news room of a large city newspaper is the newspaper library with all kinds of reference books. The San Francisco *Examiner* (circulation 257,251, population 775,357) thought highly enough of its library to glamorize it in an attractive mailing piece. The copy pointed out the number of photographs, clippings and books kept in the library and the role it plays in making accurate information available to the *Examiner* staff and the general public.

Excellent reporting is being done daily, and more needs to be said about it. Walter A. Steigleman tells about a certain reporter who, when called upon to report a state labor convention, spent three weeks in advance of the convention in reading up on the organization and the labor movement in general. As a result of this, he was complimented by both labor and management for his "understandable" stories. Later when an eclipse of the moon was to take place, the same reporter read up in advance about eclipses. His story was so meaningful that a press association picked it up verbatim and put it on the wire.[2]

Here is the very essence of good promotion. Nothing is of greater interest to thoughtful readers or of more importance to the newspaper than conscientious action of this sort. Nothing better could be presented to stimulate confidence in the paper as a faithful source of information or as an advertising medium. Accuracy in the news columns is a clear indication that the same quality prevails in the advertising columns.

---

[1] *Editor & Publisher*, Oct. 19, 1957, p. 58.
[2] *Editor & Publisher*, Sept. 7, 1957, p. 9.

Knowing Those Who Write

Still another effective means of promoting a newspaper's news-giving service is by acquainting regular and prospective readers with those who write the news. Mention already has been made of the promotion given to Arthur Daley's clever writing of sports for the New York *Times*. There is, in fact, a good newspaper promotion story in every member of a newspaper's writing staff. Most newspapers do very little to give their readers a close personal acquaintance with their correspondents, feature writers and reporters. Much more interest is thrown into a news story when the reader knows the person who wrote it.

Small newspapers seldom feature their staff members except in a special edition of some kind. Usually on its 10th, 25th or 50th anniversary, a newspaper puts out a large edition, a section of which is devoted to the newspaper. Here the pictures of staff members appear with a brief description of the work each does. But they are deserving of more frequent publicity.

T. S. Irvin, who writes the helpful promotion column in *Editor & Publisher,* believes that papers should promote their people much more than they do — especially those of the news staff.

"Too much newspaper promotion of people is of the syndicated talent, too little of the own home talent," he says. "Too many of newspaperdom's people are known only by their by-lines. Promotion ought to build up the by-lines, put flesh and blood on them, make them come alive."[3]

The Chicago *Daily News* believes that promotion of its featured writers is one of the surest ways to build reader interest. The startling response to Pat Dalton's series of articles was used in a colorful ad promoting the newspaper's public service (see Fig. 8.3). Later the fashion editor was presented in a promotion advertisement glowing with praise for her brilliant writing. "Fashionably speaking, there is only one Peg Zwecker," the ad declared. "To Midwest women she's the pipeline that tells them all — and tells it first. Revealingly, she takes her readers on exclusive excursions into the fashion workshops of New York and Los Angeles. She even hops hemispheres through the *News* famed foreign staff — putting readers in Paris and Rome — making them first-nighters at world showings of fashions." Enough to make any fashion-minded woman want to read the *Daily News!*

Large newspapers are better at this type of promotion, but still they could do more with profit.

"These are the *Herald Tribune* All Stars," said the New York *Herald Tribune* (circulation 335,466, population 7,795,471) in a large advertisement featuring its sports staff. "Each can write — and write

---

[3] *Editor & Publisher,* Nov. 10, 1951, p. 46.

expertly — on not one but several sports. When occasion demands, each can double as a sports columnist — or, if he is a columnist, as a sports reporter. On assignment, each man writes on these two scores: (1) he reports accurately and completely; (2) he writes colorfully and readably. Tough team to beat."

Thrilling stories are found in the lives of most newspaper reporters. What opportunities they provide for effective newspaper promotion!

"On Burning Decks He Stands," was the caption of a striking promotion ad for the Kansas City *Star*. The "he" referred to in the heading was Alvin McCoy, Kansas correspondent. "Al has been shot at literally and figuratively," the ad continued. "As a war correspondent for the *Star* in the Pacific, he was on board when Jap bombs blasted the aircraft carrier Franklin, killing 900 members of the crew. His

words
for wives
THAT STRUCK HOME...

"Seven out of 10 married women reading this article will be widows some day."

With this rather startling pronouncement, Woman's Page writer Pat Dalton opened a recent series of articles in the Chicago Daily News. She followed it with a thorough study of the steps to ward off financial panic and the ways to meet widowhood with poise and peace of mind.

It was the kind of public service material Chicago Daily News readers have come to expect. This time the response was more than expected.

Banks asked permission to reprint the series. Insurance companies and lawyers wrote and telephoned their praise. Business was stepped up in probate courts and law offices because hundreds of men were ordered by their wives to make out wills before returning home.

One firm put the six stories into booklet form and offered it to the public. The offer was publicized only in a one-inch box with the last article that appeared in the Daily News on Saturday.

Within a few days the firm received almost 7,000 individual requests for reprints, more than 25 times the response to previous comparable offers by the same firm on television.

In the Chicago Daily News, the women's columns are always sprightly, practical and stimulating. They help Chicago area women run their homes.

CHICAGO DAILY NEWS
MARSHALL FIELD JR., Publisher

Fig. 8.3 — The Chicago **Daily News** features the popularity of one of its Woman's Page writers as a feature in a promotion ad.

story of the holocaust and epic fight to bring the crippled Franklin to port, made available to all newspapers, is one of the classics of World War II reporting. Al also covered the Okinawa landings and the taking of Iwo Jima. Safe home from the war (he thought), Al went back to his regular job covering the Kansas legislature at Topeka. His career there came to a fiery climax in 1953 with his *Star* disclosure of a mysterious $10,000 insurance fee on a state-owned building. The story touched off a national political explosion."

Any newspaper may cause an explosion of public interest in its staff and services by featuring members in attractive, well-written promotion material of the type just described. When the public knows the more intimate facts about those who write the news, the newspaper draws closer to its community and a more friendly, cooperative spirit develops.

"Many avenues
such as mail, posters,
newspaper adver-
tisements and
carrier solicitation
can be brought
to bear on
upcoming features."

— C. H. Favor,
Circulation Manager,
Utica, N. Y.,
Daily Press

CHAPTER 9

Promoting

Newspaper Features

THE VARIOUS DEPARTMENTS devoted to special types of news and the entertainment and cultural features of a newspaper are more generally promoted than the current news that daily or weekly flows through its columns. This is not because they are more important but because they represent the "extras" provided in a newspaper to give it greater appeal.

While a reader appreciates news of quantity and quality more than anything else, he is enticed also by features that cater to his special interests and provide information and entertainment for himself and his family. The wide-awake publisher, therefore, uses various means to let the public know about these extra offerings. These features lend themselves readily to promotion because they constantly develop into new angles — sometimes sensational, sometimes outstandingly educational and often loaded with human interest. Always they can command glowing headlines in promotion material.

The features to be found in most newspapers are of eight classes:

1. Departments or pages devoted to the interests of special groups, such as the Woman's Page, Book and Music Columns, Television and Radio Listings, Sports Pages, Financial Columns and Children's Page.
2. Educational articles that usually appear serially. Among these might be a series of instructions on making out the income tax return, a series on the state parks, an analysis of the city budget, lessons in bridge playing or a discussion of educational methods used in the public schools.

3. Stories dealing with timely subjects, such as articles by renowned scientists on atomic energy or conditions in outer space, a series on home gardens or lawn care at the beginning of the growing season or articles based on a survey of city needs.
4. Magazine sections and supplements, such as Farm and Home Section, Sunday Magazine and Rotogravure Section.
5. Features of human interest, such as comics, cartoons and personal columns.
6. Fiction by well-known writers, brought to readers in daily or weekly installments.
7. Pictures, which may be presented in wide assortment throughout the newspaper or constitute a page or section devoted to a common theme.
8. Tests of knowledge and skill, including puzzles and contests of various kinds.

The opportunities to use these features as the basis of consistent promotion is very apparent. Small newspapers, as well as large ones, may make them the means of increased sales at the newsstands and more circulation in the residence sections. Give a promotion department free rein in "plugging" features and some remarkably appealing copy will be produced; also many media will be employed.

Announcements of forthcoming features often take page one, a position never available even to the best advertiser in most papers. A terse message, neatly spaced with attractive type faces, and occupying only a few inches of space, may help greatly to cut down reader turnover.

Features are ideal subjects for promotion also in trade papers, magazines and on outdoor boards. For the promotion of syndicated features, attractive material may be obtained from producers, and for local features the promotion personnel can readily create attention-compelling copy.

To Win Attention of Special Groups

Readers appreciate the newspaper that gives special attention to their needs and interests. When a newspaper announces to its women readers, "We are presenting some tasty tempting recipes for you to test in your kitchen — watch for them each Friday," it is not only creating a demand for the Friday grocery issue but it is drawing itself closer to all its women readers. When it tells football fans it will predict the scores of all conference games during the season, it wins their immediate good will, added interest, and perhaps a continuous welcome into their homes. The various departments and pages which represent the interests of special groups are "naturals" for promotion.

To introduce its Football Peach Section, which appears daily and Sunday during the football season, the Minneapolis *Tribune* (combined daily and Sunday circulation 849,949, population 521,718) did more than simply announce it through its columns. First, it sold the feature to its entire staff and sent them out to boost it. Each employee was given a windshield sticker in the form of a football bearing the inscription "Daily and Sunday Football Peach, Minneapolis *Tribune*" (see Fig. 9.1).

Fig. 9.1 — Windshield sticker used by the Minneapolis **Tribune** to promote its Football Peach Section.

Carrier-salesmen and street salesmen were alerted to make personal calls, to talk it up and sell. They were given coupon announcements to distribute and to use in explaining the extra feature (see Fig. 9.2).

"Reach for the Peach every day in your Minneapolis *Morning Tribune*," said the announcement. "Exciting action pictures — interviews with coaches and players — high school ratings — previews of Gopher opponents — reports on the pros — plus a score of other Football Peach Sports Section features."

Special announcements appeared also at the newsstands and on the billboards and were presented by radio and television. Everybody in the newspaper's circulation area was given a burst of publicity regarding the *Tribune*'s plans for covering sports during the football season.

With the same enthusiasm and efficiency, the *Tribune* promotes all its departments and features. Virginia Stafford's column of comment on enticing foods and popular dining places, Axel Hanson's discussion of farm problems, John Sherman's reviews of the top stage shows and his interviews with stars, and the newspaper's other departments, pages and columns were effectively presented in a promotion series entitled "What Makes A Newspaper Great."

The Kansas City, Mo., *Star* (circulation 334,518, population 456,662) talked big — and rightly so — about Frank Alexander's Rod and Gun column, which it says, "in season and out of season is required reading for duck hunters, bird shooters, archery fans, deer stalkers, trapshooters, coon hunters, hound dog folks and other sports followers of all ages, tastes and conditions." The *Star* claims this to be the most popular, most widely read and quoted column of its kind in the Midwest.

Full-page promotion ads in the Macon, Ga., *Telegraph* and *News* (combined circulation 62,151, population 70,252), preceding the state basketball tournament, plugged its plans for covering that event.

Fig. 9.2 — The Minneapolis **Morning Tribune** used the Football Peach Section as a feature of coupon offer to new subscribers.

Featured were pictures of tournament teams and players in action. Fans knew they would obtain full particulars from the sports pages of the *Telegraph* and *News*.

A publisher needs to keep in mind at all times the various groups represented by subscribers and, when something of special interest is about to appear he will prepare them for it. Promotion's particular service is in keeping regular readers faithful and interested as well as in obtaining new subscribers for the paper.

Features To Inform

Individual interests as well as group interests are represented in the features a newspaper offers. Nothing draws a newspaper closer to the heart of a reader than an article which gives the answer to a problem he is facing or throws light on an idea he is pursuing.

Not entirely satisfied with the facts concerning economic conditions presented in syndicated features and the stories put out by news-gathering agencies, the Atlanta, Ga., *Constitution* (circulation 193,558, population 331,314) sent Jim Montgomery, its business editor, on a 1,400-mile trip throughout Georgia to obtain from farmers and businessmen firsthand knowledge of conditions in the home state. Here was a series of articles in which all responsible citizens would be interested. The feature was well promoted during the week preceding the first installment.

At about the same time, the Atlanta *Journal*'s Pat Watters took a detailed look at the Georgia insurance rate problem, which was causing considerable controversy in the state. Here again was the opportunity for effective promotion. The *Journal* (circulation 253,470, population 331,314) used considerable space in its own pages and elsewhere to urge readers to watch for this enlightening feature.

The Atlanta papers came up with another timely feature on the high cost of political campaigns. William Bates, their political editor, explained that running for office means a long, tiring business of speech-making, banqueting, traveling and grass roots handshaking plus a heavy expenditure of money.

These three features, launched in a Sunday issue and dealing with questions of wide interest, revealed enterprise on the part of the newspapers and, because they were well promoted, won an abundance of good will for the *Journal* and *Constitution*.

The Boston *Herald* (circulation 182,816, population 801,444) used two full columns of a Saturday issue to promote outstanding features relating to five different subjects: (1) plans of the Metropolitan Transit Authority to take over and operate a branch of the Boston & Albany Railroad that would provide better transportation service for a section of the city; (2) the growing interest of women in bowling not simply because they needed exercise but because they enjoyed the sport; (3) a Roxbury nursing order that was doing much for the sick and needy; (4) a local locksmith, who had many exciting experiences to relate; and (5) a disastrous fire that swept Boston a half century before and remained vivid in the minds of many citizens.

In another Saturday issue the Boston *Herald* used two inches full page width at the bottom of Page 1 to tell about an extra-large Sunday paper with pointed articles on fancy food prepared by a prominent chef, the roles of labor, industry and politics in a time of recession, the silent maneuvers behind the sudden passage of a pre-primary convention bill by the state legislature, and the weather quirks behind the 18 roaring northeast gales that had visited the New England coast since December.

Such promotion not only increased demand for immediate issue; but it created in readers a continuous expectation for something unusual and timely in the *Herald*.

Timely Features Always Hit

When a feature can be produced that fits perfectly into the thoughts and deeds of the moment it will attract twice the attention of an ordinary news story. Given plenty of good promotion, such timely features will instantly increase circulation and draw readers closer to their newspaper.

Ideal for promotion by the Atlanta, Ga., *Journal* and *Constitution* (combined circulation 447,028, population 331,314) at the opening of the golf season was a story about Ben Hogan, the boy who started his golfing career to help pay bills at home and who now is the nation's highest paid golfer. This was the first of a series telling about men and women who worked their way up from extreme poverty to fabulous wealth.

Spring is the time of year for housecleaning, painting, remodeling and gardening as well as for playing golf. Special sections of the paper devoted to such enterprises are other good subjects of promotion. Jim Chandler, real estate editor of the Cleveland, Ohio, *Press and News* (circulation 385,000, population 914,808), calls attention to a great change that has taken place in the building trade pages within the past 20 years.[1] No longer are they edited to appeal to the trade alone. Newspapers have found that readership and circulation can be increased by directing the material on building pages to everyone who owns a home or wants to own one. Such pages then become service pages full of helpful information.

When the firing of the Sputnik brought to the attention of the world the Soviet's system of scientific education, people of the United States began to wonder about their own educational system. George Gallup, director of the American Institute of Public Opinion, began at once to gather in the thoughts of educators and parents and offered to newspapers a series of six reports on his survey. This feature, as timely as could be, was purchased by many newspapers and presented to their readers. Glaring newspaper ads, window cards and mailing pieces were used to promote it (see Fig. 9.3).

"Is a revolution coming in education?" asked the Birmingham, Ala., *News* (circulation 184,893, population 326,037) in a two-column announcement. "Since Sputnik, the issue of U. S. education has been the subject of much heated debate. To get the views of people most closely connected with the controversy, the Gallup Poll has surveyed two groups — educators in the secondary schools and parents of the nation's children. See what they say about our school system, starting Monday in a five-part series in the *News*."

The Des Moines, Iowa, *Register* and *Tribune* (combined circulation 345,146, population 177,965) used a quarter-page to promote the same feature, starting off with an interrogatory headline, "Will Russia's science triumphs revolutionize U. S. education?" "Learn what educators and parents think," it urged. "Read the series of Gallup reports daily and Sunday in the *Register*."

---

[1] *Editor & Publisher,* Nov. 16, 1957, p. 40.

The Dallas, Tex., *News* (circulation 207,156, population 434,462) carried an advance notice of the feature in three inches at the bottom of the front page.

Another timely feature put out about the same time was equally popular and equally well promoted. It was a five-part series on "Is Your Child Fit?" produced by the New York *Herald Tribune* Syndicate. This attempted to answer the quandary as to whether Americans are raising their children to be weaklings and cowards or fighting, valorous and productive citizens.

Any type of feature — scientific or fiction — touching upon space rockets and atoms and their effects was capable of much attention at that period. The Minneapolis *Star* (circulation 287,425, population 521,718) carried "On the Beach," by the late Nevil Shute, a feature

NATIONWIDE GALLUP POLL

will give you answers to these questions:

Are many high schools changing, or planning to change, the course of study?

How do school principals feel about present educational methods and the amount of work the students do?

What do parents say about the school system?

Many Sputnik-conscious U. S. citizens advocate drastic changes in the s c h o o l system. Learn what the educators and parents think. Read this series of Gallup reports daily and Sunday in the Des Moines Register, April 6-11.

Starts Sunday

in the

Des Moines Sunday Register

Coming up next week—

Is a revolution coming in U. S. education?

Since Sputnik the issue of U. S. education has been the subject of much heated debate. To get the views of people most closely connected with this controversy, the Gallup Poll has surveyed two groups—educators in the secondary schools and parents of our nation's children. See what they say about our school systems, starting Monday in a five-part series in The News.

What do teachers think of our teen-agers? The Eugene Gilbert survey has turned the tables on the young people and have asked those who should know best—the teachers—what they think of today's youngsters. This will appear Thursday. Watch for it!

The Birmingham News

Education: Its Future

"Is a Revolution Coming in U. S. Education?" is the subject of a series of six reports by George Gallup, director of the American Institute of Public Opinion.

The first of the series will appear in your Sunday Dallas News tomorrow.

It reveals educators' criticisms and suggestions for meeting the "Challenge of the Sputnik"—parents' attitude toward curricula.

You will want to read the first installment tomorrow in your Dallas Morning News.

Fig. 9.3 — Promotion advertisements in various newspapers announcing the Gallup poll on educational methods.

which attempted to show what would happen if war should wipe out almost everyone on the earth. "It's the most talked about story of the year," declared the *Star* in 9 x 12 window cards of black and yellow and in elaborate newspaper promotion (see Fig. 9.4).

Timely features are easy to promote and they always "ring the bell" with the reading public.

Promote Sections and Supplements

A Sunday newspaper is composed of many sections, each of which contains features of unusual interest. Large space generally is used in week-day issues to tell readers what they will have for pleasant and exciting Sunday reading.

The Denver *Post* (circulation 253,410, population 415,786) devotes four full columns of advertising space in each Friday issue to

Fig. 9.4 — The Minneapolis **Star** uses counter and window cards to announce a new feature starting in the newspaper.

promote coming Sunday features. From seven to a dozen of the outstanding departments or articles are played up, each with a separate head, a block of copy and a piece of art. The features thus promoted are from almost every part of the Sunday paper.

Features scheduled for the Sunday issue of the Atlanta, Ga., *Journal* and *Constitution* are promoted in two full columns of each daily issue during the preceding week. Sometimes these ads are run in color and glossy proofs are displayed in the front window of the newspaper office for the sidewalk audience.

"Here's MUST reading for you in the big Sunday Atlanta *Journal* and *Constitution,*" the ad usually begins. Then four outstanding features are described in snappy paragraphs with attention-compelling headlines. The features selected for promotion one week were:

'Bama Dreams of Bowls Again

Retired Atlanta *Constitution* sports writer, Ed Danforth, reports that alumni want nothing less than a miracle.

Foolproof Lie Detector

The state has purchased a new-type lie-detector for use in crime investigations. Jack Nelson, Atlanta *Constitution* staff writer, says it's absolutely foolproof.

Arrest Etiquette

Dorothy Cremin, Atlanta *Journal* staff writer, tells you what arresting officers have to say about the good manners of being arrested.

Teachers Still Go to School

Atlanta science and math teachers go to school the year 'round, at night and on Saturdays. An Atlanta *Journal* staff writer reports on this in-service training.

The Philadelphia *Bulletin* (circulation 695,960, population 2,071,605) advertises its Sunday issue as "Ten Sections with More for Everybody." At least three of the ten sections are promoted in each advertisement. Coming up often for special mention are its News and Views Section, *This Week Magazine* and TV-Amusements Section (see Fig. 9.5).

"It takes more than cloth to make a suit," said the *Bulletin* in one of its full-page promotions, "because cloth becomes a fine suit only through the knowledge and skill of the tailor. And to produce a great Sunday newspaper, additional features are added to the all-important element of complete, timely and accurate news coverage. *The great Sunday Bulletin adds the most interesting family of features in America.*" In this same ad four of the *Bulletin's* separate magazine sections were featured as follows:

The American Weekly

Sparkling pageant of the American scene.
Stories that glitter with spice of life.
Background stories of famous personalities.
A complete, *separate* section.

Lincoln's Lesson for Today

In 1861, Abraham Lincoln faced a challenge that threatened the survival of the nation. The country was divided; public opinion was confused; the issue of secession had overtones of foreign involvements. How Lincoln summoned America to greatness — and the lesson it holds for us today — is the theme of a powerful article by the noted Civil War historian, Bruce Catton, next Sunday in the

News and Views Section

Keep Women Out of College?

Are women's reasons for wanting a college education less important than men's? By 1968, our already bulging colleges will be besieged by twice as many applicants for enrollment. Something's got to give — so a professor comes up with a startling solution. It may seem outrageous to women, and be unpopular with men too — but he presents his case for closing college doors to women next Sunday in **This Week Magazine**

TV Puts Tab Hunter on Ice

Actor Tab Hunter is no stranger to ice skates. But it took a classic story for children — "Hans Brinker, or, The Silver Skates" by Mary Mapes Dodge — to put him on ice before TV cameras. Rex Polier tells the story of this upcoming musical comedy, costarring skating champ Dick Button, and there's an interview with Tab in next Sunday's

TV-Amusements Section

Next Sunday's Bulletin

Ten Sections with More for Everybody

Fig. 9.5 — Three important sections of the Philadelphia Sunday **Bulletin** are featured in a promotion ad several days in advance of publication.

Book of the Week
> Novels by the nation's top writers.
> Read 52 best sellers a year.
> All yours with the Sunday *Bulletin*.
> A complete, *separate* section.

The Fun Book
> Keeps kids from 6 to 60 happily occupied.
> Comics, games, puzzles, contests.
> Sunday morning entertainment for all.
> A complete, *separate* section.

This Week Magazine
> A great publication in itself.
> Centered around home and social life.
> Gives you week-long reading pleasure.
> A complete, *separate* section.

A newspaper's sections and supplements may be promoted from various angles. The Cleveland, Ohio, *Plain Dealer* (circulation 309,267, population 914,808) added considerable local interest to its *Plain Dealer* Pictorial by reproducing on the cover each week an original painting, in full color, by a well-known Cleveland artist. It then advertised reprints of the cover paintings on fine-textured paper, suitable for framing, at $1.00 each. This was a good way to draw attention to the pictorial section and develop a lot of reader interest.

When the Roundup Magazine of the Denver *Post* changed its makeup, the improved appearance and more convenient arrangement were immediately publicized.

"Roundup Magazine takes on a new look this week," the *Post* explained. "Emphasis is being placed on leisure-time activities — movies and drama, radio and television, travel and resorts, book reviews. The *Post's* editorials, outstanding editorial articles, letters to the editor and editorial columns will be in our Section AA, right behind the main news section. You'll find the Teens Today pages in Roundup this week, too, along with the regular Roundup features, such as photography, stamp column, bridge, crossword puzzle, fine arts and platter parade."

Human Interest Features Always Popular

Any feature that can bring out the smiles or cause readers to recall exciting and pleasant experiences should have liberal promotion. Readers appreciate having some chuckles sprinkled in with the serious side of the news. Whenever a new comic, a cartoon series or a column rich with human interest is about to be introduced, a great opportunity is at hand to develop interest in the newspaper and increase its sales.

Comics are susceptible to many unique forms of promotion. The mirth-provoking characters that appear in them may become boosters of classified advertising as well as of circulation, predict the weather or jump around on the sports page. They may also have a children's club named in their honor with membership cards bearing their likenesses. They even may be featured in a street parade or a carnival.

"Twin Earths," an adventure comic with saucers and space ships, "Gene Autry," first air-western adventure strip, and other science fiction comics have been tops in readership. When rockets and cowboys share the spotlight, promotion material easily takes on action and excitement.

The small cartoon, too, has become extremely popular in recent years. "Little Sport," a shallow four-column strip, has appeared on the sport pages of many newspapers. "Peanuts" doesn't have to say or do much to provoke a hearty laugh. The cheerful and humorous side of a newspaper may always be promoted with profit.

The serious side also is well presented in some newspaper comics. "Louisiana Purchase," a 52-week educational comic strip, produced in 1953 to commemorate the 150th anniversary of the purchase, was a unique treatment of history that went over with a bang. The *Register* and *Tribune* Syndicate, producers, provided excellent promotion material, and newspapers that bought it used liberal space for advance promotion (see Fig. 9.6).

——— LOUISIANA PURCHASE ———

Thrilling History of Early America Told in 52-Week Comic Strip Form

One of the most exciting, and most momentous eras of U.S. history will be portrayed in comic strip form when LOUISIANA PURCHASE starts (Date) in (Logo).

This is a unique and new treatment of history, bringing it to life and action as a real story in cartoons. The daily strip will start and will be completed in the coming year of 1953, the year of the 150th anniversary of the famed Louisiana Purchase.

LOUISIANA PURCHASE actually is the story of the whole United States at the time. It was a period of high adventure and dangerous exploits, of international politics and intrigues, and of lusty pioneering. It's the story of how the United States acquired more than a third of its land area by a new theory for acquiring territory—by purchase rather than by war.

An Account of Courage

It's an account of American courage and diplomacy and free enterprise which are just as vital to the nation today as they were at the turn of the Nineteenth Century.

John Chase, editorial cartoonist of the New Orleans States, is doing the adventure strip which will appear in leading newspapers throughout the United States and elsewhere in the world.

Author of a prize-winning book on a narrative history of New Orleans and a lecturer of many years standing, Mr. Chase is master of his subject and is skilled in the popular story-telling technique—the adventure strip.

Story Is Accurate

The historical incidents of the comic strip story are completely accurate, and the story is just as it happened. But in addition, there is wit and humor in every strip, proving Chase's theory that history really is great fun!

It's a bright and entertaining feature for children and adults alike. Watch for it in (LOGO). It starts (Date) and will continue daily through the end of 1953.

Fig. 9.6 — Suggested promotion for historical feature put out by the **Register** and **Tribune** Syndicate, Des Moines, Iowa.

Personal columns which deal with common problems, when well promoted, build readership for a newspaper. Features of this kind, however, must be given liberal advance announcement and be occasionally promoted after they have become an established part of the paper. Columnists have something different to offer in each writing. "What will they say next?" readers ask themselves, and when the newspaper gives a hint of what is coming, there is a cordial reception for it when it appears.

The Des Moines, Iowa, *Register* once lifted the curtain on Ann Landers' column in this manner:

> TOMORROW a young mother signing her letter *"Messed up at 21"* asks Ann for help with her unfaithful husband; *"Skinned"* wants to know what to do about an "Indian-giver" uncle; and an *"Unhappy Threesome"* of youngsters seek counsel on how to get along with quarreling parents. Read ANN LANDERS tomorrow and every Sunday in the *Register.*

The Cleveland *Plain Dealer* chose to tell in advance some of the distinguished persons Margaret McManus would introduce in a forthcoming column, and its promotion department came forth with this: "Miss McManus knows everyone associated with television from network residents to television stars, bit players, writers, producers and Mike, the doorman at CBS. She goes everywhere that celebrities gather. Within a few days she lunched at Sardi's with Perle Mesta, at the Harwyn Club with Jack Benny, sipped tea with George Gobel at the Waldorf. Her column, which is devoted to off-stage lives of the actors and actresses on TV, is as intimate and revealing as a photograph blown to full size. For a glimpse at Manhattan's most glamorous face read *Margaret McManus* every Saturday in the *Plain Dealer"* (see Fig. 9.7).

Any feature based on very important persons draws good readership, but to no higher degree than those which carry the smiling faces of children and their surprising sayings.

"The Cradle Roll," a service feature of the Cleveland *Press and News,* gave the circulation of that newspaper a rapid climb. More than 56,000 babies were enrolled in order that their mothers might receive from the *Press* free bulletins each month on child care. Various subjects, ranging from toilet training to temper tantrums, were discussed by Mrs. Helen Allyn Macdonald in the Cradle Roll department. Each week the faces of new members appeared in the newspaper. That, in itself, was promotion enough to keep the Cradle Roll roster growing.

"Small Talk," another interesting baby feature, was given effective promotion in the Sioux City, Iowa, *Journal-Tribune* (combined circulation 73,826, population 83,991). The testimonials of many parents were used in a full-page advertisement with a baby at the

MARGARET McMANUS

COVERS THE WIDE, WIDE WORLD OF TELEVISION

Manhattan is the heart of the television industry and it takes a top notch reporter like **Margaret McManus** to cover it for you. **Miss McManus** knows everyone associated with television from network presidents to television stars, bit players, writers, producers, and Mike the doorman at CBS. She goes everywhere that celebrities gather. Within a few days she lunched at Sardi's with Perle Mesta, at the Harwyn Club with Jack Benny, sipped tea with George Gobel at the Waldorf. Her column which is devoted to off-stage lives of the actors and actresses on TV is as intimate and revealing as a photograph blown to full-size. For a glimpse at Manhattan's most glamorous face

Read MARGARET McMANUS

every Saturday—Starting April 5—in the

PLAIN DEALER

Fig. 9.7 — The Cleveland **Plain Dealer** uses its own pages to promote a leading columnist.

center, showing that "Small Talk" draws hundreds of letters, phone calls and comments of praise and approval.

"Are you following this sparkling collection of pictures and humorous sayings?" asked the *Journal-Tribune* and then explained that it appeared every morning and evening except Sunday.

Serial Stories Hold Subscribers

Some newspapers have found a serial story to be a popular feature. Years ago, when many features were offered in plates that could be thrown immediately into the makeup without the cost of composition, most weeklies and small dailies carried continued stories. Good fiction by well-known authors is still available, but seems to be used more in the larger papers today than in the smaller ones.

Charles Dickens' "Christmas Carol" and other Christmas stories are favored features during the yuletide season. Easter also brings out Fulton Oursler's "Greatest Story Ever Told" and others appropriate to Passion Week. A feature of this kind sometimes is presented in consecutive issues until the story is completed. Sometimes it is continued from one Sunday issue to the next. In either case, it helps to sustain the reader's interest in the newspaper. Usually the installments are so arranged that they build up suspense and keep the reader constantly eager for the next installment.

Features of history, economics and politics also are offered in a series of installments. Newspaper syndicates produce features that tie in with national events or with the lives of national figures (see Fig. 9.8). The life stories of movie stars, political leaders and business tycoons always are consumed avidly by newspaper readers.

Local characters and local events may be woven into attractive features that will win an abundance of good will for the newspaper. In connection with the 100th anniversary of the town, the newspaper often carries in serial form a history of the community written by a staff member or local historian and author.

All such offerings as these require well-planned and abundant promotion. Display cards should go up at the newsstands. Carriers should be given descriptive material to present to patrons on their routes and at the time should be made to see the opportunity afforded them to increase their collections and their profits. Spot advertising on radio and television should be used extensively, and liberal space in the newspaper should be allotted for promotion.

Serial stories, when properly promoted, not only help to obtain new subscribers but they help to hold a newspaper's regular readers. Anything that may be done to prevent circulation turnover is valuable.

Pictures Need Promoting

While more attention is being given to pictures by newspapers than ever before, much remains to be done to improve this phase of supplying answers to readers' wants.

The Philadelphia Inquirer

is privileged to bring to its readers
the first publication in any form
anywhere in the free world
(*and to offer without cost
to any publication in the world
reprint rights to*)

Nikita S. Khrushchev's
Blueprint for the Future

from the Soviet Premier's
First Major Book

"FOR VICTORY IN PEACEFUL
COMPETITION WITH CAPITALISM"

The Philadelphia Inquirer is pleased to announce the exclusive publication of important sections of this new book, beginning Tuesday, September 8.

Premier Khrushchev, at our request, has granted this newspaper permission to be the first publication in the free world to publish selected portions of this volume.

In order to insure an accurate translation, conveying Mr. Khrushchev's views as he expressed them, we requested the Premier to have the translation in English made under his supervision and approved personally by him.

Because The Inquirer feels that publication of this book is of such great importance to the peoples of the free world, it is offering reprint rights to all publications, at no cost, for use 48 hours after each of the seven installments appears in The Philadelphia Inquirer.

Walter H. Annenberg

EDITOR
THE PHILADELPHIA INQUIRER

(Note: Reprints of this series in other periodicals must carry full copyright notice.)

Fig. 9.8 — Features in a metropolitan newspaper often are of nationwide significance, and the Philadelphia **Inquirer** reached a national audience with an advertisement in **Editor & Publisher**.

According to Vincent Jones of the Gannett Newspapers, photo-journalism suffers from these handicaps: (1) the cult of the single picture, (2) a secondary role in telling a story, (3) overemphasis upon speed and immediacy, (4) the big squeeze of a static, inelastic format and (5) rigid cliche notions of what constitutes a news picture.[2]

"Half-baked ideas, indifferent work with the camera, dull prints, uninspired cropping and scaling all combine to present engravers and pressmen with pictures which must convince them that if no one else cares, why should they be expected to work miracles," Mr. Jones told members of the American Society of Newspaper Editors.

He blamed newspaper editors for being either scornful or resentful of magazines in the photographic field from which there is plenty that might be learned so as to get away from the stark ups-and-downs and jagged corners that inhibit newspaper makeup.

Newspapers that are giving special attention to the making and use of better pictures should make known their successes to fellow members of the press and thus promote a movement toward more effective use of pictures. Furthermore, they should call the attention of readers to what they are doing in that line to make the newspaper more interesting.

The Des Moines *Register* and *Tribune* and the Minneapolis *Star* and *Tribune,* which are Cowles publications, have learned much about picture-taking and picture-editing from *Look,* a Cowles picture magazine of great popularity, and are pleased to say so. In an attractive booklet concerning the *Register*'s Farm and Home Magazine is this paragraph:

"A staff of 14 photographers use the latest techniques developed by the originators of *Look* magazine to bring more pictures, diagramed pictures and picture stories to Iowa readers. A staff plane and pilot-photographer speed airviews to publications offices. Pictures are unexcelled for explaining new farming methods quickly and clearly."

The Minneapolis papers' photographers often win prizes in photo contests. When this happens readers are instantly told about it, and the circumstances surrounding the prize picture are explained. A picture taken by Jack Gillis of the *Star* and *Tribune* staff, entitled "The Volunteers," won the grand prize in a Graflex contest. The newspapers explained that the picture was taken at a Minneapolis rooming house fire when, because other firefighters were busy elsewhere with a four-alarmer, the volunteers had to call for help from spectators. This picture, by reason of its timeliness, the unusual situation it revealed and its excellence, twice brought brilliant and effective promotion to the newspapers that carried it.

The Columbus, Ohio, *Star* (circulation 65,150, population 375,901) carries a great amount of news photography. Often it inserts an advertisement in the Sunday Columbus *Dispatch* (circulation 241,923,

---

[2]*Editor & Publisher,* May 12, 1956, p. 60.

population 375,901), calling attention to the *Star*'s outstanding features and announcing that it is on sale at Columbus newsstands. It is issued each Wednesday and refers to itself as "Ohio's Picture Newspaper" (see Fig. 9.9).

The picture services furnished to newspapers by the Associated Press, and United Press International are deserving of great promotion

Fig. 9.9 — The Columbus, Ohio, **Star**, a picture weekly, uses the Columbus **Dispatch**, a daily, to promote its newsstand sales.

by newspapers that use them. They help to make vital and understandable the news of the world. Photographers and reporters work hand-in-hand to give readers a wide perspective of all that is going on.

The Schenectady, N. Y., *Union-Star* (circulation 35,624, population 91,785), in a series of picture pages, showed how the Albany bureaus of the Associated Press and the United Press International worked for them in the gathering and transmission of news. A *Union-Star* photographer was sent to Albany to take pictures of the AP and UPI staffs at work.

A small weekly newspaper in southern Missouri — the Salem *News* (circulation 3,287, population 3,182) — carries an unusual number of pictures in each issue, and each picture is as bright and fresh as the Ozark sunshine of the region in which the newspaper is published. The *News* was determined to give its readers *good* pictures. It investigated thoroughly and installed equipment best suited for the work. It tested cameras and bought those that produced the best pictures. The *News* now offers to its readers a picture service unexcelled by any other Missouri newspaper. This is not only helping its prestige with its readers but it is encouraging other publishers to improve their photography and engraving.

Any newspaper that has a photographic service of this standard should promote it well — describe the equipment used, give the cost of equipment and operation and explain the rules to be followed in producing clear and interesting pictures.

Great Interest in Puzzles and Contests

Question contests, which have been the rage on television, are no more popular with TV viewers than puzzles and contests are with newspaper readers.

Crossword puzzles, quizzes, coloring and essay writing contests, brain-twisters and other tests of knowledge and skill are found in most newspapers today. Many publishers think they are carrying more features of this kind than they should, but whenever they attempt to drop one, such protest comes up from readers that they desist.

It is easy to interest children in an Easter or Christmas coloring contest. Adults, too, are attracted by question contests and crossword puzzles. The entire family may be drawn heartily into a contest of any kind where big prizes are offered.

A "Match The Twins" contest has been an exceptionally popular feature with a number of newspapers. The individual pictures of sets of twins are run over a period of time. Contestants are asked to match each picture with the picture of the other twin. The Minneapolis *Star* and *Tribune* ran this contest with a high level of prizes and strong promotion and received thousands of entries. The contestants who matched the most sets of twins received a two-week, all-expense trip for two persons to Europe or to Hawaii. In addition to the vacation trips were 230 cash prizes totaling $2,000, six regional prizes totaling more than $1,000 in United States Savings Bonds and 1,000 pairs of Ice Follies tickets.

Placards, brochures, banners, radio advertising, television advertising and newspaper advertising — all were used to promote "Match The Twins." The results were startling.

Features to interest children and young people are used extensively in newspapers to stimulate in youth the habit of newspaper reading. The Baltimore, Md., *American* (circulation 314,499, population 949,708) published each Sunday in its American Life section a 2-page, 4-column, 10-inch deep feature called "Baltimore American Notebook," which interpreted current news in simple, declarative sentences easily understandable. It was laid out so that any child could clip it from the newspaper with two snips of the scissors and then preserve it in a standard form of ring-binder notebook.

This feature was given liberal promotion. Immediately following publication of the first "Notebook," letters were mailed to principals of all Baltimore schools and those of the surrounding area, offering reprints of the "Notebook" on request. This offer was readily accepted and the service was continued through the school semester.

Features of great variety are offered in newspapers. New ideas are constantly being developed. Their benefit to the newspaper depends largely upon the extent to which they are promoted.

CHAPTER 10

Making Use of Readership Surveys

PROMOTION OF A NEWSPAPER'S FEATURES, departments and general services always is more effective when it is based on definite information regarding readers' interests, needs and desires and general conditions within the community the newspaper serves. Research, therefore, has an important connection with newspaper promotion.

Promotion should never be on a guesswork basis. Much money may be wasted if promotion is attempted without a particular purpose in mind and without complete knowledge of conditions that may assist or handicap. It is always important to know the obstacles as well as the opportunities to be faced in developing newspaper readership.

Many valuable readership surveys have been made by publishers' associations, schools of journalism, professional organizations, departmental groups and individual publishers. These, in the main, have been for the following purposes:

1. To ascertain what offerings of news, features and advertising in the newspaper are of greatest interest to most readers.
2. To find out to what extent each department and feature is read by regular subscribers.
3. To find out what features or what types of news not already offered readers are particularly desired.
4. To learn what features or types of news are of special interest to certain age groups.
5. To find out what changes are taking place in the thoughts and actions of readers.
6. To determine the public's attitude toward certain subjects of timely interest and concern.

7. To find out how the newspaper stands with other media of communication that compete with it for attention and support.
8. To enable a publisher to see how his newspaper compares with other papers of approximately the same circulation or with those published in cities of the same size.

Studies in Newspaper Reading

The most extensive readership survey made by any organization was the "Continuing Study of Newspaper Reading" conducted by the Advertising Research Foundation in cooperation with the Bureau of Advertising of the American Newspaper Publishers Association. This was a series of surveys of various daily newspapers of similar pattern to enable easy comparisons.

The system used by the Advertising Research Foundation has been followed by many newspapers other than those which participated in the original study. The School of Journalism of the University of Missouri, with the cooperation of the Missouri Press Association, made a similar study of newspaper readership for weekly newspapers of Missouri.

The plan followed is very simple, but care has to be used in approaching interviewees and in recording their answers. A crew of interviewers is sent into the newspaper territory to ascertain how closely the paper is being read. Sections of the area, representing various economic levels in their proper proportions, are chosen, and a proportionate number of homes are visited.

An interviewer places before each respondent a fresh, unmarked copy of a chosen issue of the paper and requests him to go through it, page by page, and point out those items, features and departments which he has seen or read. Each feature recognized by the respondent is then marked with a crayon.

Only adults 18 years and older are interviewed. Field workers are instructed to use only two questions in their interviewing. The first, "Did you happen to see or read any news story or feature on this page?" and the second, "Did you happen to see or read any advertisement on this page?" The emphasis is placed equally on the editorial and the advertising content of the paper. There is no tendency to stress or direct the attention of the respondent to any particular item or type of content.

The results of the interviews are later tabulated, and the percentage of the total number interviewed who read each item or feature of the newspaper is indicated. The percentages are tabulated separately for men and women readers.

Maximum value is obtained from the study when the reports, as released, are studied for trends and principles rather than for detail.

Frequent Contacts With Readers Are Important

The "Continuing Study of Newspaper Reading" was particularly useful to advertisers in evaluating position, size of space and type of copy with reference to reader response. It indicated also the kind of news service readers expect of their newspaper. It gave to advertisers a basis on which to judge the newspaper's pulling power.

In planning schedules, advertising agencies weigh heavily a newspaper's editorial content. Geyer Advertising, Inc., makes a comprehensive media study called "The Editorial Approach to People," in which it attempts to analyze the different departments of a newspaper. Among the points considered are editorial impact, editorial stability and reader loyalty.[1]

"It is important for us to know what editorial atmosphere a newspaper creates for its advertisers," says Lewis H. Happ, media director of the Geyer Company. "We like to know all we can about the readers of women's pages, sports pages, financial sections and other departments of the newspaper and what percentages of the total readers are interested in what those departments offer."

Mr. Happ contends that the editorial diet of any publication or part of it culls out for the advertiser the most desired audience at the lowest primary audience cost. This points out the importance of promoting a newspaper's news and feature services.

Some interesting facts regarding the hold of certain pages, departments and features upon readers has been revealed in newspaper surveys. A study made by the Hartford, Conn., *Courant* (circulation 104,765, population 177,397) showed that its main news section had 92 per cent readership by women and 98 per cent by men. The second section, which carried editorials, real estate news and financial columns, also enjoyed high readership by both men and women. Quite a difference in readership by men and women, however, showed up in other sections. The sports section, for example, had 90 per cent readership from men and 39 per cent from women, and the women's news section had 92 per cent from women and 70 per cent from men.

A small or medium-sized newspaper, as well as a large one, may conduct a readership survey at little expense and reap great benefits. The Easton, Pa., *Express* (circulation 46,572, population 35,632), at a cost of less than $125, conducted 300 interviews to check readership on 67 features carried in its columns.[2] It used twelve interviewers recruited through the state employment office. At a one-hour meeting the night before the survey was to take place, workers were made familiar with the survey plan, the sample, the approach, technique in

---

[1] *Editor & Publisher,* Mar. 8, 1958, p. 17.
[2] *Editor & Publisher,* Apr. 5, 1958, p. 46.

asking questions, pitfalls, marking the answers and assigning the territory.

Because information was wanted regarding readership for features only, it was felt that a one per cent sample of city zone readers would be enough to give a fair indication. Each interviewer, therefore, was instructed to take 30 copies of the issue to be used in the survey and to bring back completed reports of at least 25 interviews with men and women. In addition to finding out what features were read, the interviewers asked readers to comment concerning the general contents of the newspaper. The publisher and editor were greatly interested in the comments and were pleased with the full results of the survey.

Interviewers who worked in neighborhoods where they lived seemed to receive more accurate reports and more fluent comments than those working in strange territory. This led the *Express* to believe that older carrier-salesmen calling on their regular patrons might conduct a more satisfactory survey than employed interviewers working in unfamiliar sections of the city.

Should Learn Readers' Likes

Although it is never possible to produce a newspaper that will please everybody, a publisher wants to move in that direction as far as possible. It is advisable, therefore, to know not only the attitude of readers toward the features and services of the newspaper but what readers would like to find in their newspaper that is not there.

Some very frank statements concerning the newspaper come to a publisher unsolicited sometimes. These may be honest criticisms or practical suggestions but more often they reflect the ire of readers whose wrong-doings have been revealed by the press or whose feelings have been hurt by unintended slights or inferences. A newspaper is more likely to receive helpful suggestions when it invites comments in its own pages or by means of a personal contact survey.

Ralph Shannon, publisher of the Washington, Iowa, *Journal* (circulation 4,197, population 5,902) believes that a newspaper owner should constantly seek the counsel of readers and give full consideration to whatever they have to say. He sent four interviewers to 5 per cent of the homes receiving his paper, asking for comments, complaints or criticisms concerning the *Journal*. Some of the homes were in Washington, some in outlying towns and still others in the rural districts.

After the survey was completed, Publisher Shannon used a series of front page boxes to explain some of the points raised by readers. For example, a number commented that the price of the newspaper was too high. In his answer to this, Shannon pointed out that there was more of this type of comment 20 years ago than at present. He compared the present prices of commodities familiar to all — corn, shoes, motor cars and the like — and showed that the newspaper compared favorably in the current market.

"*Journal* rates," he said, "have been forced upward by the same trend that has caused all other prices to go up."

He also pointed out that operating costs have trebled for the average newspaper and continue to increase, so that if there is to be a newspaper for the readers, the price must be adjusted accordingly.

The opportunity thus provided to explain some misconceptions was one of the major benefits from this survey.

When the Columbia, Mo., *Missourian* (circulation 3,954, population 31,974) conducted a readership survey to ascertain reaction to its various features, it instructed its interviewers to invite suggestions for improvement of the newspaper. On the form to be filled in by interviewers were questions such as these:

> Would you like the *Missourian* better if it carried more national and international news? If it carried more stories from nearby towns?
>
> What suggestions can you make for improving the *Missourian*'s editorials? Its book reviews?
>
> Is there any comment you would like to make about the *Missourian*'s sports coverage? Its society news coverage? Its picture page?
>
> Do you see features in other papers you would like to receive in the *Missourian*?
>
> Have you any other suggestions for the improvement of the *Missourian*?

The suggestions received were presented and discussed at a meeting of the *Missourian* staff and some were adopted. Each person who presented some idea for improvement of the paper was sent a letter of thanks by the manager.

Material received from subscribers in readership surveys may become the basis of effective promotion. A publisher who does not make use of it in this way is indifferent to one of the best means of building good will for his newspaper. It is important to know readers' likes and to give careful and logical attention to their suggestions.

To Hold Interest of All Groups

Persons of different ages, nationalities and vocations read the newspaper, and if they are to be satisfied with the news and the features it brings them, the publisher must give consideration to their special interests and needs.

All readers want the news and some of the features, but few give attention to *every* feature the newspaper provides. Youth is interested in some features that have lost their glow for adults. Men turn quickly to the markets and the financial page while women are more interested in the women's news page. Older people, too, are vitally interested in

certain types of news and features that persons of middle age will
pass over quickly. Certain features that are popular with the people
in one community may not be much enjoyed by the people of another
community.

Pierre Martineau, manager of research for the Chicago *Tribune*
(circulation 868,455, population 3,620,962) says: "There has been
a decided change in the composition of people since the 1930's. People
today are getting more out of life and what they do has a direct bearing on what they read. There is the enormous middle income group,
for instance. Women's role, too, has changed. The patriarch type of
family is disappearing and there is much more of comrade-like sharing
in the home. People enjoy more participation sports, more hobbies
and do-it-yourself type of activities — particularly those who live in
the suburbs. All this goes to the guts of what constitutes news."[3]

American people also attend church services more regularly and
are more liberal in their support of religious institutions. Consequently newspapers are giving more attention to news about churches
and religion. This is revealed in a survey made by the Gannett newspapers.[4] Eight of 13 church page editors reported they were using
more and larger pictures to illustrate church news. Four listed increasingly prominent play for top wire and syndicated articles on religion. Five noted a trend toward the use of news from all faiths —
Protestant, Catholic and Jewish. Churches also have sensed the value
of church advertising and are buying more space in newspapers.

This survey gave to the Gannett newspapers excellent material
for a promotion campaign that assuredly won greater respect and regard from an important portion of their readers.

To Study Reading Trends

The Associated Press Managing Editors Association has a special
group of its members who comprise what is called a New Trends
Committee. Their responsibility is to help publishers keep their
newspapers up-to-the-minute in news, features and typography. Discussions within the committee have brought forth some interesting
comment regarding contemplated changes in newspaper makeup and
content.

One discussion was centered on women's pages.[5] Some newspapers
are making over their sections devoted to home and family life with
the purpose in view of appealing to a wider group of women. Instead of devoting so much space to local persons and local social events,
they are increasing their volume on styles in dress, child psychology,
how to reduce, popular recipes, cooking and the like. Upholding

[3] *Editor & Publisher,* Jan. 28, 1956, p. 7.
[4] *Editor & Publisher,* Feb. 1, 1958, p. 28.
[5] *Editor & Publisher,* Apr. 5, 1958, p. 34.

this plan was the Los Angeles, Calif., *Times* (circulation 476,746, population 2,243,901).

"Our aim is to interest a million subscribers instead of the members of a small club or social group," said William Stewart, editor of the *Times'* Family Section. "We give more space and pictures to BIG society and club news and the trivial is eliminated. This concept has been accepted by our women readers. Only one unfavorable letter was received during the month following the change."

Some of the smaller papers could not see the advisability of such a change.

"A woman's page, filled with advice and how-to articles, is devoid of personality," said Sam Ragan of the Raleigh, N. C., *News and Observer* (circulation 124,271, population 65,679). "It is about as lifeless as wallpaper. When you take personals, parties, brides' pictures and stories of interesting personalities out of a section you lower the interest of readers."

The best way to ascertain the reaction of readers to a change in the woman's page or any other department of the newspaper is to conduct a survey — find out what features on the page or in the department are enjoyed most and what additional features readers would like to see there. A publisher should rely more heavily on the interests and feelings of his own readers than on the experience of a publisher in another town. He should go directly to subscribers for their opinions and ideas before accepting fully the counsel of an outsider, even though the outsider has been successful in his own community in providing his readers' needs.

Young people represent another group that should receive special consideration. With youngsters giving so much time and attention to radio and television programs, the question often has arisen as to how much time they give to newspapers and whether or not they will ultimately lose the habit of reading newspapers.

The Research Division of the School of Journalism of the State University of Iowa conducted a survey in Des Moines to find out how well teen-age boys and girls read the newspaper and to what extent their interest in news varies as they grow older. More than 300 pupils in each of grades five, seven, nine and eleven, and 115 third graders took part in the study. A major part of the study was financed by the Des Moines *Register* and *Tribune* (combined circulation 345,146, population 177,965). The highlights of the study were as follows:

a. From 97 to 99 per cent of the pupils in grades five, seven, nine and eleven, and 85 per cent of the third graders, said they read a daily newspaper.

b. More boys than girls said they liked to read about murders and robberies, accidents, fires and floods, but more girls than boys said they liked reading about love triangles and divorce.

    c. The boys' three top choices in types of news were sports, crime-police-gangsters and auto wrecks, while the girls' top choices were Hollywood, sports and Des Moines news.

    d. The favorite sections of the newspaper for all youngsters surveyed were the comics, sports and movie-radio news.

    e. Girls' interest in women's features and society increased sharply from fifth through eleventh grades; girls of all ages showed some interest in columns on love and personal problems.

    f. Small interest was shown in the so-called "educational" content of the newspaper — editorials, public affairs columns, book reviews and the like.

The South Bend, Ind., *Tribune* (circulation 108,793, population 115,911) conducted a similar survey, attempting to learn how much time teen-agers spend each day in reading the newspaper as well as to find out what features interest them most. When asked how much time they spent in reading a certain issue of the *Tribune,* 37.7 per cent of the boys and 56.8 per cent of the girls said they spent thirty minutes or less; 51.9 per cent of the boys and 37.5 per cent of the girls said they spent from thirty minutes to an hour.

The survey showed that teen-agers read a great deal in the newspaper besides the comics. In fact, one 8-line item on page one, concerning the death of a Boston quadruplet, was read by 93 per cent of the girls — more than saw any comic strip or cartoon. There was hardly a story, feature or advertisement in the newspaper, regardless of size, that did not receive some readership.

Surveys to determine the interests of special groups are important in maintaining a close relationship with all readers. They serve as a guide for the promotion department in focusing its appeal to groups where readership build-up is needed.

Must Keep Up With Changing Times

Newspapers, of course, cannot rely permanently on the facts revealed in a single survey. They must contact readers often in order to keep up with changing needs, interest and moods. The Chicago *Tribune* carries on day-to-day research and faithfully applies what it learns. The promotion of its Sunday magazine, its editorial page and even its comics is devoted primarily to adaptations brought about through continuous surveys.

Too many newspapers, however, are prone to follow a pattern with few changes from year to year, indicating that they are doing little toward finding out better ways to serve their readers. An indication of this is the general sameness in the Sunday issues of American newspapers.

Sexson E. Humphreys of Ohio University, using the Sunday issues of 26 newspapers published on the same date, analyzed them to see in how many ways they were alike.[6] He found that nine sections were common to most: (1) a general news section in all papers, (2) comics in 25 papers, (3) a separate sports section in 21, (4) a women's section in 20, (5) a syndicated magazine distributed with 17, (6) a television section in 15, (7) a classified advertising section in 15, (8) the newspaper's own magazine or rotogravure supplement in 15 and (9) sections emphasizing editorial comment, often with special added feature material, in 12 papers.

The interests of people in one community, of course, are similar to those of another community, but never in all respects the same. The similarity in all Sunday newspapers indicates that even the large newspapers might take a livelier interest in the special wants of their readers.

Newspaper surveys sometimes reveal shocking facts. A public opinion survey made by the National Association of Science Writers six months before the Soviets launched Sputnik I showed that less than half of the American public had ever heard of space satellites.

Those interviewed were asked, "Have you heard anything about plans to launch a space satellite, sometimes called a man-made moon? From what you've heard, what is the purpose of launching these space satellites?"

Of the 1,919 adults questioned, 54 per cent said they had never heard of space satellites. Only 20 per cent had any real idea of what such satellites would accomplish. The rest had vague knowledge of those "man-made moons" but knew little of their purpose.

"These statistics are significant because they provide a base for measuring how much of the items on the satellite phase of the International Geophysical Year had gotten through into people's memories," said Hillier Krieghbaum, chairman of the survey committee. "Coverage about satellites had been considerable up to the survey time but all of it was small compared with that after the Soviets put their Sputniks into the sky."

Newspapers, sensing this increased interest in space exploration, have since given greater space to science news and have promoted this new step extensively. They have also caused studies to be made of America's offerings in scientific knowledge and research. Some newspapers have made full-scale surveys of courses offered in public schools of their areas. The Stroudsburg, Pa., *Record* (circulation 8,950, population 6,361) mailed questionnaires to every teacher, school administrator, school board member, teachers college faculty member and P. T. A. group in its area.[7] The questions were based on the major issues described at a conference called by the Governor of Pennsyl-

---

[6]*Editor & Publisher,* Jan. 11, 1958, p. 13.

[7]*Editor & Publisher,* Feb. 22, 1958, p. 50.

vania to consider the extent to which the state's system of education was adequate or deficient. Out of this survey, the *Record* evolved a picture of "Education — 1958" as it existed in an average county of the state. It presented timely facts of statewide importance and interest.

To properly fulfill its purpose and at the same time maintain its stability a newspaper must keep up with the needs of the times and the changing thoughts and interests of its readers.

Must Meet Competition

Publishers need to be kept conscious of their opportunities and their responsibilities. Surveys will keep them from falling into the rut of self-satisfaction and retrogression.

In 1957 Dr. George Gallup's American Institute of Public Opinion conducted what was believed to be the "first national study of the role of newspapers in the field of communications." Seventy-four major questions were used to learn what the public actually thinks about the newspaper press, not only by itself but also in relation to other communication media. This survey revealed the need for newspapers to make important changes in content and package.

"News must be made more pleasant and easier to read," said Dr. Gallup. "At present the approach is too formal, too stiff. When I say 'easier to read,' I do not mean merely the choice of simple words and phrases. I mean the use of imagination and study, study and more study to change the entire method of news presentation to conform with what the public wants. The time can come when, with changes in television and no changes in newspapers, the power of the press can be weakened. And that should never happen."

Dr. Gallup did not question the public's appreciation of newspapers but he warned against self-satisfaction on the part of publishers. The survey revealed that newspapers must be conscious of changes and move forward with the progress of the world. It suggested also that they must promote themselves more. They don't tell their readers often enough all they are doing for them and the costs of the services performed for them. They are much too modest. At least that was the feeling of Prof. Emery H. Ruby, who directed the survey for Dr. Gallup.

The Los Angeles, Calif., *Mirror-News* (circulation 307,412, population 2,243,901) employed the Los Angeles Poll in 1957 to conduct a reader-viewer survey in its circulation area.[8] The most striking fact to come out of this survey was that residents of Los Angeles spent more time reading newspapers and less time in front of television sets than they did in 1955. The common reasons given by respondents who had increased their reading time were:

---

[8]*Editor & Publisher,* Nov. 23, 1957, p. 16.

"I'm more interested in what's going on."

"I have more time to read."

"Newspapers are more interesting and more important."

In summarizing the results, Walter H. Eaton, director of the survey, said: "The average person appears to feel guilty, ashamed, embarrassed, if he now spends less time reading newspapers. It is also apparent that television, for the average viewer, is a means of relaxation, an expression of lethargy or an escape from loneliness. Essentially, it's a passive medium. But newspapers are read in a spirit of inquiry and positive interest to learn what's going on. The newspaper is an active medium."

In both Minneapolis and Des Moines, newspaper readers were asked whether they thought television ever would take the place of daily newspapers. Nine out of ten replied "No."

The same readers then were asked to specify what they got out of newspapers that they don't get out of television. An average of 60.7 per cent said "more news and more detailed coverage" or "more local and regional news"; 18.5 per cent specified "more time for reflection," or "time to reread"; 8.4 per cent named "advertising" and 4.8 per cent "editorials." But only 2.3 per cent made any reference to "comic strips" or "cartoons."

Most reader-viewer surveys reveal that television is sought for entertainment and the newspaper for information — a fact that may be used effectively in newspaper promotion.

Publishers Learn From Each Other

Publishers learn from each other as well as from the readers of their newspapers. From reading each others' newspapers and drawing comparisons, they decide on many of the changes they institute. Particularly will they do this if they notice any drop in reader interest. Then they are anxious to find out if the same unfortunate situation is facing other newspapers of their class and, if so, what they are doing to correct it.

After analyzing the contents of a group of metropolitan newspapers over a publication period of 50 years, Dr. Frank Luther Mott, journalism historian, remarked: "When circulation holds up, it seems like tempting fate to change the offering." But when circulation begins to drop, papers become willing to engage in research and experimentation. Moreover, so far as smaller papers especially are concerned, Dr. Mott points out that "imitation of successful newspaper practices is the oldest and most consistent secondary cause of newspaper trends."

State press associations and other regional groups of newspaper publishers often make surveys of their members to see what innovations have been instituted in the way of features and news handling and which have been the most successful. It is not unusual for a publisher to conduct a survey among publishers whom he knows to see if they are facing problems similar to his own. Often a publisher will subscribe to a dozen or more papers in order to study their contents, manners of handling news and features, and general typography.

Good ideas for newspaper betterment and also for newspaper promotion are obtained in this way. Readership surveys help to illuminate the way ahead. Research determines the future. It has become so important a factor in newspaper publishing that some papers, particularly the larger ones, have departments devoted entirely to research, separate and apart from the promotion department.

Promoting
Advertising Services

CHAPTER 11

Medium for
Total Advertising

ONE-THIRD OF ALL AMERICAN ADVERTISING DOLLARS go to newspapers. This is strong evidence of the high regard in which
newspapers are held by the advertising public. It is also the incentive
for greater promotion of advertising in newspapers — particularly for
the selling of the newspaper as an effective, exclusive medium.

The Newspaper Advertising Executives Association and the Bureau
of Advertising of the American Newspaper Publishers Association
have instigated, within the past few years, several campaigns which
reveal the results that may be obtained from total selling through
newspapers. All these campaigns have been closely related, each giving
force and speed to the total selling movement. They have been identified by *Editor & Publisher*[1] as "Operation Step-up," "Project Follow-
Thru," "Operation Screening," "Operation Exec" and "Operation
Bootstrap."

"Operation Step-up," the first campaign, was instituted in 1958. It
was a sales-training program in which more than 8,400 newspaper
advertising salesmen participated. This was followed, in the same
year, with a refresher course in selling known as "Project Follow-
Thru." Realizing the importance of throwing efficiency into the sales
force, a third campaign, known as "Operation Screening," was developed to improve the selection of advertising salesmen. Then out of
this came the thought that advertising managers might do a better
job in directing and training their salesmen, and "Operation Exec"
resulted. A three-volume kit for managers was developed, dealing with

---

[1]*Editor & Publisher,* Jan. 17, 1959, p. 6.

compensation for salesmen, sales controls for the advertising director and training techniques for new salesmen.

These related campaigns made the year an important one in getting newspaper personnel on fire for effective total selling. Newspapers invested $100,000 in these tooling-up efforts in addition to giving particular attention to the development of better selling within their own organizations.

Newspapers then were ready for greater progress in 1959 and launched a campaign known as "Operation Bootstrap," which included five important steps in total selling:

1. The united efforts of associations of publishers, advertising executives, special advertising representatives and promotion managers in setting forth the merits of newspaper advertising and in instituting selling campaigns.
2. The close cooperation of manufacturers, distributors and retailers in pushing the sale of a single product or a special line of goods through newspaper advertising.
3. The tying together of all forms of newspaper advertising —retail, national and classified — in building sales volume.
4. Cooperative campaigns of advertising and selling through newspapers by merchants engaged in the same line of business.
5. Exclusive use of newspapers for advertising a single product or line of goods.

Newspaper Groups Unite Forces

In launching the 1959 campaign for total selling, George Lemons, president of the Newspaper Advertising Executives Association, called attention to the unity of thought and effort that prevails in the newspaper industry. Working together with the Bureau of Advertising and the NAEA in the promotion of better newspaper selling are the American Association of Newspaper Representatives, National Newspaper Promotion Association and the Association of Newspaper Classified Managers.

"We have the most powerful sales force in the world," Mr. Lemons said. "We have twelve hundred representatives, two thousand national advertising salesmen, four thousand classified advertising salesmen and twelve thousand retail salesmen."

That truly is a remarkable sales force, and when they can be lined up together in a promotion campaign, much is certain to happen. And much did happen.

Four major promotions were planned and carried out. These were in the automotive, food, appliance, and health and beauty fields. Leaders in these fields were enthusiastic about the results obtained and the future effects of the campaigns upon their lines of business.

"Great benefits will come to us and to the consuming public from the cooperation of newspapers in spotlighting the importance of food in our economy," said Charles B. Shuman, general manager of the National Food Conference.

Dean Chaffin, president of the National Automobile Dealers Association, expressed appreciation for the lift provided automobile dealers by newspapers all across the land. "In addition, we are grateful for the generous cooperation and support rendered our efforts to eliminate false, misleading and unethical auto advertising," he said.

The initiative and vision of newspapers was lauded, too, by Joseph F. Miller, managing director of the National Electrical Manufacturers Association. "This will provide great opportunity for the appliance industry," he declared.

Manufacturers of health and beauty items also gave hearty cooperation to the campaign and derived their share of the benefits.

By the full cooperation of newspaper sales and promotion forces, total selling of newspaper advertising became effective in four important business fields, and an abundance of prestige and good will was gained for newspapers.

Push Sales of Single Items

In developing the sale of a single item or a certain brand of goods, the newspaper again becomes an effective medium. It reaches its maximum efficiency when distributors and retailers join heartily with the manufacturer in advertising the product and pushing its sale. When those who distribute the item and those who stock it for retail sale line up with the manufacturer in promoting it, astonishing results are obtained.

"Buying is more than wanting and knowing," explains Walter Kurz, advertising manager of the Chicago *Tribune* (circulation 868,455, population 3,620,962). "The consumer moves through a complicated process from desire to consummation. Many steps intervene. Much information must be integrated into the mind before the purchase is completed. Advertising in the newspaper — and only in the newspaper — does all this. It creates desire, tells about the product, builds the brand image, tells where the retailer is, when the merchandise is available and how much it costs. The manufacturer, the distributor and the retailer can join hands in the newspaper to create and satisfy consumer demand. The newspaper is the one advertising medium in which total selling, the distributing process, consumer demand and buying process can converge."[2]

No item of merchandise that goes on the market receives maximum sales push until all the forces behind it — manufacturer, distributor and retail outlet — give their full unified support in promoting it. And right here is where all types of newspaper advertising may step into the total selling arena.

---

[2] *Editor & Publisher*, Jan. 24, 1959, p. 24.

National Helps Local Advertising

National advertising may give valuable support to local advertising. Classified advertising may be used to develop greater newspaper readership and thereby give greater power to all newspaper advertising. And everything that helps the newspaper helps national advertising. Here is a complete round of helpful cooperation. The chain should never be broken and it constantly needs strengthening.

"In all selling of newspaper advertising we must place first the sale of the medium," Arthur H. (Red) Motley, president and publisher of *Parade Magazine*, told members of the National Advertising Executives Association at their 1959 winter meeting. "This calls for cooperation between the various groups in selling newspaper advertising — advertising representatives, syndicates formed to sell comics or magazine sections, as well as the local and national advertising departments of newspapers themselves."

He outlined six steps as a practical guide to more and better selling of the newspaper medium:

1. No sale of newspaper space without an intelligent, effective sale of the power of newspaper advertising generally.
2. More intensive contacts with younger men in advertising departments and advertising agencies by newspaper advertising salesmen.
3. Easy-to-understand rate cards to encourage use of the newspaper medium.
4. Discounts for volume, frequency and continuity in order that the newspaper may conform to the general practices of all advertising media.
5. Narrowing of difference between the local and the national rate.
6. Better training of salesmen in the techniques of explaining their product, showing its advantages and closing the sale.

Anything that can be done to keep national, retail and classified advertising pulling together will go far toward developing an effective plan of total selling.

Cooperative Campaigns Produce Results

Another type of total selling that has proved effective is a cooperative campaign of newspaper advertising by merchants in the same line of business.

One of the best examples of this was the "You Auto Buy" campaign, started by the newspapers of Cleveland, Ohio, in 1958 to help motor car dealers stimulate the fading sale of automobiles. This produced an estimated sale of $15 million worth of new and used cars in one week in that city — a result astonishing enough to cause auto dealers in many other cities of the country to follow suit. This became one of the greatest cooperative campaigns ever conducted in newspapers.

This revealed a golden opportunity for dealers in other lines of merchandise as well as for motor car dealers, and it presented a challenge to newspapers. It demonstrated how newspaper advertising on a cooperative basis could help retailers of the nation move merchandise quickly and keep sales at a high level.

The idea took hold with even greater enthusiasm and more astonishing results in 1959. Retailers moved ahead of manufacturers in the use of newspapers to place their products' images in buyers' minds. With equal diligence, the newspaper advertising men of the nation gave their aid in determining consumer wants and in preparing compelling copy. The total result was better advertising, better marketing and greater sales.

What the results would be from the standpoint of sales was made plain in 1958 when groups of merchants who used newspapers almost entirely had remarkable sales increases despite the prospects for a mediocre business year. Food stores had an increase of $2\frac{1}{2}$ billion dollars in sales over 1957. Drug stores, whose major reliance is on newspaper advertising, had a gain of 4 per cent. Apparel stores, which use almost nothing but newspaper advertising to move their goods, experienced a total sales increase of $3\frac{1}{2}$ per cent. Department store sales also showed a total gain for the year. These four groups of merchants, which depend almost exclusively on newspaper advertising to ring their cash registers, taped a grand sales total of 95 billion dollars for the year.

It is not surprising, therefore, that in planning a 1959 campaign, newspapers were considered for total selling and that several leading groups of merchants did the job on a cooperative basis.

An Exclusive Medium

Another angle that naturally worked itself into this total selling campaign was emphasis on the newspaper as an effective exclusive advertising medium for many lines of business. The Bureau of Advertising produced promotion material, and merchants testified to results obtained from their exclusive use of the newspaper in moving goods to consumers.

In an attractive brochure the Bureau of Advertising explained how the newspaper might be used as a total selling medium and stressed four points:

1. The daily newspaper is the only medium that reaches the total market; that is, it is the only medium with which an advertiser can deliver his selling message to over 85 per cent of the adults throughout the United States and Canada.

2. The daily newspaper does a total servicing job of the total buying population; that is, it is used by almost every family as the Total Shopping Guide.

3. The daily newspaper is on hand to do its selling job for the advertiser 24 hours a day — every week and every month of the year.

4. The daily newspaper is the only medium which offers advertisers total marketing help with distributors, retailers and consumers.

The Newspaper Advertising Executives Association makes plain, however, that total selling is not for daily newspapers alone, but that it is designed to help bolster a broad group of weekly papers as well. To make total selling a success, all newspaper advertising people must give greater attention to marketing. They must be stronger in the competitive field and promote newspaper advertising as the best means of selling more goods at lower cost. Total selling is for everybody in the newspaper advertising business.

In support of total selling, it was not difficult to obtain the co-operation of merchants who had experienced the benefits of exclusive newspaper advertising.

Forrest Arthur, president and general manager of the Buttrey Associates department store in Great Falls, Mont., told members of the NAEA that if he were suddenly restricted to one and only one advertising medium, he "would board up the display windows, discontinue all interior and departmental selling displays, eliminate all informative show cards, discontinue all sales meetings and sales incentives, stop all telephone selling, and continue an aggressive business-building advertising investment in the newspapers."

"It is a wasteful folly to advertise a product nationally with a king-size appropriation," he added, "and not realize fully that the final selling of the product must be done locally — by the local newspaper." And to the same group of advertising executives, Joseph J. Foy, president of Spartan Store, Inc., Grand Rapids, Mich., said: "Without newspapers all advertising in the long run would be pretty weak."

Testimonials came from many other sources during the year. George R. Abrams, vice-president and advertising director for Revlon, told *Editor & Publisher*:[3] "We have always considered newspapers a prime medium, especially for introducing new products. In supporting established brands, newspaper advertising enables us to tell a complete story as does no other medium."

William D. Tyler, vice-president and creative director of Benton & Bowles, Inc., lauded the use of big space in newspapers. "It is the greatest thing the newspaper has to offer today," he said. "No one

---

[3]*Editor & Publisher,* Jan. 31, 1959, p. 20.

else can offer such a great big piece of paper on which to tell a simple story so powerfully, so dramatically." And from Chester D. Palmer, Jr., advertising manager of Johnson Motors, came this: "Newspapers have always been our basic medium and our thoughts concerning them have never changed."

A Program of Wide Scope

Total selling of the newspaper as an exclusive advertising medium, therefore, reaches its maximum success when it includes:

1. The united efforts of publishers, advertising executives, special representatives and promotion managers.
2. The close cooperation of manufacturers, distributors and retailers.
3. The concerted use of retail, classified and national advertising.
4. The united push of merchants in the same line of business.
5. A clear picture of newspapers as sufficient for great selling in any field. Such is the wide scope of promotion for newspaper advertising.

A combined movement of this kind in no way lessens emphasis on retail, classified and national advertising as individual services. It only demonstrates that better results can be obtained when forces combine to do an all-out job. Each service not only lifts itself but all others by its own bootstraps. It then becomes a more vital promotion factor.

CHAPTER 12

Promoting
Retail Advertising

RETAIL ADVERTISING PRODUCES MORE REVENUE for the newspaper than any other type of advertising. The territory from which it is drawn is conveniently reached and prospective buyers are easily persuaded.

These facts would seem to spell out a great promotion opportunity fraught with astonishing results which should induce newspapers to give it extensive promotion. The strange fact is, however, that many newspapers give less promotion to retail advertising than to either general advertising or classified.

Publishers, like other businessmen, are inclined to consider lightly what comes easily and put their greater efforts on what requires the heavy pull. In assuming this attitude they fail to reach the full possibilities of retail advertising volume for their newspapers.

A newspaper's reputation as an advertising medium for home merchants is determined largely by reiterated information, misinformation or lack of distributed information on its merits as such. This reputation can grow through continuous, concerted effort on the part of the promotion department or can be damaged by the absence of such effort. A well-developed program in its behalf is important. There are, in fact, four groups to whom promotion should be directed in developing retail advertising:

1. The advertising staff.
2. Individual merchants of the community in which the newspaper is published.
3. Various retail groups.
4. The community at large.

PROMOTING ADVERTISING TO SALES FORCE

The first important step in promoting retail advertising is for the publisher to sell himself and his advertising department on the importance of retail advertising to the newspaper and the home merchants, and at the same time become convinced that steady, well-organized promotion, kept always at high pitch, is essential in obtaining maximum volume.

It is not difficult for a publisher to obtain enough advertising from the merchants of his community to produce something that citizens may be willing to call a newspaper. But it requires persistent, hard-hitting, convincing selling to derive sufficient steady income from the sale of retail advertising to develop that something into a healthy, growing instrument of public service.

A progressive publisher is never willing to stand still. He is constantly seeking new ways to improve his paper and his community. If he is to realize these aims, he must sell advertising and it must be mainly to firms that do business in the community where the newspaper is published. He must have an adequate number of salesmen and keep them constantly in the selling groove.

Here is where a promotion department becomes helpful. It steps in to aid the advertising manager by:

1. Impressing on advertising salesmen the dependence of the newspaper upon local advertising to produce needed income.
2. Giving advertising salesmen the necessary sales facts and tools to convince merchants and manufacturers of the newspaper's result-giving power.
3. Keeping the department constantly supplied with new and practical ideas for developing advertising on a scientific plan.
4. Keeping before salesmen a calendar of events and special days to which advertising may be tied to produce extra volume.
5. Stimulating good salesmanship with bonuses and commissions.
6. Stimulating competition between salesmen by use of contests and goals.

Build Up Faith in Advertising

Rising costs and a narrowing profit margin create a challenge to survival for many newspapers, especially for those in a competitive field. Therefore, it is important for those in the advertising department to know how vital it is to keep the newspaper's available space filled with advertising. Salesmen need to know how valuable advertising is to the newspaper they represent as well as its value to the merchants for whom they prepare copy and plan campaigns.

The promotion department can help the advertising manager in bringing this point home to his salesmen by setting before them charts showing the percentage of the newspaper's total income they are expected to provide. For most newspapers more than 60 per cent of supporting revenue must come from advertising. But more important even than this is for advertising salesmen to understand the high value of the product and service they are selling.

John S. Knight, in an address to the Southern Newspaper Publishers Association, lamented the lack of faith of so many advertising salesmen in the newspapers they represent.

"Editorial departments are literally showered," he said, "with 'support copy.' In addition, many so-called special sections carry more free publicity than advertising space. Do you know any advertisers who make this demand of the local television station? Do you read any 'free blurbs' in *Life, Look,* the *Saturday Evening Post* or the news magazines? Of course not. Their advertising departments sell the worth of the book because they believe in it."

This same sort of belief must be instilled in the newspaper's advertising staff, and the promotion department must provide the needed information and inspiration.

"If you would look at the book shelves in the home of a typical space salesman, you would not find half a dozen books on salesmanship," said Van L. Phillips, sales consultant, to members of the Inland Daily Press Association. "Yet these men consider themselves professional salesmen representing the newspaper industry."

To overcome this situation, Phillips has assisted the Newspaper Advertising Executives Association in developing a sales training program for newspaper advertising staffs. It is known as "Operation Step-up." Instead of being a lecture course, it is a sales-training program requiring the active and continued participation of trainees. It is designed not only to train new members of the staff but also to improve the salesmanship of experienced and older members.

Give the Salesmen Some Tools

Any publisher may improve the efficiency of his advertising department by training members of the sales force, keeping them informed of the importance of their work and providing them with up-to-the-minute ideas that may be applied in their selling. The art of being diplomatic and at the same time sincere is another valuable business asset. To develop these important abilities in a newspaper's advertising sales force is a responsibility that rests mainly with the newspaper's promotion department.

Elmer E. Ferris in his book, "Developing Sales Personality," says that "every man should work out his own method" but that it would be well for him to "handle the phlegmatic temperament with deliberation, the sensitive with deference, the open-minded with frankness, the cautious with proof." A promotion department may not be expert in all these categories of sales approach, but it at least can supply the proof of benefits from newspaper advertising that may be needed to convince the cautious.

It can load an advertising salesman with the ammunition he may need to win in battles with most minds. When properly equipped, it is easy to prove that advertising accomplishes the following:

1. Paves the way for sales.
2. Humanizes a company in the eyes of its prospects.
3. Creates and nourishes a desire for the product featured.
4. Builds confidence and belief.
5. Neutralizes normal buying fears.
6. Resells customers who have already bought.
7. Prepares the ground work and opens the road to new trade.
8. Constantly builds a widening mass market.

Keep Abreast of New Ideas

One of the greatest helps to a newspaper in keeping abreast of new ideas is the Bureau of Advertising of the American Newspaper Publishers Association. Among the many important services it provides for newspapers is an Annual Time Table of Retail Opportunities. This is in two parts:

1. A "Full Power Newspaper Advertising Plan Book," containing facts and figures to be used in planning and selling, and work sheets — one for each month of the year.
2. An easel presentation, "How to Cut the Cost of Getting More Business." This shows how to use sales records for effective planning and budgeting of advertising.

Here is a service that an advertising salesman finds pleasure in explaining to his clients. It aids greatly in focusing the attention of retailers on the fundamentals and mechanics of timing advertising for high turnover operation at full markup and maximum profits. It contains a special advertising quiz designed to test the effectiveness of any individual merchant's advertising timing, a listing of traditional merchandising events and promotion dates which offer strong merchandising and advertising opportunities, and outlines of basic steps to be followed by retailers in achieving more productive advertising.

A newspaper, of course, needs to adapt any such advertising service or plan to its local situation. This may be done readily by the promotion department. Some newspaper chains compile for their newspapers a monthly bulletin containing suggestions for selling advertising that otherwise might not be considered at all. Current events, as well as special days, often present opportunities for producing effective advertising for the various lines of business represented in a newspaper's community. This sort of service may be provided for any newspaper by its promotion department and put into operation in its advertising department. The additional inches of advertising thus produced may be surprising.

The advertising department may be helpful also to home town merchants by passing along to them selling plans that have been used with success in other communities. *Sales Management Magazine,* for example, compiled in 1951 a "Portfolio of Selling Plans" to help merchants and manufacturers maintain sales at a high standard during the Korean War period. A newspaper's promotion department can prepare for its advertising department at any critical time a similar collection of timely suggestions to be passed along by advertising salesmen to their clients. Anything that will increase sales for the merchants will increase advertising in the newspaper.

Provide Special Incentives

Contests and incentives in the advertising department often bring in new advertising contracts and additional linage. A survey by the newspaper's promotion manager among publisher friends would reveal many effective ways of conducting such contests and many incentives that might be used.

By simply instituting the common plan of keeping before advertising salesmen the monthly linage figures of the preceding year and urging that they beat them, the Houma, La., *Houma Courier,* issued on Friday, and the *Terrebonne Press,* issued on Tuesday (combined circulation 11,488, population 11,505), doubled their advertising volume, and their advertising manager increased his salary by 350 per cent. Additional income was provided also for salesmen. This kept before the advertising staff a constant challenge, and they continually strove to go far beyond the previous year's record, according to John B. Gordon, publisher.

Gordon believes also in letting his advertisers know that the newspaper's entire staff is working in their behalf. He prepared and presented to actual and prospective advertisers, both local and national, an 8-page folder containing pictures and stories about all persons on the annual $100,000 payroll. "Forty-eight busy hands are constantly working at the pleasant task of bringing to YOU and YOUR CUSTOMERS the *Houma Courier* and the *Terrebonne Press* every Friday and Tuesday," the folder proclaimed on its title page (see Fig. 12.1).

The Niles, Ohio, *Times* (circulation 6,422, population 16,773) pays its advertising salesmen a bonus of $2.50 for every 3-month contract they sell and $4.50 for every yearly contract, regardless of whether it is a new order or a renewal. Each contract, however, must be for more than five inches a week.

48 busy hands

are constantly working at the pleasant task

of bringing YOU and YOUR CUSTOMERS

THE HOUMA COURIER

and

THE Terrebonne Press

Every FRIDAY and TUESDAY

That's right folks, 48 busy hands, wielded by 24 trained workers, are engaged on a full-time basis to write and produce your newspapers. That doesn't include the 31 part-time workers who do rural correspondence and special writing. Neither does it include the mailing crew, which works late at night, nor the 16 bread delivery men who start as early as 4:30 a. m. to distribute the Courier and Press throughout Terrebonne's rural areas. Space limitations restrict us to the introduction of full-time workers, and it's a crew that any publisher would be proud to introduce.

Fig. 12.1 — Front page of a folder issued to regular and prospective advertisers by the Houma, La., **Houma Courier** and **Terrebonne Press**.

The South Haven, Mich., *Tribune* (circulation 3,039, population 5,629) sets a minimum goal of 10,000 column inches per year for each of its advertising salesmen. As soon as the goal is reached, the salesman receives a $50 bonus, and for all that he sells within the year above the goal, he receives $25 per thousand inches. Under this plan, a girl on the sales staff during four months of one year earned a bonus of $100 or more per month, according to Donald V. Schoenwether, general manager.

The Lawrence, Kans., *Journal-World* (circulation 10,755, population 23,351) pays in addition to a weekly salary a commission on the amount of advertising sold. For whatever a salesman brings in up to the first 1,000 inches, he receives a penny an inch, and for all above 1,000 inches he receives one and one-half cents per inch. To prevent trouble over whether or not to hold out a page on the last day of the month and insert it on the first of the next month, the newspaper pays half a cent per column inch on the net gain for the year. Dolph Simons, Jr., general manager and promotion manager, says that during the first year, this plan produced an increase of 10 to 15 per cent in advertising volume each month.

George W. Rogers, business manager of the Salem, Ohio, *News* (circulation 9,980, population 12,754), has used many incentive plans, most of which have been on a short-term basis. He believes that three months is the desirable limit of time for any contest or incentive plan. However, one year he carried through a commission plan based on the gain over the previous year, which proved very successful. For the first thousand inches produced by his sales staff he paid seven cents an inch, for the next thousand six cents an inch, and for all inches above that he paid five cents per inch. The money thus accumulated by the advertising department was put into a "kitty," of which 90 per cent was distributed evenly among the salesmen. The 10 per cent remaining was given to the salesman who showed the greatest percentage of gain in his contract accounts.

Many small dailies and weeklies have found an incentive plan of some kind valuable in stimulating advertising sales. A survey of 130 weekly papers covering a wide area of the United States revealed ten different means of paying advertising salesmen:

1. Straight salary (by far the most popular means of payment).
2. Straight commission (rarely used).
3. Salary plus stock in the company paid as a bonus.
4. Salary plus bonus based on percentage of gain.
5. Salary plus bonus based on percentage of gross.
6. Salary plus commission on gross.
7. Salary plus commission on sales above pre-determined minimum.
8. Commission with a minimum base.

9. Salary with commission scaled according to increased linage.
10. Commission with varying percentages paid for renewals, contract advertisers and special editions.

A promotion department may give other valuable assistance to the advertising manager in developing incentives for advertising salesmen. Bulletins outlining effective sales practices and providing up-to-the-minute suggestions on sources of advertising may be prepared and submitted. The Bureau of Advertising's "Nine Points for Effectiveness in National Newspaper Advertising" furnishes the pattern for some good suggestions leading to better results from retail advertising. In fact, the bureau's following points apply to retail as well as to national advertising:

1. Newspaper advertising reaches more people than any other medium.
2. People like advertising in a newspaper better than in any other medium.
3. Newspapers deliver more "ready to buy" prospects than any other medium.
4. Newspaper advertising gets more action than any other medium.
5. Newspaper advertising offers more local selling flexibility than any other medium.
6. Newspapers give more flexibility in selling copy than any other medium.
7. Newspaper advertising offers better retail merchandising than any other advertising.
8. Newspaper advertising is a safer and surer investment than advertising in any other medium.
9. Newspaper advertising produces more sales per dollar of advertising costs than do other media.

Material of this kind assembled by the promotion department and passed along to the advertising department helps to keep the salesmen sold on their newspaper as an effective medium for local merchants.

PROMOTING ADVERTISING TO MERCHANTS

In addition to helping the advertising manager stimulate his salesmen's faith in advertising and put fire into their efforts, the promotion department must turn its attention directly to merchants and firmly convince them of the merits of newspaper advertising. This may be done through:

1. Personal contacts.
2. Presentation of salient facts.
3. Campaigns and special days.
4. Assistance in copy preparation.

Personal Contacts Develop Cooperation

Promotion may be a ready partner with advertising in creating demands for items featured in the newspaper's advertising columns.

The promotion department should impress upon merchants the importance of cooperation from window dressers, display artists and sales clerks in giving emphasis within the store to the merchandise advertised. In some instances, the newspaper's promotion manager has been permitted to appear before the sales forces of leading advertisers to explain to them ways in which the store's advertising helps them to greater sales and how by close cooperation with the advertising they can help both themselves and their employers.

Many advertising efforts have failed because the store's sales force has not been informed on sales points of the products advertised. Failure to coordinate advertising and selling lessens the effectiveness of both advertising and within-the-store service — and usually the full blame is unjustly imposed on advertising. An alert and active promotion manager will see that proper cooperation exists within the store to enable advertising to bring maximum results.

Advance Preparation for Special Days

Whenever the Des Moines, Iowa, *Register* and *Tribune* (combined circulation 345,146, population 177,965) sponsors a special sales day or campaign for Des Moines merchants, its promotion department spends as much time in getting the sales forces of participating stores in the spirit of cooperation as it does in selling advertising space to store managers. Its promotion of White Elephant Day, an annual event at the Iowa capital, is a good example of how it instills enthusiasm into store owners, sales managers, window trimmers, display artists and clerks.

Far in advance of the sales day, it showers the merchants with broadsides, announcement cards, folders and letters explaining what the event will mean to them if they will join hands with the newspaper in a "smash promotion" (see Fig. 12.2). A 4-page tabloid, *The Jumbo News*, explains how crowds will throng the streets and stores, how full-margin sales will be made along with the disposal of "lowball" items, and how cash registers all over town will ring. Cooperation from merchants and their full sales forces is emphasized. A check list of all that should be done in preparation for the event includes the following:

1. *Extra selling help* for this one day. Office or service people provide a good source for extra help, and frequently no additional payroll is necessary.
2. *Survey inventory* to line up merchandise. Nooks and crannies on every floor and in the basement or warehouse should be thoroughly checked. It's surprising what merchandise will turn up in a search like this.
3. *Tell all personnel* about this event well in advance. There's no substitute for well-informed sales people, and it's a good idea to let everybody know what's going on.

4. *Be sure to tell* service departments (delivery, credit, etc.) about White Elephant Day, so they can better prepare for an additional load.

5. *Plan advertising* as far in advance as possible. Retailers have found that when they can show advance proofs for sale ads several days in advance, the sales people are better equipped to handle the extra crowds.

6. *Use specific quantities* in advertising of White Elephant Day specials. Such phrases as "Just 8 left" or "One to a customer, please" give authenticity to W.E.D. advertising.

7. *Strongly consider hourly specials.* It's wise to set aside certain items to go on sale "at 3 P.M. only" or "for lunchtime only." This helps to keep traffic steady all day long, and gives working people opportunity to shop too.

With promotion and within-the-store cooperation such as this, a store's advertising is bound to bring results.

All set for WHITE ELEPHANT DAY?

If you're ready now, you're going to have a rousing stem-winder of a sale on July 24.

If you're not, there's still plenty of time to prepare for this fabulous one-day event! Keep in mind, you'll do plenty of full-margin business, even though your White Elephant Day low-ball items will go first and fast.

Don't leave anything to chance. The better you plan, the more successful White Elephant Day will be in YOUR store. Get going NOW, and make W.E.D. work. If you need help, be sure to call your regular Register and Tribune representative. He's anxious to help make your W.E.D. sale a real smasheroo.

DES MOINES REGISTER AND TRIBUNE
Retail Advertising Department   **CHerry 3-2111**

COPY DEADLINE
is Friday, **July 19**, but get your copy in earlier, if possible. And please order your W.E.D. window banners and countercard toppers by **July 16**, so they can be produced in plenty of time. Also . . . don't forget to give your R and T man your list of hot specials for the FREE full-page promotion ad.

g. 12.2 — One of the many forms of promotion used by the Des Moines, Iowa, **Register** d **Tribune** to encourage merchants to make plans well in advance of a special sale day.

Help To Plan Advertising Budgets

A newspaper's promotion department may also assist merchants in planning their advertising budgets. Many merchants do not really know how much they should spend for advertising. They give no particular thought to the matter, but go along from month to month inserting an ad occasionally without any real aim in mind for obtaining maximum results.

Research studies made by Harvard and Northwestern universities reveal that various lines of business have found the following percentages of gross sales to be minimum satisfactory expenditures for advertising:

Department stores	2.3%
Grocery stores	1%
Meat markets	1%
Drug stores	1%
Hardware stores	1%
Men's wear stores	3.3%
Women's wear stores	3.1%
General merchandise	1.5%
Shoe stores	2.9%
Cleaning and dyeing	3.3%
Jewelry stores	3.1%
Electrical shops	2.7%
Specialty stores	3.8%
Furniture stores	5 to 6%
Florists	5%
Millinery shops	2.2%
Music stores	3.3%
Restaurants	3.1%
Tires	1.5%
Stationery, books	1.4%

Many manufacturers and wholesalers share advertising costs with merchants who handle their goods. They willingly pay for half of the advertising in the local paper and provide attractive copy to be run as "blocks" in the merchant's general advertising or as individual ads. To obtain this advertising, however, merchants must request it and when the ads have been run must furnish the manufacturers with tear sheets and receipted statements to show that the merchant has taken care of his part of the deal.

Because many other business matters demand his attention, a merchant may not give close attention to this part of his advertising program and consequently may not receive all the advertising assistance to which he is entitled. By keeping a close check on all manufacturers who share in advertising costs and by keeping merchants informed and by seeing that orders are sent in and checking copies supplied, a promotion department may add a nice sum to the newspaper's annual income from advertising and at the same time render a valuable service to advertisers.

Set Up Definite Schedules

Another way to expand advertising is to help merchants set up definite schedules to be followed throughout the year.

The Madison, Wis., *Capital Times* and *Wisconsin State Journal* (combined circulation 93,795, population 96,056), through their promotion and advertising departments and with the assistance of the Retail Division of the Bureau of Advertising, developed for a men's wear store in Madison an eight-step advertising planning procedure that became a model for many stores, both large and small, in that and other areas. These were the steps:

1. A study was made of the national buying pattern to see how it applied locally to this particular store. To aid in this, the newspapers prepared a chart of department store sales from month to month throughout the country as reported by the Federal Reserve Board. From the same source were also gleaned the percentages of business realized monthly in the men's clothing departments of the department stores in the Federal Reserve District where the store was located.
2. The sales of each month and the buying habits of the store's customers were considered, and, with this information at hand, specific objectives were outlined for each month by the store's executives.
3. The amount of advertising support necessary to reach the objectives was determined.
4. An advertising space budget was set up for each month.
5. On the basis of the previous year's sales and on possible sales opportunities as revealed in Federal Reserve data, a definite amount of advertising linage was allotted to each department.
6. After checking the previous sales of various items in each department, advertising space was allotted to each item according to its need for sales build-up.
7. The pricing of items sold in the store was given careful consideration. High quality promotions were alternated with advertisements stressing utility at lower prices.
8. Special consideration was given to customary weather conditions and local community events in determining the timing and frequency of specific advertisements.

The Green Bay, Wis., *Press-Gazette* (circulation 40,137, population 52,735) increased materially the volume of local advertising carried in its columns by helping merchants to plan their advertising on the basis of sales volume and sales possibilities. One salesman gave full time to developing planned campaigns. A copywriter with creative ideas developed attractive copy. The timing of each store's campaign was determined well in advance.

Prepare Effective Copy

It is in the preparation of effective copy that a promotion department may be of most value to a newspaper. Better art techniques, greater legibility and more attractive layouts are common goals today for newspaper advertising. Color, too, is finding its way rapidly into the advertising columns of daily and weekly papers, and local pictures are used in greater quantities. Publishers and merchants realize that the personality content of an advertisement is as important as the items it features.

A study made for the Chicago *Tribune* (circulation 868,455, population 3,620,962) by Social Research, Inc.,[1] brought forth these major facts concerning retail advertising:

1. In addition to the continuous task of selling goods immediately, every ad has the long-range job of helping create a store personality that will attract the most customers from the store's potential market.
2. A store's personality can be communicated through a general style of advertising, physical appearance of the ads, art, style, tone, whiteness or blackness of copy, and layout techniques.
3. Advertising should match the over-all character a store is striving to maintain. Since a store must keep up with its market, the store image must be changed as the people change.
4. Personality characteristics communicated to women by department store advertising include the store's appearance, size, location, reliability, policies, and attitude of salespeople.
5. The average woman shopper decides whether or not a particular store's character is suitable to her by the impression she gets from the store's advertising.
6. An advertisement may exclude part of the store's logical market by being too high styled or too low styled.

A well-organized promotion department becomes the motivating force for the newspaper's entire sales organization. It often is called upon to step in where advertising salesmen leave off. If a regular staff salesman cannot sell his client, he knows that the promotion manager may come up with a new angle and create for him a reasonable solution and a convincing presentation.

Develop New Accounts

The promotion department is helpful to the advertising department also in developing new accounts. Business firms not accustomed to advertising may be converted to regular advertisers or induced to widen the scope of their advertising if given some special study and attention.

---

[1] *Missouri Press News,* June, 1957.

Some utility companies do not fully understand the good will opportunities as well as the sales opportunities available for them in newspaper advertising. Often to great advantage they can supplement their advertisements of appliances with advertisements concerning various phases of their service to customers.

When California in 1954 had one of its coldest winters and some discomfort was experienced in homes equipped with under-sized furnaces, gas utilities used newspaper space to say that this was not due to low gas pressure but to inadequate equipment. The gas supply was normal but, b-r-r-r, the weather was just plain cold, the ads explained. This was accepted by gas patrons as a fair explanation.

An alert promotion department may quickly make a regular advertiser out of a firm moving into the community. A personal call from the newspaper, a news story concerning the firm's coming, its plans and policies, and some flowers on its opening day may establish immediately an important business relationship between the newspaper and the business. The newspaper may also develop a special section of announcement advertising, including a history of the firm, advertisements of its introductory offers, and some warm greeting ads from the Chamber of Commerce, service clubs, the city administration and leading firms of the community.

PROMOTING ADVERTISING TO GROUPS

A promotion department may be particularly helpful in promoting advertising to groups of merchants as well as to individuals. If men in the same line of business can be brought together at a luncheon and the promotion manager with representatives from the advertising department can appear before them with a well-developed plan of attractive advertising that will serve the interests of all, a united response to the ideas presented likely will follow. Merchants ordinarily enjoy pulling together on worthwhile projects. When it is in a movement from which each has a fair opportunity to benefit, the response is certain to be hearty.

Then, too, a sales effort before a group requires a more carefully organized and more effective presentation than for a single merchant. More is at stake. If the advertising proposal to a group is rejected, the newspaper loses more than if it were turned down by an individual. The promotion man called upon to face a group of businessmen realizes that more is expected of him than if he were trying to sell advertising to a single merchant in his place of business. Consequently, he puts in more time in preparing his presentation. Some research may be required. Charts, displays or exhibits may seem to be the most effective means of selling the idea. Some preliminary conferences with leaders of the group may be advisable. Nothing must be left undone to sell the advertising program to the group.

Research Is Sometimes Needed

Some research is often required to make a newspaper's presentation effective. When facts and figures relating to the experiences of merchants of the same class can be presented, the sales appeal is more persuasive and convincing.

The need for better merchandising and advertising in the retail building material field was clearly set forth in a presentation by the Chicago *Tribune* following a study of consumer attitudes regarding lumber yards. The findings in this survey pointed to an undersold market largely due to unimaginative lumber dealers. The study showed, among other things, that lumber yards needed to use a different type of advertising — a type that would create for the business a pleasing personality as well as a reputation for reliable merchandise and reasonable prices.

Most home improvement plans are initiated by women. Indeed, much buying at lumber yards today is by housewives. Consequently, the places that sell lumber should be made attractive and at the same time suggestive of what may be done to provide pleasing surroundings in the home. The same consideration for feminine taste should be given to the firm's advertising.

Clinic for Advertisers

The Sharon, Pa., *Herald* (circulation 23,217, population 26,454) went at this matter of group selling in a pleasing and effective way when it conducted a series of eight workshop clinics to show its retail advertisers how it handled their copy and sent their advertising on its way to build business for them. Those who participated were grouped according to their line of business.

Each workshop started with a luncheon and was followed by a tour of the newspaper plant. Merchants thus became acquainted with the mechanical processes through which a display ad passes from the time it is received from the advertiser to the time it is taken from the press and placed in the hands of carriers to be delivered to the homes of actual and prospective customers.

Following each tour, advertisers viewed the film, "How To Prepare Better Newspaper Ads," which was jointly sponsored by the National Retail Merchants Association and the Newspaper Advertising Executives Association and supervised by the School of Retailing of New York University. At the close of each workshop, copies of two booklets — "How To Prepare Better Newspaper Advertising" and "A Picture Visit to the Sharon *Herald*" — were distributed to the advertisers.

As a good-will builder for the newspaper and as an effective means of selling retail advertising, the eight clinics, attended by 125 merchants, were successful. Gratifying results were realized because the project was well planned and the sales story was well presented.

Promoting National Home Week

The Minneapolis *Star* and *Tribune* (combined circulation 502,252, population 521,718) drew a special group of Minneapolis merchants into a successful cooperative advertising and trade promotion campaign when it instituted a city-wide observance of National Home Week. However, instead of calling the merchants into a meeting to receive instruction and demonstration as the Sharon *Herald* had done, the *Star* and *Tribune* threw their talent for analysis and persuasion into direct-mail material and newspaper advertising.

In a large broadside, folded twice for convenient mailing, it announced on the outside fold in bold type: "Coming in September, one of the greatest sales promotion events of the year." Then the message continued: "The Minneapolis Sunday Tribune's National Home Week section will command the attention and interest of more than 615,000 Upper Midwest families who read the Sunday Tribune, providing you with an ideal opportunity to present your advertising message to the thousands of Upper Midwest families planning on home building or home improvement."

On the other side of the sheet appeared reproductions of layouts for four promotion ads to appear in both the *Star* and *Tribune*: a series of teaser ads to appear the week prior to National Home Week, a double-page ad to appear on Sunday in the National Home Week section, and two dominant follow-up ads to keep reader interest high throughout the campaign.

To give the promotion a more personal touch, a thin slab of mahogany wood went to prospects in another mailing with this inscription: "The most important plank in your advertising program — National Home Week, September 22–29."

Advertising salesmen, of course, followed up with calls on dealers in furniture, appliances, hardware and home decorations; also on architects, contractors, builders, plumbers and electricians, from whom were obtained orders for individual ads. National Home Week was well observed in Minneapolis, and the newspapers and merchants all profited.

National Trade Groups Assist

National trade organizations appreciate the efforts put forth by newspapers to interest members of their groups in advertising and give valuable assistance in producing attractive copy and in obtaining sales cooperation.

During the first four months of 1958, 69 daily newspapers and three weeklies, representing a combined circulation of 20,000,000 in

23 states, ran 77 special boat show supplements containing 742 pages of advertising and editorial matter regarding speed, pleasure and fishing boats. The National Association of Engine and Boat Manufacturers and newspapers worked hand in hand in this promotion project.

The Home Improvement Council, composed of manufacturers, contractors, dealers, utilities and others engaged in the repair-remodel-replace industry, received liberal newspaper cooperation in promoting its campaign to institute remodeling and repairs in 40 million American homes. The council provided mats for ads and news content and the newspapers contacted local merchants, explaining the movement and obtaining orders for space.

The Bureau of Advertising originates many campaigns that promote advertising by groups. Such campaigns not only increase sales but they bring about a closer relationship between dealers and newspapers.

The Bureau of Advertising in 1958 issued a salute to retail druggists — the nation's "men in white" — which was carried in more than 800 newspapers. This advertisement was a tribute to "the dedicated pharmacists across the land who stand ready to give you exactly what the nation's 225,000 doctors order." It explained also that the druggist, in addition, is a retailer of many diversified products and for that reason invests 73 per cent of his total advertising budget in newspapers.

Other promotions by the Bureau of Advertising to bring groups of merchants into closer relation with newspapers have been in behalf of grocers, service station operators and automobile agencies. These have all contributed prestige to the newspaper as a vital advertising medium.

"Car dealers and newspapers have much in common," says the bureau. "Both are upstanding local citizens vitally interested in local affairs. Back of almost every civic affair you'll find the local car dealer supporting it with all his weight, and right beside him, backing civic endeavors with equally ardent support, is the newspaper. Car dealers, like others, have learned that the newspaper puts plenty of weight behind an advertiser's sales message, too. That's why newspapers each year carry the biggest share of automobile advertising."

Other Plans for Group Advertising

A promotion department has a multitude of opportunities throughout the year to use special days and events to advertise the newspaper's services available for groups as well as individual merchants (see Fig. 12.3).

The New Brunswick, N. J., *Home News* (circulation 39,554, population 38,811) issued 37 special sections and pages in one year. The most fruitful was a "January Financial Review," featuring industrial developments, municipal improvements and banking expansions of the area. Special pages, sponsored mostly by space buyers who normally would not have used the newspaper, provide from 10 to 15 per cent of the newspaper's annual income from advertising. Such promotions as "National Baby Week," "Fire Prevention Day," "Father's Day," "Spring Opening" and "Do It Yourself Day" produce annually a gratifying amount of additional revenue.

Fig. 12.3 — Many newspapers use this type of promotion to tie their advertising service in with special days or events.

There is never a likelihood of running out of "special days," but if that should happen, a new one could readily be created. The Charleston, W. Va., *Gazette* (circulation 70,592, population 73,501) exhibited its resourcefulness when it promoted a "Dog's Day Sale" to combat the customary summer slump in business. The promotion was built around a sad-eyed basset hound christened George, and the slogan for the days was "Let George Do It." Arrangements were made for a dinner meeting at which merchants might discuss plans. Invitations to this meeting were delivered to 100 merchants by a smiling model leading sad-eyed George by a leash. On the day of the sale crowds gathered hours before the stores opened and sharp buying continued throughout the day.

Newspapers often may induce stores located in certain areas to take space in full or double page advertisements to promote special sales days at their shopping center. Suburban stores in some areas have followed this plan so extensively and successfully that downtown stores have instituted sales days to combat the efforts of their outlying competitors. Here again is where a newspaper's promotion department may develop additional advertising through group-selling.

Organizations Find Group Advertising Pays

One of the best examples of results accruing from promotion of a newspaper's advertising service to a group of businessmen is the great change that has taken place in the attitude of bankers toward newspaper advertising within the past few years. It required some hard selling and continuous promotion to make the community newspaper the home town bank's favorite advertising medium, but that has been brought about in most communities where newspapers are published. Each year since 1950 banks have been spending more advertising dollars in newspapers. Banks today use much printer's ink to sell savings and thrift, trust services, loans for all kinds of business development, and the advantages of dealing with a bank for specific and complete financial assistance.

The Educational Foundation of the Pennsylvania Bankers Association has issued for bankers a helpful pamphlet entitled, "Effective Newspaper Advertising for Banks." It records results from readership surveys, discusses the value of newspaper advertising and reproduces attractive and result-getting ads. This has been reprinted by the Pennsylvania Newspaper Publishers Association for distribution to interested newspapers.

Political candidates represent another group that may easily be induced to use advertising. The Flat River, Mo., *Lead Belt News* (circulation 3,978, population 5,308) at the beginning of each political campaign announces in a 3-column display ad its publicity fees for political announcements (see Fig. 12.4).

City governments, like bankers, have awakened to the advantages of advertising their special services. Instead of presenting their annual financial statements in small type and occupying a few columns of space, many cities have arranged with their home town newspapers to issue supplements of several pages, containing stories and pictures to show taxpayers how their money has been spent for civic improvements and the convenience and comfort of citizens.

A committee of Colorado publishers, headed by Clyde Moffit of the Fort Collins *Coloradoan* (circulation 7,669, population 14,937) appeared before members of the Colorado Municipal League in Denver and showed city officials how they could achieve greater public confidence by using more newspaper space to tell their stories of public service. The publishers exhibited a number of special sections which various newspapers had issued for their city administrations.

PUBLISHING FEES
for
Political Announcements

Congress	$35.00
State Senator	25.00
State Representative	15.00
Prosecuting Attorney	20.00
Magistrate Judge	20.00
Probate Judge	20.00
Judges of The County Court	15.00
Presiding Judge County Court	20.00
Circuit Cleck	20.00
County Clerk	20.00
Collector of Revenue	25.00
County Surveyor	15.00
Recorder of Deeds	20.00
County Treasurer	20.00
Circuit Judge	25.00
Member County Committee	5.00

An order for an announcement to be published weekly carries with it a news item calling attention to same. All statements the candidates desire must be in two weeks before the Primary Election and signed by them. All cuts must be furnished by the candidate. Those receiving the various nominations will be entitled to their own write up, signed, two weeks prior to the general election.

All fees are payable in advance

CARDS — PLACARDS — MATCHES

The Lead Belt News

Phone GE 1-2233   Flat River

Fig. 12.4 — A weekly newspaper promotes political advertising by publishing well in advance its scale of prices for political announcements.

They explained that a complete and attractive report would gain the attention of readers and in addition would serve as a deterrent to false talk about buck-passing at the city hall. They pointed out also that extra copies of the supplement could be printed at little additional expense and be made available to civics classes at high schools, thereby acquainting youth with their city government. The presentation by the publishers was listened to with obvious interest and some cities immediately accepted the suggestion.

PROMOTE ADVERTISING TO COMMUNITY

Some peppery shotgun firing of promotion needs to be aimed at the entire community as well as some very pointed rifle shots at advertising salesmen, merchants and trade groups if the newspaper is to be firmly established as the ideal advertising medium.

Newspapers should never cease to impress upon all the people of their trade areas the valuable advertising service made available by their experienced copywriters and advertising salesmen. Retail advertising may be effectively promoted communitywide through:

1. The newspaper's own columns.
2. Radio and television.
3. Lectures and demonstrations.

Should Use Its Own Columns

Full-page, half-page and quarter-page ads, prepared with a purpose beyond that of being simply space-fillers, should be used to tell the full story of the newspaper's ability to reach buyers of the area and convince them of the merits of trading at home stores (see Fig. 12.5).

"They're buying tonight from Hartford stores," said the Hartford, Conn., *Times* (circulation 120,161, population 177,397) in a full-page promotion advertisement showing a couple at home reading the ads in the newspaper. "Yes, they're sitting at home making buying decisions from the pages of their home newspaper. That's why advertisers last year bought 24,404,549 lines of advertising in the Hartford *Times*. They chose the most effective, resultful way to reach the thousands of high-income-level families in this rich market area." And the ad also said that 80.9 per cent of the 139,879 families in Hartford and 29 surrounding towns read the *Times* daily. Here was an advertisement read with equal interest by readers and advertisers.

The merchants of Little Rock as well as the *Arkansas Gazette* (circulation 84,011, population 102,213) were given effective promotion in a full-page ad entitled "Little Rock Business Has Always Been Bigger Than Little Rock — or Pulaski County — or Little Rock city and trade area."

"Arkansans come to Little Rock to buy, sell and shop for the many advantages only a metropolitan trade and cultural center provide,"

"It's been proved at Director's that advertising is essential for business success"

FINE FURNITURE, appliances and floor coverings have been a tradition at Director's Furniture Company for over 46 years. Recently established in its new location at Yamhill and SW Third, this store enjoys the patronage of thousands of families in Portland and the surrounding area. It has always sought to make the best available buys in the market . . . and then pass those savings along to its customers. Director's stocks merchandise made by the best known manufacturers in America . . . and sells at appealing prices. Naturally Director's attributes much of its success to long use of advertising in this market area.

Mr. Frank Director has been president of Director's Furniture Company since 1932 and associated with that company for well over four decades. Mr. Director attended Portland schools in his youth, and gained his first business experience delivering Oregon Journals to downtown customers in this city during the first World War. Associated with Mr. Director in the operation of Director's Furniture Company are Sol Director and Samuel Soble.

Director's has consistently used the Oregon Journal as the advertising medium to tell their story to Portlanders. Frank Director says:

"It has been proved to us that Journal readers are buying readers . . . and advertising in The Journal is necessary for our continued progress."

Fig. 12.5 — The Portland **Oregon Journal** uses testimonial promotion to stress the advantages of newspaper advertising.

You reach people by using the newspaper that reaches their hearts . . .

the Oregon Journal

HOME-OWNED AND
PUBLISHED IN THE INTERESTS
OF THE PACIFIC NORTHWEST
AND ITS PEOPLE

the ad proclaimed. "To keep up with Arkansas and Little Rock interests, they depend on the *Arkansas Gazette*. Arkansans have been doing this for 137 years."

Shown also were charts reflecting the audited circulation leadership of the *Gazette*.

The Pittsburgh, Pa., *Post-Gazette* (circulation 274,765, population

Fig. 12.6 — Promoting the convenience provided by newspaper advertising in planning well-organized and economical shopping.

676,806) often carries full-page promotion, showing how shoppers watch for ads from merchants in various lines of business.

Other facts to impress upon the public are: The variety of advertising offered by a newspaper, the care and attention given by the publisher to truth and honesty in the newspaper's advertising sections, the convenience in buying what is offered in the newspaper (see Fig. 12.6) and results obtained by leading merchants through newspaper advertising.

Make Effective Use of Radio and Television

In communities where television advertising is available, newspapers should use this means of winning favor with the general public. Tributes may be paid to the Retail Merchants Association and its efforts toward community improvement. Although not directly featuring the newspaper's worth as an advertising medium, such promotion builds an abundance of good will and in the long run yields direct returns.

Some filming of activities within the newspaper's advertising department would provide another effective television presentation.

Radio, too, is a practical means of reaching the public with important facts concerning the newspaper's advertising service. Attention may be directed to outstanding announcements by merchants. Results from advertisements in the newspaper may be related. Special sales events in which many merchants cooperate may be emphasized.

A well-organized and well-trained promotion department can work out promotion programs on television and radio that will go far in building advertising volume for the newspaper.

Reach Public Through Demonstrations

The power of newspaper advertising may be presented with telling force before service clubs, women's organizations and youth groups. Representatives of the promotion and advertising departments should make themselves available at all times for public appearances. Clubs are always glad to have local speakers appear before them to explain services available to the community.

A speakers' bureau within the promotion department can render a vital public service and be a great help in promoting retail advertising. Talks before groups should stress the time saved and the money saved by keeping close tab on ads in the local newspaper. Special demonstrations also may be arranged by the promotion department to reveal to the community the benefits accruing to it from the home town newspaper and advertising merchants.

CHAPTER 13

100 Tested Ways
To Increase
Advertising Linage

ANY PUBLISHER, advertising manager or promotion manager may increase advertising linage in his newspaper tremendously by being alert to new ideas and methods. Merchants who are not regular users of newspaper advertising often are induced to buy space when good copy based on current events or original ideas and tied in with their lines of business is prepared by the promotion department and presented to them by the advertising department. Regular advertisers may be persuaded by the same means to increase their customary volume. The following ideas and plans have been employed successfully by wide-awake dailies and weeklies:

CO-OPERATIVE PAGES AND SECTIONS

1. **Business Picture Page** — The Lynn, Mass., *Item* (circulation 22,129, population 99,738) ran once a month for three years a picture page headed "Latest Pictures of Greater Lynn Business Firms." Each page contained pictures and ads from nine business firms.

2. **High Fidelity Section** — The Chicago *Tribune* (circulation 868,455, population 3,620,962) published a 16-page section containing 33,000 lines of advertising by 27 firms. The editorial content included a history of the phonograph, features of hi-fi recording and a discussion of installations and packaged sets.

3. **Plumbers Co-operate** — The Marshall, Tex., *News Messenger* (circulation 11,582, population 22,327) carried for members of the Plumbing and Heating Contractors Association a large ad which tied up with the city plumbing and gas code.

4. **Shopping Center Section** — The Delwood Shopping Center ran in the Austin, Tex., *American-Statesman* (circulation 53,411,

[154]

population 132,459) a special 8-page section devoted to the center's anniversary party, at which special values and prizes were offered.

5. Do-It-Yourself Co-op — Twenty-four independently owned hardware stores of Louisville sponsored a double page ad on "do-it-yourself" items in the Louisville, Ky., *Courier-Journal* (circulation 216,645, population 369,129) .

6. Appeal to High School Grads — The Des Moines, Iowa, *Register* and *Tribune* (combined circulation 345,146, population 177,965) ran a full page of ads from colleges, hospitals, chiropractic schools, colleges of osteopathy and others addressed to high school graduates and soliciting their enrollment.

7. Heating and Ventilating Section — When the American Society of Heating and Ventilating Engineers met in Houston, the Houston, Tex., *Chronicle* (circulation 192,062, population 596,163) tied in with 8 pages of advertising on air conditioning, different kinds of refrigerators, water heaters and the like.

8. Avenue Merchants — The St. Louis *Post-Dispatch* (circulation 380,495, population 856,796) featured bargains of Franklin Avenue merchants in a full page containing ads from 19 stores. By going together, the stores were able to make a greater splurge than if they had advertised individually.

9. Directory of TV Dealers — The San Angelo, Tex., *Standard-Times* (circulation 32,848, population 52,093) published a directory of television dealers. Thirty-five dealers were listed. Names of sets were in black type.

10. To Offset "Bootlegging" — When "bootlegging" of new cars by independent dealers became a great problem, authorized new-car dealers individually and co-operatively used space in the Dallas, Tex., *News* (circulation 207,156, population 434,462) to advertise the merits of buying through franchised dealers.

11. Livestock Show Edition — The Pauls Valley, Okla., *Democrat* (circulation 3,978, population 6,896) encouraged farm youth and obtained a nice volume of additional advertising by issuing a special edition featuring a Junior Livestock Show.

12. Promotes Bank Credit — The Buffalo, N.Y., *News* (circulation 287,446, population 580,132) published a 16-page tabloid advertising supplement for a bank in connection with the launching of a shopper credit service. Listed in it were 2,000 stores affiliated with the credit service.

13. Weekly Auto Page — The Orange, Tex., *Leader* (circulation 7,332, population 21,174) carried in its Monday issues, for a period of time, an automotive page to feature cars sold by local dealers.

14. Treasure Hunt — Three hundred dollars' worth of merchandise was given away in a Treasure Hunt conducted by Newberg, Ore., merchants in cooperation with the Newberg *Graphic* (circulation

2,785, population 3,946). The newspaper listed in a half-page announcement the merchants who were taking part and also carried individual advertisements by participating merchants.

15. Safety Appeal — By publishing an article entitled "Don't Drive a Death Trip," reprinted from *Look* magazine, the Westport, Conn., *Town Crier and Herald* (circulation 6,448, population 11,667) was able to sell two pages of tie-up ads to garages and service stations prepared to check cars for safety.

16. Financed at Home — The Waxahachie, Tex., *Light* (circulation 5,318, population 11,204) carried a series of full-page ads for local banks featuring financing and insurance for car buyers. It contained pictures of all cars sold in Waxahachie with the announcement that "these cars can be seen, bought, financed and insured right in the old home town."

17. Co-op for Service Stations — Service stations located on a main highway carried an attractive cooperative ad in the Three Rivers, Tex., *News* (circulation 620, population 2,026). The headline, "In Three Rivers, a City Growing Bigger and Better, We Line Both Sides of Highway 281."

18. Little Money Goes Long Way — The Hollis, Okla., *News* (circulation 1,700, population 3,089) carried a page of small ads for local merchants who wished to feature money-saving items. The headline was "Our Little Ads Make a Little Money Go a Long Way."

19. Hot News About Cooling Appliances — Omaha merchants cooperated with the Omaha, Nebr., *World-Herald* (circulation 125,805, population 251,117) to give readers an interesting and appealing 12-page section featuring air conditioners, refrigerators and freezers.

20. Checked Values — All items advertised by merchants for sale during a "Bargain Day" were checked by the Drumright, Okla., *Derrick* (circulation 2,073, population 5,028) and granted a "seal of approval." Invoices were checked to verify the original cost of all articles, and the paper was able to report that nearly every article was offered for sale at or below wholesale cost.

21. Say It With Flowers — The Pasadena, Calif., *Star-News* (circulation 38,521, population 104,577) had no difficulty in interesting florists, nurserymen and seed stores in a section devoted entirely to California flowers. This ran to 44 pages.

22. Report on Human Side — A special report on the "human side" of the Great Northern Paper Co. was published as a separate supplement in the Bangor, Me., *Daily News* (circulation 72,625, population 31,558). The 16-page offset report was printed on "Jet," a bright groundwood paper developed by Great Northern.

23. "Stinker Day" — This special day, observed each year by the merchants of Albion, Nebr., is a "stinker day" for the publisher of the Albion *News* (circulation 2,872, population 2,132). On this day merchants set up sidewalk stands, in front of their stores, to sell at low prices merchandise they couldn't sell at regular prices during the year. These values were well advertised.

24. For Specialty Men — "Patronize the Specialty Man" was the headline for a 52-times-a-year ad which ran in the Waco, Tex., *Citizen* (circulation 7,450, population 84,706). The reliability of these specialists was vouched for by the newspaper.

25. Quiz Page — A full page headed "Know These Numbers?" was published in the Snoqualmie, Wash., *Snoqualmie Valley Record* (circulation 1,800, population 806). The ad listed the telephone numbers of 22 prominent business firms, and readers were asked to identify them.

26. Church Advertising — In the Independence, Mo., *Examiner* (circulation 10,713, population 36,963), churches advertise their Sunday programs in paid space the same as movie theaters. Before substituting paid advertising for free notices, the publisher presented the idea to the Ministerial Alliance and received endorsement.

27. Outboard Marathon Section — The Milwaukee, Wis., *Sentinel* (circulation 184,302, population 637,392) issued a 12-page tabloid section in connection with the annual marathon outboard racing classic it sponsors.

28. Let's Have a Picnic — The Milwaukee, Wis., *Sentinel* ran, on July 1, a page in four colors advertising bread, sausage and soft drinks as ideal for picnics.

29. Gourmet Guide — The San Francisco, Calif., *Chronicle* (circulation 225,429, population 775,357) annually issues a detailed directory of all restaurants in San Francisco environs. One year this section ran 52 pages.

UNIQUE APPEALS

30. White Elephant Show — The El Paso, Tex., *Times* (circulation 58,066, population 130,485) carried a striking full-page ad announcing a "White Elephant Show" for a leading department store. Preceding the listing of a host of attractive items was this appeal: "Everywhere we look little elephants . . big white elephants . . even some shady irony-colored big and little elephants . . We're told that even in the far off corners of darkest Africa are no bigger herds of elephants than we have assembled here . . the reason, you see, is that we have over 54 years' experience in trapping only that rare and long-lasting breed which our buyers can spot so easily . . and they're here and ready for you to lead by the tail from our doors . . so bring your peanuts . . that's all it takes . . and take them, please." The Chicago *News* (circulation 547,796, population 3,620,962) developed this idea after World War II. Many papers have used it.

31. "Hire a Professional" — To combat the "do-it-yourself" trend, painters and decorators ran a campaign in the Fort Lauderdale, Fla., *News* (circulation 53,491, population 36,328) aimed at not "overdoing it yourself." Copy was based on sane and sensible appeal with the criterion, "If you can stand on the floor, go ahead . . but if you have to climb or use ladders, hire a professional."

32. Lucky Thirteenth — The Fort Lauderdale, Fla., *News* used a double page to feature Friday the 13th items at thirteen stores. Each store advertised items at 13¢, $1.13, $13.13 or some derivative.

33. Siamese Auction of Furniture — The Galveston, Tex., *News* (circulation 17,627, population 66,568) carried a Siamese Auction for a furniture store. Values up to $318 were started at $99.50 each, and a $3 reduction per day followed, ending at $30.50 if not taken before it reached that level.

34. Daily Ads for Memorial Park — The Seaside Memorial Park ran a series of ads in the Corpus Christi, Tex., *Caller-Times* (circulation 71,477, population 108,287) for several months. The ads featured the various advantages of Memorial Park services.

35. Hooked — The Toledo, Ohio, *Blade* (circulation 183,143, population 303,616) taped a large fish-hook on a promotion piece with this headline, "Here's what you need to pull them in." The gist of the copy was that merchants could pull in people to their exhibit at the *Blade*'s Annual Home and Travel Show by advertising on special Home and Travel Show pages of the *Blade*.

36. Local Girl in Flour Promotion — Ten independent grocers promoted the sale of a certain brand of flour in a unique page advertisement in the Portsmouth, Ohio, *Times* (circulation 25,238, population 36,798). Featured in the ad was a local high school girl who had been the winner in a state-wide cherry pie baking contest.

37. Considerable Reductions — A merchant who was discontinuing business and was selling his stock at "considerable reductions," emphasized the "considerable reduction" idea by making his full-page ad in the Beaver-Rochester, Pa., *Beaver Valley Times* (circulation 23,815, population 13,557) all white space except for some copy 2 columns by 5 inches in the very center of the page.

38. "Piggy-Back Sale" — In an advertisement in the Highland Park, Ill., *News* (circulation 6,600, population 16,808), a gift store advertised its stock at 20 per cent off, cash and carry. "Nothing will be delivered anywhere," the copy read. "If you can't carry it out piggyback, you can't buy it."

39. Alphabet Ads — When a bottled-gas company wished to run a series of ads in the Marshall, Minn., *Messenger* (circulation 5,089, population 5,923), emphasizing its better service, the publisher developed a 50-inch alphabet ad — "A is for Appliances," "B is for Best," etc.

40. Recipe Ads — A local dairy presented recipes from readers in a series of advertisements in the Markdale, Ontario, *Standard* (circulation 1,357, population 986). Each recipe, of course, featured the dairy's products. A prize of $5 was given each week for the best recipe submitted.

41. Old-Fashioned Days — Pictures of the early days in Alpena, Mich., were run in conjunction with ads in the Alpena *News* (circulation 8,638, population 13,135), stressing Old-Fashioned Days bargains. The promotion produced 4,184 column inches of advertising over a period of three days.

42. Contest Promotion — To advertise its photographic supplies, a Clintonville, Wis., druggist offered a free camera to the person turning in the best snapshot each week. The winning picture then was run in an advertisement in the Clintonville *Tribune Gazette* (circulation 2,883, population 4,657).

43. House Organ — A small industry in Burgettstown, Pa., used a page each month in the Burgettstown *Enterprise* (circulation 2,620, population 2,379) as a house organ for its employees. The newspaper charged the full-page rate and also was paid for making cuts.

44. Employees Wrote Copy — A Pontiac dealer in Butler, Pa., decided to do something to cut down accidents. So he invited each of his employees to write a 200-word essay on the subject, offering prizes for the best, which he ran at space rates in the Butler *Eagle* (circulation 22,236, population 23,482).

45. Cordial Column — Humorous quips, interspersed with such bold sales pitches as "New shipment of ladies' fall dresses at $5.95," were included in a feature called "Cliff's Cordial Column" in the Hardin, Mont., *Tribune-Herald* (circulation 2,208, population 2,306).

46. News-Ad Pictures — Newsy pictures of merchants selling their wares were used in an interesting advertising feature in the Canby, Ore., *Herald* (circulation 2,050, population 1,671). Merchants featured paid for pictures and space.

47. Church Promotion — A bank in Buffalo, Okla., ran in the *Harper County Journal* (circulation 1,716, population 1,544) a series of eight ads containing pictures and historical sketches of Buffalo churches.

48. Mystery Man — A Mystery Man identification contest proved surprisingly popular in the Skowhegan, Me., *Somerset Reporter* (circulation 2,748, population 7,422). Nineteen merchants participated in a full-page ad which ran for 19 consecutive weeks. The owner or an employee of one of the stores, pictured in mask, appeared each week on the page. Caption of the page was: "Who is the Mystery Skowheganite?"

49. Face in the Crowd — Shoppers on the town's streets and in the stores were pictured in a series of full-page "Trade at Home" ads in the Russellville, Ala., *Franklin County Times* (circulation 3,651, population 6,012). In each of the pictures of shoppers crowding the stores and streets a face was circled, and the shopper who found his or her face so designated could claim $5 by going to the newspaper office.

50. Gets Husband's Attention — The wife of a local attorney ran an ad in the Salem, Ill., *Times-Commoner* (circulation 4,250, population 6,159) to call her husband's attention to things which needed to be done around the home. She knew she could reach him in this way because he always read the newspaper thoroughly.

51. "Doing the Town" — A lively column called "Doing the Town" was written each week for the Marysville, Wash., *Globe* (circulation 1,260, population 2,259) by its advertising manager. The column featured people the ad man met while on his rounds. It called attention also to many stores and products.

52. Appreciated Reminders — "Just to Remind You" was the title of a bank ad run weekly in the Batesville, Ark., *Guard* (circulation 3,356, population 6,414). In the ad were such reminders as license purchasing deadlines, tax payment deadlines and dates of local events of general interest.

53. Cheaper Than Post Cards — Stressing the fact that it costs ten times as much to reach people by post cards as it does to use a post-card-sized advertisement in a weekly newspaper, the King City, Mo., *Tri-County News* (circulation 1,859, population 1,031) devoted an 8-page section to an analysis of its readership made by the University of Missouri School of Journalism and the Missouri Press Association.

54. Different Approach for Dollar Days — Dollar bills were mailed to every major retail store in the area by the Bell, Calif., *Bell-Maywood Industrial Post* (circulation 8,600, population 15,430) on the occasion of that community's annual Dollar Days. Merchants were urged to use the accompanying dollar to advertise in the paper. The promotion produced one-third again more advertising than the newspaper carried for previous Dollar Days.

55. Identification Contest — Identification contests in advertisements have proved popular in the Chester, S. C., *News* (circulation 3,569, population 6,893). A dry cleaner gave cash prizes and free dry cleaning to those who identified portions of photographs of local citizens. Each week other portions of the photos were added to make it increasingly easy.

56. "Come and Get It" — A column called "Come and Get It" is highly popular in the West Springfield, Mass., *Record* (circulation 3,143, population 20,438). Run separately from regular classified advertising, the column lists items which people wish to give away.

57. Best Ad Contest — A good plan for getting ads read was worked out by the Oakland, Nebr., *Independent and Republican* (circulation 1,695, population 1,456). Calling the idea a "Newspaper Jury Contest," readers were asked to pick the best ad in the paper and tell their reasons for selecting it. Prizes were offered for the best answers.

58. Post Card Solicitation — An increase in classified advertising volume has resulted from a double-post-card method of solicitation used by the Gatlinburg, Tenn., *Press* (circulation 2,119, population 1,301). Ads suited to the Gatlinburg trade are clipped from other publications, pasted on one part of the double post card, along with a notation as to insertion cost for the same ad in the *Press*, and mailed to the prospective advertiser.

TYING IN WITH SPECIAL EVENTS

59. Used Car Show — The Indianapolis, Ind., *Star* (circulation 208,562, population 472,173) and the Indianapolis motor car dealers sponsored a Used Car Show which drew 73,000 visitors, brought in a good amount of advertising from dealers and resulted in greater good will for the newspaper.

60. V.F.W. Story — The Abilene, Tex., *Reporter-News* (circulation 31,761, population 45,570), in a full-page advertisement, presented the local V.F.W. organization as one of the largest groups of foreign war veterans in the country.

61. Help for Income Tax Payers — The First National Bank of Minneapolis carried in the Minneapolis *Star* and *Tribune* (combined circulation 502,252, population 521,718) an attractive advertisement in March explaining how the bank would lend money for income tax payments on low-cost payment plan.

62. New Thanksgiving Angle — The Ludington, Mich., *News* (circulation 5,853, population 9,506) sold a cooperative page to run on the Monday before Thanksgiving. A streamer headline announced "We all have many things to be thankful for," and 21 advertisers used space to list some of the items that should have made the paper's readers more joyful.

63. New Type Christmas Ad — A pictorial story was told in a full-page cooperative ad in the Le Mars, Iowa, *Sentinel* (circulation 6,065, population 5,844). A local couple, Bob and Betty, were featured looking over gift suggestions with 14 store owners or managers. Each picture had cutlines with selling copy.

64. St. Pat's Day Promotion — The Beaumont, Tex., *Enterprise* (circulation 64,993, population 94,014) sold double-column ads with St. Pat's Day specials to go on a full page printed in green.

65. Legion Drive Promotion — The Big Spring, Tex., *Herald* (circulation 9,529, population 17,286) sold a page to local citizens to promote American Legion membership drive. The ad had 25 sponsors.

66. Coloring Contest — An "Around the World" coloring contest was run as an Easter feature by the Coquille, Ore., *Coquille Valley*

Sentinel (circulation 2,310, population 3,523). This was open to children from 14 different countries represented in the community. Each picture was sponsored by a local merchant and three prizes were given.

67. Wedding Section — A special "Wedding Section" to help newlyweds plan their homes brought into the columns of the Clinton, N. Y., *Courier* (circulation 3,350, population 1,630) a nice volume of additional advertising.

68. Furniture Style Week — The San Jose, Calif., *Mercury-News* (circulation 100,830, population 95,280) issued a 12-page section featuring new furniture styles and announcing an open house for local furniture stores held on one evening from 7 to 10 o'clock.

69. Baseball Souvenir Edition — The Cincinnati, Ohio, *Post and Times-Star* (circulation 265,831, population 503,998) issued a 52-page section commemorating the 75th anniversary of the National League. The edition carried 38,031 lines of paid advertising, of which 20,336 were retail and 17,695 general.

70. Blueprint for White Christmas — The Pittsburgh, Pa., *Post-Gazette* (circulation 274,765, population 676,806) produced a special White Christmas Section to tie in with the United States Steel Corporation's "Operation Snowflake." The section contained over 50,000 lines of advertising.

71. Rotary Anniversary Section — The Drumright, Okla., *Journal* (circulation 2,093, population 5,028) issued a special section observing the Rotary club's 48th anniversary. Businessmen belonging to the club carried ads in the section.

72. Planning Calendar — The Chicago, Ill., *American* (circulation 467,557, population 3,620,962) gave to each of its principal advertisers a Retail Sales Planning Calendar showing all the special days and weeks of each month.

73. Christmas in May — Every retailer knows that Mother's Day shopping volume is second only to Christmas, so the Des Moines, Iowa, *Register* and *Tribune* featured it as "Christmas in May" with a volume of advertising that created extensive buying.

74. Happy New Year — A double-page advertisement wishing a Happy New Year to Jewish friends and patrons was run during the week of the Jewish New Year in the Somerville, N. J., *Somerset Messenger-Gazette* (circulation 10,363, population 11,571). The page consisted of boxes 2 columns by $2\frac{1}{4}$ inches in which local merchants and service establishments extended their greetings.

75. Washington's Birthday Sale — A single day of honest values is featured by the Des Moines, Iowa, *Register* and *Tribune* and the Retail Merchants Bureau of the Chamber of Commerce. This usually has proved to be the greatest one-day retail promotion of the year.

PROMOTING COMMUNITY PROGRESS

76. C. of C. Progress Report — The Denton, Tex., *Record-Chronicle* (circulation 9,040, population 21,372) published a 12-page section devoted to accomplishments of the year by the Chamber of Commerce. The C. of C. took a half page on the front cover, and several other large congratulatory ads were inside next to interesting news copy.

77. City's Annual Report — The Des Moines, Iowa, *Register* and *Tribune* carried the city's annual report in an 8-page tabloid section. It was in news-style format with many good pictures, and the cost for this was no greater than for the printing and distribution of the report in booklet form.

78. "City In Action" Section — The Sherman, Tex., *Democrat* (circulation 13,921, population 20,150) published a 32-page tabloid section featuring the development of the local community. About two-thirds of the ads in the section were from industries and utilities which seldom advertised.

79. Shop at Home — "What Draws the Crowd to Steinbach?" was the headline for an advertising feature in the Steinbach, Manitoba, *Carillon News* (circulation 4,719, population 2,688). Copy gave reasons for shopping locally. The feature carried a border of sponsors' names, listing most of the merchants in the town.

80. Plan and Plant Section — The Dallas, Tex., *News* ran a tabloid section of 20 pages urging readers to "Plan and Plant a Tree." This was in connection with a campaign to beautify the city. Advertisers gave liberal cooperation.

81. "Good Town" — To increase local linage, the Marshall, Minn., *Messenger* stressed different lines of business in a series of double-page ads on the theme "This Is a Good Town To Shop in." For example, every shoe store in town was represented in one ad under the heading, "Marshall Is a Good Shoe Town."

82. Outdoor Living Issue — The Des Moines, Iowa, *Register* and *Tribune* put out an Outdoor Living Issue to promote the recreation and scenic resorts of Iowa and Minnesota. Featured in it were the Iowa Sports and Vacation Show, the Baseball Season Opener, the Drake Relays, and Cleanup, Paint and Fix It Week.

83. Back to School Issue — The Des Moines, Iowa, *Register* and *Tribune* features school news and advertising in an annual Back to School Section of its Sunday paper.

84. School Dedication Edition — When the Painesville, Ohio, *Telegraph* (circulation 18,672, population 14,432) issued a School Dedication Edition, 105 advertisers participated. Seventy-five out-of-town firms, who provided material or did work on the school building, were solicited by mail.

85. Save the Soil Edition — The Omaha, Nebr., *World-Herald* issued a special section to point up its $1,000 worth of awards in a soil-saving campaign. It contained an abundance of farm equipment advertising and a great story on the protection of American resources.

86. Community Promotion — Signature ads, such as community promotion ads, are sold on an annual basis, rather than singly, by the Worthington, Minn., *Globe* (circulation 9,653, population 7,923). The confidence of the merchants is such that the newspaper is permitted to decide the theme of each ad and to prepare the copy.

87. Vacation Section — The Port Huron, Mich., *Times Herald* (circulation 31,203, population 35,725) issued in June a "Blue Water Edition," in which 24 cities advertised their resort attractions.

88. Market Information — The Winston-Salem, N. C., *Journal-Sentinel* (circulation 74,833, population 87,811) issues, at intervals, a series of data releases on the Winston-Salem Market under the heading, "Know Your Market."

SALUTES TO GROUPS AND INDIVIDUALS

89. One-a-Day Club — Every advertising salesman for the Washington, D.C., *Post* and *Times Herald* (circulation 390,104, population 802,178) who sold a contract for retail advertising every day of the year became a member of the "One-a-Day Club." Each member was awarded a wrist watch in recognition of his achievement.

90. Salute to Waitresses — The Lubbock, Tex., *Avalanche-Journal* (circulation 55,002, population 71,747) used a cartoon about waitresses to sell to a creamery a large ad saluting the waitresses of Lubbock and the South Plains.

91. Family Album — A weekly feature about successful businessmen, with pictures of them when they first came to town, as well as up-to-date pictures, proved popular in the Klamath Falls, Ore., *Herald and News* (circulation 14,091, population 15,875). The feature was called "Family Album." In addition to having reader interest, it built good will with the newspaper's advertisers.

92. Record of Anniversaries — The Woodburn, Ore., *Independent* (circulation 1,602, population 2,395) keeps a card file of the anniversaries of business firms, which forms the basis for some real space selling.

93. Pats on the Back — An automobile dealer used space in the Littlefield, Tex., *County Wide News* (circulation 3,891, population 6,540) to give a weekly "pat on the back" to a local club, group or individual for outstanding civic work.

94. Women's Supplement — A special supplement called "A Tribute to Women" was published by the Mission City, British Columbia, *Fraser Valley Record* (circulation 2,166, population 3,010). It gave the background of women's organizations and outlined their activities. Advertisers featured merchandise of special appeal to women.

95. Welcome to Newcomers — A "Welcome Newcomers" page, listing 20 families which had recently moved to town, was run in the Independence, Mo., *Examiner*. The page, sponsored by 33 merchants, contained an aerial photo of the business district, descriptions of the town's facilities and organizations, and a brief historical sketch. Important coming events also were listed.

96. School Section — When asked to devote a page to high schools preceding graduation, the Utica, Mich., *Tri-City Progress* (circulation 18,312, population 1,196) offered an 8-page section instead. A page was devoted to each of the seven high schools in the district. On the front page were pictures of all the schools. The section contained congratulations to graduates from merchants.

97. Salute to Campus Section — The Riverside, Calif., *Press* (circulation 27,684, population 46,764) saluted the Riverside campus of the University of California with a 48-page special section containing a large volume of attractive advertising.

STRESSING NEWSPAPER SERVICE

98. Scheduled Calls — A regular schedule for making advertising calls helped to obtain advertising for the Lakeview, Ore., *Lake County Examiner-Tribune* (circulation 2,110, population 2,831). By doing this, the publisher developed the habit among advertisers of expecting the advertising salesman on a certain day at about the same time, and often copy was ready for the salesman when he arrived.

99. Buttons — Because a local radio station was working hard to obtain advertising from local merchants, the Hanover, N. H., *Gazette* (circulation 1,050, population 6,259) ran ads comparing the value of radio and newspaper advertising. One of the ads had this headline: "Nobody can turn the button off on the Hanover *Gazette*."

100. "Klassified Korner" — "Your Key to Writing Real Estate Copy That Sells" was the title of an informative folder distributed to real estate dealers by the St. Paul, Minn., *Dispatch* (circulation 119,683, population 311,349). It contained a list of good phrases and adjectives for headlines and copy.

Want Ads Sell..

Concrete Mixer Sold

MIXER, concrete, 2 wheel trailer with large box. AM2-2907.

"Ran the ad two days and had too many replies to count them," said Mrs. Wendell Craig of 1722 East 14th St., Des Moines, Iowa. "Really had good results. Didn't realize want ads got such good response."

Piano Sold

PIANO, upright, $25. Good condition stL5-7263.

"Had 16 telephone calls and sold the piano the first day. Could have sold 2 or 3 of them," said Jack Kimball of 716 37th St., Des Moines, Iowa.

Outboard Motor Sold

16 H. P. Johnson Outboard motor. Cheap. 2700 State St. AM2-1236.

"Had wonderful results, said Mrs. Raymond Robinson of 2700 State St., Des Moines, Ia. "We're still getting mail on our ad."

YOU CAN SELL YOUR UNUSED ARTICLES TOO!

Register and Tribune want ads are famous for producing results. Offer your unused articles for sale in want ads. Interested buyers look through the want ads every day for almost every kind of item. Write the Register and Tribune want ad department or in Des Moines call CH 3-2111.

DES MOINES REGISTER and TRIBUNE WANT ADS

Fig. 14.1 — Illustrated testimonials emphasize the variety of articles that may be sold through classifieds.

CHAPTER 14

Promoting
Classified Advertising

A CLASSIFIED ADVERTISEMENT is a small item from the standpoint of the space it occupies and the single unit revenue it produces for the newspaper. But when a number of these small ads are collected on a newspaper page or on several pages daily or weekly, they stir up a vast amount of reader interest, render satisfactory service to a host of people and produce substantial income for the newspaper.

To make classifieds produce satisfactory profit, volume is required. To produce volume, almost continuous promotion is necessary, and that promotion must be pointed in two directions:
1. Toward the general public — those who have needs and wants for which classifieds can supply the answers.
2. Toward those within the newspaper organization who are responsible for the sale of classifieds and for seeing that they yield maximum returns.

PROMOTING CLASSIFIED ADVERTISING TO GENERAL PUBLIC

Promotion of classified advertising to the general public is a matter of education as well as salesmanship.

A large percentage of those who supply the market for classified ads are persons who seldom feel the need to advertise and who do not comprehend the satisfactory results that may be obtained from classified advertising. Then, too, there are persons seeking employment, retail establishments, utilities, factories and other business institutions — many of which use large display space to advertise their goods and services but which are inclined to disregard the opportunities made available to them by the classified department.

Des Moines
Register and
Tribune
WANT ADS!

ECHO POINT

the
MARKET PLACE
OF ALL
IOWA !

ECHO POINT

Here's proof:

1. People from ALL of Iowa's 99 counties use Register and Tribune Want Ads.

2. Last year, 78,500 Want Ads came from OUTSIDE Des Moines.

3. Hundreds of people and businesses from every corner of the state have been using Register and Tribune Want Ads for years. Some customers date back to 1930!

RESULTS DO IT!

The reason for the state-wide popularity of Register and Tribune Want Ads is that they bring RESULTS! You, too, can get the same fast results, if you want to SELL — BUY — TRADE — HIRE — RENT — FIND!

COST IS LOW!

The results are low-cost results! For instance, a two-line ad in the daily Register and Tribune costs less than 4 cents to reach 10,000 families. In the Sunday Register, a two-line ad costs but 3 cents to reach 10,000 families.

Use this handy Want Ad order blank
Fill it out now and mail today!

WANT AD RATES

The Des Moines Register and Tribune Want Ad Department.

Enclosed find $———— Please run my ad for

————— days.

See for yourself why
Register and Tribune Want Ads are
called the Market Place of All Iowa!

Fig. 14.2 — The Des Moines **Register** and **Tribune** prove want ads provide a profitable market for many things no longer needed by their owners (see p. 166) and that readers in all 99 counties take advantage of this service.

To obtain response from prospects such as these, promotion of a very vital kind is needed. Friendly pokes, convincing pointers, stiff jabs and strong testimonials — delivered in effective sequence and often — are needed to make them become happy, regular users of classified advertising. How home needs and personal wants may be satisfied and how businesses of all kinds may be benefited through the use of the classified section must be presented with sufficient punch and sincerity to compel action. Promotion helps in all this by acquainting the general public with:

1. The various services offered by the classified section.
2. The eagerness with which readers scan the classified pages.
3. The volume of wants that are represented in and may be answered by the classified section.
4. The systematic and attractive makeup of the classified pages so that advertisers readily obtain the attention of prospects.
5. The prompt, satisfactory results obtained by those who use classifieds.
6. The importance of giving complete and understandable details in classified ad copy.
7. The reasonable cost of classified advertising.
8. The easy and convenient ways in which classified ads may be inserted.

Many Services To Be Emphasized

When a person inserts a classified ad in the home town newspaper, he seldom considers the great variety of wants or offerings that will become neighbors to his little advertisement. But when he begins to scan the page and section in which his ad appears he sees the variety of needs the newspaper answers.

Tree trimmers, lawn mower sharpeners, lawn sodders, floor sanders, workers in concrete, carpenters, bricklayers, plasterers, radio and television repairmen, auto mechanics, plumbers, wallpaper hangers, painters, sheet metal workers, blood donors, salesmen, bookkeepers, stenographers, typists, clerks, housemaids, baby sitters, switchboard operators, cooks, farmhands — all offer their services in the "Situations Wanted" columns, and persons needing help from this diversified crowd express their wants under "Help Wanted." Those wanting help and those needing work meet in the classified section and help each other.

Whatever a person wants to buy, whether it is something new or something used, most likely is offered in the classified section...anything from a baby buggy to an airplane, from a guinea pig to an elephant, from a bathing suit to a mink coat. Many things no longer needed in the home are quickly converted to cash through want ads (see Figs. 14.1 and 14.2). Homes and apartments of all styles and sizes

— near the downtown business district or at the suburban lakeside —
are for sale or for rent, and the money needed for the deal is offered
at low interest rates. For centuries classified ads have served effectively, and they still startle their users with prompt results inexpen-
sively obtained.

In a series of promotion advertisements, the Charlotte, N. C.,
Observer (circulation 154,179, population 134,042) vividly and con-
vincingly revealed that *"Observer* Want Ads Sell Everything from A
to Z." Each advertisement in the series featured a letter in the alphabet and a marketable item for which the letter stood. A was for "Automobiles" and Z was for "Zithers" (see Fig. 14.3).

To emphasize the great variety of services offered by their classified sections, the Springfield, Ill., *Illinois State Journal* and *Illinois
State Register* (combined circulation 72,930, population 81,628) ran
a series of promotion ads under the heading "Want Ad Wonders" (see
Fig. 14.4).

"Want Ad Locates Missing Heiress to Uncle's Fortune," announced
one ad. Others had these headings: "Want Ads Reach Ghoul Who
Stole Rich Man's Body," "Husband Uses Want Ad to Praise Wife on
55th Birthday," "McCormick First Used Want Ads to Publicize
Reaper" and "Man Finds Sister Missing 52 Years Through Want Ad."

Tales equally strange and interesting concerning the variety of
services offered by classified ads may be found in any community and
turned into effective classified promotion by an alert promotion department.

"Always read the want ads," urges the Birmingham, Ala., *News*
and *Post-Herald* (combined circulation 279,782, population 326,037)
in a box on its front page. "Each day on the average, 1,426 individual
paid want ads are published in the *News* and *Post-Herald*. Think of
this wide diversification of wants and offers — think of the interesting
bargains in cars, trucks, farms, homes, business opportunities, jobs,
merchandise! Never pass up this highly profitable feature of the paper.
Turn to it now and convince yourself."

The Birmingham, Mich., *Eccentric* (circulation 12,489, population
15,467), a weekly newspaper circulated in suburban Detroit, loses no
opportunity to promote its classified pages. Inserts regarding want
ads are used with correspondence from the circulation department.
These are sent out with renewal notices so that readers are reminded
of quick classified results at little cost (see Fig. 14.5).

The New Milford, Conn., *Times* (circulation 3,990, population
5,799), another weekly carrying a page or more of classifieds, does
the most of its promoting of classified advertising by telephone. "At
one time we used direct mail forms," says John W. Nash, editor, "but
because this was not too effective we settled down to simple telephone
solicitation and follow-up. This follow-up consists of a very thorough

"Observer want ads sell everything from A to Z"

IS FOR ZITHERS

It's entirely possible (and quite probable) that you aren't a zither player. But chances are you do have a musical instrument or two that are carry-overs from the younsters' high school days. Instead of their cluttering up closets, sell these instruments and use the money for something more useful.

By advertiisng in the classified columns of The Charlotte Observer, you're bringing your sales message to the attention of a vast audience. Larger circulation coverage is why The Observer's classified pages are known as the biggest, busiest, sellingest marketplace in the two Carolinas.

To place your "For Sale" ad in The Observer, mail it . . . bring it . . . phone it . . . or place it through any of 50 other newspapers in the Carolinas.

To place your Want Ad, dial **FR 7-7474** **The Charlotte Observer**

FOREMOST NEWSPAPER OF THE CAROLINAS

Fig. 14.3 — A wide variety of salable articles were attractively featured in a promotion series in the Charlotte, N.C., **Observer.**

system of dealing with each ad placed with us. If, for example, we receive an ad for a bicycle for sale for one insertion, a duplicate of the order is placed in the follow-up folder and prior to the next week's issue the advertiser is phoned, inquiring about results and suggesting a re-run of the ad if the article has not been sold. If the advertiser seems dissatisfied with the results, we immediately suggest a change of copy to increase its appeal. In addition to this we search through area newspapers for logical prospects and solicit the business directly."

Classifieds Appeal to All Readers

Prospective advertisers should continuously be reminded that the classified pages rank next to the newspaper's best news pages in readership interest. In an address before the Association of Newspaper Advertising Executives, Worth Wright, classified advertising manager of the Pasadena, Calif., *Star-News* (circulation 59,785, population 104,577) called attention to the universal appeal of classifieds. He pointed out that they interest the person who wants to buy a mansion of $50,000 or a modest cottage of $5,000, a late model car at $3,000 or a jalopy at $300, a grandfather's clock for $500 or an inexpensive alarm clock. They appeal alike to persons of wealth and those of small means. Day by day they carry the news of exceptional values and day by day they are searched by persons who want to buy.

Fig. 14.4 — One in a series of promotion ads carried in the Springfield **Illinois State Journal** and **Illinois State Register** to illustrate that classified ads have been profitable for more than a century.

Even persons who may not have money with which to buy, but who someday will be more fortunate, read the classified pages. In planning their future, newlyweds may visualize living in a handsome cottage in the choicest residence section (see Fig. 14.6). Are the homes pictured in their dreams available, and how much will one cost or for how much would it rent? The classifieds give the answers. People often are anxious to know if homes in their section of the city are being offered for sale. The classifieds tell. Curiosity causes many readers to turn to the classified pages as they would to the news pages to see what of human interest they contain — and seldom are they disappointed.

Real sympathy goes out to the little girl who advertises that her puppy has strayed away and won't somebody help her bring him back, and there is a longing to help the 10-year-old boy who has studied hard and wants a violin for his birthday.

All surveys indicate high readership for classifieds. In a survey made by Raymond A. Kamper & Associates for the Louisville, Ky., *Courier-Journal* and *Times* (combined circulation 392,224, population 369,129), 652 respondents checked their frequency of reading the classified section as follows: Almost always, 20.2 per cent; usually, 24.7 per cent; sometimes, 75.9 per cent. Of the 11.9 per cent of persons interviewed who were in the highest income bracket, 84 per cent placed themselves in one of the three categories, thus stating that they read classifieds with some frequency.

High readership is a point that should be strongly emphasized in promoting classified advertising — and it is being done by many newspapers. For example, the Portland *Oregon Journal* (circulation 182,956, population 373,628) on its classified page showed a horseshoe ringing the peg and with it this bit of business counsel: "Make your pitch where and when it counts most! Over 600,000 readers are reached daily...It's a ringer — a *Journal* classified action ad!"

Volume Indicates Efficiency

The large number of classified ads carried in American newspapers is a strong testimony of their efficiency. Millard Cope, publisher of the Marshall, Tex., *News Messenger* (circulation 11,582, population 22,327) estimates that more than 300,000,000 classified advertisements appear each year in United States newspapers — nearly two ads for every man, woman and child in the country. So many persons would not spend money for classified advertising if it did not bring results.

When for the fifth consecutive year, the Los Angeles *Times* (circulation 476,746, population 2,243,901) published more lines of classified advertising than any other newspaper, it used a 2-column box on the front page to advertise the fact that the *Times* was pre-eminently popular with users of its classified ads (see Fig. 14.7). Its classified linage count for that year was 20,823,586, while the Miami, Fla., *Herald* (circulation 270,573, population 249,276) was second with 16,547,814 lines.

The Charlotte, N. C., *Observer* has developed an immense volume of classified advertising from a wide territory by arranging with small newspapers in the area to accept classified ads that will appear in the *Observer*. This service is extensively advertised (see Fig. 14.8).

"Help Wanted" ads alone in New York City newspapers during the first 120 days of 1958 ran up to 330,000 — an average of over 2,700 job offers per day.

The number of classified ads carried by small daily and weekly newspapers also is almost phenomenal. Many of these smaller papers carry more than a page a day — sound evidence of classified advertising's ability to produce satisfactory results for readers in all areas.

A large volume of classified ads recommends a newspaper not only to its readers but also to business firms which use its display columns.

"Each transaction that begins with classified creates a long chain of economic reverberations which are felt by the people who make appliances and automobiles, soap and slip covers and those who sell insulation and insurance," says Daniel L. Lionel, classified advertising manager of the New York *Herald Tribune* (circulation 335,466, population 7,795,471). "It is this chain that links classified to display and, properly used, can provide every newspaper with a powerful and dynamic sales weapon for display advertising."[1]

Many users of classified advertising later become customers for large display space in the newspaper. On the other hand, many purchasers of large space use regularly a liberal volume of classifieds.

The newspaper that carries a large amount of classified advertising is looked upon by national advertisers as a good medium through which to gain more customers and increase sales for their products. Mr. Lionel stressed this fact at the Annual Sales Clinic conducted by the Philadelphia, Pa., *Inquirer* (circulation 619,381, population 2,071,605). He told advertising salesmen: "The ads that appear daily in classified represent the people's choice of a medium that can influence the buying and selling of valuable goods and services. It is a vote of confidence backed by hard dollars. Even more significant to the national advertiser is the fact that by its very nature the bulk of classified is placed by local people for local consumption. National advertisers are aware of the fact that no one knows better how to influence Philadelphians than the people who live in Philadelphia."

A newspaper's prestige and power are revealed to a large extent by the volume of classified advertising carried in its columns — a fact that no promotion manager should overlook.

------

[1] *Editor & Publisher,* Jan. 12, 1957, p. 18.

Fig. 14.5 — The promotion and circulation departments of the Birmingham, Mich., **Eccentric** boost each other by inserting these reminders in subscription expiration notices; they promote the classified ad page, and remind subscribers what they will be missing if they fail to renew.

Appearance of Section Is Important

Another factor that may influence the effectiveness of a newspaper's classified section is its general appearance and arrangement.

Are the ads set in type easy to read, and are the headings of the various classifications in type bolder than the type used in any other way on the page? Furthermore, does each ad appearing in each classification have a guide word to indicate its contents, and are these individual ads arranged in alphabetical order in their proper classifications? These are vital points in gaining readership for the classi-

fied columns. The classified section should be just what its name implies — an orderly arrangement of personal wants and their answers.

While some publishers have broken away from a few of the more
common standards for classified sections, most of them believe that the
section's effectiveness may be greatly hampered by allowing logotypes,
illustrations and borders to appear in ads of the section. H. L.
Meaker, classified advertising manager of the Binghamton, N. Y., *Press*
(circulation 66,978, population 80,674), believes firmly that when a
newspaper allows multiple-column ads and ads with cuts to appear on
its classified pages it does so at the expense of the readers.

Great pressure is sometimes brought to bear on newspaper publishers to induce them to run display ads on the classified page. If
accepted, they should be pyramided at the lower right hand corner
just as they would be positioned on a regular news page. Nothing
should be permitted in the various classifications that would give advantage to one advertiser over another or that would handicap the
reader in promptly finding the answers to his wants.

In order to obtain reader endorsement for a clean, attractive and
convenient classified section, every newspaper that maintains one
should explain that it is kept on a high standard for the public's benefit. A newspaper's promotion department may help to increase volume
and win good will for the classified section by explaining to readers
that all ads are carefully indexed and arranged in alphabetical order
under standard classifications for the readers' particular convenience.
This would help to eliminate some misunderstandings that salesmen
often find hard to explain away.

The Philadelphia *Inquirer* was greatly pleased by favorable reaction to a change in type face and other improvements in the general
makeup of its classified section. "The legibility of the new type is
excellent," said the Philadelphia Guild of Opticians in a letter to
Joseph H. Hopkins, classified advertising manager. "The bold face
headline on each advertisement also brings about easier reading by
making every advertisement separate and distinct. We congratulate
the *Inquirer* on this forward step." It was a good letter to use in
promoting the *Inquirer*'s new dress for its classified section.

Nothing Talks Like Results

The variety of services they offer, the reader interest they command, the great number of column inches they occupy and the convenience their system of classification provides are all points to be
featured in promoting classified advertising, but nothing talks so
loudly or means so much as results. Here again, classifieds score.

It is the custom in the classified departments of most newspapers
to call an advertiser on the day his ad expires to see if he has obtained
satisfactory results or if he wishes to continue the ad a few days longer.
Wonderful testimonials are obtained in this way, and wise is the

is there a new home in your dreams?

Start making them come true ... check the hundreds of Homes For Sale ads daily in the Register and Tribune

It's a thrill to plan for a newer, bigger, better home!

Dreaming about a new home and planning for it is almost as much fun as actually owning one.

And since you'll probably never buy anything more important than your next home, your plans should have a logical beginning place.

Why not start reading through the Homes for Sale ads in the Des Moines Register and Tribune Want Ad

section? Classifications 70 and 71 are the largest single source of home buying ideas. Just think, every week you'll find nearly 1,500 different homes offered for sale.

It makes no difference what kind of home or location you want, or what price you want to pay. You'll find the home of YOUR dreams listed conveniently in the Register and Tribune Want Ad section.

Your dream home is waiting for you ... read the Homes For Sale Want Ads in the
Des Moines Register and Tribune

Fig. 14.6 — The classified page should be promoted as a market place for desirable homes — new or used, immediate or future.

promotion manager who publishes them in order that the general public may have specific evidence of classified's pulling powers.

Testimonials for classified advertising are the best promotion that can be provided. They are easily obtained and are unquestioned evidence of result-giving power. The Toronto, Ontario, *Star* (circulation 307,928, population 667,706) has produced a 32-page booklet entitled "True Stories of Want Ad Results." It contains outstanding result stories gleaned by W. D. Sutherland, classified advertising manager, from other papers as well as his own. It is a remarkable selling tool abounding in human interest as well as a convincing evidence of the pulling power of classified advertising.

The New York *Herald Tribune* often runs several testimonials in a single promotion ad (see Fig. 14.9), and the San Francisco, Calif., *Chronicle* (circulation 225,429, population 775,357) sometimes runs the picture of a happy advertiser who has had unusual results from *Chronicle* want ads (see Fig. 14.10).

Not much space is required to print testimonials, but they carry a lot of weight. Three inches of display space in the Chicago *American* (circulation 467,557, population 3,620,962) is all that was needed to tell how a classified ad of 15 words, costing $2.22, sold a boat for

TIMES LEADS ENTIRE NATION IN CLASSIFIED ADVERTISING

For the fifth consecutive year, the Los Angeles Times last year published more lines of classified advertising than any other newspaper in America, according to a report from Media Records, official newspaper linage measuring service.

The Times' total classified linage count of 20,823,586 lines exceeded the total classified linage published by the second-place Miami Herald by 4,275,772 lines. The Times led such newspapers as the Chicago Tribune and the New York Times by more than 7,000,000 lines of classified advertising.

In Los Angeles, The Times published 59.0% of the total classified linage placed in all four metropolitan papers during the year.

The Times also led the nation in the number of individual classified ads published with a total of 2,874,793 ads.

Fig. 14.7 — The Los Angeles **Times** uses published reports of its national leadership in volume of advertising to promote the **Times** classified section.

$95 (see Fig. 14.11). The Baltimore, Md., *Sun* (combined daily circulation 410,945, population 949,708) uses liberal space to tell its story of results from classifieds (see Fig. 14.12).

A pleased reader and classified ad patron of the Birmingham, Ala., *News* and *Post-Herald* sent the classified advertising manager this letter:

> We ran a three-line ad in the "Help Wanted" column in the classified section of your papers on Wednesday, January 22, and the response was so tremendous that we wanted you to know the result. During the next four days, a steady stream of applicants came into our store to apply for this position, and by Saturday noon we had counted 147 people that had applied in person, plus over 100 calls on the telephone. We filled the opening on the first day. Another good example of "advertising pays."

To be sure, the letter was reproduced on an important news page with the suggestion that "others should become acquainted with the pulling power of *News* and *Post-Herald* Want Ads."

The immediate sale of a motorcycle after a small ad appeared in the Portland *Oregon Journal* brought joy to a regular subscriber who called in by phone to say: "Lots of calls — sold right away." This testimonial, when published with the fact that "thousands of *Journal* readers are earnestly searching and anxious to buy," brought other ads into the *Journal's* classified columns.

The Des Moines, Iowa, *Register* and *Tribune* (combined circulation 345,146, population 177,965) in their promotion material often point to classifieds as the quick means to ready cash (see Fig. 14.13).

The promptness of results from classifieds is a point that may be well emphasized in promoting classified advertising service. The Charlotte, N. C., *Observer* ran a series of promotion ads on the first-day results from ads that had appeared in its classified columns. "Sold the First Day Advertised Through this *Observer* Want Ad" was the catch line. This brought such good response that the *Observer* occasionally substituted a testimonial for a "Found" ad (see Fig. 14.14) which stimulated greater use of that service.

Should Make Ads Understandable

To produce all the results expected, an advertisement must be wholly understandable. The importance of this is stressed by the Des Moines, Iowa, *Register* and *Tribune* in attractive mailings to prospective advertisers at intervals throughout the year.

"Do abbreviations in your classified advertising REALLY save money?" asks the *Register* and *Tribune*. "Is there a chance that prospects for your merchandise or services fail to act on your classified ad because they cannot understand it? And do you think you would get better results if your ads were easier to read, easier to understand, and more natural?"

Classified ads also should be kept as fresh and newsy as the items that appear in the news columns of the paper. Those who advertise regularly need to comprehend the importance of changing copy. Too many ads in the "Merchandise" or "Miscellaneous" classifications are simply business cards that remain the same from day to day. This lack of change dulls interest in the ads and lessens reader response.

An active and alert promotion department can do much toward building classified volume by inducing advertisers to give more attention to preparation of copy. This is educational work of extreme value to both the newspaper and the advertiser.

Low Cost Appeals to Advertisers

Just as it is important for the advertiser to feature in his classified ad the price of the article he is offering, so it is good business to emphasize the reasonable cost of classified advertising in the newspaper's promotion of its classified section.

Transient ads are the backbone of the classified section. Special promotion should be given them in order to keep the volume high. These ads come from persons who do not know very much about copy or understand rates when quoted on the basis of lines, words or inches.

In order to clear up for its transient advertisers any confused ideas they may have about rates, the Bristol, Tenn. and Va., *Herald Courier* and *Virginia-Tennessean* (combined circulation 27,588, combined population 32,725) carries a classified ad rate box, which reproduces ads of various sizes and shows their costs (see Fig. 14.15). Another good rate box, which can be used to send ads in by mail, is used by the Utica, N. Y., *Observer-Dispatch* (circulation 46,067, population 101,531). This is highly effective in communities where many ads come in from farmers and others who live outside of town (see Fig. 14.16).

Some newspapers have found it advantageous to make a special rate for a few days at certain periods of the year in order to bring new advertisers into the columns. An annual "Want Ad Week," during which period four insertions may be offered for the price of three or six for the price of four, often is used to restore volume. This special week usually is observed in the early months of the year when volume has reached a low ebb and needs rapid build-up. The promotion department can be a great help in making such a campaign successful.

To bring payments in quickly, most newspapers allow a liberal discount on the price of a classified ad if paid for within seven or ten days. This should be well advertised. It not only helps to avoid money losses but it gives the newspaper an opportunity to promote classified advertising from the discount rate standpoint.

You... CAN PLACE OBSERVER CLASSIFIED ADS

through **50** *North and South Carolina*

HOMETOWN NEWSPAPERS

Your **hometown newspaper**

HERE'S WHERE YOU CAN PLACE AN OBSERVER CLASSIFIED AD

IN NORTH CAROLINA

AHOSKIE—Roanoke-Chowan News
BURNSVILLE—Yancey Record
CHAPEL HILL—Chapel Hill Weekly
CHERRYVILLE—Cherryville Eagle
DANBURY—Report
DURHAM—News Journal
ELIZABETHTOWN—Bladen Journal
ELKIN—Elkin Tribune
FAIRMONT—Times-Messenger
FARMVILLE—Enterprise
GREENSBORO—Democrat
KERNERSVILLE—Kernersville News
LEAKSVILLE—Leaksville News
LENOIR—News-Topic
LINCOLNTON—Lincoln County News

MONROE—Monroe Journal
MORGANTON—News-Herald
NEWLAND—Avery County News
PINEHURST—Pinehurst Outlook
RAEFORD—News-Journal
RUTHERFORDTON—Rutherford County News
SELMA—Johnstonian-Sun
SPINDALE—Spindale Sun
STATESVILLE—Record and Landmark
TABOR CITY—Tabor City Tribune
TRYON—Daily Bulletin
VALDESE—Valdese News
WADESBORO—Messenger and Intelligencer
WALNUT COVE—Stokes Record
WEST JEFFERSON—Ashe County News

IN SOUTH CAROLINA

ABBEVILLE—Press and Banner
ALLENDALE—The County News
BAMBERG—Bamberg Herald
BEAUFORT—Beaufort Gazette
BENNETTSVILLE—Marlboro Herald-Advocate
CAMDEN—Camden Chronicle
CLOVER—Clover Herald
CONWAY—Horry Herald
DILLON—Dillon Herald
FOUNTAIN INN—Tribune
GREER—Greer Citizen

KERSHAW—Kershaw News-Era
LAKE CITY—Lake City News
LANDRUM—Landrum Leader
LAURENS—Laurens Advertiser
PAGELAND—Pageland Journal
ST. GEORGE—Dorchester Eagle-Record
SENECA—Journal-Tribune
SIMPSONVILLE—Times
WINNSBORO—News and Herald

For the convenience of its thousands of out-of-town Classified advertisers, The Charlotte Observer has an arrangement with 50 North and South Carolina hometown newspapers to accept and place Classified Ads in The Observer—at no extra charge.

This arrangement provides the unique advantage of personal service even though the advertiser and The Observer may be hundreds of miles apart.

It saves time, too, eliminating back-and-forth correspondence. Everything is handled at one time—wording of ads for best results, calculating linage and most effective schedules, handling payment.

This easy selling service puts the selling power of Observer Classified Ads within easy reach of advertisers throughout North and South Carolina. The classified advertising volume in The Observer provides the greatest marketplace in the Carolinas for jobs, services, buying, selling, swapping opportunities of every conceivable kind!

Residents of Gaston County can place Observer classified ads through our Bureau in Gastonia . . . 220 W. Airline Avenue, Dial UN 4-4319

WHEREVER YOU LIVE . . .

USE 𝕮𝖍𝖆𝖗𝖑𝖔𝖙𝖙𝖊 𝕺𝖇𝖘𝖊𝖗𝖛𝖊𝖗 CLASSIFIED ADS

Fig. 14.8 — Weekly newspapers of the surrounding area accept classified ads for the Charlotte, N. C., **Observer.**

Convenience, Too, Is a Factor

The ease and convenience with which a classified ad may be inserted is something more that should be strongly emphasized in classified promotion.

Some papers give "one day service." A telephone call to the newspaper in the morning may bring buyers to the advertiser's home by evening of the same day. A statement of the cost together with a coin

SOLD FUR COAT!

"A Trib Want Ad soon sold my fur coat...in spite of bad weather on the days my ad appeared."

Mrs. Adeline Greene, New York City

BOUGHT USED PIANO!

"Had a dozen or more replies...for action, put a Want Ad in the Trib!"

Mrs. Doris Bock, Flushing, N. Y.

SOLD USED PIANO!

"Sold my piano quickly through a Trib Want Ad."

Lucie Wallace, New York City

to place your TRIB
WANT AD
call PE 6-4000
ask for an Ad-Taker and charge it

Fig. 14.9 — The New York **Herald Tribune** frequently uses testimonials to show that classifieds satisfy the customers.

card to carry the payment is mailed at once to the advertiser, who is allowed a discount if paid within a given time. It is all so easy!

Any newspaper may tell its readers: "Our classified department is as near to you as your telephone, and buyers for what you want to sell will come to you with your newspaper or within a few hours after it leaves the press." Usually credit privileges are allowed patrons who have telephones.

To make it easy for readers to compile want ads, figure the cost and send in orders by mail, many newspapers, especially the smaller ones, carry a display advertisement containing a blank order form and the schedule of rates. The Hope, Ark., *Star* (circulation 3,400, population 8,602) has had good response to this kind of promotion (see Fig. 14.17).

PROMOTING CLASSIFIEDS TO SALES FORCE

Promotion's service to the classified department is not entirely that of acquainting prospective advertisers with the many ways in which classifieds may answer their wants and needs promptly, conveniently and economically. It performs another great service by impressing upon the newspaper's sales force the merits of classified ads and by assisting them to formulate workable plans for building classified volume. Excellent opportunities to be helpful are found in:

1. Training salesmen.
2. Providing incentives for salesmen and ad-takers.
3. Developing forms and providing equipment for monitoring sales.
4. Furnishing information to advertising agencies.
5. Revealing sources of classified ads.
6. Studying possibilities for expanding volume in each classification.
7. Instituting special campaigns to build volume for each issue.

Provide Training for Salesmen

No one can sell classified advertising without first of all being sold on it himself. Publishers have learned that the selling of classifieds is a particular job and that too many persons are started out in that field without being fully convinced of classified advertising's importance and without understanding the special techniques required.

A classified advertising manager does not always have the time needed to present to his force all these ideas for better selling. But if the newspaper has an aggressive promotion department, the needed assistance is available to train salesmen and to keep them continually interested in swelling classified totals.

Louis E. Reinhold, president of the Richmond Advertising Agency, says that classified ad salesmen are too much interested in merely selling an ad for the next day's paper. He suggests a three-point program:

1. Instead of selling an ad for tomorrow's paper, encourage the dealer to set up a consistent program of advertising based on a monthly budget.

2. Attempt to include in all copy an individual personality for the advertiser. Although the dealer is probably an expert merchant, his knowledge of specialized advertising techniques is likely to be only perfunctory. He will appreciate sound suggestions.

3. Urge the dealer to deliver to the full extent of his advertising claims. Only in this way will classified advertising retain its reader following.

In selecting its classified salesmen, the Chicago *Tribune* gives applicants personality and aptitude tests. Those chosen then are trained by the newspaper in preparing copy and in selling. They are told to sell more than an advertisement — to sell a campaign.

Telephone solicitors for the *Tribune* are put through a rigorous course in telephone techniques and sales language. A training program, all on tape recordings, covers classifications, censorship rules, rates, deadlines, type sizes, full run circulation, blind ticket procedure, errors, tact in explaining censorship rules, selling voluntary ads and soliciting transient ads. A manual is given to each solicitor, pointing out that she is an adviser to the advertiser, not just a sales person, and her job is to tell the customer how to achieve the best results from his advertising.

Karl Kirchhofer, author of "The Art of Telephone Selling," says: "In personal selling of advertising space, both classified and display, various elements enter into the picture," such as the first impression you make on the person you are trying to sell, the confidence you display in your general demeanor and the interest and consideration you reveal in your voice.

Large newspapers conduct schools of instruction for their ad-takers and salesmen. They train them in the meaning of words, the construction of sentences and in the assembling of facts — all that is required to make an attractive and result-producing advertisement. For business firms that use classified advertising extensively, they provide specific instruction in the preparation of copy and concerning the best times to advertise. General information on how to write classifieds for best results also is carried from time to time in the newspaper. Advertisers must know that they cannot depend on type alone to bring answers to their want ads. They must put something into the type that will arouse interest, hold attention and drive to action. It is possible, too, in classified, as in display advertising, to put something of the personality of the individual or firm into the copy.

Sales Management, weekly magazine for marketing executives, issues an attractive booklet entitled "How To Pack Pull Into Your Classified Advertising Copy," which tells about everything a person needs to know in order to put punch and drive into classified advertising. It is written by T. Harry Thompson, an advertising agency executive, and is sold in quantities to newspapers for distribution to their classified advertisers. This very practical booklet presents the

Fig. 14.10 — A picture with a testimonial gives authenticity to classified promotion in the San Francisco **Chronicle**.

Charles P. Wakefield, 3973-23rd Street, San Francisco, says:

"I sold my child's chifforobe with a Chronicle Want Ad"

Sell YOUR spare things for money!

GA 1-1111   LY 3-7654   HI 4-1414   GL 4-8282

following ten tests by which an advertisement may be checked to assure it of readership and response:

1. Does your copy begin with "A" or some other letter well forward in the alphabet, to put you near the top of the column? Classified is "classified" alphabetically.

2. Does your headline or opening sentence contain some key-word like "salesman," "draughtsman," "tool-maker" or "farmhouse" for quick identification of your want?

3. Is there a "grappling-iron" in your headline or first sentence to reach out and grab a busy scanner of type? Try to write a "stopper." Classified must say it with words, without benefit of illustration.

4. Is the copy *long* enough to complete the standard cycle of Attention, Interest, Desire, Action? The same principles of selling apply to these capsule ads as to the larger display ads.

5. Have you used too many abbreviations, some of which the reader puzzles out or skips entirely, passing on to the next ad? Over-abbreviation is false economy.

6. Did you scribble your classified ad between trains, on the back

Boat-plywd, 15½ ft. $95. Call aft.
4:30 P.M. Sat. All Sun. OL 0-0000

This ad in The Chicago American
cost $2.22. Sold boat for $95!

You, too, can sell, rent, buy, trade, with lowest cost Person-to-Person want ads. Run 2 lines for 2 days for $2.22 in The Chicago American. (Or, for only 78c more, run same ad for 3 days.) Pay just half the cost of ads in other papers, get fast results. Same low rates apply seven days a week.

To advertise tomorrow, call ad
taker until 8:00 p.m. tonight

Andover 3-1234

Fig. 14.11 — Small promotion ad in the Chicago **American** shows large return from a low-cost classified.

Fig. 14.12 — Proof of results is always good promotion for classifieds.

of an old envelope, and telephone it to the paper? Don't merely "dash it off." Take time to think it out, then write it, making every word work.

7. Have you written the copy from your own point of view, instead of the reader's? Have you told him the things that he would like to know, rather than just what *you* want? Remember his eternal question: "What does it mean to *me?*"

8. Is your copy lively and human, the way you would talk it? Or formal and dull, like a bill-of-lading?

9. Is the copy sincere? Will it instill belief? Does it even admit a minor "fault" or two, to underscore this sincerity? Readers are better informed today...quicker to spot a "smoothie."

10. Are you sure you don't wish to sign your firm name, instead of using a blind box-number? The fact that you require another salesman or executive or short-order cook is no disgrace. Even though reputable publishers refuse to accept dishonest or misleading advertisements, few readers are willing to "tell all" to a masked stranger, however honorable he may be and doubtless is.

The Chicago *Tribune* (circulation 868,455, population 3,620,962) has prepared a series of "How To" booklets for business classifications that may benefit from liberal classified advertising. In a 24-page issue for used car dealers it gives these pointers on "How To Write Ads That Bring Real Buyers":

1. *Get the Reader's Attention* — Promise him something sensible; use short, snappy phrases; ask pointed questions; tie your copy in with news events, seasons and holidays.

2. *Tell the Reader What Benefits Your Car Will Give Him* — Use words that appeal to his wants and emotions. He may want a car to drive to work, to keep up with the Joneses, to carry the groceries, to satisfy a boyhood ambition or to feel the thrill of having 180 horsepower at his command. Tell him you can satisfy his desires.

3. *Tell the Reader Why Your Car Will Please Him* — Direct your ads to special buyers. One buyer for each car is all you need.

4. *Help the Reader To Believe You* — Use a natural, friendly style; don't exaggerate; stick to specific offers backed by real benefits.

5. *Tell the Reader Your Selling Price, and Justify It* — Put a price on every car you advertise. Leave out the price and you cut your response more than half. Tell what the car will cost and be sure to show that it's worth it.

6. *Get the Reader To Come Out and See You TODAY* — Invite him warmly; give your name and address, and mention any intersection or landmarks that would help him to visualize your location; include your phone number and the hours and days you are open.

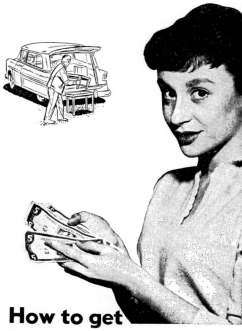

Fig. 14.13 — Speed and economy are sure-fire materials for classified promotion, and get better results when variety and imagination are used in presenting them.

How to get
Extra Cash
in a hurry...

Use a fast-acting, low-cost
Register and Tribune Want Ad

It's so easy....

Advertise the things you no longer need. In practically no time at all, people will beat a path to your door with extra cash. You can use it to buy newer items you've wanted.

How do Register and Tribune Want Ads work so effectively for people who use them? Well, every day, thousands of R and T readers check the Want Ads thoroughly, searching for things they want to buy. That's one reason why they're called the market place of all Iowa.

Right now people are looking for:

- Furniture
- Appliances
- Sports equipment

- Baby things
- Lumber
- Animals, pets
- Livestock

- Farm machinery
- Office equipment

- Television
- Radios
- Phonographs

3 easy ways to order your Register and Tribune Want Ad:

PHONE—In Des Moines, dial CHerry 3-2111

COME IN—Use the handy Want Ad counter in the main floor lobby, Register and Tribune building, 715 Locust

MAIL—Send your ad to: Want Ad Department, Des Moines Register and Tribune, Des Moines 4, Iowa

LANDLORDS:

Empty rooms or apartments cost you money. Find tenants fast and at low-cost with a Register and Tribune Want Ad. Try one the next time you have a vacancy.

Fig. 14.14 — The Charlotte, N. C.,
Observer features the less-used
services of the classifieds.

It Has Happened Again!

FOUND

the First Day
ADVERTISED

through this OBSERVER WANT AD

Mr. Dowd of Dowd Heating Co., Charlotte, found his canvas bag the first day
he placed his ad. **"I was pleased to find
my bag so soon,"** says Mr. Dowd.

Here's another example of the pulling power of Observer Want
Ads! They get results, but fast! So, whether you want to buy, sell,
rent, hire or trade, Observer Want Ads will do the job for you
quickly and economically. Not every item offered gets "first day"
results, however. It depends on timing, price, and other factors.

The cost is just 26c a line per day for an ad which runs seven
days. You can cancel the ad after the first day, or as soon as you
make a sale, and pay only for the number of days run.

When you place your ad, just ask the friendly ad taker to
"charge it."

The Charlotte Observer

Foremost Newspaper of the Carolinas

TO PLACE YOUR WANT AD
Dial FR 7-7474 in Charlotte . . . UN 4-4319 in Gastonia

Given in the sales pamphlet also is a collection of phrases that may be used in describing the comfort, safety, power, equipment and appearance of the car to be advertised. Highly valuable also are examples of what Chicago car dealers considered to be the best ads they ever ran in the *Tribune*.

The Birmingham, Ala., *News* and *Post-Herald* carry on their classified pages these six rules to use in "Writing Want Ads for Best Results":

1. By using consecutive insertions your ad is assured maximum reader attention. Ads inserted 3, 7 and 30 times get better results than intermittent insertions.

2. In writing an ad, copy must be clear and specific. General terms waste the reader's time and do not tell him anything about your offer.

3. Take the reader's view, and ask yourself what you would like to know about your offer. The answer will make a good want ad.

4. Be sure the first word of your ad names the article or service you have for sale.

5. Every want ad should contain the name, address and phone number (if possible). Make it easy for the prospect to reach you.

6. Make your advertising truthful; it enables you to obtain quicker action from prospects and eliminates controversies. The *News-Herald-Post* does not knowingly print any untruthful advertising.

Plan Incentives for Salesmen

A never-lagging interest in developing classified linage and a continual eagerness to see the classifications lengthen and bring new names into the classified pages are essential to a successful classified advertising department. It is important, therefore, that careful supervision be provided and that incentives be offered occasionally.

The publisher of a small daily paper had the habit of counting the ads on the classified page each day. He considered there should be at least 200 ads on the page, and whenever the count ran below that mark, he called his classified ad manager into counsel and planned some sort of campaign or incentive that put fire into the sales force. On larger papers the promotion department takes care of details such as this. A good promotion manager is full of ideas for contests, bonuses and other types of awards that will stimulate classified selling.

The Toronto, Ontario, *Star* divides its salesmen into two groups with a supervisor over each group. The supervisor confers daily with each member of his group to see what accounts he has developed and how his results compare with goals that have been set. Each salesman makes a daily report on the business he turns in and a weekly report on problems arising in his territory.

Herald Courier

Virginia-Tennessean

WANT-AD RATES

This is a 6-line ad. It costs only
$5.88 for 7 days, $3.84 for 4 days,
or $1.20 for 1 day.

CHEVROLET — 1948 Aero sedan.
New royal blue finish. Upholstery
clean. Good tires. Radio and heat-
er. Low mileage. Motor's just been
tuned and serviced. A steal at $1,095.
Private owner. Phone 0000.

This is a 5-line ad. It costs only
$4.90 for 7 days, $3.20 for 4 days,
or $1 for one day.

MAGNOLIA DR., 000—Mod. 2-bed-
room brick home and attached
garage on 92x139 corner lot. Beau-
tifully decorated inside and out.
Can be financed for $10,500. Ph. 000.

This is a 4-line ad. It costs only
$3.92 for 7 days, $2.56 for 4 days,
or 80c for 1 day.

TYPEWRITER—1952 Smith-Corona
sterling portable with tabulator.
Used only a few weeks. Bargain
price: $70. Call Smith at N-0000-J.

This is a 3-line ad. It costs only
$2.94 for 7 days, $1.92 for 4 days,
or 60c for 1 day.

CAMP STOVE WANTED — Used
2-burner Coleman gasoline camp
stove. Call John Doe at S-0000.

Sunday Only 25c per line

Minimum Charge 3 Lines
5 Average Words Per Line
Contract Rates Upon Application

All ads start in the morning Herald
Courier and appear in the morning
and in the afternoon Virginia-Tennessean on the same day.

Call

192

For Want-Ads

Fig. 14.15 — Rate box that shows both size and cost proves helpful to prospective advertiser.

The Los Angeles, Calif., *Examiner* (circulation 356,496, population 2,243,901) has for each salesman a set of daily report forms, a
different form for each day of the week. While the information that
the salesman is required to fill in each day remains the same, the 4-
page form provides the salesman with a suggested set of goals for each
day. For example, on Monday the following message appeared:

Fresh beginning for a new week. Challenging opportunities today to
show advertisers the advantages of 30-time orders; to point out to advertisers whose ads expired with yesterday's paper that the more times an ad
appears the more people will see it, and the better the opportunity for
results. New prospects enter the market EVERY day.[2]

Important To Monitor Sales

Monitoring classified sales is a matter that should never be treated
lightly. The promotion department can devise report forms that will
keep salesmen active and that will give the classified advertising manager a clear picture of what is being accomplished.

[2]*Editor & Publisher,* Apr. 7, 1956, p. 32.

The Montreal, Quebec, *Gazette* (circulation 110,018, population 1,109,439) keeps an accurate record of calls made and the number of orders obtained by each classified salesman. The system is described in an article by Daniel L. Lionel in *Editor & Publisher*.[3] John M. Henderson, classified advertising manager of the *Gazette*, says in a letter to Lionel:

> We have the salesman fill out a list of ten planned calls every morning before leaving the office. The results of these calls plus any additional calls he may make are included in the same report the following morning before his planned list is again made out. This completed report is checked by the sales manager and myself after which the information on it is transferred to a permanent card which is maintained for each account.
>
> At the end of the month the actual billed linage is transferred to this same set of cards along with the linage measured for all the large accounts from the competing newspaper. A monthly report then is arrived at. This provides us with the number of calls made by the salesman on every account, the linage obtained from each account, the amount of linage run by the same account in the same month of the previous year, and the approximate amount of linage run by the account in the other paper. In addition, a progressive signal on each card enables us to tell at a glance how long it has been since a salesman called on an account.
>
> This accumulated data is then used to discuss the territory with the salesman at an individual meeting each month, at which time a decision is reached as to whether the amount of calls is satisfactory, whether more or less should be made and what we anticipate the account will run in the current month. This provides the salesman with a pretty fair breakdown of what his accounts are doing and of what he is doing with them. It is also the basis for any changing of territories, establishing of quotas and and the like on our part.
>
> Altogether, we find it a very essential and very effective means of keeping track of the individual accounts as well as the salesman's efforts. Certainly we have no difficulty in having the boys keep good records and a full report on the basis of help we are able to give them in planning their time and effort.

The promotion department also should make a careful study of the general arrangement of the classified advertising department and its equipment in order to see what might be done to add to its efficiency.

To assist in reaching a five-year production goal, Har M. Henry, classified advertising manager of the San Jose, Calif., *Mercury-News* (circulation 100,830, population 127,564) set up a separate phone room and a two-position switchboard. "One doesn't have to move into a new building or take over another guy's operation as classified manager to have an excuse to thoroughly set up a five-year production plan and estimate the number of people who will help produce it," says Henry.

---

[3]*Editor & Publisher*, May 12, 1956, p. 64.

Give Agencies Full Information

A newspaper's promotion department can help greatly in obtaining classified advertising in the national advertising field. Special advertising representatives want facts concerning the newspaper and its territory that they can present to advertising agencies. Representatives sometimes become rather disgusted with the information that some newspapers think is vital in obtaining contracts.

UTICA DAILY PRESS
UTICA OBSERVER-DISPATCH
Classified Adv. Department
Oriskany Plaza   Ph. 2-1111
COUNTER SERVICE
8:30 a. m. to 5:00 p. m.
Except SUNDAYS

WANT AD
MAIL-O-GRAM
WRITE YOUR AD BELOW
(three inch space with blank lines was left here)

**Name, address, phone number counted as part of ad.
50c service charge for box number at this office.**

NAME ....

ADDRESS ....

CITY .... **STATE** ....

NUMBER OF DAYS ....

CASH AD PRICES

Words	1 Day	4 Days	7 Days
Up to 15	1.13	3.36	4.29
16 to 20	1.47	4.35	5.71
21 to 25	1.76	5.28	7.14
26 to 30	2.02	6.14	8.57

To place an ad by phone call
AD-TAKER 2-1111
BRANCH OFFICES:
ROME — 127 N. Washington, Ph. 99
ILION — 1 E. Main, Ph. Ilion 1
HERKIMER — 103 E. Albany, Ph. 1777

Fig. 14.16 — Rate box used by the Utica, N.Y., **Observer-Dispatch** and **Daily Press** makes it convenient for out-of-town readers or users to mail in classifieds or telephone them to branch offices.

"Much of the material is just bragging about relatively minor conditions," a special representative once told a group of publishers. "When papers give us percentages of coverage, as many do, we wish they would be more careful to see that the circulation figures are reasonably comparable with the family figures instead of current circulations percentaged against five-year obsolete family figures."

He said that much more should be given on the character of the newspaper than is usually given. Quite often a space buyer is asked to give an appraisal of the influence of the newspaper on the community. A good description of the character of the newspaper in 200 words or less prepared by the promotion department would be useful.

It is important for the promotion department to develop a complete plan for promoting classified advertising in the national field. The plan should be for a year or at least several months. This applies to research or promotional material whether in the form of presentations, direct mail or trade paper campaigns.

Point Out Advertising Sources

The promotion department again may be helpful to the classified department by constantly searching for and directing attention to new sources of classified advertising.

Opportunities to sell classified advertising often bob up from unexpected sources. When in 1954 the U.S. government arranged to dispose of surplus real property, it opened up a new source for classified advertising and newspapers were quick to take advantage. The division handling this detail for the government reported excellent results from the advertising. For some items the government received more than the appraisal value.

Again in 1957, when a long awaited FHA directive cut down payments on homes and increased interest rates for mortgages, there was another opportunity to increase volume in the real estate and loan classifications.

New sources, however, usually are the result of some solid, quick thinking on the part of the promotion manager or the classified advertising manager. The following are some outstanding examples.

The Philadelphia, Pa., *Bulletin* (circulation 695,960, population 2,071,605), determined to increase the number of ads from homes in its territory, offered "2 lines 2 days for $2" and backed it up with elaborate and extensive promotion. The results desired were accomplished.

The Toronto, Ontario, *Globe and Mail* (circulation 215,570, population 667,706) planned a "Household Service Directory" in its classified section and promoted it heavily. A series of ads in the paper urged readers to consult this new, exclusive directory. Seven outdoor billboards, strategically located, drew the attention of motorists

HOPE STAR

MAIL-IN CLASSIFIED AD ORDER

The Quick and Inexpensive Way To Do Business

INSTRUCTIONS: Put your Classified Ad Words in Squares Below . . . one word to the square. Put the number of days you want your Ad to run in square at bottom. Then figure your cost.

EXAMPLE: 15 words runs 3 days......90c — 6 days......1.50

NAME . . . . **No. of Days Ad Is To Run**

ADDRESS . . . .

BOX NO. . . . . PHONE . . . .

Clip and Mail — Check . . . . . . Cash . . . . . . Money Order . . . . . .

Here's How You Figure Your Total Cost . .

	1 Time	3 Times	6 Times	One Month
UP to 15 words	.45	.90	1.50	4.50
16 to 20 words	.60	1.20	2.00	6.00
21 to 25 words	.75	1.50	2.50	7.50
26 to 30 words	.90	1.80	3.00	9.00
31 to 35 words	1.05	2.10	3.50	10.50
36 to 40 words	1.20	2.40	4.00	12.00
41 to 45 words	1.35	2.70	4.50	13.50
46 to 50 words	1.50	3.00	5.00	15.00

Fig. 14.17 — The Hope, Ark., **Star** adds to its rate box a blank form to make word counting easy and accurate.

and pedestrians. The advertising on outdoor billboards and in the newspaper then was reproduced in a neat, slick paper, 2-color, 6-page folder and sent to potential advertisers. In a short time this promotion made the "Household Service Directory" a profitable, volume-producing feature.

Any new feature or classification that may be introduced requires careful planning and extensive promotion. In providing these, a well-organized, well-directed promotion department is highly valuable.

Keep Classifications Well Filled

A study of the various classifications represented in a newspaper's classified section reveals that in each classification volume goes up naturally at some periods of the year and down at others. This is not pleasing to the classified advertising manager, who wants to keep volume constantly high. How may the customary dips in certain classifications be avoided? The person with the best answer is the promotion manager. He seldom disappoints.

If used car linage is down, something needs to be done there. The promotion manager has a suggestion. How about inducing all motor dealers to unite in a community-wide used car sale? To give more than ordinary force to ads run at regular rates in the used car columns, the newspaper will prepare attractive copy and use half-page and quarter-page space to promote the campaign (see Fig. 14.18). In this way the classified section will receive extra reader attention for a number of important days, used car dealers will be stepped up in their selling and realize pleasing results, and the volume of used car advertising will go to a new high.

A similar campaign may be conducted for real estate dealers in the spring when people have their minds on homes in the suburban areas where they may grow flowers and vegetables.

Holiday weekends provide the opportunity to promote the sale of resort cabins or rentals at hotels. There is a season for everything offered on the classified pages, and an aggressive promotion manager never misses a chance to show the classified department how it may build volume in one or several of the classifications.

Build Everyday Volume

Building volume for every issue of the week as well as in every classification is the classified department's responsibility. Sunday newspapers carry a larger volume of classifieds than weekday issues. This is not altogether because Sunday is a better day to obtain the attention of readers. It is partly due to the large amount of promotion given the Sunday classified section and the very small amount given weekday advertising.

To help the weekday volume, the Los Angeles, Calif., *Mirror-News* (circulation 307,412, population 2,243,901) came forth with

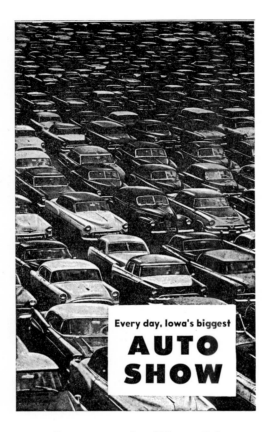

Every day, Iowa's biggest

AUTO SHOW

See it in the Want Ad section of the Des Moines Register and Tribune

It's so easy to shop for a newer, better car.

Simply turn to the Want Ad section of any Register or Tribune. There you'll find literally several hundred cars for sale, listed conveniently in classifications 35 and 36.

Station wagon, convertible, sports car, foreign car, second car . . . you're sure to find what you want quickly and easily in Iowa's biggest auto show. Remember, this show is on EVERY DAY in the Want Ad section of the Des Moines Register and Tribune.

Find the car you want; turn to the Want Ad section, classifications 35 and 36

Fig. 14.18 — A newspaper can boost linage sales in any section of the classifieds by promoting that section in attention-getting ads of its own.

"Wonderful Wednesday," a unique classified value day, and promoted it by every available means. Eye-catching cards were placed at all *Mirror-News* stands. Outgoing mail was stamped with colorful teaser stickers. Spot announcements went out on radio and television. Busses and street cars carried display cards. Attention-getting display ads and feature stories appeared in the newspaper.

This may have been a greater promotion expenditure than the feature's money yield merited, but it gave the classified section a tremendous boost and went far toward establishing the *Mirror-News* as a right medium for all-time advertising of common wants and needs.

The means that may be employed to promote classifieds are unlimited, and unfortunate is the newspaper that does not use them.

"Promote classified
continuously and
endeavor to make
every staff member,
from front office
to mechanical department,
classified-minded."

— C. VERNE McKINNEY,
Publisher,
Hillsboro, Ore.,
Argus

CHAPTER 15

50 Tested Classified Advertising Promotions

THE FOLLOWING PROMOTIONS of classified advertising indicate the wide variety of means that may be employed to popularize classified and increase volume:

TO INCREASE USED CAR SALES

1. Selected Used Cars — The Boston, Mass., *Record* (circulation 369,809, population 801,444) carried a full page of used car advertising under the heading, "Selected Used Car Values." The name of car and price were set in 10 point bold face. The rest of each ad was in agate.

2. Color in Classified — The Columbus, Ga., *Ledger* and *Enquirer* (combined circulation 52,221, population 79,611) ran three pages of automotive advertising, carrying tags and arrows in color.

3. Free Pony Ride — A motor company advertised in the Louisville, Ky., *Courier-Journal* (circulation 216,645, population 369,129) a free pony ride for any child visiting a used car lot with parents.

4. Pay After Christmas — Used car dealers of Newark, N. J., made holiday sales by advertising nothing down and payments after Christmas — an obvious appeal to those who shop heavily at Christmastime.

5. Two Cars to a Family — The Portland *Oregon Journal* (circulation 182,956, population 373,628) sent automobile dealers a series of colorful circulars urging them to exploit Portland's market for second cars by placing ads aimed at potential 2-car families.

6. Easter Used Car Parade — Dealers in some towns have taken advantage of the Easter theme by throwing in an Easter bonnet for the wife or sweetheart of the purchaser.

[200]

TO SELL REAL ESTATE

7. **Classified Tie-in** — A large department store shared with real estate dealers the cost of classified ads when they allowed to be inserted in copy the line, "Only ____ blocks from _____ store."

8. **Family Scene** — A promotion on classified advertising in the El Paso, Tex., *Times* (circulation 58,066, population 130,485) was an ad containing a family scene with pictures of attractive homes in the background. The headline was "Wise people turn to the classified section to find a home for the family."

9. **Key to Good Selling** — "Your Key to Writing Real Estate Ad Copy That Sells" is the title of an information folder distributed to real estate dealers by the St. Paul, Minn., *Dispatch* and *Pioneer Press* (combined circulation 210,007, population 311,349).

10. **"Buy Home Near School"** — The Sioux Falls, S. Dak., *Argus Leader* (circulation 50,658, population 52,696) ran a full page of classified advertising under the heading "America's Two Great Institutions — the School and the Home."

11. **"March of Homes"** — The Seattle, Wash., *Times* (circulation 214,927, population 467,591) conducted in March what it called a "March of Homes." Homes ready for sale were opened for inspection and listed twice in the classified section: first, under the cut of a weather vane rooster in the realtors' ads, and second, by districts, in an omnibus ad.

12. **"Fix Up Your Home"** — The Denison, Tex., *Herald* (circulation 12,252, population 17,504) obtained extra classified volume by selling a "Fix Up Your Home" promotion which ran every other day for a month.

TO SELL MERCHANDISE

13. **Free Chicks** — A feed company in Denison, Tex., had a great run on chick starter when it advertised in the Denison, Tex., *Herald* free chicks with each 25-lb. order.

14. **"We're Stuck"** — A furniture company put so much faith in the ability of the Long Island, N. Y., *Newsday* (circulation 288,483, population 672,675) to produce quick results that it ran a solid classified page to push home furnishings. The heading was, "We're Stuck."

15. **Trade-in Sale** — The Portland *Oregonian* (circulation 233,856, population 373,628) advertised for a furniture store a trade-in sale with an offer of from $30 to $50 for an old set on purchase of a new dining or breakfast set. The store offered also a 10-pound turkey with each set purchased during the sale.

16. **For Credit Accounts** — Under the heading, "Specials at the Stores," a department store ran this ad in the Haverhill, Mass., *Gazette* (circulation 10,363, population 47,280): "Ancestors may be necessary to get on certain societies' books, but not on ours. We invite you to

join the thousands of women who so thoroughly enjoy the time-saving convenience of their charge accounts here. We welcome the business of career girls, coeds, young married couples, nice newcomers to Haverhill or long-established dowagers. Come in and be surprised at how simple it is to say 'charge it' at our store.''

17. After-Christmas Campaign — The Marshall, Tex., *News Messenger* (circulation 11,582, population 22,327) put on a special campaign for furniture and automotive classifieds to counteract the customary after-Christmas drop in linage.

18. Feminine Appeal — The Wichita Falls, Tex., *Record-News* (circulation 28,241, population 68,042) appealed to thrifty housewives when it ran a promotion ad depicting a woman with a background of dollar marks and the heading, "More Dollars in Her Purse — She Reads the Classified Ads.''

19. Classified Budget Wheel — Jack Henderson, circulation manager of the Montreal, Quebec, *Gazette* (circulation 110,018, population 1,109,439) has designed what he calls a "Budget Wheel." It consists of two pieces of cardboard, one yellow and the other green, one smaller than the other, mounted on a common axis so that they revolve. The gadget enables the advertiser to select a linage bracket into which his budget falls, and he can then work out the cost per insertion of varying sizes.

20. ABCZ — The classified advertising department of the Los Angeles *Mirror-News* (circulation 307,412, population 2,243,901) has published a 30-page study of Los Angeles as a market for classified advertisers. The booklet is called "ABCZ — Formula for Successful Classified Advertising in Los Angeles Today.''

TO EMPHASIZE CLASSIFIED SERVICE

21. Millionth Ad — The Portland *Oregonian* gave a check for $100 to a Portland housewife when she inserted an ad, which happened to be the millionth of the year.

22. Newsy Want Ads — The Shreveport, La., *Times* (circulation 87,184, population 127,206) used an unusual page-1 box promotion featuring news highlights from newsy classified ads.

23. Letter-Writing Contest — The Toronto, Ontario, *Star* (circulation 307,928, population 667,706) offered $1,000 in prizes for best letters telling in simple language how want ads helped writers. Later the letters were presented in an attractive booklet, making a beautiful want ads promotion piece.

24. Convincing Testimonial — The Battle Creek, Mich., *Enquirer-News* (circulation 37,170, population 48,666) reproduced an ad featuring the opening of a model home and a testimonial letter in appreciation of the fine results obtained. The heading was "It's Results That Count.''

25. Good Classified Fillers — The Gary, Ind., *Post-Tribune* (circulation 54,517, population 133,911) selects illustrations from mat service and prepares copy for promotion ads on classifieds. The ads urge readers to go through their attics and basements, pick out things they no longer need and sell them quickly with a *Post-Tribune* want ad.

26. To Catch the Eye — "More Eye-Catching and Better Returns" was the heading for a promotion ad in the Detroit, Mich., *Free Press* (circulation 456,117, population 1,849,568). It contrasted the old-style close-set classified ad with the airy attractive display style now used in the *Free Press*.

27. Pushes Telephone Sales — To coincide with the Newspaper Color Conference held in Chicago in 1957, the Chicago *Tribune* (circulation 868,455, population 3,620,962) published a full-color advertisement to promote telephone sales of classified ads.

28. Three More Days, If — The Paris, Tex., *News* (circulation 10,418, population 21,643) guaranteed results to the extent that if the advertiser didn't get a satisfactory response using three to six continuous insertions, the ad would be run free for three additional days.

29. Split the Cost — The Denison, Tex., *Herald* found it easy to sell a co-op ad on "Fix-up Your House for Winter" when it ran the ad on the last Sunday of September and the first Sunday of October, thereby billing half in September and half in October.

30. Leadership Contest — Claiming to be the only paper in the entire Southwest to publish a million classified ads in one year and to have gained that distinction for eight successive years, the Houston, Tex., *Chronicle* (circulation 192,062, population 596,163) sponsored a contest with $400 in prizes to persons making the best guesses on the number of ads that would be carried in the current year.

31. Copy in Hand — The Elk City, Okla., *News* (circulation 4,986, population 7,692) insists that its classified salesmen always have copy in hand when calling on a prospect.

32. Plenty of Insertions — Don Schneider, advertising manager of the Dallas, Tex., *Times Herald* (circulation 178,848, population 434,462), in speaking to an ad seminar in Dallas, said that 60 per cent of the results on rental ads are obtained from the first four insertions and that the greatest injustice to an advertiser is to not sell him enough insertions.

33. Safety Campaign — Classified advertising was used to good advantage by the Big Spring, Tex., *Herald* (circulation 9,529, population 17,286) in connection with a safety campaign. An ad occupying 6 full columns and sponsored by business firms explained safety rules.

34. An Old Owl Said — The Spokane, Wash., *Spokesman-Review* (circulation 91,208, population 161,721) carried a unique full-page ad with a reverse heading and Ben Day background to promote classified ads. The heading was "Be Wise — Advertise in Want Ads," and the illustration was a cut in the shape of an owl from the classified page.

35. Abbreviations Reduce Results — A survey made by the Minneapolis, Minn., *Star* and *Tribune* (combined circulation 502,252, population 521,718) revealed that excessive use of abbreviations in classified ads reduced their selling power materially.

36. A Want Ad Talks — The Minneapolis *Tribune* (circulation 214,827, population 521,718) carried an attractive full-page promotion for classified ads. The heading was "I Am a Want Ad," and the message was a heart-to-heart sales talk on what want ads can do.

37. Free Ads for Kids — The New Rochelle, N. Y., *Standard-Star* (circulation 18,288, population 59,725) each year for a limited number of days runs want ads free for boys and girls age 16 and under.

38. Double Time — The San Angelo, Tex., *Standard-Times* (circulation 32,848, population 52,093) opened numerous new accounts when it offered, for one week only, "twice as long for same price."

39. What Happens to Want Ad — The Houston, Tex., *Chronicle* used a full page with seven photos to show how a want ad is handled from the time the ad-taker gets it until the time it goes to press.

40. Result Summary Form — The New York *Herald Tribune* (circulation 335,466, population 7,795,471) has found it useful to supply advertisers with "Classified Advertising Result Summary Forms" with which to keep a record of results obtained from advertising.

41. Zone Page Repeaters — Classified ads in the Los Angeles *Mirror-News* (circulation 307,412, population 2,243,901) may be repeated in the same issue on "zone pages" at a rate of 10 cents a line additional to the advertiser's regular rate.

42. Above-Door Promotion — The Medford, Wis., *Star-News* (circulation 5,031, population 2,799) gives classified advertising some excellent promotion with a sign on its shop front which says "The Newspaper That Want Ads Built."

43. "Teen-to-Teen" — The Washington, D. C., *Star* (circulation 258,434, population 802,178) carries a sales and swap column in its "Teen" Sunday supplement in which youngsters may insert a 3-line ad for 25¢ plus 10¢ for each additional line. This column is called "Teen-to-Teen."

44. Prizes for Testimonials — The Tarentum, Pa., *Valley News* (circulation 23,192, population 9,540) gave away 100 passes to the movie, "Oklahoma," for best letters of 25 words or less telling "Why I like to read *Valley News* Want Ads."

45. Checks All Expirations — The Milwaukee, Wis., *Journal* (circulation 361,856, population 637,392) checks each classified ad expiration when it comes through from the accounting department before it is returned to the sales girl. Often it is accompanied with suggestions for change of copy or classification.

46. Promotes Results — The Santa Rosa, Calif., *Press-Democrat* (circulation 30,503, population 17,902) put a young woman on the telephone to call at random 50 advertisers to ask what success they had had with classified ads in the *Press-Democrat*. The results of this casual survey were published in a half-page promotion advertisement.

47. "Remember Results" — The Charleston, W. Va., *Gazette* (circulation 70,592, population 73,501) stamps on the back of all bills for ads that brought results this reminder: "Remember, the *Gazette* brought you results. When you need us again, dial 60-611."

48. Hidden Names — To draw readership to its classified page, the Wakarusa, Ind., *Tribune* (circulation 1,190, population 1,143) hides names among the ads and gives a free movie ticket to each person who discovers his name.

49. Classified Front Page — When the Campbell River, British Columbia, *Courier* (circulation 1,835, population 1,986) received enough want ads to fill a page, it ran them on the front page and thus drew special attention to the newspaper's remarkable increase in classified volume.

50. Pink Classified — The Arlington Heights, Ill., *Herald* (circulation 6,710, population 8,768), which sometimes runs eight pages of classified ads, prints the section on pink paper.

"The scope and quality of
your research and
how well you can actually
document the advertising
values you claim . . .
will determine your share
of national adver-
tising linage."

CHAPTER 16

Promoting General Advertising

— ARTHUR A. PORTER,
Media Director,
J. Walter Thompson Co.

SUCCESSFUL PROMOTION of general (or national) advertising requires coordinated planning in three principal areas:

1. Important contacts outside the newspaper's immediate territory.
2. Well-planned use of various communications media.
3. Strong emphasis on many points of advertising service.

MUST PROMOTE IN WIDE AREA

General advertising is sold in a much wider field than is local advertising (retail or classified). Most of it comes from outside sources, sometimes far distant. In order to obtain maximum volume, selling and promotion must be directed consistently and forcefully to five groups, each having some influence in placing newspaper schedules:

1. Local merchants who stock nationally advertised products.
2. Salesmen for manufacturers, distributors and wholesalers who "work" the newspaper's territory.
3. The newspaper's special representatives in the national advertising field.
4. Advertising agencies that plan schedules and place orders for national advertisers.
5. Advertising executives of firms seeking distribution for the products of their company in the newspaper's territory.

Promotion Begins at Home

The Bureau of Advertising of the American Newspaper Publishers Association, which devotes its full energies to selling newspaper advertising to national firms, emphasizes the fact that, in reality "all advertising is local."

Preliminary efforts toward obtaining an advertising schedule for a newspaper are in the field the newspaper serves. Results from the same advertising must be realized in the same area. There are other steps between these in obtaining and processing a schedule of general advertising, but success depends largely on a proper launching and a resultful ending, both of which take place in the territory the newspaper serves. Local effort starts it off and local results determine its success. To that extent at least, all general advertising is local.

If it were possible to impress upon newspaper publishers the importance of keeping all retail establishments in their area fully acquainted with the advertising service their newspapers are able to give above that of other media, a great deal more general advertising would appear in newspapers today. This is a matter that demands more attention than most publishers realize. Many schedules are placed on television and radio or in magazines because promotion or advertising departments have lagged in keeping merchants conscious of superior service provided by newspaper advertising.

A retailer may see in some national magazine a colored advertisement of an item he stocks. It is a beautiful ad. He clips it from the magazine and pastes it in his window. Unless he has been previously well fortified, he may conclude that magazines offer the quickest and best means to move merchandise from his shelves. The reaction, however, is different, when the merchant is given facts concerning the circulation of magazines and newspapers in his area. Usually the number of copies of any one of the best magazines sold in a newspaper's community is no more than one-seventh or one-tenth of the newspaper's circulation. Colored advertising in magazines is effective in bringing patronage to a merchant only in proportion to the number of homes it reaches in the merchant's trade territory.

A cosmetics manufacturer once had a survey made of drugstores in a large city to find out their advertising media preferences. Seventy per cent of those surveyed preferred radio spots, but only 40 per cent *knew* that the manufacturer already had a program on the air. They expressed a preference for advertising that had appeared before them but failed to get their attention. This shows how easily a manufacturer may be influenced by the blind preferences of retailers who give no thought at all to what constitutes attractive advertising. It shows also the importance of keeping merchants showered with information concerning the newspaper's services.

Much needs to be done by a newspaper at its home base before it can expect to receive advertising from manufacturers, jobbers and distributors located at distant industrial centers or from advertising agencies. The high points of a required program are well outlined in a formula that was presented to members of the Northwest Daily Press

Association by Thurman M. Salada, former national advertising manager of the St. Paul, Minn., *Dispatch* and *Pioneer Press* (combined circulation 210,007, population 311,349) :

1. Get local retailers, brokers, wholesalers, jobbers and manufacturers' agents to write letters to manufacturers in behalf of their LOCAL newspapers.
2. Don't hesitate to dig up and equip your salesmen and folks you're working on with FACTS about the wealth, buying power, retail and service outlets, and other pertinent features of your town and trade area.
3. Get on the program of sales meetings and conferences to tell the newspaper story in your most effective and convincing manner.
4. Help your advertisers — with store surveys, telephone surveys, whatever they need or want to help do a better distribution job.
5. Follow through on all local tie-in possibilities; localize your national advertising with tie-in space, store displays, etc.
6. Work with all local outlets in making the advertising functional — get actual sales results. However small or intermittent a schedule, results will make it grow. Personal calls are better, but good pointed sales letters to everybody concerned in an advertising campaign help a lot.
7. Watch trade paper announcements, sales meetings, general media of all kinds, for tips and leads and hints as to where space can be effectively sold.

Keep Close Contact With Salesmen

Just as important as keeping local merchants informed concerning the advantages they may derive from advertising placed in the local newspaper by national firms is the matter of keeping salesmen for these companies sold on the newspaper's ability to help them increase sales with advertising. Salesmen always have the opportunity to wield some influence in the placing of advertising schedules in newspapers published in towns where they call regularly on merchants and receive orders. A salesman's request or recommendation regarding advertising goes far with a manufacturer and his advertising executive. Therefore, a continuous easy contact with salesmen is important to any newspaper.

A newspaper's first opportunity to obtain the good will of a salesman is when he makes his first visit to the area to obtain sales outlets for the merchandise he represents. He wants to call on all merchants who may be interested in handling the type of goods he sells. If the newspaper will supply him on arrival with a route list of merchants in the town and close-in territory, it will render to him the most important service it can provide for him on his initial trip. A route list is a classified tabulation of business firms with the names arranged in order according to street addresses so the salesman, using it as a guide, may move from one business house to the next with greatest convenience and speed. Along with the route list may be presented also some material concerning the community and the newspaper for the salesman to take back with him to the main office. In this initial contact, with the right technique and thoroughness, much can be accomplished for the newspaper.

Other opportunities for contacts with salesmen will arise from time to time if advertising salesmen and promotion men are alert and active. District managers, brokers, wholesalers and distributors who hold regular meetings with their sales staffs often are glad to have an advertising man come in and explain how well-planned newspaper advertising will enable them to increase sales in their territory. This is particularly helpful when a schedule on the manufacturer's product is to appear soon. Then the newspaper representative can explain why the newspaper was chosen for this campaign and how, by close cooperation with the advertising, members of the sales force can build up for themselves better sales records and greater commissions. A flip-chart presentation is very practical and the cost is small. A slide or film presentation is more dramatic and, of course, more expensive.

For a large group meeting, particularly if representatives from the local radio and television stations as well as newspaper representatives are to attend, newspapers have found it effective to have some of their outstanding editorial talent present. A few words from the chief editorial writer, a popular local columnist and perhaps the editor of the women's page will help salesmen to see that their company is buying more than white space when it takes advertising in the newspaper — it is buying the talent of fine writers who give the newspaper a distinctive personality and great reader appeal.

Keep Special Representative Informed

In this business of developing general advertising, another person to whom particular attention must be directed is the newspaper's special representative. Some newspapers pay little attention to him except to send him his check when commissions become due. They believe he knows his business, which is generally true, and that he can be left alone to do it. But how does he know when opportunities for advertising development in the newspaper's territory are springing up and what improvements the newspaper may be making in its plant to give better advertising service if the newspaper does not keep him informed?

A chatty letter from the advertising manager to the special representative, telling him that a new linotype is being installed at the newspaper, the town bank is expanding its building and 300 new homes are being erected in a new addition to the town, keeps the special representative mindful of his client and supplies him with some choice reinforcement for his sales talk when he presents the newspaper's claim for a place on the next schedule to be issued by an agency for an important item marketable in the newspaper's area. A monthly report, containing material of this kind, would be appreciated by any special representative.

Newspapers that have no special representatives but who depend upon their state or regional press associations to represent them in the national field also find it important to keep press associations fully informed concerning conditions in their home communities. They should supply information when it is requested and should voluntarily send promotional material to the press association.

Occasional visits by the special representative to the newspaper also are effective in keeping a line of contact between the newspaper office and distant prospects. An annual luncheon meeting of the special representative with the newspaper's local advertising salesmen helps to clear up misunderstandings that may exist regarding the treatment of general and local advertising and to determine what can be done locally to help the special representative sell more general advertising. Such a meeting, held at the newspaper plant, impresses upon the special representative the fact that he is a vital member of the newspaper's sales force.

Just as important as occasional visits by the special representative to the newspaper plant are visits by the publisher or advertising manager to the special representative's office or offices, usually in New York, Chicago, Detroit or Los Angeles. A visit to the New York office particularly is important because many orders go out to newspapers from advertising agencies located there. Several days may be profitably spent with the special representative in making calls on agencies.

Important To Call on Agencies

When a newspaper publisher, advertising manager or promotion manager calls on media directors of advertising agencies to present his claim for advertising, he helps not only himself but the newspaper profession in general. He helps to keep media departments mindful of newspapers as economical and effective means of carrying the advertiser's message directly to those in the home who buy for family needs.

The advent of television has brought new competition, whose claims for the advertiser's dollar are eloquently and forcefully presented. The newspaper's bid must be presented with full vigor and attractiveness. Important improvements in newspaper publishing have taken place in recent years to give added effectiveness. Newspapers that have substituted bright, new, more easily read type for the old type faces or have installed equipment to provide color printing, must pass along to prospective advertisers and those who prepare schedules the information that they are prepared to give this additional attractiveness to their news and advertising columns. Unless advertisers and advertising agencies are informed of these improvements, the old picture of inadequate and outmoded facilities remains before them.

The customary presentation of circulation figures and linage totals is not enough. Means should be provided for the space buyer to receive some intimate facts about the newspaper. Such an arrangement is as important to the newspaper as to the space buyer, and here is where a newspaper's promotion department is important.

Reach Advertising Executives Also

Already, it becomes evident that the promotion of general advertising requires thoroughness. A publisher or advertising manager generally feels he is well along the way to success when he has established an organized routine of contacting and selling local merchants and salesmen for national firms and advertising agencies. But the job really is not completed until advertising executives of manufacturers, wholesalers or jobbers are included among those to be called upon and informed regularly.

The man who directs the advertising of a manufacturing firm with items to sell in the newspaper's territory has a lot of questions he would like answered, such as: What other brands of the same item are offered in the newspaper's area? What stores have the greatest trade and would therefore be the best outlets for his product? On what days do people do most of their shopping? What are the prospects for population growth? To what lengths will the newspaper go to obtain dealer cooperation with the advertising? These are all matters of great importance to the prospective advertiser, and when satisfactory answers can be given, a newspaper stands a better chance of receiving schedules of advertising.

MUST PROMOTE BY MANY MEANS

To keep these various individuals and groups continually impressed with the newspaper's ability to create consumer demand in its area, a newspaper must do more than make personal contacts with them. Something needs to be done between calls to keep them mindful of the newspaper's ability to serve. Principal avenues for effective promotional contacts are:

1. Direct mail material
2. Advertising and news columns of trade journals
3. Radio and television
4. Bureau of Advertising
5. Press associations

Use Effective Direct Mail

To begin with, a newspaper should supply every advertising agency and prospective national advertiser with a convenient brochure containing facts concerning the newspaper's market. The American Association of Advertising Agencies and the Bureau of Advertising have devised a form that is followed by most newspapers. The size is 8½ x 11½ inches with a 1-inch strip on the back fold carrying the name of the town in which the newspaper is published.

On the front is a map of the area served by the newspaper (see Fig. 16.1). On the inside are listed the major towns of the area with populations, number of families, number employed, family buying income and amount of retail sales. Other facts include nationalities and ages of residents, number of families owning homes, number of homes with telephones, electricity, gas, radio, television, mechanical refrigeration, hot water service and central heating. It lists occupations, businesses and professions represented, total bank deposits, retail and wholesale sales, estimated total payroll, educational institutions, parks, recreation centers, churches, theaters, assessed valuation of real estate, tax rate, postal receipts, gross farm income, bank deposits, climate conditions, rates for light, power, heating and water.

Another folder to go inside this one should contain facts about the newspaper: its history, personnel, circulation, size, features and advertising rates.

Other material sent by the newspaper may be filed inside these so that the advertising agency or advertiser may be constantly accumulating and developing a better picture of the newspaper and its territory. Promotion material should contain convincing facts but it should have originality and humor to attract attention to it. Agencies are interested in other material beside circulation figures and linage totals. This was emphasized by A. G. Ensrud, media director of J. Walter Thompson Agency, in an address at a regional meeting of the National Newspaper Managers Association. He said that under ideal conditions a space buyer should know every newspaper in which he buys space as intimately as he knows the newspapers of his home town. Newspapers, he believed, should do a better job of presenting basic material, and should present also material that would reflect the influence of the newspaper on its readers and its community.

"The kind of space we buy is an intangible in itself — we cannot store it in a warehouse," he said, "and the intangible item of reader interest is the most important thing we buy."

To show national advertisers what type of people read the Memphis, Tenn., *Commercial Appeal* and *Press-Scimitar* (combined circulation 353,229, population 396,000), those newspapers took a map of Memphis and divided it into 14 districts. Then in superimposed

STANDARD MARKET DATA

FOR

FORT DODGE, IOWA

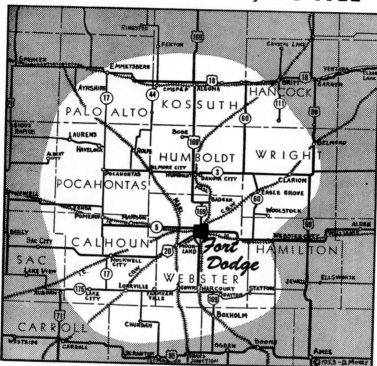

RETAIL TRADING ZONE . . .

The Fort Dodge Retail Trading Zone includes Calhoun, Humboldt, Pocahontas and Webster counties in their entirety; portions of Boone, Greene, Carroll, Hamilton, Hancock, Kossuth, Palo Alto, Sac and Wright counties, all in the state of Iowa, according to the June 30, 1953 report issued by the Audit Bureau of Circulations, Chicago.

Prepared with Approved Revisions in Conformity with Standard Market and Newspaper Data Forms of the
AMERICAN ASSOCIATION OF ADVERTISING AGENCIES and BUREAU OF ADVERTISING, A. N. P. A. by

FORT DODGE MESSENGER AND CHRONICLE

Messenger Founded 1856

REPRESENTED NATIONALLY BY JANN & KELLEY, INC.

Chronicle Founded 1884

MEMBER IOWA DAILY PRESS ASSOCIATION

Fig. 16.1 — Front page of Standard Market Data Form, featuring a map of retail trading zone reached daily by the Ft. Dodge, Iowa, **Messenger** and **Chronicle.**

Fig. 16.2 — Front page of a booklet for national advertisers put out by the Louisville, Ky., **Courier-Journal** and **Times** to show business expansion plans of 28 leading firms.

type they pointed out whether the districts were industrial, commercial or residential, how many newspaper reader families there were in each district, and what percentage of these read the *Commercial Appeal* and *Press-Scimitar* exclusively.

The Louisville, Ky., *Courier-Journal* and *Times* (combined circulation 392,224, population 369,129) put out a booklet showing plans for expansion by 28 leading business firms (see Fig. 16.2). This too was vital information for advertisers and undoubtedly found a permanent place in agency files.

When the Air Force base at Oklahoma City added 10,000 employees to bring the total employment to 23,093, thus making up the state's largest payroll, the Oklahoma City *Oklahoman* and *Times* (combined circulation 259,311, population 243,504) presented this information to national advertisers in an attractive folder. On its cover was a picture of air force bombers raining down dollar bills on mid-town Oklahoma City with the slogan "Oklahoma City Target for Three Million Dollars Every Other Friday." No better fact than this could be presented to stimulate advertising.

To reveal to national advertisers the reading preference of corporate officers and executive personnel, the *Wall Street Journal* (circulation 536,313, population 7,795,471) conducted a survey which showed that more of them read the *Journal* than the New York *Times*, *Time* magazine or *Life*. This high preference was a good selling point for the *Wall Street Journal* with top men of big business.

The Des Moines, Iowa, *Register* and *Tribune* (combined circulation 345,146, population 177,965) issues to agencies and national advertisers a weekly bulletin entitled "Iowa's Expanding Economy." One issue revealed that total construction contracts in Iowa for the year were 6 per cent ahead of the previous year. Iowa bank deposits were up 5.6 per cent, savings bond purchases topped the national state average and federal tax payments were 20 per cent ahead. Such facts keep before advertisers the picture of a healthy, growing community with money to spend for consumer wants and needs.

Direct mail may be used effectively by a newspaper of any size to carry important market information to prospective newspaper advertisers. Three weekly newspapers of suburban Philadelphia — the Ambler, Pa., *Gazette,* the Hatboro, Pa., *Public Spirit* and the Willow Grove, Pa., *Guide* (combined circulation 26,543, combined population 15,353) — set forth in attractive brochures and other mailing pieces their merits as advertising media for firms which desire to draw trade from their circulation areas.

On the front page of this folder in color is a photograph of three attractive young women sitting on a fence panel reading the three newspapers, and beneath the picture is the line, "Vital to Suburban Living."

You can sell it <u>everyday</u> in
The Cleveland PLAIN DEALER

The only Cleveland Newspaper that sells the city and the 26 adjacent counties

Here's how the Cleveland Market sells 4½ **billion dollars**

RETAIL SALES IN CLEVELAND AND ADJACENT COUNTIES*			
COMMODITY	CLEVELAND CUYAHOGA COUNTY (000)	26 ADJACENT COUNTIES (000)	TOTAL (000)
Total Retail Sales	2,247,897	1,999,804	4,247,701
Retail Food Sales	549,318	484,163	1,033,481
Retail Drug Sales	85,930	55,457	141,387
Automotive	382,082	390,920	773,002
Gas Stations	120,031	157,081	277,112
Furniture, Household Appliances	124,695	102,572	227,267
(Source, Sales Management Survey of Buying Power, May 10, 1957)			

*Akron, Canton and Youngstown's Counties are not included in above Sales.

Represented by Cresmer & Woodward, Inc., New York, Chicago, Detroit, Atlanta, San Francisco, Los Angeles. Member of Metro Sunday Comics and Magazine Network.

Fig. 16.3 — The Cleveland **Plain Dealer** takes a full page in **Editor & Publisher** to advertise its tremendous market area.

"Every hour one new family makes its home in our suburban area," begins the text which features a map of the area covered by these newspapers. Then it continues, "They become completely absorbed in a new pattern of living and each member of the family finds new friends. The axis of the earth for them goes through their own neighborhood. They are eager to know what is going on. They constantly consult the only media designed for them: the Ambler *Gazette*, the Hatboro *Public Spirit* and the Willow Grove *Guide*. A new concept of buying comes with this move to the suburbs. It's a concept that so many here have had for a long time...they count on one of these community newspapers for thorough reporting and complete shopping information. Take a long, keen, continuing look at maintaining your marketing momentum through these three accepted and trusted community newspapers. You'll find you'll get acceptance, coverage and retention and you'll become inextricably woven into the fabric of the lives of these people."

Advertise in Trade Journals

Trade journals are other effective media through which to promote newspaper advertising to manufacturers and wholesalers anxious to establish new outlets or increase sales in certain areas (see Fig. 16.3).

Industry's chief executives, advertising managers and advertising agency men read regularly the various magazines devoted to advertising. Such magazines as *Tide, Newspaper Rates and Data, Mediascope, Sales Management, Advertising Age, Printer's Ink, Western Advertising* and *Editor & Publisher* are good media for a newspaper to use in promoting its newspaper service to advertisers in the national field.

Tide, issued monthly, carries news regarding market conditions, sales promotion in various fields, new media trends and advertising results. Tying in with its advertising of newspapers, it provides reports from tape-recorded retail executive studies. This is objective and valuable in vividly portraying the complete image of the function performed by newspapers for national advertisers who must have a follow-through on their campaigns at the retail level.

Standard Rate & Data Service, Inc., is a national authority on media information pertaining to newspaper advertising. It sponsors two valuable publications — *Newspaper Rates and Data* and *Mediascope.* Its *Newspaper Rates and Data,* an authoritative and up-to-date classified directory of newspaper space-buying information, is found on the desk of every large advertiser or agency representative, accessible always for handy reference. It lists some 1200 daily and Sunday newspapers in the United States and its possessions, plus U.S. foreign-language newspapers, general and comic supplements, reli-

Fig. 16.4 — A cartoon enlivens a promotion advertisement used by the Atlantic City, N.J., **Press** in **Advertising Age.**

gious and Negro newspapers, suburban and community newspapers. Publishers have found it useful in comparing rates and services with other newspapers. *Mediascope*, issued monthly, deals particularly with media planning techniques and data, organization matters, general trends and prospects.

Sales Management, a monthly magazine for those in advertising sales and service, contains a wealth of information on markets. It issues an annual *Survey of Buying Power*, which is of great assistance in establishing sales quotas, analyzing markets and potentials, developing advertising appropriations and programming media. It is estimated that over $200 billion of goods and services are distributed annually by companies using the survey. A number of papers build their national sales stories on *Sales Management*'s projection of local market income, retail sales, population and buying power.

Advertising Age, a weekly business newspaper, covers the entire field of advertising and marketing. Its aim is to report developments and trends in the promotion programs of advertisers, with emphasis on marketing and advertising research, merchandising and media strategy, the role of advertising agencies and other significant facts concerning the operations of advertisers. In addition to sports news reporting, *Advertising Age* features a large group of commentators, most of them specialists who discuss copy, media, merchandising and

Fig. 16.5 — The Spokane, Wash., **Daily Chronicle** and **Spokesman-Review** advertise their market area in **Printer's Ink.**

other subjects of importance to advertising and marketing, many of them controversial. It contains also valuable statistical information regarding agency billings and expenditures.

Printer's Ink, which for many years has been a reliable source of information for advertisers, executives and publishers, is issued weekly. It presents the highlights of each advertising week, showing trends and developments in advertising, marketing and sales promotion. The services of advertising and the value of well-planned campaigns, with plenty of appropriate illustrations, are presented in this magazine.

Western Advertising is edited to appeal to all factors in the advertising industry, with particular emphasis on advertising agencies and advertising managers. The monthly edition of this magazine contains depth articles on advertising campaigns, marketing personalities and the various functions of advertising. A weekly news issue of eight to sixteen pages gives a brief summary of the preceding week's advertising developments in the West.

Editor & Publisher, the "newspaperman's bible," is another magazine read by industrial leaders and their advertising representatives as well as by publishers and editors. It carries news important to them: circulation figures, successful campaigns, merchandising policies and other vital facts connected with advertising in newspapers.

All of the above magazines are used effectively by newspapers in promoting their advertising service and in developing national advertising accounts (see Figs. 16.4, 16.5, 16.6 and 16.7).

Use Care in Preparing Copy

Promotion managers need to select their media and prepare their copy for promotion campaigns with the same care and skill that advertising agencies take in planning advertising for their clients. The promotion manager of a midwestern daily that drives hard for general advertising gave these suggestions to a group of newspapermen as a guide in planning advertising for trade papers:

A. *Define Your Objectives*
   1. Select a basic sales idea for your campaign and develop it dramatically, presenting in each advertisement a major reason why advertisers should use your paper.
   2. Once you have a basic sales idea and campaign theme, stay with it. It takes time for even an outstanding campaign theme to penetrate the consciousness of all your prospects. Don't succumb to "new-itis."

B. *Make Your Story Complete*
   The next step in planning an advertising campaign is deciding what to say. Tell them:
   1. The complete story of your circulation.
   2. Your coverage of your market.

3. Market data, so they can evaluate the importance of your market: retail sales in total and by product and brand, retail facilities, employment statistics, etc.
4. Your editorial objectives, methods and achievements.
5. A breakdown of your readers by age and sex, income levels, educational status, buying habits, home ownership, reading habits and loyalties.

NOW...MORE THAN EVER

SOLID CINCINNATI READS THE CINCINNATI ENQUIRER

Just ask your

MOLONEY, REGAN & SCHMITT

Representative

for the facts

Fig. 16.6 — In a **Mediascope** advertisement, the Cincinnati **Enquirer** uses few words in heavy type to stress its importance as a market place for national advertising.

6. Volume of advertising you carry, in total and by major classifications.
7. Advertising success stories.
8. Merchandising and promotion service you offer.
9. Rates and costs.
10. Your history and personnel.
11. Market and reader surveys available.

C. *Make Your Copy Specific*
1. Make your copy factual and interesting. Talk directly to your prospect (not down to him or up to him). Talk his language. Copy should never be hazy and should avoid purple passages.
2. Stress one sales point in each advertisement, but tell enough about that point so your reader will quickly understand what you are driving at.
3. Help your reader solve a problem by giving him useful information or helpful ideas. Emphasize what you can do for him, not what he can do for you.
4. Determine the length of your copy by your sales story, not by any arbitrary ideas of the relative merits of short or long copy.
5. Ask your reader to act; to write for literature or send in an order.

D. *Keep Your Prospect in Mind*
Remember that you are dealing with a professional group inclined to be overly critical of layout. So:
1. Use headlines that lead naturally and logically into the copy. Make the main point of your advertisement in the headline. Use stoppers, but don't leave your reader suspended in midair; carry him easily into the copy.
2. Use honest, dramatic and convincing pictures that illustrate your sales story, not just ornament it.
3. Select type faces for easy reading and clean appearance.
4. Use color when it contributes to the sales story, not merely to make the advertisement pretty.
5. Have your layout make the advertisement easy to read and understand with headline, illustration, copy and typography in unity.
6. A family resemblance in the advertisements of the campaign will make a greater impact on the reader. Get that resemblance by effective use of headline, layout, picture treatment, typography and logotype.

E. *Give Sales Support to Advertising*
1. Mail reprints of ads in campaign to those on prospect list and in sales organization.
2. Make reprints of all advertising a definite part of salesmen's kits so they can leave them with customers and prospects they call on.

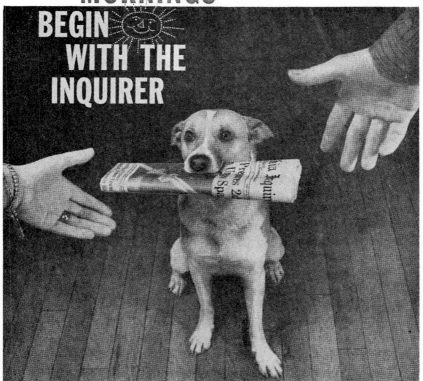

GOOD MORNINGS BEGIN WITH THE INQUIRER

DOGS' BEST FRIENDS are a majority in Inquirer families. Take the case of the foundling Fidos at the City Pound. Each year, on page three, The Inquirer sponsors a campaign themed: "Adopt a Dog for Christmas." And how the readers of this newspaper respond! For The Inquirer awakens emotions as well as minds. It, frankly, tugs at heartstrings . . . inspires its readers, as it informs, amuses and entertains them. Such a climate provides a welcome atmosphere for advertising. And advertisers know it well . . . have made The Inquirer first choice in Delaware Valley, for 24 consecutive years!

The Philadelphia Inquirer
Constructively Serving Delaware Valley, U. S. A.

NEW YORK	CHICAGO	DETROIT	SAN FRANCISCO	LOS ANGELES
ROBERT T. DEVLIN, JR.	EDWARD J. LYNCH	RICHARD I. KRUG	FITZPATRICK ASSOCIATES	FITZPATRICK ASSOCIATES
342 Madison Ave.	20 N. Wacker Drive	Penobscot Bldg.	155 Montgomery St.	3460 Wilshire Boulevard
Murray Hill 2-5838	Andover 3-6270	Woodward 5-7260	Garfield 1-7946	Dunkirk 5-3557

Delaware Valley, U.S.A.—14 county Retail Trading Area . . . home of 5,200,000 people . . . Philadelphia is the hub.

Fig. 16.7 — The Philadelphia **Inquirer** instills some human interest into its promotion advertisement in **Sales Management.**

3. Post proofs of all ads used in campaign on bulletin boards in sales offices of advertisers and in advertising directors' offices. This reminds salesmen of promotional activity and will impress visitors.
4. Reproduce advertisements in house organ.

F. *Check Results of Promotion Campaign*
Find out from available sources the benefits derived from campaign. Check:

1. Recognition of your newspaper before and after campaign.
2. Recognition of your theme after advertising appeared.
3. Number and quality of inquiries and traceable sales.

Most advertising men will find time to read a well-written, attractive advertisement about a newspaper. They are glad to learn something new about any medium that absorbs thousands of their dollars. None of them will willingly read something they already know, or something that doesn't matter. They are interested in good copy and good promotion because these are parts of their business.

When Leo McGivena was called upon to handle an advertising campaign in trade journals for the New York *Daily News* (circulation 2,056,521, population 7,795,471) he decided that the advertising should be timely, lively and newsy. There would be no conventional series, written and okayed months before publication. If possible, each ad would be as fresh and timely as the current issue of the newspaper it promoted. McGivena said he wanted to give the *News* character, to make more advertisers more conscious of the *News*, to provide them greater knowledge and understanding of the newspaper.

Following the announcement of his aim, he began work on copy. He explained some of the ways in which the *News* gets close to the people of New York. Statistical material was presented in an interesting as well as informative way. The size of circulation, though immense, was not as impressive as the fact that every day more than 2 million people came up to the newsstands, laid down their money and walked away with the *News*. The campaign gave advertising men a keener sense of the *News* as a vital advertising medium and provided a good pattern for other newspapers planning to promote their advertising services in trade journals.

To show advertisers that it circulates in a community where business is good, the Macon, Ga., *Telegraph* and *News* (combined circulation 62,151, population 70,252) prepared and ran in trade publications a series of advertisements containing statements by leading Macon businessmen (see Fig. 16.8). "Business Is Good in Macon, Georgia" was the headline for each testimonial. These ads were reproduced on 8 x 11 enamel sheets and enclosed in a jacket on the face of which appeared pictures of six Macon business executives. This presentation of how they felt about the Macon market was sent to leading advertising agencies and executives. The follow-up ad in a trade journal was a full page entitled "Everything's 'Peachy' in Middle Georgia" (see Fig. 16.9).

Fig. 16.8 — A prominent businessman endorses a promotion advertisement of the Macon, Ga., **Telegraph** and **News** showing that business is good in their area.

Where CIRCULATION and PAYROLLS keep GOING UP

CONSISTENT, CONTINUOUS GAINS EVERY YEAR
Bring the Macon Market and the Macon Newspapers
hand-in-hand to the FOREMOST POSITION IN GEORGIA!

Check these MACON Sales Points:

★ Trading center for 28 Counties in Rich Middle Georgia
★ 487,800 POPULATION
★ $520,679,000 Effective Buying Power
★ $370,563,000 Retail Sales
★ $79,000,000 annual payroll employing 18,000
    (Warner Robins—Largest Military Payroll in Georgia)
★ Four New Banks opened in 1957
   72% increase in Deposits in Five Years
    (Estimates from 1957 Sales Management)

You can

COVER MIDDLE GEORGIA

only with the . . .

MACON TELEGRAPH and MACON NEWS
MORNING SUNDAY EVENING
National Representative: THE BRANHAM CO.

Fig. 16.9 — The Macon **Telegraph** and **News** carry their enthusiastic promotion to the national market with an advertisement in **Editor & Publisher**.

"We do not have a large budget for promotion," says Hugh P. Harper, promotion manager, "but we are represented in all the trade publications that are used by media men. Because of this consistent advertising program we were able to show increases while other newspapers 'talked recession.' Yes, it pays to advertise your own newspaper."

The Joplin, Mo., *Globe* and *News-Herald* (combined circulation 42,455, population 38,711) let manufacturers, distributors and advertising agencies know it was ready to answer all their questions regarding the Joplin market when it provided for them an attractive 4-page "question and answer" folder loaded with vital information. With a piercing glance directed straight at the reader, the intent businessman on the cover raised the oft-quoted query, "Are you from Missouri?" (see Fig. 16.10), while the inside pages continued the "Show Me" theme by analyzing the Joplin market as to extent of territory, business volumes in various classifications, industrial developments, newspaper circulation and the like. Copies of this went directly to sources of national advertising.

The Mount Holly, N. J., *Herald* (circulation 10,474, population 8,206), one of the enterprising weeklies of the eastern states, goes after general advertising as persistently as a metropolitan newspaper. It gives manufacturers, wholesalers and advertising agencies full facts concerning its trade area (see Fig. 16.11).

Might Use Television and Radio

Not many newspapers make use of television or radio to promote their advertising services to national firms, but there are good possibilities in that field, according to Newman F. McEvoy, medium director for Cunningham & Walsh, Inc.

McEvoy believes that newspapers may give important aid to their national advertising staffs by using television along with newspapers, trade journals and direct mail. TV advertising is good, he says, and so is newspaper advertising, and when used together they add strength to each other. He believes that publishers should attempt to obtain tie-in advertising in their newspapers for everything that goes on television.

"If I were a newspaper publisher," he said in *Editor & Publisher*,[1] "I would study TV in my city very carefully and make suggestions to advertising agencies for areas where any TV program needs extra support. I would horn in on every promotion device running on TV so that every deal (10¢ off, 2-for-1, money back offers, etc.) which was broadcast on TV would hopefully be made available to my readers.

---

[1] *Editor & Publisher,* July 12, 1958, p. 10.

are you from Missouri?

Fig. 16.10 — "We're ready to show you," says the Joplin **Globe** and **News-Herald** from the "Show Me" state.

"Newspapers alone, as we all know, can do a superb job. However, they might be regarded as a STATIC medium in contrast to the dramatic action of television. Again critically we might say that, although television is a FAST ACTION medium, its message evaporates all too quickly in the flood of competing TV messages. A little more positively...we might say that a hardworking combination for the advertiser is the reference ability of the newspaper AND the dynamic quality of television. Consider a typical package goods promotion...it can be sold dramatically on TV, and newspapers can literally nail it down locally."

A publisher should never allow his competitive feelings toward television and radio to prevent him from using those media to promote his own business when it seems advantageous to do so. Although it seems unlikely, there may be areas best reached by radio or television in the promotion of a newspaper's advertising service.

Bureau of Advertising Always Helpful

Another helpful ally of newspapers in promoting general advertising is the Bureau of Advertising of the American Newspaper Publishers Association. Through its careful analysis of newspaper influence and its selling of newspaper advertising in the national field, it has brought to newspaper advertising high respect and constantly increasing recognition. The success of newspapers and the help they receive from the Bureau of Advertising have long been the outspoken envy of the radio and television industries.

When the Bureau of Advertising launched its sales efforts in the national field, it turned its guns first on the top 100 national advertisers, many of whom afterward made newspapers their major advertising medium. Soon it launched another offensive to sell newspapers as a national medium on the local front. In a booklet entitled "More Profit From National Advertising," it outlined a sharply stepped-up program of research, sales and promotion material for newspapers' local use.

The work of the bureau since has been notable in the production of a steadily growing reservoir of sales ammunition. Extremely helpful to newspapers have been:

1. Data concerning consumption of different grocery, drug, toilet and household products in various areas of the country.
2. Studies of month-by-month and year-by-year sales and preference trends and distribution of brands.
3. A continuing study of newspaper reading.
4. Information on how much various types of business should invest in advertising and how the expenditures should be budgeted.
5. Studies regarding retail classifications and a wealth of statistical information on the planning of seasonal advertising programs.
6. Business-building bulletins to arouse the interest of the legal profession and security dealers in local national advertising.
7. A directory of research studies conducted by American daily newspapers.
8. An index to county markets and media data.

The availability of these data through the bureau has provided an exceptionally effective promotional tool for newspapers.

MOUNT HOLLY HERALD
LINEAGE CHART

POPULATION
GROWTH
Burlington County
New Jersey
1940-1960

MOUNT HOLLY HERALD
Circulation Chart

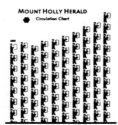

POPULATION AND TRADE

	Mount Holly City Zone	Retail Trading Zone	Mount Holly and Trading Area
POPULATION			
Total—Special Census Report—	8,206	31,961	40,167
FAMILIES	2,355	8,360	10,175
Families Owning Homes	1,370	5,666	7,036
Families Renting Homes	985	2,694	3,679
AUTOMOBILES (Registrations)	3,625	12,050	15,675
TELEPHONES	2,826	10,032	12,858
BANKS	2	7	9
Deposits	$15,503,000	$38,661,000	$54,164,000
RETAIL TRADE:			
Number Retail Establishments—	124	310	434
Number Employees—	390	960	1,350
Annual Retail Sales—	$14,324,000	$26,876,000	$41,200,000
Annual Retail Sales—	$16,093,000	$28,972,000	$45,065,000

ROSS ANDERSON SURVEYS — ASK FOR MORE DETAILS

ANNUAL FAMILY EXPENDITURES

	Per Family	Mount Holly City Zone	Retail Trading Zone	Mount Holly and Trading Area	Readers of The Herald
TOTAL ANNUAL					
EXPENDITURE	$4,697.00	$11,061,000	$39,267,000	$50,328,000	$42,014,000
Food	1,521.00	3,582,000	12,716,000	16,298,000	13,605,000
Apparel—Including Footwear	537.00	1,265,000	4,489,000	5,754,000	4,803,000
Household—Including Services	514.00	1,210,000	4,297,000	5,507,000	4,598,000
Fuel, Light, Refrigeration	206.00	485,000	1,722,000	2,207,000	1,843,000
Housing and Maintenance	522.00	1,229,000	4,364,000	5,593,000	4,669,000
Miscellaneous	1,397.00	3,290,000	11,679,000	14,969,000	12,496,000
GENERAL MERCHANDISE					
TOTAL	540.00	$1,271,000	$4,514,000	$5,875,000	$4,830,000
Department	330.00	777,000	2,759,000	3,536,000	2,952,000
Dry Goods and General	126,000	297,000	1,053,000	1,350,000	1,127,000
Variety	84,00	197,000	702,000	899,000	751,000
AUTOMOTIVE TOTAL	$832.00	$1,960,000	$6,955,000	$8,915,000	$7,442,000
Motor Vehicles—Total	698.00	1,644,000	5,835,000	7,479,000 •	6,244,000
New Cars	458.00	1,079,000	3,829,000	4,908,000	4,097,000
Used Cars	170.00	400,000	1,421,000	1,821,000	1,521,000
Trucks—New Only	70.00	165,000	585,000	750,000	626,000
Accessories and Parts Total	104.00	245,000	869,000	1,144,000	930,000
Tires, Replacement—Total	30.00	71,000	251,000	322,000	268,000
GASOLINE AND OIL—TOTAL	270.00	636,000	2,257,000	2,893,000	2,415,000

ROSS ANDERSON SURVEYS — ASK FOR MORE DETAILS

MOUNT HOLLY HERALD KEEPS PACE!

Fig. 16.11 — This New Jersey weekly attractively displays statistics to prove the steadily expanding markets of its trade area.

Cooperation With Press Associations Important

And while considering organizations that may be helpful, state and regional press associations must not be overlooked. Small newspapers have found them exceedingly beneficial in developing newspaper advertising in the national field. A wide-awake press association provides an easy, effective and economical way of promoting the market areas of weeklies and small dailies. It not only issues attractive material concerning the markets served by its newspaper members, but it places advertising, gathers tear sheets and sends one invoice for all newspapers to each advertiser who accepts the blanket coverage provided. The advertiser or its agency then can pay for advertising in all state papers with one check mailed to the press association. For example, the Missouri Press Association will accept and fully process one space order for advertising in its 394 daily and weekly newspaper members and accept a single check in payment. When the remittance has been made by the advertiser to the press association, the association in turn issues individual checks to the newspapers which carried the advertising.

Promotion material put out by a press association usually includes:

1. A folder explaining the newspapers' market and coverage (see Fig. 16.12).
2. A pamphlet describing the cooperation given advertising by newspapers carrying schedules.
3. A directory of newspapers belonging to the press association. This gives the circulations, rates, days of publication, page sizes and names of publishers.
4. A map showing the location of each newspaper and how, as a group, they cover the state.

These are the customary means employed to promote newspaper advertising to manufacturers, wholesale firms, jobbers and others who seek wide distribution for their goods.

POINTS TO BE EMPHASIZED

The media and means to be employed in promoting national advertising in the national field and the persons to whom such promotion should be particularly directed have been discussed in the preceding sections of this chapter. Remaining still to be outlined and discussed are the points that should be given particular emphasis in a newspaper's efforts to draw advertising from firms seeking additional outlets and greater sales for their manufactured products. A few of these already have been touched upon, but their importance warrants

why **MISSOURI** newspapers

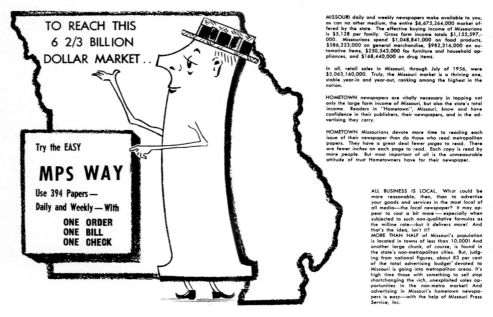

TO REACH THIS
6 2/3 BILLION
DOLLAR MARKET...

Try the EASY

MPS WAY

Use 394 Papers —

Daily and Weekly — With

ONE ORDER
ONE BILL
ONE CHECK

MISSOURI daily and weekly newspapers make available to you, as can no other medium, the *entire* $6,675,264,000 market offered by the state. The effective buying income of Missourians is $5,128 per family. Gross farm income totals $1,155,597,-000. Missourians spend $1,048,841,000 on food products, $586,223,000 on general merchandise, $982,316,000 on automotive items, $250,543,000 for furniture and household appliances, and $168,440,000 on drug items.

In all, retail sales in Missouri, through July of 1956, were $5,063,160,000. Truly, the Missouri market is a thriving one, stable year-in and year-out, ranking among the highest in the nation.

HOMETOWN newspapers are vitally necessary in tapping not only the large farm income of Missouri, but also the state's total income. Readers in "Hometown", Missouri, know and have confidence in their publishers, their newspapers, and in the advertising they carry.

HOMETOWN Missourians devote *more time* to reading each issue of their newspaper than do those who read metropolitan papers. They have a great deal *fewer pages* to read. There are *fewer inches* on each page to read. Each copy is read by *more people*. But most important of all is the unmeasurable attitude of *trust* Hometowners have for their newspaper.

ALL BUSINESS IS LOCAL. What could be more reasonable, then, than to advertise your goods and services in the *most local* of all media—the *local newspaper*? It may appear to cost a bit more — especially when subjected to such non-qualitative formulas as the milline rate—but it *delivers more!* And that's the idea, isn't it?
MORE THAN HALF of Missouri's population is located in towns of less than 10,000! And another large chunk, of course, is found in the state's non-metropolitan cities. But, judging from national figures, about 83 per cent of the total advertising budget devoted to Missouri is going into metropolitan areas. It's high time those with something to sell stop shortchanging the *rich, unexploited* sales opportunities in the *non-metro market!* And advertising in Missouri's hometown newspapers is *easy*—with the help of Missouri Press Service, Inc.

Fig. 16.12 — Outside of folder put out by the Missouri Press Association to emphasize the value of Missouri papers as desirable media for national advertising.

further discussion. There are at least five such points to be emphasized:

1. The newspaper's market.
2. The newspaper's coverage of its market.
3. The merchandising service offered by the newspaper.
4. The use of color in making newspaper ads attention-compelling.
5. The flexibility of newspaper advertising.

Must Sell the Market

A manufacturer must, first of all, be sure there is a market for his product in the newspaper's territory before he will consider the placing of advertising in the newspaper. Therefore, great emphasis is always placed on the newspaper's market in any attempt to obtain general advertising.

"Iowans have money; they'll spend it," said the Des Moines, Iowa, *Register* and *Tribune* in an attractive 2-color mailing piece at the beginning of the vacation period. That statement was supported with the following facts to show further that conditions were right for the sale of vacation goods in Iowa:

> ...Bank deposits in Iowa total more than two and a quarter billion dollars.

> ...The number of visitors to Iowa state parks increased from 2½ million to nearly 7 million since 1949.

> ...Nearly 60 per cent of Iowa families will take vacations during the year.

> ...Land-locked Iowa is only 35th in the nation in water area, but Iowa is ninth in the per capita use and purchase of outboard motors.

> ...Iowans, aged 12 and over, each year spend 28½ million dollars for fishing...14 million for hunting.

> ...Iowa boasts more Izaak Walton League members than any other state.

> ...As in other urban centers, Iowa cities' suburbs are growing fast; suburban area growths as high as 400 per cent have taken place.

Such information left no doubt in the minds of national advertisers that outdoor living was big business in Iowa (see Fig. 16.13).

Coverage Also Is Vital

When a manufacturer is convinced that there is an available market for his product in a certain area, he wants next to know what is the best media to use in convincing residents of the quality of his product and their need for it. He wants to know how well the newspaper covers that market.

"Coverage of the market and quality of the coverage are the most important factors for an advertiser to consider in making up his schedule," said Fred Barrett, an outstanding media director, in a panel discussion sponsored by *Advertising Agency Magazine*. And Gordon Buck, another well-known media director, added as other vital factors: "Distribution profiles, same for product merchandising support, retail advertising by retailers carrying the product, duplication with competitors and other media, and cost per thousand."

Of all factors to be considered in selecting an advertising medium, nothing is of greater importance than coverage of the market. The Des Moines *Register* and *Tribune* spends thousands of dollars annually to promote its "intensive, penetrating market coverage." It and the Kansas City, Mo., *Star* and *Times* (combined circulation 663,656, population 456,622) claim delivery to virtually 100 per cent of the homes in their metropolitan areas. The Santa Cruz, Calif., *Sentinel* (circulation 14,030, population 21,970) claims it reaches 93 per cent of the families living in its trading area.

Fig. 16.13 — Page from material put out to promote advertising vacation merchandise in the Outdoor Living Issue of the Des Moines **Register** and **Tribune**.

Community growth and circulation increase both bring a newspaper into favor as an advertising medium. Therefore, when Broward County, in which the Fort Lauderdale, Fla., *News* (circulation 53,491, population 62,906) is published, recaptured its lead in the Florida population sweepstakes, the newspaper, to be sure, let this fact be known to prospective advertisers. It ran a display advertisement headed "Population Gain Here Tops State" in its own columns, then had reprints of it made to mail to national advertisers and advertising agencies. Another mailing featured the newspaper's growth in circulation. An increase of 155 per cent in 6½ years made an excellent promotion story.

Merchandising Service Is Expected

Important also in the development of general advertising is the merchandising cooperation given to advertising by the newspaper's advertising and promotion departments. Anything the newspaper can do to bring local selling support to products advertised in its columns helps keep advertisers satisfied users of newspaper space.

The Santa Cruz, Calif., *Sentinel,* three times a first award winner in state merchandising contests and a certificate of merit winner in *Editor & Publisher*'s 23rd Annual Newspaper Promotion Contest, presented its merchandising story and some pertinent facts concerning its advertising services in an attractive 4-page folder, which it handed out to sales representatives when they came to the newspaper's office (see Fig. 16.14). Copies were mailed or delivered in person also to key personnel and selected agencies by the newspaper's special representative. Fifteen hundred copies were produced and the total cost, including pictures and printing, was under $200, according to Norman L. Powell, advertising director. Several sizable schedules for the newspaper were traced to this promotion.

The following ten salient points in the *Sentinel*'s merchandising program evidently are what made this a successful effort:

1. When a national schedule is received by the *Sentinel*, the merchandising wheels begin to turn.
2. Jumbo postcards announcing campaigns and national ads are prepared and mailed to retail outlets in the Santa Cruz trading area. Specific features of the advertising campaign are stressed, along with information regarding availability of tie-in mats and cooperative allowances.
3. Tie-in proof sheets showing all the tie-in mats available for a national product are personally given to the advertising manager or owner of retail outlets who regularly advertise in the *Sentinel.*

4. "Advertising News," an editorial column, is available to advertisers for news items concerning their products, promotions, premium offers and personnel. There is no charge for this well-read *Sentinel* feature.

5. An up-to-date grocery-drug route list is available for the asking. Revised yearly, this handy pocket-sized booklet includes address, phone, name of owner or manager, size of store and whether or not it is a regular *Sentinel* advertiser.

6. Surveys are conducted by staff members of the *Sentinel* for store distribution, sales and brand preference of products. There is no charge for this service, which is available to *Sentinel* advertisers upon request.

7. Point-of-sale displays are set up with the cooperation of the *Sentinel* and the store.

8. Colorful "As Advertised in the Santa Cruz *Sentinel*" shelf and display cards are distributed to local retail advertisers. A large space on the card is left open for product and price. Retail advertisers are urged to feature nationally advertised products on these cards.

9. A bonus is awarded to each salesman who obtains tie-ins for national advertisements scheduled for the newspaper.

10. Tear sheets of tie-ins for advertised products are sent monthly to the *Sentinel*'s national representatives and are available to agencies and companies through them. Free tear sheets are also available in a file located in the display advertising department of the *Sentinel*.

A newspaper's promotion department can well afford the giving of time to induce local merchants to display items nationally advertised, particularly those featured in the paper's own columns. It can help to obtain counter and window displays and to line up the store's sales force behind the advertised items. It can keep the advertising manufacturer informed regarding the quantities of his goods stocked in local stores.

The Bureau of Advertising gives valuable assistance to newspapers in keeping local dealers informed concerning additional results to be obtained from cooperation with newspaper advertising. It has available to newspapers for use before local groups a 20-minute color slide presentation specifically tailored for showing to the field sales force of a packaged goods manufacturer running a newspaper campaign. It shows how salesmen may increase their sales totals by inducing dealers to put up and keep up more displays and to stock more of the product.

Other important presentations provided by the Bureau of Advertising are entitled "The Daily Newspaper: Its Influence on American Life and Business," "This Little Product Goes to Market," and "What Happens When Newspapers Don't Hit Town." Each shows why manufacturers may safely depend on newspapers to build and maintain public acceptance of their products.

3 Time Winner!
BEST NATIONAL
MERCHANDISING

In state-wide competition, the Santa Cruz Sentinel has earned first award
for Best National Merchandising for three consecutive years.

Above is pictured some of the plaques awarded to the Santa Cruz
Sentinel for advertising excellence. At right, the awards most
coveted by any newspaper . . . Best National Merchandising
The Santa Cruz Sentinel has won this award three years in a row.

We Merchandise Your Advertising..

HERE'S WHAT HAPPENS WHEN YOUR PRODUCT
IS ADVERTISED IN THE SANTA CRUZ SENTINEL

Fig. 16.14 — Front page of folder prepared by the Santa Cruz, Calif., **Sentinel**
proving its excellence in merchandising.

Demand for Color Increasing

Color in advertising, a service now provided by most daily newspapers, has been another strong factor in obtaining general advertising for newspapers. Interview data disclose a ratio of 3 to 1 in favor of color over black-and-white when it comes to a direct question of response to advertising. The demand for color is becoming so great, in fact, that the day is approaching when new achievements in newsprint textures, inks, plating, engraving and high speed press work will furnish an ROP color product not unlike that of the glossy magazines.

When a newspaper can reproduce for a manufacturer in his advertising the brand name used on all his products in actual color, newspaper readers are brought much nearer to buying the product than if the ad were simply in black and white. The inviting and convincing words of the advertisement are instantly revived in memory when the item is observed in stock at stores where readers do their shopping.

Therefore, newspapers that are equipped to produce advertising in color have an important item to promote. By means of color they are able to obtain some schedules of general advertising that otherwise might not be obtainable.

"Color moves people," says the Columbus, Ohio, *Dispatch* (circulation 181,410, population 375,901) in a promotion advertisement. "It adds that extra punch to make sales objectives and quotas easier. That's why year after year the volume of color advertising in the *Dispatch* grows! We're so positive of the future of color advertising that we have made a long-range investment in the most modern high-speed color presses...and the buildings to house the equipment" (see Fig. 16.15).

"Color packs the wallop of a shillelagh," adds the Washington, D. C., *Post* and *Times Herald* (circulation 390,104, population 802,178). "In city after city across the nation split run tests, coupon returns and advertiser comments bear out the fact that ROP newspaper color packs a mighty wallop. Color increases readership by 50 per cent to 150 per cent and, in some cases, better than 200 per cent over black-and-white for only slight additional cost."

Realizing the importance of color in newspaper printing, the Buffalo, N. Y., *News* (circulation 287,446, population 580,132) pioneered in a new concept of color printing when it erected its new $8,000,000 plant in 1958. By means of "right angle placement" of printing units, color is possible on eight pages anywhere from the first to the last page. New flexibility was attained by placing a color printing unit and its companion black ink printing unit at right angles to lines of other printing units, with a folder on each side. Choice of

Fig. 16.15 — The Columbus, Ohio, **Dispatch** demonstrates its faith in the future of color advertising with a colorful ad of its own.

position for color pages is made with the use of an angle-bar roller that can be set to take the web of newsprint from the color unit to the folder at any desired page location. In providing for advertisers this timely service, the *News* deserves wide publicity and promotion.

Flexibility a Great Newspaper Asset

Another point favorable to newspaper advertising that has not been adequately featured in the promotion of general advertising is a newspaper's flexibility and ready adaptability to seasons of the year, competitive situations and geographic variation in market and brand potential.

Richard Blun in *Advertising Agency Magazine* laments the tendency of national advertisers to become stereotyped in their use of newspaper advertising. There has been little apparent inclination to explore the manifold possibilities inherent in the very nature of the medium.

"The physical nature of the newspaper, the composition of its audience, and the manner in which its widely varied audience approaches it, provide almost unlimited opportunity for 'beamed' copy appeals, for change of pace, for purposeful variations in size," Blun adds.

"In a newspaper, the variety of editorial content — whether its news matter or features — reflects the variety of life itself. In its relationship to the reader, the newspaper is a constant friend providing timely information on virtually every phase of any reader's interest and daily activity. And in fulfilling this function, the newspaper also forms a common denominator for family and community values: The interest standards, living habits and desires of the local community and its place in regional and national communities."[2]

Although not so readily inclined, weekly newspapers are in as good a position as daily newspapers to give service to national advertisers. By their own efforts, they may increase their national linage. Alan R. McGinnis, chairman of the board of Klau-Van Pieterson-Dunlap, largest advertising agency in Wisconsin, told members of the Wisconsin Press Association: "For years I have carefully watched and studied readership of country weeklies and have made a number of mental and statistical comparisons between their readership and other media that are circulated for the hundreds of thousands. It is my opinion, although not officially documented, that subscribers of weekly newspapers will come closer to being cover-to-cover readers than those of any other printed medium available."

Success in developing national advertising requires promotion of a newspaper's market and coverage, its ability to make advertising attractive, its willingness to give liberal merchandising service and its adaptability to all situations that may affect sales. This must be done over a wide area in a variety of media.

---

[2] *Advertising Agency Magazine,* Oct. 25, 1957, p. 2.

PART IV

Promoting the Newspaper's Circulation

CHAPTER 17

Promoting
Circulation by Mail

MANY NEWSPAPERS HAVE FOUND promotion by mail to be an effective means of building circulation. However, in order to obtain maximum returns, special care must be used in compiling a current mailing list, in preparing copy and in mailing the material at timely periods. There are three questions to be answered, and this is the logical order:

1. Who may be best persuaded by mail solicitation?
2. How should copy be prepared to produce prompt results?
3. When is the best time to make mailings to prospective subscribers?

GROUPS BEST REACHED BY MAIL

Every publisher should have a mailing list that includes the names of all persons in his newspaper's area who are not subscribers — a list of prospects to whom he may send attractive announcements and appeals with the intention of winning them as regular readers. Mailings should go to them at specific intervals, and extra mailings should be made whenever the newspaper begins a new feature, institutes a new type face or adds a section. Direct mail will wonderfully reinforce the selling efforts of salesmen and carriers. To compile an accurate, complete mailing list and keep it alive and up to date is quite a task, requiring constant and careful attention, but it pays well for the effort expended.

Mail solicitation may be applied in promoting circulation to all

[243]

classes of readers but it is more successfully applied in obtaining subscriptions from:

1. Farmers and other rural residents.
2. Former residents.
3. Vacationists.
4. Servicemen.
5. College students.
6. Newlyweds.

How To Obtain Rural Subscribers

The newspaper that doesn't cultivate the friendship and support of rural residents is missing a good opportunity to build circulation. Here is a class of people who appreciate attention and deserve it. They are easily reached and persuaded through mail solicitation.

Wallace Seigenthaler, circulation director of the Nashville, Tenn., *Banner* and *Tennessean* (combined circulation 220,617, population 174,307) pointed out this potential newspaper market to circulation managers at a convention in Shreveport, La. "We have never given mail circulation the consideration it rightly deserves," he said. "We have treated it as a sort of balancer. If we lost a thousand on carrier delivery, we would work up some kind of a special offer to farmers and bring the total back by mail. This meager and intermittent consideration is an indictment against us. We need to reach a standard for mail circulation promotion as we have done for other branches of our business." He contended also that publishers have not fully appreciated farmers as newspaper readers. "The day of the hick farmer is gone," he added. "Those folks out there on the farm are pretty much the same as the folks on Main Street."

The mailing of sample copies to all rural route boxholders at least once a year is certainly a worthwhile project. Somewhere in the issue thus mailed should be a strong promotion advertisement explaining what the newspaper offers from day to day or week to week of special interest to rural dwellers. An order blank should appear in a corner of the ad to be conveniently clipped out, filled in and mailed. A personal letter from the editor or publisher to each boxholder, preceding the mailing of the sample copy or immediately afterward, would add still more to the effectiveness of the promotion.

The Eau Claire, Wis., *Leader* and *Telegram* (combined circulation 25,792, population 36,058) have been unusually successful in building rural circulation by mail. After several experiments, they have developed a system that yields a 2 per cent return or better and adds approximately 1,500 subscribers per year.

In August, 1955, Willard Tomashek, circulation manager, sent a 25,000 boxholder mailing within a radius of 60 miles of Eau Claire. This brought in 548 new subscribers and 122 renewals. In November another mailing went to the same boxholders and this added 533 more new subscribers and 118 renewals. In February, 1956, another mailing returned 522 new subscribers and 123 renewals. Again the next year similar mailings were made with satisfactory results.

The mailings gave readers an opportunity to receive the *Leader* or *Telegram* for two weeks free if they subscribed immediately. They further offered a 13-month subscription for the yearly rate of $9, 8 months for the 6-month rate of $5, and 5 weeks for the monthly rate of $1.

"We worded the offer in terms of 'from now' until a certain date and it drew quick response," says Mr. Tomashek. "The offer's pulling power was also increased by giving readers a choice of rates. The offer was enclosed in a No. 10 Kraft window envelope. 'Coupon Enclosed' was printed under the window. The 3-part mailing cost $3,300 a year." [1]

"GET ACQUAINTED" OFFERS

Sometimes a special "get acquainted" offer to rural prospects brings quick and satisfactory returns. The Cleveland, Ohio, *Plain*

Fig. 17.1 — Direct mail promotion makes it easy for rural residents to become subscribers of the Cleveland, Ohio, **Plain Dealer.**

The CLEVELAND PLAIN DEALER

Good Reading for ALL the Family!

FOR MOTHER	FOR DAD	FOR BOYS and GIRLS
HELEN ROBERTSON for meal-planning ideas and tasty recipes	GORDON COBBLEDICK nationally recognized sports writer	ASK ANDY Inquisitive dwarf with a giant's mind
CECIL RELIHAN advises on home furnishing and decoration	JAMES E. DOYLE conductor of rib-tickling Sports Trail	UNCLE RAY'S CORNER constructive fun every day
LOUISE DAVIS the last word on Cleveland society	JOHN BRYAN authority on Cleveland's business activity	YOUNG HOBBY CLUB youngsters learn by doing
ELIZABETH BIRKLEY complete coverage of women's clubs	WILLIAM F. McDERMOTT the world is his playground	JUNIOR EDITORS interesting and instructive coloring series
WINIFRED GOODSELL for years the authority on fashions	PHILIP W. PORTER people, politics, prudence	BOYS AND GIRLS PAGE youth finds its voice on Saturday

It's just too good to miss!

IMAGINE! The PLAIN DEALER

6 DAYS-A-WEEK

Only **25c**

↓ FILL OUT THE CARD BELOW AND MAIL IT—NOW! NO STAMP IS NECESSARY ↓

Motor Route Manager:

Please enter my subscription to

☐ The Daily and Sunday Plain Dealer at 45c per week

☐ The Daily only Plain Dealer at 25c per week

The Daily delivered by mail—the Sunday by automobile.

Name_____

Road_____

City_____ R. F. D._____

I understand that the carrier will collect each Sunday via the envelope system please provide a receipt card.

---

[1] *Publication Management*, Sept., 1958, p. 46.

**WE REPORT
THIS AREA
EVERY WEEK
WATCH FOR IT**

Exclusive News

**FROM YOUR AREA
EVERY WEEK**

News about your church, local gov't,
social affairs, new babies, new
residents, etc.

**THIS IS THE FIRST OF 4
COPIES OF THE ECCENTRIC
YOU WILL RECEIVE. WE HOPE
YOU ENJOY THEM AND BECOME
A REGULAR READER.**

MARY RUTH ROSS
32461 BEACONSFIELD
MIDWEST 6-4726

☐ **TRIAL OFFER: 4 MONTHS for $1.00**

Yes!... Send The Eccentric

☐ I ENCLOSE $...............
☐ BILL ME LATER

☐ 1 YEAR @ $3.00
☐ 2 YEARS @ $5.25
☐ 3 YEARS @ $7.50

NAME ....
(PRINT PLAINLY)

STREET ....

CITY ....

Fig. 17.2 — Promotional material mailed out by the
Birmingham, Mich., **Eccentric** helps the news correspondents
get subscriptions in outlying areas.

Dealer (circulation 309,267, population 914,808) realized good results from a mailing piece set up in the form of a personal letter in ordinary handwriting. It said simply this:

> Dear Friend:
> You can enjoy one of America's finest newspapers — The Cleveland *Plain Dealer* for just 25¢ *per week.* Here's good reading for all the family. Wonderful features for Mother, Dad and the youngsters, too.
> IMAGINE! Getting the *Plain Dealer* 6 *days a week for just 25¢.* Don't miss this! Fill out the card below — and mail it. Do it NOW! You'll always be glad you did.

On the back of the mailing piece was a listing of features that provided good reading for ALL the family — Mother, Dad and children — and a handy order form on a postage-paid return post card (see Fig. 17.1).

The Birmingham, Mich., *Eccentric* (circulation 12,489, population 15,467), a suburban weekly, serves 90 per cent of its subscribers by mail. It has news correspondents in sixteen areas, who not only contribute news but who are continually selling subscriptions. They are paid a commission on all orders obtained. The newspaper assists them by mailing sample copies and promotion material to prospects (see Fig. 17.2). "We make circulation promotion as important as supplying the news and serving advertisers," says George R. Averill, editor and publisher.

The Winterset, Iowa, *Madisonian* (circulation 3,980, population 3,570) conducted a subscription letter campaign which J. C. Moore, publisher, says produced almost a 50 per cent return.[2]

Four letters, together with sample copies, were sent out weeks apart to an accurate list of 765 non-subscribers on rural routes in the newspaper's territory. The first letter follows:

> Howdy, Neighbor:
> And we are all neighbors in Madison County. Crops have been good this year. Livestock prices have been on the upgrade, and that is just as important here in the *Madisonian* office as it is to you.
> Fact is, when you farmers have a bad year, it reflects darned quick on any business in Winterset.
> We are sending you a month's free subscription to the Winterset *Madisonian,* Madison County's official newspaper. Naturally we hope you will like it enough to become a regular subscriber.
> But anyway, this month is on us with no strings attached.
> Enjoy having a copy of the *Madisonian* for your very own for the next four weeks. We sincerely hope you like it.
> The Winterset *Madisonian*
> P. S. Incidentally, we also hope you can save a little "egg money" reading the many want ads, farm sales and grocery advertisements.

---

[2] *American Press,* Feb., 1958, p. 14.

In two weeks the second letter went out in the following form:

> Here we are again!
> Haven't said a word for a whole two weeks.
> But we do hope you are enjoying this month of *Madisonian* reading.
> We hope the ads have saved you some money.
> Next week we are going to make you a dilly of an offer.
> We think you need the *Madisonian,* and we know we would like to have you as a subscriber.
> We'll save this reverse inflation pitch of ours until next week. Be looking for it.

A week later Letter Number 3 was sent to all on the list who had not already subscribed to the newspaper:

> Here's the bargain you've been waiting for...
> We'll mail the Winterset *Madisonian* to your farm home every week from now until April 1 — or a period of 5½ months — for just one dollar.
> *You save 50 per cent on regular subscription price.*
> This offer available to Madison County farm residents only.
> So...take advantage of this special bargain offer. Have the *Madisonian* come regularly to your home all winter and into spring.
> DO IT NOW...just tear off the handy order blank...tuck it, with $1, in the postage paid envelope, and keep the *Madisonian* coming to your home until April 1.

The above letter brought in 309 new subscribers within ten days. Then two weeks later the newspaper made the final call in the following letter, from which it received 61 more orders, making a total of 370 new subscriptions:

> HAVE YOU MISSED THE *MADISONIAN?*
> Of course, we certainly hope you have. We want you to welcome the *Madisonian* to your farm home every week, on a regular basis.
> So...here's our final reminder of how you can subscribe to your official county newspaper and
> *Save 50 Per Cent on Regular Subscription Price.*
> Receive the paper every week from now until April 1 for just $1.00.
> But DO IT NOW...offer absolutely expires on November 6. Just tear off the handy order blank...tuck it, with $1 in the postage paid envelope attached to this letter, and keep the *Madisonian* coming all winter and into spring through the farm sale season.

USE INSTALLMENT PAYMENT PLAN

Many newspapers that serve wide rural areas have found an installment purchase plan effective in building circulation with farmers who between crops do not have ready money in substantial amounts. The opportunity is given to pay $1 down and $1 a month until the full price of a year's subscription is paid. If the annual subscription price is $7, the subscriber simply makes $1 payments for seven consecutive months and pays nothing the remaining five months of the year.

One newspaper announced the plan to rural boxholders in a 2-color letter, as follows:

> It costs so little now to receive the *News* daily by mail! A *dollar* will start the paper to you tomorrow — and then you pay as you read.

Here's How It Works

YOU simply send in one dollar ($1.00) each month for seven months and the last five months of the year you pay nothing.

YOU receive the *News* for a whole year and pay for it in seven easy $1.00 installments.

EACH month of the seven we will send you a reminder together with a business reply envelope for your convenience in paying. If you would rather pay all at once or at weekly intervals, you may do this also. A dollar at a time is all that is necessary.

WE ARE enclosing a card for you to fill out and return to us in the envelope provided. We know you will want to take advantage of this fine offer, particularly when you consider what the *News* gives you — world news by the Associated Press and United Press, city and county news, society news, church and school news, sports, radio and television listings, daily markets, weather reports, weekly Farm Page, daily picture page, leading comics, comment by prominent columnists, and an abundance of other features.

THIS installment offer is for present subscribers as well as new ones. If you want to change to the $1.00 a month plan and pay as you read, sign the card and send it in.

YOU pay for your telephone and for your gas and electric service by the month. Why not pay for your newspaper the same way? The *News* provides this opportunity.

SEND IN YOUR ORDER TODAY

The La Crosse, Wis., *Tribune* (circulation 32,514, population 47,535), which has a large number of subscribers on the installment plan, uses a double post card as a statement and as a record of payments made (see Fig. 17.3).

Former Residents Are Good Prospects

Persons moving from a community ordinarily do not like to break community ties. If they have long been readers of the home town paper, a warm attachment to it has developed. To break away from it is like saying "good-by" to an old friend. If they do not continue to receive the paper, they will not know what old friends and neighbors are doing. Every person who moves out of a newspaper's immediate area to a distant community is a circulation prospect, easily persuaded to have the paper follow him.

Carriers know when persons move out of the city. If they are unsuccessful in obtaining orders to continue the paper to them at their

PAY as you READ

Mail your payment of $1.00 or more with this card. Use the business reply envelope enclosed. It requires no postage.

This same card with another self-addressed envelope will be sent back to you on the 25th of the month as a reminder that another $1.00 payment is due on the first of next month.

Your payments will be recorded below showing the date each payment is received at our office. Send this card with your remittance the first of each month, and we will mail it back on the 25th of each month until your final payment is received, following which we will return the card to you as a receipt. Payment of more than $1.00 may be made at any time in which case your subscription will be paid up that much sooner.

THE LA CROSSE TRIBUNE   La Crosse, Wisconsin

Subscription is for one year   See expiration date below name

Date Paid	Amount	Payment		Date Paid	Amount
	$1.00	1	7		$1.00
	$1.00	2	8		$1.00
	$1.00	3	9		$1.00
	$1.00	4	10		$1.00
	$1.00	5	11	**PAID IN FULL**	Free
	$1.00	6	12		Free

Do not write on this side of card

Fig. 17.3 — Combination statement and record of payments used by the La Crosse, Wis., **Tribune** for subscriptions purchased on the installment plan.

new homes, the mail subscription department should be notified. After a few days away from old neighbors, former residents become anxious to know what is going on in the community where they formerly resided. Mother perhaps is anxious to know whom the missionary society at her church elected to succeed her as program chairman. Daughter wants to read about her chum's wedding which was planned before the family moved away. Dad and Son always will be interested in the home town baseball league where Brother was captain of the All Stars. This contact of interest is a tight one and works wonders in keeping persons on the subscription list when they move away.

Rural correspondents also know when families move away from the rural communities they represent, and should send in items concerning departures. Someone in the mail subscription department should have the responsibility of clipping all such items to be used as the basis of mail solicitation.

Every newspaper reader has relatives or friends who at one time lived in the home town. Local subscribers may be of great help to the circulation department and extend a courtesy to their friends by telling the publisher about them and their interest in the home town. C. W. Brown, publisher of the Oconomowoc, Wis., *Enterprise* (circulation 4,270, population 5,345) offers each subscriber the privilege of naming a friend to receive the paper free for two months. This personalized sampling really clicks, according to Brown.[3]

A mailing list of former residents is valuable. Names should remain on it for a year after persons have left the community. New names may continuously be added. Well-worded and attractively compiled solicitation letters will bring results.

An efficient promotion department knows exactly the right approach and wastes no time in making it.

Vacationists Want Home News

Persons leaving their communities temporarily, as well as those leaving them permanently, like to have the home town newspaper follow them. It is important for business and professional men, even when they are to be gone a short time, to keep in touch with what is taking place in a commercial and financial way, and air mail will bring the newspaper promptly to any destination.

Persons going away to the mountains or the seaside for a vacation may be persuaded to have the newspaper follow them. Those planning to spend a few months abroad may arrange to have the newspaper sent by air mail so that they keep up to date with all that takes place at the home base.

Newspapers published in university towns are sent to distant lands each season to professors who are there on Fulbright scholarships or on other teaching arrangements. The Columbia, Mo., *Missourian* (circulation 3,954, population 31,974), daily community newspaper produced by faculty and students in the School of Journalism of the University of Missouri, continually goes to such professors.

Carriers are instructed to obtain vacation orders from their customers before they leave town. If subscribers do not wish to have the paper sent to them at their vacation spots, copies may be held for them and delivered when they return. Thus, they miss none of the local news that was published while they were away, and the newspaper does not experience a "summer slump" in circulation.

For Servicemen a "Letter From Home"

Men and women in the military service, who are separated from their families and friends during training and service, welcome their home town newspaper almost more than anything that might be sent them. It is like a daily or weekly letter from home and contains much more about home town happenings than would be contained in a letter.

---

[3] Frank W. Rucker, *Newspaper Circulation — What, Where and How,* Iowa State University Press, Ames, Iowa, 1958, pp. 151–52.

Some papers have gained great good will by making a special rate to servicemen. Often the firms that employed them before their military duty will pay for having the paper sent to them. Parents, however, are more likely to respond to a subscription appeal.

The Denver, Colo., *Post* (circulation 253,410, population 415,786) during World War II sent papers to men in training camps at the low mail rate usually reserved for persons residing within the Rocky Mountain area. It recognized that from a morale-sustaining viewpoint the man in service had great need for his home town newspaper, and parents, wives and other relatives were encouraged to sponsor subscriptions for men in uniform.

A reduced rate, however, is not always needed to obtain subscriptions for servicemen. Although the Milwaukee, Wis., *Journal* (circulation 361,856, population 637,392) made no special concession in handling GI mail, it at one time had more than 500 subscriptions going to servicemen.

Students Like Home Newspaper

Those of another group away from home who appreciate the home newspaper when they can receive it regularly are college students, and when schools open in the fall there is an opportunity for an alert circulation manager to boost his paid subscription total. Parents may be persuaded easily to make the newspaper a "back-to-school" gift for sons and daughters who have enjoyed all summer the pleasant privilege of reading the family newspaper.

The Honolulu *Star-Bulletin* (circulation 97,680, population 284,034), in an advertisement 2 columns wide and 10 inches deep, promoted subscriptions of this kind, and as a result the *Star-Bulletin* went regularly to many Hawaiians attending American colleges. The advertisement said: "The student attending a mainland school needs many things that are different from what he is accustomed to in Hawaii. Help his adjustment by writing often . . . and don't forget the *Star-Bulletin*."

Beneath this was a coupon giving prices for both daily and "Saturday only" subscriptions, together with space for filling in the student's name and address and the name of the donor.

High school students, as well as college students, appreciate the home newspaper more during their school period than at any time of the year. Many newspapers have developed greater newspaper reading among this group by sending copies of the paper to schools for use in various classes.

The La Crosse, Wis., *Tribune* carried a 10-part series of articles portraying the newspaper's value and adaptability to classroom work and later produced the series in booklet form. The booklet was used in the fall in its mailings for school subscriptions.

"Daily newspaper reading presents an opportunity for teachers to make students aware of the total picture of news happenings and features," said the *Tribune,* "first by scanning the newspaper thoroughly and following up by reading items which catch their interest. Integration of the newspaper with any subject or unit tends to make pupils more familiar with events and trends, thus increasing their perception and finally broadening their reading interests."

The Eau Claire, Wis., *Leader* and *Telegram* have 250 rural schools on their paid subscription list. These subscriptions were obtained by mail solicitation. Each fall, beginning with the September 1 issues, papers are mailed to all schools. A letter and a statement for a subscription covering the school period are sent to each school. The teacher is requested to submit the statement to the school clerk. If the school board does not care to accept the proposal, the teacher is asked to mark "cancel" on the statement and mail it back to the newspaper office. About 95 per cent of the schools "O.K." the subscription.

The Eau Claire papers also run ads in their columns soliciting subscriptions for students going away to college.

Good Start for Newlyweds

Every opportunity should be taken by a newspaper to become at once the friend and companion of "newlyweds." Announcements of engagements and weddings appearing in the newspaper may be the basis for a valuable mailing list. A month's subscription free to newly married couples has been used by some newspapers to gain orders for continuous delivery (see Fig. 17.4).

The Detroit, Mich., *Times* (circulation 391,295, population 1,849,568) has printed an attractive congratulation card, which is mailed to newly married couples. By returning the postage-paid reply card, the young couple may receive the first four weeks as a gift from the *Times.*

Furthermore, what would be nicer as a wedding gift than a year's subscription to the home newspaper? Why not promote it?

TYPE OF COPY IS IMPORTANT

Success in promoting circulation by mail requires well-prepared, sharply pointed copy as well as a good list of prospects. Broadsides, post cards and circular letters all may be used individually or collectively, but the results obtained from them depend more upon the quality of the mailing piece than upon the number of pieces sent out.

Most newspapers use direct mail to obtain subscription renewals. A cross-section survey of United States newspapers in 1956 showed that 84 per cent used this method to keep subscribers on their lists. However, only 32 per cent were using direct mail to obtain new subscribers.

NEW BRIDES

Your Newspaper FREE
for One Month

Every new bride who will establish her new home in Iowa
after this date may have entirely free as a gift one full
month's delivery of the Des
Moines Daily Register or the
Des Moines Tribune. Just fill
out the coupon below and mail
to Circulation Department, Des
Moines Register and Tribune,
Des Moines 4, Iowa. Kindly
give as much advance notice
as possible.

- - - - - - - - - - - - - - - - - -

Yes, we gladly accept your
NEW BRIDE OFFER:

Name ....

Town ....

Street or R.F.D. ....

Date of Marriage ....

Daily preferred ....

(Register or Tribune).
Please start delivery

.... Date

Fig. 17.4 — This notice is carried on alternate weeks in
the Home and Family section
of the Des Moines Sunday
Register.

The increase in postage rates in 1958 had further effect on mail solicitation, causing some publishers to do less of it and others to give more
attention to the *type* of material they used in selling by mail.

Should Stress Features and Services

Dr. Ralph D. Casey, for many years director of the University of
Minnesota School of Journalism, believes firmly that promotion managers of newspapers should tell prospective readers more about what
is being done for them on the news front.

"The newspaper in its present-day form," says Dr. Casey, "is a bundle of utilities. It provides for the reader news, features, editorials, interpretative articles, encyclopedic material, entertaining and amusing content and, of course, advertising. While not underrating any one of these utilities, I think we must confess that the news is the primary staple, and in saying this I am reflecting, I think, the view of the average reader."

The solid achievements of reporters and editors should not go unnoted, he adds: "I believe the public can come to recognize outstanding news getting and news writing in terms of personality, but what is missing in the promotion picture is a solid series on what the service of news in our contemporary lives means in the lives of readers."[4]

Louis B. Seltzer, editor of the Cleveland, Ohio, *Press and News* (circulation 385,000, population 914,808) believes that newspapers need to have greater concern for the welfare of their readers and should draw nearer to them in warm interest.

"Too many newspapers in America are viewed by their readers as cold, remote, impersonal business establishments packaging news and comment, to be delivered for a circulation and advertising price," Seltzer told the New York professional chapter of Sigma Delta Chi. "The warmth, the understanding, the cordiality between the paper and the people is lacking, and where it is lacking the people can easily turn to other instruments for news and comment — which is precisely what will happen."[5]

This warmth of feeling, coupled with the newspaper's ability to give valuable service, must be expressed in direct mail material. The prospect must be convinced that the newspaper's interest in him is beyond that of merely obtaining his subscription dollars.

Many of the larger newspapers advertise extensively their outstanding features, such as health column, editorial page, scientific articles and surveys pertaining to local problems (see Fig. 17.5). These go out as broadsides or as supplements to letters.

The Omaha, Nebr., *World-Herald* (combined morning and evening circulation 246,588, population 251,117) has a large mail circulation and does much solicitation by direct mail. About four times a year — every three months — it re-solicits its "kill" list, which contains the names of former subscribers who did not renew their subscriptions. This newspaper uses no reduced-rate offers but makes a combination rate with magazines.

In its mail solicitation, the *World-Herald* calls attention to its late-wire news, pictures of national and international events and local happenings in sports, politics, science, world problems and agricultural progress.

---

[4] *Editor & Publisher,* Nov. 19, 1955, p. 32.
[5] *Editor & Publisher,* June 2, 1956, p. 74.

Good Health
for all the family

Dr. Walter C. Alvarez, the Plain Dealer's distinguished medical columnist, brings you and your family the benefit of fifty years in medicine. As former Professor of Medicine at the Mayo Foundation and now editor of "Modern Medicine" and "Geriatrics," he is aware of the health problems that confront every American home.

He believes that the public has a right to share the latest medical knowledge. By dispensing current and accurate information to Plain Dealer readers he seeks to quiet the anxiety that stems from doubt. His columns have stimulated sympathy and support for urgently needed medical projects. They have also encouraged doctors to keep up with medical advances.

Dr. Alvarez advises persons with an ailment to confide in their doctors and not to labor under the assumption that they have contracted some dread disease or require surgery.

"Some people make themselves ill," he remarked. "And sometimes life's strife and strain cause sickness. In most cases everything depends on a person's nerves and good sense.

"Many people induce their own headaches and heartaches. They make themselves ill with fear, usually unjustifiable fear. When your doctor tells you that you haven't contracted heart disease or cancer, don't search for these ailments in yourself—go home, rejoice, be of good cheer."

• • •

Dr. Alvarez' acceptance by the medical profession was evidenced when he addressed Plain Dealer readers at the Music Hall last year. A dozen of Cleveland's leading medical authorities shared the stage. Their ovation was as enthusiastic as the audience's.

Dr. Alvarez has become the family doctor's colleague in thousands of Cleveland homes. He visits Plain Dealer families every Sunday, Monday, Tuesday and Friday.

Good reading for all the family
in the

CLEVELAND PLAIN DEALER

For Home Delivery • Phone MAin 1-4500 • Ask for Circulation

Fig. 17.5 — The Cleveland **Plain Dealer** uses direct mail to promote many of its special features in a program planned to stress "Good reading for all the family."

Special Offers Bring Action

Most newspapers, however, supplement their promotion of features and services with a special offer of some kind in order to drive the prospect to immediate action. Sometimes it is a premium, again it may be a short-time discount offer or a tie-up with a charity in which the community is vitally interested.

The New Orleans, La., *States-Item* (circulation 162,805, population 570,445) once carried on a subscription drive in cooperation with the Crippled Children's Hospital Board. For a period of one year, the hospital was paid 60 cents for each new 18-weeks subscription.

In order to promote its new and renewal subscriptions, and at the same time its classified advertising service, the Columbus, Kans., *Modern Light* (circulation 720, population 3,490) offered four average-sized want ads free with a new or renewal subscription. The want ads could be run at different times, and the offer was restricted to county residents.

With each new or renewal subscription, the Forest Grove, Ore., *Washington County News-Times* (circulation 3,398, population 4,343) gave a 5 x 7 portrait of the subscriber, to be taken by a local photographer.

An unusual offer to rural subscribers was made by the Carmi, Ill., *Times* (circulation 5,794, population 5,574). A front-page item in sample copies mailed to boxholders announced: "We pay 75 cents per dozen for your eggs in trade for a one, two or three year subscription to the *Times*."

Farm women put the pinch on "Mister" to resubscribe for the Goodlettsville, Tenn., *Gazette* (circulation 2,438, population 1,590) when the newspaper gave 500 orchids, flown from Hawaii, to the first 500 subscribers to renew. The orchids were delivered on Sunday, in time for church services.

Twice each year the Peoria, Ill., *Journal Star* (combined morning and evening circulation 97,785, population 111,856) conducts direct mail promotion offering a discount for one and two year subscriptions; the offer goes to new prospects as well as to old subscribers for renewals.

A Good Letter Is Essential

Broadsides and circulars may be used, but a warm, friendly letter, using vivid, forceful words to describe the interesting news and features the newspaper has to offer, is the best means of obtaining subscriptions by mail.

Robert Bauer, circulation manager of the Muscatine, Iowa, *Journal* (circulation 9,799, population 19,041) believes that every mailing should contain a letter.

"It is the cornerstone of your entire mailing," he says. "Without it, you are just handing out a circular. With it you can make an individualized sales presentation, give your message warmth and personality, talk to your prospects as if they were right across the counter from you. In this type of selling you need a personal touch. Make the over-all appearance of your letter come as close to a personally typed letter as possible. Always use a facsimile or handwritten signature — NEVER TYPE. Interest depends also upon the wording and typography. Too many long paragraphs are not likely to be read. Make the letter physically attractive and easy to read. Use generally short simple words and sentences."

Most successful letter writers believe it pays to use such devices as indented paragraphs, asterisks, dots and the like, in the letter to break up sentences.

Jack Holm, city circulation manager and former circulation promotion manager of the Davenport, Iowa, *Democrat* and *Times* (combined circulation 51,327, population 74,549), who has had remarkable success with mail solicitation, presents the following important points regarding the style and content of direct mail material:

1. The most effective direct mail pieces include an outgoing envelope, a letter, an order form and a reply envelope. All four are needed for best results.

2. As a general rule, white envelopes are the best for outgoing mail. Color has a commercial significance, while white resembles personal mail.

3. For the average newspaper direct mail letter, one page is regarded best. If your letter hits Mr. Farmer's place right after a 4-foot snow in January, he would probably read two or three pages. Such a solicitation, however, is not normal, and most modern-day farmers are not going to read an average two or three page letter.

4. Study the physical appearance of your letter. Never make your paragraphs too long or too solid. Use punctuation to break up the copy. Use underlining and indentations judiciously, and be sensible in your use of marginal notations, pointers and postscripts.

5. If the budget allows use a second color in the letter, especially to emphasize a special offer or some noteworthy inducement.

6. Begin your letter with a good opening sentence — one that will immediately attract attention. Then keep your copy moving. In closing, tell the prospect once more what your offer will do for him and that it is for a limited time only.

7. It is generally considered more practical and effective to use an attached order form than a separate order form. In this, use live words to get across the urgency of the message.

8. Business reply envelope should be different in color from the stock on which the letter is written. Goldenrod, canary and pink are popular.

The Cleveland, Ohio, *Plain Dealer* realized a good return from the following letter, which adheres to most, if not all, the fine points usually outlined by expert letter writers:

Dear Friend:

We're mighty proud of our newspaper...and rightly so. Perhaps it's because today, more than ever before, the **PLAIN DEALER** has become a symbol of good reading to the families of Cleveland and suburban communities.

It's just neighborly to want to share the good things in life with others. That's why we are sending you, absolutely **FREE**, a sample copy of the PLAIN DEALER for a two-week period. This is our way of sharing Cleveland's favorite newspaper with you and your family.

The treat is on us. Our pleasure will be in your enjoyment of the many wonderful features which appear in the PLAIN DEALER columns. There's something for everyone. Thought provoking editorials, up-to-the-minute market news and the best sports and comics...a parade of women's features and the tops in radio and television news. They're all here plus the warmth and authority that has endeared our paper to the most discriminating readers.

But then, read the PLAIN DEALER for two weeks...and see for yourself. We're so sure you will want to become a regular subscriber, we are enclosing a business reply card for your convenience.

The daily and Sunday PLAIN DEALER will be delivered to you for as little as 45 cents per week...the daily by mail, the Sunday paper by motor route carrier. No advance payment is necessary — our carrier representative will collect each week.

We would like very much to have you join the PLAIN DEALER family. Won't you read with us...nearly everyone else does.

William J. Kitchin
Delivery Service Bureau Manager

The order form was a postage pre-paid card with the following:

Motor Route Manager:
Please enter my subscription to
___ The Daily and Sunday Plain Dealer at 45¢ per week
___ The Daily only Plain Dealer at 25¢ per week
The Daily delivered by mail — the Sunday by automobile.
Name_____
Road__ _____
City_____R. F. D._____
I understand that the carrier will collect each Sunday via the envelope system. Please provide a receipt card.

RIGHT TIME IS IMPORTANT

For promoting circulation by mail there is a right time as well as a right method. Although, with effective promotion material, results may be obtained at any time of the year, there are some months that seem to be better than others for influencing certain types of prospects.

Some Months Better Than Others

For selling subscriptions by mail to rural boxholders, the "R" months generally have been considered best. September, October and November seem to rank about equally. So do January, February and March. In reaching the farmer, a good time to mail is during a stretch of inclement weather. Then he cannot get out in the field and has time to look at his mail.

December probably is at the bottom of the list of "R" months in direct mail because of the holidays, although the Christmas gift idea often brings good returns. Some weekly papers and small dailies have allowed a regular subscriber to send without cost a 6-months subscription to a friend or relative as a Christmas gift when he renews his own subscription for a year. The recipient of the gift must be a resident of the newspaper's territory. Thus new names are added to the mailing list and a high percentage of them renew their subscriptions when the 6 months have expired.

During one holiday season the Lansing, Ill., *Journal* (circulation 4,268, population 8,682) offered a free Christmas tree with a year's subscription. The paper purchased a shipment of trees from 4 to 6 feet tall and notified the subscribers when the trees arrived. Each subscriber was allowed to make his own selection.

Sports and Politics Are Drawing Cards

Seasons of the year when sports are uppermost in the minds of Americans is a good time to promote circulation.

To promote its coverage of the football season at Baylor University, the Waco, Tex., *News-Tribune* and *Times-Herald* (combined circulation 50,325, population 84,706) sent a mailing to 9,000 Baylor alumni, offering a 3-months subscription for $3. This netted a return of 500 out-of-territory subscribers. At another time these newspapers sent a special 2-part mailing to members of nearby riding clubs calling attention to stories being carried regularly for persons who love horses. A third series of mailings was sent out in the spring featuring the large amount of fishing news from Lake Whitney, a large fishing resort about 50 miles from Waco. All yielded good returns.

A political campaign year is another good time to promote circulation. Persons want information concerning the issues and the candidates.

"You need a big-time state newspaper in an election year," said the Des Moines, Iowa, *Register* and *Tribune* (combined circulation 345,146, population 177,965) in a letter sent to a long list of rural prospects. The full text follows:

Tell Us Which One
You Like Best.

Did you know that both the Des Moines daily REGISTER and the Des Moines daily TRIBUNE are MORNING newspapers? BOTH give rural readers late news the SAME day. BOTH have a large following in all parts of Iowa.

Our local Route Man thought you would like to read sample copies of both of these morning papers. So with his compliments we are going to send you...

3 sample copies of the Des Moines daily TRIBUNE
and then
3 sample copies of the Des Moines daily REGISTER

After enjoying the samples, will you either tell the route man which you like the best or fill out the enclosed card so you can continue getting one of these papers?

3 WEEKS FREE TO THOSE WHO PICK THE TRIBUNE

BECAUSE MANY FAMILIES ARE NOT AS WELL ACQUAINTED WITH THE DES MOINES TRIBUNE AND DUE TO THE FACT THAT 3 SAMPLES ARE NOT ENOUGH TO BECOME FAMILIAR WITH IT, WE ARE MAKING AN EXTRA LIBERAL OFFER FOR YOU TO TRY IT. You will get 3 full weeks free with your order for at least 6 more weeks.

Check the daily REGISTER on the enclosed card and you get 2 WEEKS FREE with your agreement to continue 6 more weeks. That's also a big bargain for you.

You Need a Big-Time State Newspaper in an Election Year.

The way to judge any article is to USE IT. Will you urge members of your family to read and enjoy the samples and HELP YOU DECIDE? But be sure to choose one of them for it is MORE IMPORTANT THAN EVER BEFORE to have a newspaper in your home that will give you the COMPLETE STORY — world wide — nationally and state. It takes a paper with its own WASHINGTON, D. C. NEWS OFFICE — special service from the NEW YORK TIMES — and a big staff here in Iowa to do it.

Of course you may also make your decision on the entertainment, comics, women's features and sports. Both papers have lots of them. Take your choice.

Mail Card for Quick Action

You do not need to send a single penny with your order. On this route we have the easy pay-by-the-week plan. Our Sunday Route Man will collect for the paper after the free time. He may already be delivering your Sunday paper and you can pay for both at the same time. He will see you to make these arrangements.

Yours very truly,
H. O. Monahan
Subscription Manager

Other seasons and occasions are timely for obtaining subscriptions by mail. To this the progressive promotion manager is alert, taking advantage of every opportunity. He knows who is to be reached and how and when it should be done.

CHAPTER 18

Promoting Circulation Through Carriers

MOST PUBLISHERS of daily papers, and some of weekly papers, consider the best avenue for promoting circulation is through "little merchant" carriers, the size of whose income depends upon the number of subscribers they maintain on their routes. "Little merchant" carriers are independent contractors who buy copies of the paper from the publisher and sell and deliver them at a profit to residents of a designated area. They buy at wholesale and sell at retail as a merchant does, and their success depends primarily upon businesslike handling of their routes. Youngsters 12 to 18 years of age have found selling, delivering and collecting under this plan to be remunerative part-time work with excellent experience in the handling of money and in dealing with the public.

This means of building circulation is highly successful where newspapers, through their circulation and promotion departments, provide:

1. Care in selecting boys for the position.
2. Well-planned training in selling, delivering and collecting.
3. Special incentives and appropriate recognition for outstanding efforts.
4. Campaigns and contests in which boys may engage with interest, fairness and enthusiasm.
5. Wholesome activities for the display of physical and mental skills and for the general development of character.

[262]

ENLISTING CARRIER-SALESMEN

The first important step in developing a satisfactory carrier organization is the enlisting of intelligent, active, ambitious, dependable boys. In order that carriers of the right caliber may be obtained, their duties and the rewards that may come to them need to be fully explained, emphasized and widely publicized. This is of primary importance.

Every community has many boys of the right age, mentality and character to handle newspaper routes efficiently and to earn for themselves a much-appreciated income. However, publishers must realize there are other opportunities for these vigorous lads to find part-time employment with satisfactory returns. There is strong competition for the services of healthy, courteous junior and senior high school boys. These boys also have ideas of their own regarding work to be done, and they have certain school activities outside the classroom in which they wish to engage. They must be "sold" on the general rewards of newspaper route work and must be convinced that such a position will not greatly interfere with other things they want to do and that their parents will approve.

Therefore, publishers succeed only if they approach seriously and scientifically this problem of building a strong carrier organization.

A newspaper promotion department finds one of its greatest opportunities to be of real service right at this point. The wide-awake promotion manager promotes carrier service in every way possible, particularly through:

1. Public schools.
2. Youth organizations.
3. Parents.
4. Newspaper's own columns.
5. Radio, television and other means of communications.

Public Schools Give Assistance

Public school administrators and teachers realize that wholesome employment which does not encroach upon school activities is good for school boys. Those who are constantly doing something for themselves and for others frequently become better students. In turn, newspaper publishers realize that boys who do well in school usually are good newspaper carrier-salesmen. Most newspapers require their carriers to maintain satisfactory records in school. The school and the newspaper in this way pool their efforts to help the boy.

"We have a mutual problem," Dr. Clara E. Cockerville, assistant superintendent of schools in Armstrong County, Pennsylvania, told members of the Interstate Circulation Managers Association. "You are responsible for the first work experience of thousands of teen-age boys. We, through the schools, are responsible for the formal learning experiences of those same boys. We have mutual friends."

Dr. Cockerville emphasized another point that should be adhered to by newspapers in dealing with carriers. "Before you begin to think of boys as carriers, you must think of them as boys," she said. "You cannot ask only, 'How is Johnny delivering the papers?' But you must ask, 'What is route work doing for Johnny?' Your observance of Newspaperboy Day, the sweaters your boys wear to show they represent a paper, the rewards your boys can attain — these are things youth need. As you use them you build boys as well as circulation."

When newspapers assume this attitude toward youth they have no difficulty in obtaining assistance from schools in enlisting high-class boys for delivery service. This, too, is a relationship of which the newspaper and its carriers may be proud and concerning which wide publicity should be given. What better promotion of the carrier-salesman position could be presented than to say it has the endorsement of school authorities?

The Hamilton, Ohio, *Journal-News* (circulation 26,036, population 57,951) realized this when it used a photograph of a carrier, with testimonials from him and the superintendent of schools, to show how a newspaper route helps a boy in school.

When four carriers for the Fostoria, Ohio, *Review-Times* (circulation 5,923, population 14,351) received scholastic honors, the newspaper presented them with lithographed certificates which paid tribute to their fine work both as little merchant carriers and as students in school. This presentation during a school assembly gave added recognition to the helpful cooperation between school and newspaper.

Publicity and public recognition of this kind impress upon the youth of the community and their parents the merits of newspaper carrying. Such promotion is a great aid in carrier enlistment.

Youth Organizations May Help

Members of youth organizations, such as Boy Scouts, 4-H Clubs, Key Clubs and Y Clubs, usually make successful carrier-salesmen. The rosters of such clubs provide an excellent list of prospects to whom may be sent attractive mailings regarding carrier services and activities.

A newspaper's promotion department should keep in close contact with such groups and at every opportunity present to them the advantages of becoming newspaper carriers, pointing out that the qualifications for becoming a good carrier-salesman are about the same as for membership in any character-building youth organization.

The Minneapolis *Star* and *Tribune* (combined circulation 502,252, population 521,718) realized this when it ran a full-page house ad congratulating the Boy Scouts of America on their 40th anniversary, giving a special salute to the more than 3,000 *Star* and *Tribune* carrier-salesmen who were members of the Scout organization. The article showed a Scout at salute in the foreground with the same lad in the background, newsbag on shoulder, carefully folding up a paper for delivery. Cuts of nine outstanding carrier Scouts with identifying cutlines gave credence to the close character-building activities of the two organizations.

Parents Should Be Interested

In addition to building up close relations between its circulation department and youth organizations of the community, the Minneapolis *Star* and *Tribune* constantly seeks the assistance of parents in interesting their boys in operating newspaper routes. Parents of boys already in the carrier organization are among the circulation department's chief assistants in keeping the carrier ranks filled with industrious, personable boys. Letters received from parents in appreciation for what newspaper carrying experience has done for their sons provide excellent promotion. In an advertisement that was particularly appealing the *Star* and *Tribune* used pictures of a carrier and his parents with a letter from the father saying what great benefits had come to his son by handling a *Star* and *Tribune* route.

Letters from parents in tribute to a newspaper for what it has done for their carrier sons are not hard to obtain. Many come in voluntarily — others are written when parents are invited to do so.

A newspaperboy promotion contest was the means used by the Des Moines, Iowa, *Register* and *Tribune* (combined circulation 345,146, population 177,965) to obtain letters on "Why I Like My Son To Be a *Register* and *Tribune* Carrier." A total of 469 letters were received when parents were asked to estimate the business training, personality development and character-building experience gained by their sons through the newspaper route. Cash prizes of $25 each were awarded for the best letters received from a father and a mother.

A slightly different angle on the parent theme was introduced by the Schenectady, N. Y., *Union-Star* (circulation 35,624, population 91,785) on Mother's Day. Mothers of carriers were asked to write essays on "What a *Union-Star* Newspaper Route Has Meant to My Son." The mother who wrote the best essay was invited to take her family out for a Mother's Day dinner at any restaurant or hotel of her choice with the newspaper picking up the check. Three other mothers received orchids in recognition of the excellence of their letters. A special award went to a dad who wrote commending the helpful training the paper route had given his boy, explaining that the lad's mother was no longer living.

The *Union-Star* also published on Father's Day a quarter-page advertisement entitled "Newspaperboys Extend Best Wishes to Dads Everywhere on Father's Day," with a signature line, "Lads of Today — Dads of Tomorrow — The Schenectady *Union-Star*."

Efforts of this kind cause parents to become interested in carrier positions for their sons.

Use Newspaper's Own Columns

One of the best ways to promote carrier service and have on hand a ready list of applicants for carrier positions is to tell in the newspaper's own columns about the interesting experiences of active carriers and the special recognitions given them from time to time. The Dayton, Ohio, *Daily News* (circulation 144,687, population 243,872)

Fig. 18.1 — Stories about carrier-salesmen which appear in the Dayton, Ohio, **Daily News** make effective promotion to use in enlisting good carriers.

publishes a story at least once a week about the achievements of one of its carriers. These stories build prestige and encourage good boys to want routes (see Fig. 18.1).

"Newspaperboy Day" — a day set apart to pay tribute to carrier-salesmen — is observed annually by most newspapers. Naturally it brings forth an abundance of effective carrier promotion. A glance at the promotions used in a single year reveals a wide and interesting variety.

The Bloomington, Ill., *Pantagraph* (circulation 39,384, population 34,163) carried a double-page advertisement over the personal signatures of its 306 carriers. With a striking layout, it fairly screamed for attention, telling the number of families served each day by these carriers and the benefits the boys received from their route work.

The Dallas, Tex., *Times Herald* (circulation 178,848, population 434,462) used a full page to honor "today's newspaperboy" as "tomorrow's leader," and featured a series of pictures from the life of one of its carriers, pointing out the many benefits this individual received from being a carrier-salesman. It was an impressive tribute to the *Times Herald*'s entire carrier organization.

The Elkhart, Ind., *Truth* (circulation 22,253, population 35,646) built a "Newspaperboy Day" ad around President Eisenhower's quotation, "No American president . . . could ever get along without boys like you." It featured one of the newspaper's carriers as typical of the 200 who deliver the *Truth*.

The Mobile, Ala., *Press* and *Register* (combined circulation 107,846, population 173,849) used pen-and-ink drawings of active carriers to illustrate the social side of being a carrier-salesman. Further information of a more serious nature was brought out in the copy.

Not to be outdone by larger daily newspapers, the Rocky Ford, Colo., *Gazette* (circulation 2,231, population 4,087) devoted a full page to pictures of its carrier force. Each lad was fittingly introduced to *Gazette* readers.

Promotion of carrier service is by no means confined to "Newspaperboy Day." Newspapers often run promotion ads in tribute to their carriers. Sometimes the important part they play in the daily production of the newspaper is emphasized. The Detroit, Mich., *News* (circulation 463,469, population 1,849,568) did a particularly good job of this in its pictorial magazine. The front cover showed a *News* carrier and the center spread pictured the process of newspaper publishing and the part that the carrier plays in getting the paper to homes of its readers.

"It's Great To Be a *Pantagraph* Carrier," said the Bloomington, Ill., *Pantagraph* in a compelling carrier promotion. Featured standing in a row were small cartoon characters. The first was a youngster with newspaper in hand. Next in order came two full-fledged carriers with filled newspaper bags, a school boy growing into a college man in cap and gown, a successful businessman carrying a brief case and finally a comfortably retired gentleman with cane in hand. Thus, the evolution that might naturally spring from a carrier-salesman position was uniquely illustrated.

The Woonsocket, R. I., *Call* (circulation 24,963, population 50,211) built a compelling promotion advertisement around four of its carriers who were honor students at Mount St. Charles Academy. Over pictures of the boys appeared these captions: "An Ambitious Newspaperboy," "A Religious Newspaperboy," "An Interested Newspaperboy" and "A Studious Newspaperboy." An accompanying story told about the lads' scholastic and extra-curricular activities with continual reference to the fact that their newspaper routes had offered training and financial aid toward their education. The accumulative effect of the repetitive captions built up a favorable and positive impression.

The enjoyment of outdoor life experienced by boys who earn spending money by carrying papers was featured in a full-page ad in two colors in the Sunday comic section of the Des Moines, Iowa, *Register* and *Tribune*. "The R & T carrier-salesman earns his own money for vacations, sports, fishing and camping," was the legend of this striking ad. A coupon for more information regarding carrier work was inserted at the bottom of the page.

The high character of newspaper carriers often is revealed in stories concerning their heroic acts. The Garden City, N. Y., *Newsday* (circulation 288,483, population 14,486) awarded a $25 Savings Bond to each of two carriers, one for arousing a family from a burning building and the other for pulling a drowning boy from a creek. The Toronto, Ontario, *Star* (circulation 307,928, population 667,706) in a news story paid tribute to a carrier who notified a stationmaster of a broken rail in time to flag down an approaching train and thus avoid a serious accident. The Brockton, Mass., *Enterprise and Times* (circulation 41,681, population 62,860) told how two of its carriers warned tenants in a burning building.

Such publicity presents carriers to the public as alert young men of high character, and helps to make carrier activity dramatically desirable for boys of carrier age.

Use Radio and Television

Another effective way of interesting boys in carrier positions is through radio and television. Newspapers have used these media of communication for a variety of programs stressing the advantages of carrier experience and allowing carriers to tell their own stories.

Selected carriers have been interviewed by circulation managers, local radio personalities and public officials. Carriers' parents also have told of the benefits their sons have derived from carrier service. Scholarship winners have been invited to tell about their scholastic records as well as their newspaper route achievements. Carriers have been given opportunities to appear in quiz contests and on talent shows. The Toronto, Ontario, *Globe and Mail* (circulation 215,570, population 667,706) conducted a Carriers' Television Contest, in which cash and merchandise prizes totaling $7,500, were awarded.

Businessmen and public officials, who formerly were carriers, have told on radio and TV how their early training as carriers helped them in later years. Newspaper officials, too, have made talks about their carrier organizations and what their papers were doing for the boys. Many newspapers also have used spot announcements to center attention on newspaper work.

When the youth of a community listen to programs such as these, their interest is aroused in becoming carrier-salesmen. Promotion of every kind is needed to keep the ranks filled.

TRAINING CARRIER-SALESMEN

A promotion department's second great step in promoting circulation is in training carriers to be efficient in selling, delivering and collecting. This is the most important service it can render to the circulation department and it includes:

1. Acquainting carriers with the newspaper.
2. Conducting carrier workshops.
3. Instructing in salesmanship.
4. Providing carriers with sales helps.
5. Injecting enthusiasm into regular carrier meetings.

Carrier Must Know Paper He Represents

To instill in carrier-salesmen some pride in the institution they represent and in the newspaper they are to sell and deliver, is an important responsibility of a newspaper's promotion department.

Each carrier needs to know how the newspaper is produced and who, besides himself, will have a part in its making. It is important for him to meet the publisher, editor and heads of departments, and to observe the operations in each department. A tour of the plant with answers to all questions that may arise in his mind and handshakes with the most important members of the staff make him feel that he is a vital cog in the organization.

On the last Saturday of each month all boys who, within the preceding 30 days, have joined the carrier force of the Pueblo, Colo., *Chieftain* and *Star-Journal* (combined circulation 41,389, population 63,685) are taken on a tour of the newspaper plant and entertained at lunch by the general manager. Between the tour and lunch, the boys have a 45-minute meeting with the circulation manager, district managers and regular carriers. Definite suggestions are made regarding delivery service, selling and collecting. The circulation manager and district managers conduct sales demonstrations and present a skit to illustrate courteous collecting. The boys are made acquainted also with the newspaper itself — the average number of pages it contains, the important features, its thorough coverage of the news, the savings that may be realized by shopping from the ads, and the price of the paper delivered to a customer's home.

The day proves to be a most interesting one for each new carrier. He is impressed by the machines that mold lines of type in the composing room and the large press that spins out whole sections of the paper fully printed, cut and folded. He appreciates the friendliness of those he meets, knows what is expected of him and has high regard for the newspaper and its staff. He is off to a good start.

Fig. 18.2 — A little fun is injected into the serious discussions at sales meetings and workshops of the Des Moines **Register** and **Tribune**.

Workshop for Carriers

The more thorough the preliminary training, the more likely the carrier is to be successful and happy in his work. Many newspapers conduct for their carriers, supervisors and agents a workshop, consisting of two or three evening sessions packed with intensive training (see Fig. 18.2).

For three successive winters the Beaumont, Tex., *Enterprise* and *Journal* (combined circulation 91,048, population 94,014) conducted a training school for carrier salesmen with the assistance of the Lamar State College of Technology. This was planned to acquaint carriers with the importance of their work in relationship to that done by other members of the newspaper's force. Topics for discussion included explanations and helpful information on service, selling and collections. The country circulation manager spoke on "More Profit Through Better Service," the city circulation manager discussed "More Profits Through Better Collections" and the circulation manager spoke on "More Profit Through Better Selling."

All of the current city carriers, new carriers going on routes the first of the following month, substitutes, all boys interested in routes, and carriers from major distributing points within a 25-mile radius of Beaumont were invited to attend and more than 100 carriers enrolled. This training brought pleasing results.

"We very definitely experienced an increased interest in giving good service and collections were better," said Frank W. Arnold, circulation manager. "One thing that greatly interested me was the increased curiosity on the part of carriers, their parents, other boys and the general public. Our applications for routes increased. Parents began asking more questions. Our distributors evidenced more enthusiasm and our entire department seemed to have received a shot in the arm."[1]

An interesting feature of one session was a discussion panel of leading businessmen who had carried routes in their youth. The workshop was good promotion and made carriers more familiar with the newspaper, the business and civic leaders of the city and the local college.

At a University of Wisconsin Circulation Seminar, the late Ed Mill, circulation director of the Davenport, Iowa, *Democrat* and *Times* (combined circulation 51,327, population 74,549) described a school for carriers which he conducted on the second Saturday of each month. This was attended by all boys who had been recruited for routes during the preceding month.

Mill explained to the new boys that they were part of a team of 740 carriers in business for themselves, the same as merchants on main street. He explained that the circulation department had but one thing to sell — *Service* — and then went into a pitch such as this: "Did you ever notice around our newspaper office how many different people are employed, and wonder what in the world kept them all busy? The majority of these people are getting the paper ready to turn over to you for the final step — that of getting it into the hands of the subscriber. In addition to the people you see in the office, hundreds of other people all over the world are gathering news to place in the paper. That's how important your work as a carrier is and why you should give the best service possible. We can have the best editor, the best equipment, the best advertising men, and the best circulation department, but if you as a carrier fail to give good service, all is lost."

Train Carriers in Salesmanship

The Davenport newspapers emphasize salesmanship in all their carrier meetings. They put showmanship into their programs and dramatize sales ideas with cartoons, drawings and pictures.

"We constantly sent bulletins on better sales methods to our carriers," said Mill. "In carrier campaigns we sent additional bulletins listing objections they would receive, then we gave answers to these objections."

---

[1] *Circulation Management Magazine*, May, 1955, p. 10.

The circulation department of the Denver, Colo., *Post* (circulation 253,410, population 415,786) outlines sales talks for its carriers and supervisors. These talks get down to specific questions and answers and even suggest that all-important opening sentence. The sales talk then swings into a description of the many fine features in the paper, stressing easy-to-read makeup, features for all the family, sports pages, the radio and television listings, comics, editorials, classified ads, etc. Good carrier service and monthly collections also are described.

The Minneapolis *Star* and *Tribune* stress salesmanship in a booklet entitled "What Are You Doing Tomorrow Morning?" Attractively printed and illustrated in colors, it is both a solicitation piece to be shown to the prospect and a sales text for the carrier. The principal character in the book is Erwin, impish, blues-chasing carrier for the *Star* and *Tribune*. He proceeds to tell a lady what his morning paper can do to brighten her life and make the day more interesting and profitable. Interspersed with quoted sales talks are illustrated items of various features in the paper. It all adds up to impressive sales talk presented in a humorous fashion that will appeal to the boy and help him to sell more papers.

The Dallas, Tex., *News* (circulation 207,156, population 434,462) gives to each new carrier a small book of instructions entitled "How To Be an A-1 Dallas News Carrier-Salesman." This gives the boy full details concerning selling, collecting and delivering. Each point is well illustrated so that all instructions are fully understood (see Fig. 18.3).

The Dayton, Ohio, *Daily News* believes that definite instructions are as important for branch managers as for carrier-salesmen. It has prepared for branch counselors an illustrated booklet, stressing human relations, the points to be considered in selecting new boys, the honor and merit program and other matters pertaining to sales, service and collections.

Enthusiasm Important in Carrier Meetings

Regular meetings of the circulation manager and district managers with carriers, when properly conducted, are strong factors in developing a pleasant and effective working relationship. Such meetings with the boys must be more than mere meetings. Attendance will begin to wane immediately if the sessions are not made intensely interesting and helpful. Discussions, even those regarding the most serious carrier problems, need not be dry and tiresome. They may be full of zest and surprises, and thus hold interest and attention. Lively programs at all meetings and some unexpected attendance prizes and refreshments occasionally will cause carriers to wonder what will be happening at the next gathering of their group.

WHEN TO MAKE WEEKLY COLLECTIONS

SUN	MON	TUE	WED	THU	FRI	SAT
11	12	13	14	15	16	17

Never let bills double up. Weekly collections are due on Friday and Saturday of each week. If you are late in collecting from a weekly customer, always explain that it's for last week's bill and that you'll be around again next Saturday for the current week. This word of explanation will save you many difficult collection situations.

WHEN TO MAKE MONTHLY COLLECTIONS

	SUN	MON	TUE	WED	THU	FRI	SAT
M A Y	22	23	24	25	26	27	28
	29	30	31				
J U N E				1	2	3	4
	5	6	7	8	9	10	11

Monthly bills are larger and even more important to collect on time. Monthly collections are due when the last day of the month rolls around. Work it out with your customers so that all bills will be paid by the fifth of each month.

IF YOU INCREASE YOUR SUB LIST BY ONLY 2 EACH MONTH SEE HOW IT PAYS OFF

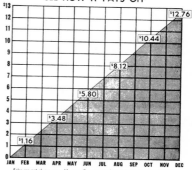

Sales are not always easy. However, the more people you ask to take The News, the better chance you have to increase your profits. Suppose you started adding two new subs each month the very first month on the route. At the end of only five months, you would be making $5.80 more each month. In one year's time, you would be earning $12.76 more profit each month than when you first took your route over. This system will work. Try it, and remember, the way to do it is to make calls, calls, and more calls. YOU can.

ABOUT CHECKS...

? ? The News is not responsible for checks received on your route. You are the loser when checks are bad. Therefore, you should be very careful about cashing checks for more than the subscriber owes. Unless you are very sure of the people, tell them you must keep your money for change.

OK Payment by check is a convenience that you should extend to your customers. Take checks for only the amount of the bill. Since it is not a large amount, rarely will you run into trouble.

Do you have a
WEEKLY ROUTE?

Example:

| YOUR WEEKLY PAPER BILL | YOUR WEEKLY CUSTOMERS PAY A TOTAL OF THIS MUCH EACH WEEK | YOUR MONTHLY CUSTOMERS PAY A TOTAL OF THIS MUCH EACH MONTH |

The News requires paper bills be paid in full on weekly routes. Many routes have both weekly and monthly pay customers. If you have such a route, you might wonder which type you have.

Suppose your paper bill for the week is $25.00 and suppose you have enough customers who pay by the week that you collect $27.00, which is more than enough to pay the weekly bill. You have a weekly route and pay your bill each week. At the end of the month, the money you collect from people who pay by the month is yours. In short ... if your weekly collections are enough to pay for your papers by the week, you have a weekly route and pay your bill each week.

Fig. 18.3 — Excellent illustrations accompany directions in the instruction booklet the Dallas, Tex., **News** gives beginning carriers.

Carrier and parent participation in staging the program is a strong factor in developing perfect attendance. The more a circulation manager or district manager may do to make his carriers feel that it is *their* meeting and not *his,* the nearer he is toward obtaining and maintaining their cooperation.

The three goals to work toward in carrier meetings are *attendance, interest* and *action.* The boys must be present, their interest must be aroused and held, and the program must be presented in so impressive a way that they will be driven to action. Each meeting throughout must carry a high degree of enthusiasm. A wide-awake promotion manager knows how all this may be accomplished.

EXTRA INCENTIVES FOR CARRIER-SALESMEN

Training, of course, is among the first requirements for success in newspaper selling and delivering, but most publishers and circulation managers have learned that some attractive incentives also must be provided from time to time to keep carrier-salesmen interested and up to standard in their work. The most common incentives are:

1. Entertainment passes.
2. Merchandise premiums.
3. Cash prizes.
4. Special day offers.
5. Trips.
6. Scholarships.

Passes Are Popular

All youngsters like to attend places of entertainment. The movie at the local theater is a great drawing card on week-end nights. Baseball and football games, rodeos, ice shows and circuses are exceedingly popular. A carrier will gladly put in extra hours and use extra salesmanship to obtain a new subscriber or two if it will win for him a pass to an event like these.

"Trips to major league baseball games using chartered buses is the best producing promotion we can use," says I. A. Myers, circulation manager of the Marion, Ind., *Chronicle* and *Leader-Tribune* (combined circulation 22,687, population 35,344). "Other successful incentives have been trips to amusement parks, hockey games and football games." The South Bend, Ind., *Tribune* (circulation 108,793, population 115,911) has found the Annual Ice Capades in Chicago its most popular and resultful incentive for stepping up carrier selling. A fun-filled day is offered to each carrier who obtains 10 "starts" for eight weeks at $2.80 each. The winners go by bus to Chicago's Forum Cafeteria for lunch, then to the Ice Capades. On the return trip they stop in Gary at Wilson's Bar-B-Q for dinner.

Fig. 18.4 — Football premium offer to carriers by the Cleveland **Plain Dealer** for subscription increases.

The Pasadena, Calif., *Independent* (circulation 25,623, population 104,577) makes carriers feel that they are regular members of the news staff by offering them a "press card" when they obtain a certain number of new subscribers. The card carries the word "Press" overprinted in red and says: "Good for one general admission to any of the following Amusement Centers, Moving Picture Theaters, Miniature Golf Courses, Bowling Alleys, Roller Skating or Ice Skating Rinks and Swimming Pools." These cards are redeemed at full price by the newspaper. This plan appeals to the boy's pride in his newspaper connection, and for that reason is very effective.

Merchandise Premiums, Too, Bring Results

Merchandise premiums and prizes in great variety may be offered carriers for turning in extra subscriptions, and always are popular.

The first thing one sees upon entering the circulation department of the New Orleans, La., *Times-Picayune* and *States-Item* (combined circulation 357,163, population 570,445) is an array of merchandise items that would excite the imagination of any teen-age boy. A variety of paraphernalia, especially selected to appeal to carriers, is attractively displayed in modern show cases in the newspapers' "premium store."[2]

The "premium store" was first opened in 1954, when the *Times-Picayune* Publishing Company used the merit and demerit system of carrier promotion and employed district managers, with carriers under contract to the company. It served as a constant means of promotion, since carriers could come up to the department at any time and actually see and select articles for which they wished to work. This method was particularly successful with new carriers. At the time a boy came in to be interviewed to go on a route, he was shown the "premium store" and the wonderful prizes he could earn.

Many newspapers have a special window and counter for display of premiums offered to carrier-salesmen. They also issue to carriers catalogs provided by supply houses, showing various merchandise items that may be won by carriers who obtain new subscriptions.

Sporting goods have a strong appeal in the proper season — football in the fall (see Fig. 18.4), basketball in the winter and baseball in the spring. The Rockford, Ill., *Register-Republic* and *Star* (combined circulation 83,973, population 92,927) one autumn used goldenrod sheets — 11 x 17 inches printed in blue and folded into four pages 8½ x 11 inches — to announce its "Annual Pigskin Frolic Offer." It offered a football for 10 points in a selling contest, a trip to the Wisconsin-Northwestern football game for 25 points or both prizes for 35 points.

---

[2] *Circulation Management Magazine,* July, 1954, p. 27.

Fig. 18.5 — Handing out bicycles to premium winners is a big event with the Des Moines **Register** and **Tribune**.

The Cleveland *Press and News* (circulation 385,000, population 914,808) one winter offered to each carrier who turned in four subscription orders, an interesting basketball package, including a rubber basketball, goal and net, gym bag and sweat shirt.

Another attractive offer by the Cleveland *Press and News* was a Radiocraft Easy-To-Assemble Kit. This included a beautiful preassembled plastic cabinet, a sensitive station tuner, regulation head phone, battery and diode detector and transistor amplifier. This was earned with a reasonable number of subscription orders and gave to the winning carrier the fun and excitement of building and listening to his own radio.

Bicycles sometimes are given as premiums, but because of the cost the number of subscriptions required to own one is so high that a carrier must have much self-confidence and courage to win (see Fig. 18.5). Bicycle attachments, such as headlight, speedometer and carrier, are more popular offerings.

Carriers Like Cash Prizes

Some circulation and promotion managers have had better success by offering cash prizes than by giving merchandise premiums. Many lads would prefer to receive money and then buy with it what they want. The Michigan City, Ind., *News-Dispatch* (circulation 14,110, population 31,663) has its carriers vote each year on what they want as awards for new subscriptions.

The Houston, Tex., *Post* (circulation 198,636, population 596,163) promoted many sales by carriers when it offered a $15 cash award for a route increase of 10 daily and Sunday subscribers. "This is to encourage you to spend more time selling yourself and your newspaper," the circulation manager told each carrier. "We will be glad to furnish you five samples each morning — pick out five homes where the people will be up — attach the two-week sample card to the sample copy — just knock on the door and say: 'Good morning, I am the independent distributor of the Houston *Post*. I am leaving you a free copy with an order card. I think you will enjoy reading the *Post*. If you do, just drop this order card in the mail. I have already put a stamp on it.' Ask your sales manager about this on his next visit with you. This method will produce business for you. We want you to be a Winner."

Five calls a week formed the basis of a summer selling campaign put on by the Cleveland *Press and News*. Each new 3-month subscription entitled a carrier to $1 in cash, plus a chance at winning the prize of the week, which was either a bicycle, camera, some piece of sports equipment or other type of merchandise.

Special Days for Selling

Certain seasons and days of the year are more conducive to selling than others. The Bartlesville, Okla., *Examiner-Enterprise* (circulation 8,576, population 19,228) gave 2-dollar bills for subscriptions turned in on Friday, the 13th. This was double the usual commission of $1, and served to dispel the unlucky day idea.

The Cleveland *Press and News* found the Christmas and New Year's season a good time to put on a selling contest with carriers. It issues a holiday order book containing 25 order blanks. Interesting prizes become Christmas gifts which carriers may earn for themselves, their mothers or other members of their families.

The South Bend, Ind., *Tribune* makes certain days of the year memorable with appropriate prizes for carriers who are willing to compete for them. At Easter it offers a 10-pound, tender, cured ham for six new subscriptions (see Fig. 18.6). For Mother's Day a carrier may win for his mother a gift of nylon hose by turning in three orders for the *Tribune*. And for Valentine's Day, two pounds of deli-

Earn a HAM for EASTER!

OFFER MARCH 16 to 30

for only 6 starts

10-lbs. Tender Cured!

SOUTH BEND TRIBUNE:
Here are my 6-new starts...signed up for 8-weeks, at 35¢ a week.

1 _____
2 _____
3 _____
4 _____
5 _____
6 _____

CARRIER'S NAME _____
ADDRESS _____

SEND ME _____ PAPERS.

Fig. 18.6 — South Bend, Ind., **Tribune** carriers sell subscriptions and earn Easter hams.

cious chocolates packaged in a lovely heart-shaped satin box may be earned for the carrier's mother, sister or girl friend. Attractively illustrated posters are used in promoting these special offers.

Carrier-salesmen are particularly anxious to earn extras for Christmas, and the Oakland, Calif., *Tribune* puts on a special campaign at this season (see Fig. 18.7).

Trips Arouse Great Interest

Of all the incentives that may be offered carrier-salesmen to arouse interest and spur them into productive activity, trips are perhaps the most successful. For many boys a trip on the train, a bus or an airplane is a novel experience. Few have ever eaten in a dining car or spent a night in a hotel, and to spend a night in a sleeping car is another thrill.

"Our entire circulation department is thoroughly sold on trips.

HEY FELLOWS!
SANTA'S BRINGING
GIFTS
AND
'CASH
FOR
XMAS'

Just in time for Christmas. This is your opportunity to get EXTRA CASH for gifts and two very fine presents for yourself.

YOUR CHOICE FOR
10 SUBSCRIPTIONS

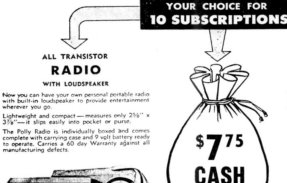

ALL TRANSISTOR
RADIO
WITH LOUDSPEAKER

Now you can have your own personal portable radio with built-in loudspeaker to provide entertainment wherever you go.

Lightweight and compact — measures only 2⅝" x 3⅞" — it slips easily into pocket or purse.

The Polly Radio is individually boxed and comes complete with carrying case and 9 volt battery ready to operate. Carries a 60 day Warranty against all manufacturing defects.

$7⁷⁵
CASH

ALL WOOL MELTON
WARM UP
JACKET

Matching knitted cuffs, collar and waist band with contrasting white stripe.

Snap front with leather pocket trim and full rayon lined.

Sizes: Boys: 12 — 14 — 16 — 18 — 20

Mens: Small — Medium — Large

Colors: Forest Green — Royal Blue — Flame Red

SPECIAL "CASH FOR XMAS"
DECEMBER 2 TO DECEMBER 15 ONLY

$2⁵⁰ CASH FOR 3 SUBSCRIPTIONS

You will receive CASH for three or more subscriptions you turn in to start December 2 to and including subscriptions starting December 15, 1959.

PLUS 75¢ for each additional subscription turned in during this "Cash for Xmas" period.

A newspaperboy earning a jacket or radio by December 15, 1959 will be entitled to 75¢ for each subscription over 10 starting by December 15, providing the subscriptions are not used for other 10 subscription prizes. The 75¢ per subscription will not be paid for subscriptions over or under 10 after December 15.

GET ALL 3 FOR 30 SUBSCRIPTIONS AND YOUR OVERPOINTS COUNT FOR EXTRA PRIZES, CASH

The jacket, the transistor radio or the $7.75 cash for 10 subscriptions is available to all Tribune newspaperboys qualifying from December 2 to January 1, 1960.

Each newspaperboy is limited to a total of three (3) prizes. He may take one of each (jacket, transistor radio or $7.75 cash) or he may take all of one item.

Jackets and radios earned by December 15 will be delivered prior to Christmas.

See your district advisor for the SPECIAL value of CONTRACT subscriptions towards your prize.

Oakland Tribune

Fig. 18.7 — The Oakland, Calif., **Tribune** gives carriers an opportunity to earn both cash and merchandise at Christmastime.

You might say we're trip happy," says Ray Gilliland, circulation director of the Lancaster, Pa., *Intelligencer-Journal* and *New Era* (combined circulation 79,603, population 63,774). "Our carriers produce more orders on trip offers than any other type of offer."[3]

The Lancaster newspapers have taken their carriers by train to New York City and Washington, D. C., by overnight steamship to Williamsburg, Va., and by plane to Miami Beach, Fla. Five times or more they have taken their boys to Hershey, Pa., hockey games, baseball and football games in Philadelphia, and on trips to Atlantic City, the Philadelphia Naval Shipyard and World Series games. In all trip offers, every boy who turns in an order receives a cash or merchandise prize of some kind. This increases interest in the contest and helps also to bring down the cost per order. By offering trips, the Lancaster newspapers increased their daily circulation by more than 3,000 within a year.

An outstanding event in the lives of carriers for the Detroit, Mich., *News* one year was a 5-day safari to the national capital. This included visits to the White House, Smithsonian Institution, Mount Vernon and a tour of the Naval Academy at Annapolis.

The Davenport, Iowa, *Democrat* and *Times* provided a 9-day, all-expense-paid trip to a Colorado dude ranch with side trips to Denver and Boulder.

A trip to Chicago to see a baseball game, eat a chicken dinner in China Town and visit the airport is a great annual event for carriers of the South Bend, Ind., *Tribune* (see Fig. 18.8). Sometimes an extra event develops for this trip (see Fig. 18.9).

The Detroit, Mich., *Times* (circulation 391,295, population 1,849,568) provided for three top winners in a carrier subscription-selling campaign, a 3-week trip to England, Scotland, Ireland and Wales via TWA Constellation. One hundred other carriers spent five days in New York, while 300 others had a 3-day deluxe trip to Niagara Falls and Buffalo.

The Little Rock *Arkansas Gazette* (circulation 84,011, population 102,213) urged its readers to help its carrier-salesmen win a trip to Spain and Portugal by air or a trip to New York by airliner (see Fig. 18.10).

A long trip covering several days and many points of interest is not always necessary to arouse the interest of carriers. Small newspapers may as readily obtain results from a trip to the state capitol, a famous close-in resort (see Fig. 18.11) or historical spot. Distance does not always determine the worth of a trip as a circulation-builder. Boys enjoy the companionship of each other and always learn something new and interesting about any place they visit. They'll work hard for a large number of subscriptions to qualify for any kind of trip that is offered.

---

[3]*Circulation Management Magazine,* Apr., 1956, p. 12.

Fig. 18.8 — Great importance is placed on the South Bend, Ind., **Tribune**'s annual trip to Chicago for carriers who have added 8 new subscriptions.

Scholarships Have Great Appeal

Scholarships provide another type of incentive to carrier efficiency that ranks closely in popularity with trips. Hundreds of high school boys, who otherwise would not be able to continue their education, are permitted to attend the best colleges and universities through scholarships provided by newspapers.

Four types of scholarships are offered to carrier-salesmen by the Minneapolis *Star* and *Tribune*:

1. Travel scholarships to continental Europe, covering all basic expenses. These awards are sponsored by the *Star* and *Tribune* and the American Field Service International Scholarships. They are separate from similar awards granted through high schools.

2. Summertime camping scholarships to Camp Rising Sun, Rhinebeck, N. Y. These awards are granted to youths who are top scholastic students from the United States and 15 foreign countries. These are sponsored by the Louis August Jonas Foundation, Inc., and the *Star* and *Tribune*.
3. $250 scholarships to 16 outstanding carrier salesmen. These grants, which are held in trust until needed, are awarded directly by the *Star* and *Tribune* and may be used for tuition, fees and expenses at any accredited college, university, business or trade school.
4. Several scholarships offered carrier salesmen by a number of schools, universities and colleges participating in the *Star* and *Tribune* International Scholarship Program. Most of these scholarships are renewable from year to year until graduation.

All scholarship applications are studied by a board of *Star* and *Tribune* judges who select a group of finalists on the basis of scholastic ability, citizenship and ability as carrier-salesmen. From the finalists are determined the winners of all four types of awards. Names of the winners are announced in the summer of each year.

Many other newspapers offer similar scholarship plans. Great pride is taken by publishers in the boys who have won such scholarships, completed their education and gone out to take important positions. No type of promotion for newspapers so highly dignifies the position of carrier-salesman or wins greater good will from the general public.

Fig. 18.9 — The South Bend **Tribune** plays up an extra event in carriers' annual trip to Chicago.

...I want all of you Tribune carriers to be my guests at The Breakfast Club broadcast while you're on your big Boat Trip to Chicago! Don McNeill

We're all invited!...so get those 12-starts NOW.... and be with the gang on the 2-Day Michigan City-to-Chicago-and-return Boat Trip!

YOU

can help your Gazette Carrier-Salesman win a trip to Spain and Portugal by air

or a trip to New York by airliner

As a participant in the Gazette "Young Columbus" event, now in progress, your Gazette carrier-salesman is working toward this Grand European Tour award, organized jointly by Parade Magazine which appears in the Sunday edition of the Arkansas Gazette, and globe-circling TWA Airlines.

A total of 60 American carrier boys will be treated to a thrilling all-expense-paid experience. They will be flown overseas aboard a giant TWA Jetstream airliner; where, after four days in Lisbon and surrounding country, they will tour by bus across Portugal and Spain to Madrid. The party will be returned by air to New York on Sunday, April 13th. This is an adventure that almost certainly will never come their way again.

There are other prizes too. In addition, there will be four trips for Gazette carrier-salesmen by air to New York for five days.

All Gazette carrier-salesmen know how the prizes are to be awarded. You can help one of these deserving boys by helping him find one or more new subscribers. He'd appreciate your help as soon as possible!

Arkansas Gazette.

Fig. 18.10 — The Little Rock, Ark., **Gazette** promotes a trip for carriers by air to Spain and Portugal or to New York.

The Charleston, S. C., *News and Courier* and *Post* (combined circulation, 92,109, population 70,174) promote strongly such a program and keep a close check on their scholarship winners. Their first college-scholarship boys graduated in 1958, and luster was shed on the scholarship program by acceptance of these graduates at the Philips Exeter Academy, by a visit from the associate director of admissions of Yale University and by the many school honors won by their newspaperboys.

"The first college graduates did us proud," said C. B. Williams, circulation manager, in *Editor & Publisher*.[4] "One of them finished cum laude, and for good measure, received one of ten military medals awarded cadets over the entire nation. A second graduate had the distinction of being chosen president of the senior class. Three of our boys will study at Exeter on scholarships this fall. Three already graduated from this school are now at Princeton, Harvard and the Naval Academy. Those at Princeton and Harvard are there on scholarships."

One of the 1958 scholarships offered by the Charleston newspapers went to a boy who placed first in a highly competitive 2-state examination for an additional scholarship. Another winner was second honor graduate from one of the largest high schools. The third scholarship was given to a Negro boy with a fine record both in school and as a carrier.

The offering of scholarships serves to raise the character and efficiency standards of those in the carrier service. It helps also to draw into the ranks boys with ambition and ideals.

CAMPAIGNS WITH CARRIERS

In addition to prizes and premiums, effective incentives to subscription selling are well-planned and managed campaigns with carriers as chief salesmen. Much selling enthusiasm and effort may be developed through:

1. Seasonal selling.
2. Territorial promotions.
3. One-day drives.
4. Quantity campaigns.

Select the Right Time

Circulation managers realize that certain seasons of the year are better than others for selling subscriptions by carriers or special salesmen. If a newspaper considers it advisable to launch an extensive circulation campaign, it usually is done in the fall when the

---

[4] *Editor & Publisher,* July 26, 1958, p. 46.

IT'S EASY FOR YOU TO EARN THE BIG TRIP TO RIVERVIEW PARK!

YOU CAN DO IT THIS WAY!

1. Secure just 5 or more NEW SUBSCRIBERS on your route between the dates of April 27-28 and May 18-19.

2. Be SURE to have the new customers you secure SIGN THE SPECIAL RIVERVIEW PARK order blank that is provided with this folder . . . because this order blank must be sent to the office along with your order for newspapers. Note that it is designed so that you can mail it easily. This is the only way that an accurate record can be kept of the new orders you secure.

3. Remember to have one of your parents or your district manager 'O.K.' this special order form before sending it to the office.

4. Additional order blanks will be furnished regularly. You need not wait until you have secured the full five orders before you send in your order card.

5. Customers who stop the paper during this contest because of vacations, move-outs, illness, etc., will NOT count against you in this contest. All you need to DO TO QUALIFY FOR THIS EXCITING TRIP IS SECURE 5 BRAND NEW ORDERS from persons who have not taken the paper in the last 30 days!

Fig. 18.11 — A day at an amusement park is an incentive easily promoted with carrier-salesmen.

spirit of activity pervades the atmosphere. Then is the time when persons are looking toward the winter months when they'll want to do more reading and will have more time for it. Salesmen will have enthusiasm for selling and prospects will be in the mood to buy.

The Des Moines *Register* and *Tribune* successfully link together several contests for their annual fall campaign beginning in September and ending in December. Carriers step readily from one contest into the next with increasing enthusiasm and with added earnings. This campaign one year included (1) the launching of the annual Red Necktie Club for carriers and dealers, (2) a 1-week free deal for all who placed orders during the contest, and (3) a contest around Thanksgiving and Christmas, with dressed poultry for prizes.

Only carrier-salesmen who met the requirements for increasing the number of patrons on their route, and dealers who increased their daily and Sunday draw at their stands were entitled to membership in the distinguished Red Necktie Club (see Fig. 18.12). The principal rewards were having their names printed in the Sunday *Register* (circulation 504,188, population 177,965) as those who had attained their goals. A double-page space was required to list all who reached quotas.

To induce a quick response from prospects, carriers were privileged to offer one week's delivery of the paper free to persons who would sign orders for eight-week subscriptions. This helped the carrier-salesmen in their sales talks and was a great aid in getting names on the dotted line.

The holiday contest gave each carrier the opportunity to win a dressed chicken or turkey for his family's Thanksgiving or Christmas dinner. Considerable showmanship was used in promoting this offer. A live turkey was placed on display in the carriers' assembly room; a choice turkey and frying chicken, each wrapped in cellophane, were borrowed from a grocery store and displayed at a carriers' meeting, using decorations of fall leaves, pumpkins, corn stalks, ears of corn and bittersweet.

Interest was further stimulated with offers of special bonuses to carriers who went above certain volume levels in their selling.

A similar selling campaign, known as the Fall Food Parade, was put on by the Cincinnati, Ohio, *Enquirer* (circulation 205,461, population 503,998). This included telephone selling as well as house-to-house solicitation, and for each additional subscription obtained, a carrier was given a certain number of points toward prizes offered in the contest. Turkeys, hams and more than 200 items of canned foods were offered. These food prizes and the number of points required to obtain each were announced in a handsome Fall Food Parade booklet given to each carrier.

Selling in Specified Areas

The circulation of a newspaper is never in balance throughout its territory, with more receiving the paper in one district than in another. The alert circulation manager or promotion manager knows exactly which homes are receiving the paper and in what section of the newspaper's circulation area some building up is needed.

All the help that can be mustered is thrown into selling campaigns launched in the weaker circulation areas. Carriers who have routes there are urged to add to their list of patrons; carriers are brought in from other areas to assist; and special salesmen, too, may be employed. The cooperation of the news and advertising departments likewise is obtained.

The whole staff of the Franklin, La., *Banner-Tribune* (circulation 5,554, population 6,144), a semiweekly, worked together in a campaign to expand distribution to the entire parish in which the newspaper is located. The publisher, Robert J. Angers, Jr., personally went out and knocked on doors. He also gave his advertising manager, pressman and two others in the back shop an opportunity to do some selling. Later he hired a full-time circulation manager, and all stayed active in the campaign for eight months.

"We sold the paper strictly on its merits," says Angers, "without giving any soup bowls, utensils or any other kind of premium. Personally I sold somewhere around 1,000 subscriptions. The long and short of the story is that we increased the list 71 per cent. It was an interesting experience conducted on a very simple formula."

Now throughout the parish the *Banner-Tribune* has blue and white tubes before the homes of all rural subscribers. These spread out 28 miles one way, 20 miles another direction and about 15 another way, with a lot of streets and country roads in between.

The added circulation increased the newspaper's gross business and in a short time the publisher paid off the mortgage on his newspaper and sold his commercial printing business. This would have been impossible without the added income from circulation, according to Angers.

Put Punch Into Single Day

All that may be accomplished even in a single day of well-organized promotion is astonishing.

Carrier-salesmen for the Hackensack, N. J., *Bergen Record* (circulation 81,574, population 29,219) have been led into almost unbelievable activity and results through 1-day sales efforts. A Telephone Order Day, in which all carrier-salesmen took part, brought in over 1,000 orders. Special selling on Washington's Birthday added 750 more subscribers.

THE NOVEMBER
RED NECKTIE
OFFER

ON THE ROUTE

COLLECTING

MOOSE HUNTING

AT PARTIES

AT GAMES

AT SCHOOL

SEE WHAT YOU GET FOR YOUR 2 INCREASE!

1. YOU GET
OFFICIAL REGISTER AND TRIBUNE
RED NECKTIE

A picture can't possibly describe this brilliant, fluorescent red, bow tie. Show your friends and customers you are one of the star Register and Tribune carrier salesmen for November.

2. YOU GET
YOUR REGISTER AND TRIBUNE
RED NECKTIE MEMBERSHIP CARD

Every Red Necktie winner, will get the official Red Necktie Club Membership card. You'll carry it in your billfold for years to come.

3. YOU GET
YOUR NAME PRINTED
IN THE
SUNDAY REGISTER

On December 9, the Des Moines Sunday Register, will print YOUR NAME in the Red Necktie Club Membership list. Thousands of families will look for the name of their carrier salesman on the honor roll.

SEE INSIDE FOR SWELL PRIZES YOU CAN EARN WITH ADDITIONAL INCREASE

Fig. 18.12 — The Red Necktie Club sponsored by the Des Moines **Register** and **Tribune** has been a popular organization for many years. Numerous other prizes are given for additional subscriptions.

The carriers' selling ability was thoroughly tested in a one-day campaign which the circulation manager called "The Big Day." Fifty awards were selected, varying in value from a free movie ticket to a $3 baseball. These awards were numbered from 1 to 50 with each fifth prize having a high monetary value. Saturday was the day selected and the campaign continued from 8 o'clock in the morning until 8 o'clock in the evening. The newspaper office was open during that time to receive orders obtained by carriers. All new starts had to be telephoned to the office. Prizes were awarded in the order the telephone calls were received.

"The response astounded all of us," said Edward L. Bennett, circulation manager. "By 8 o'clock Saturday night we had received 569 new orders. They were all good orders, too, and helped us to show a substantial circulation increase."

Drive for Definite Increase

Special efforts to add a certain number of subscribers within a limited time have proved successful with many newspapers.

In November of each year the *Bergen Record* puts on a campaign for a circulation increase of 1,000. It starts with a kick-off breakfast at a local restaurant for all home delivery adult personnel. After a nice breakfast, quotas are announced for each district and for each carrier. Each is told how many new subscriptions he must bring in each day and each week in order to make possible the 1,000 increase. If the 1,000 goal is reached, a steak dinner is provided.

Each year that this contest has been conducted the campaign goal has been reached and the publisher has eaten steak with the circulation and promotion department personnel.

ACTIVITIES FOR CARRIERS

The spirit of loyalty and interest among carriers is further promoted by various activities in which they may display physical and mental skills and engage in friendly contests. When the various hobbies and talents of boys can be brought out into the open they provide wholesome entertainment and recreation for boys and parents. Many newspapers have kept their carrier forces intact and lively with interest by sponsoring:

1. Talent shows with carriers as the participants.
2. Bands and orchestras composed entirely of carrier-salesmen.
3. Hobby fairs with carriers competing for prizes.
4. Sports contests between carrier teams.
5. Book clubs to stimulate interest in reading.

Like To Display Talents

It is surprising what a talent show will bring forth from a group of newspaper carriers. Always some boys can sing well, impersonate, play a musical instrument or whistle. Others are good at cowboy stunts, dancing, acts of magic. Some carrier groups have been sufficiently talented to charge admission for their shows and raise a nice sum of money for their favorite activities.

The Cleveland, Ohio, *Press and News* conducted an annual talent search for entertainers during the month preceding the carriers' annual party. On one occasion 100 acts were auditioned, from which nine were selected to appear on a party program. These winners in the preliminary contest competed at the party for prizes of $75, $50 and $25, and a consolation award of $5 to each of the other contestants. An applause meter determined the winners.

Have Own Musical Organizations

In communities where it has been possible to obtain a qualified bandmaster, carrier bands and orchestras have been formed. When the newspaper outfits them in bright new uniforms and presents them in programs at public meetings, pride in their connection is greatly enhanced, and in addition they have received fine musical instruction.

The most popular activity of carriers for the New Bedford, Mass., *Standard-Times* (circulation 61,527, population 109,189) is its 40-piece band composed entirely of *Standard-Times* carriers. The boys perform with enthusiasm and receive high commendation and applause at every appearance locally and at important community gatherings in various towns within the newspaper's circulation area.

Out of the same group has come a *Standard-Times* Orchestra, which appears before smaller audiences and helps further to promote the newspaper in the area it serves.[5]

Hobbies in Great Variety

There is no better way to develop friendships among carriers than to bring them together through mutual interests in their hobbies. Boys are interested in building many things, ranging in scientific and mechanical technique from a bird house to a miniature sputnik. Most surprising will be the variety of their collections — match folders, colored rocks, stamps, autographed baseballs and more.

---

[5] Frank W. Rucker, *Newspaper Circulation — What, Where and How,* Iowa State University Press, Ames, Iowa, pp. 77–78.

A well-conducted hobby show, possibly with prizes, will interest other fine boys in becoming carrier-salesmen, and will supply material for the news department, for each boy and his hobby is the background for an intensely interesting news or feature story.

The Atlanta, Ga., *Journal* (circulation 253,470, population 331,314) annually stages a free hobby fair for all its carriers. The event is held in the YMCA with judges selected on the local level, and all boys are invited to bring their parents and friends.

Another Interest Is Sports

The great interest of carriers in sports is shown not only in their attendance at games and contests but by engaging in various contests themselves. With a carrier organization of from 50 to 300 boys, it is possible to organize almost any kind of a team — baseball, basketball, football or archery. Aquatic sports also are popular.

Newspapers that encourage their carriers to participate in clean sports not only bring publicity to the newspaper but provide important physical and moral development for the boys.

Book Clubs Stimulate Reading

Always, too, in a carrier organization are boys who like to read. The Elizabeth, N. J., *Journal* (circulation 50,331, population 112,817) sponsors a Newspaperboys Book Club, whereby carriers may obtain books of educational value at reasonable prices. To introduce the club, it issued a booklet with brief reviews of 36 books. "You now have the opportunity to build a wonderful library of books that are fun to read, books that will help you achieve your future ambitions," the circulation department explained with a suggestion to each carrier that he "let his District Adviser show him how easily he might earn these truly worthwhile, enjoyable, educational awards." (See 18.13.)

SETTING UP A COMPLETE PROGRAM

A look at the various activities that may be pursued with carrier-salesmen shows that to set up a complete promotion program for them is a heavy responsibility, but the newspaper that plans every detail with thoughtfulness and precision and never lags in putting through its program will reap generous returns. A good example:

The Hackensack, N. J., *Bergen Record* relies heavily on its carrier organization in maintaining a high circulation volume. Its success in that effort is the outcome of a well-constructed and well-executed program, which consists of:

1. *Carrier Achievements.* Boys are given ranks according to their accomplishments on a plan similar to that of the Boy Scouts. The ranks in order of importance are: (1) Honor Carrier, (2)

Elizabeth Daily Journal

Newspaperboys Book Club

INVITATION TO KNOWLEDGE

Fig. 18.13 — Front page of booklet explaining the Book Club for newspaperboys sponsored by the Elizabeth, N.J., **Journal**.

Ace Carrier, (3) Star Carrier, (4) Regular Carrier, (5) Recruit.

2. *Sports Events.* Carrier-salesmen participate in softball, basketball, tennis and ping-pong tournaments.

3. *Carrier Sales Promotion.* This runs for 307 days and includes: (1) a circulation prize catalogue, from which carrier may select prizes he wishes to obtain; (2) standing offer of a trip to Washington, D. C., for a certain increase in patrons; and (3) short trip each month to various places in or near New York City, for two or three orders.

4. *Gimmick Promotions.* These include such contests as Telephone Order Day, Last Man Contest, and the like.

5. *District Adviser Promotions.* This consists of incentives for adult personnel. Typical is a bean-steak dinner contest, in which the winners eat steak and the losers eat beans.

6. *Newspaperboy Publicity.* This program is designed by the International Circulation Managers Association to draw public attention to the many opportunities offered boys through newspaper route management.

Edward L. Bennett, circulation manager of the *Bergen Record,* tabulates the minutest details that must be given attention in carrying out this full program:

CARRIER ACHIEVEMENT PROGRAM

1. Creative work.
   A. Study and up-date the present program when necessary.
   B. Always be alert for a better plan.
2. Supplies: T-shirts, jackets, sweaters and trophies.
   A. Inventory and order.
   B. Maintain stock.
   C. Make weekly issues to carriers who qualify.
   D. Arrange for sewing on of emblems.
3. Rank cards.
   A. Type on carrier's name.
   B. Have Circulation Manager sign.
   C. Withdraw and issue cash which regular carriers qualify for.
4. Arrangements for annual banquet.
   A. Secure hall.
   B. Contract for meal.
   C. Arrange decorations.
   D. Arrange seating.
   E. Prepare awards for presentations, etc.
5. Arrange the annual basketball tournament.
   A. Secure basketball courts.
   B. Secure officials.
   C. Coordinate with Home Delivery Department district advisers for the timing of the events.
   D. Supervise the tournament.
   E. Present awards.
6. Conduct the softball tournament.
   A. Secure softball field.
   B. Secure officials.
   C. Coordinate with Home Delivery Department district advisers for the timing of the events.
   D. Supervise the tournament.
   E. Present awards.
7. Arrange and conduct the tennis tournament.
   A. Secure tennis court.
   B. Secure officials.
   C. Coordinate with Home Delivery Department district advisers for the timing of the events.
   D. Supervise the tournament.
   E. Present awards.
8. Arrange and conduct the ping-pong tournament.
   A. Secure hall for ping-pong tournament.
   B. Secure officials.
   C. Coordinate with Home Delivery Department district advisers for the timing of the events.
   D. Supervise the tournament.
   E. Present awards.
9. Administer the Vocational Guidance program.
   A. Give adequate publicity.
   B. Secure advisers.
   C. Endeavor to improve the program.
10. Administer the Scholarship program.
    A. Give adequate publicity.
    B. Secure judges.
    C. Endeavor to improve the program.

TRIP PROMOTIONS

1. Creative work.
   A. Be constantly on the watch for trips that would interest and appeal to carrier boys.
   B. Make contacts, secure prices, dates, etc.
2. Maintain liaison after the trip has been decided upon.
   A. Notify all concerned how many boys qualified for the trip.
   B. What time they can expect the bus to arrive, return, etc.
3. Arrange for food or box lunches when necessary.
   A. Decide menu for the lunch, secure enough for the number of the boys qualifying for the trip.
4. Order buses.
   A. Requisition buses.
   B. Determine where the bus will leave from.
   C. Make sure bus drivers have correct information.
5. Prepare itinerary for some trips.
   A. Compile information from available spots to visit.
   B. Arrange a time schedule for stops.
6. Compile list of winners for the trips.
   A. Receive the 13-week orders and requests for trips from the district advisers.
   B. Compile a list of winners for the trips.
   C. Type stencil of the same, mimeograph and issue copy of the winners to all concerned.
7. Conduct the trip.
   A. Accompany boys on trips. See that all prior arrangements for the trip have been properly carried out, and that the carriers are properly received at their destination.

NOTICES TO CARRIERS

1. Mimeographed notices.
   A. Copy must be written.
   B. Layout must be made.
   C. Stencils must be prepared.
   D. Notice must be run off on the mimeograph machine.
   E. Notices must be counted for the various 36 districts.
   F. Issue notices to the district advisers.
2. Notices to be printed.
   A. Layout and copy must be prepared.
   B. Requisition prepared.
   C. Signature of circulation manager obtained.
   D. Follow-through must be maintained so notices will be received in time for dispatch to district men.
   E. Notices must be counted.
   F. Notices must be distributed to district men to issue to carriers.
3. Bulletin board material.
   A. Charts must be prepared for each trip and contest to create enthusiasm among the district men and supervisors for that promotion.
   B. Charts must be posted daily.
   C. Requests for photographs of trips by carrier boys.
   D. Requests for publicity on the trips conducted.

PRIZE PROMOTIONS

1. Maintain liaison with sources of prizes.
2. Develop new sources of prizes.
3. Process prize orders weekly.
4. Distribute prizes when they are received.
5. Return damaged or missent prizes.
6. Prepare visual prize displays such as prize boxes.

CASH PROMOTIONS

1. Receive requisitions from carriers for cash.
2. Tabulate winners.
3. Requisition cash.
4. Distribute cash.
    A. Insert cash in envelope.
    B. Address envelope to proper carrier.
    C. Obtain a receipt for cash.

SPECIAL PROMOTIONS

1. Major details.
    A. Details for promoting with staff.
    B. Details for promoting with carriers.
    C. Creating enthusiasm.
    D. Critique.
    E. Report of cost, methods used and results.
2. Copy and layout.
    A. Doorknob hangers.
    B. Sample literature.
    C. Collection cards.
    D. Various forms.
    E. Carrier manuals.
    F. Training notices.
    G. Carrier Christmas cards.
    H. Letters to carriers at Christmastime.
    I. Stand sales window cards.
    J. Prepare conventions displays.
    K. Keep promotion books up to date.
3. Newspaperboy publicity.
    A. Create, design and prepare layout and copy for carrier ads.
    B. Write and send to editorial department stories of newspaperboy trips and events.
    C. Prepare and conduct a large-scale promotion annually for National Newspaperboy Day.
4. Carrier newspaper.
    A. Furnish material for contents.
    B. Write copy and heads.
    C. Prepare layout.
    D. Secure pictures and engravings.
    E. Coordinate with mechanical department.
    F. Supervise distribution.

Careful attention to such details as these brought results for the *Bergen Record*. It is not surprising that this newspaper in 1958 received the *Editor & Publisher* Circulation Award and in 1957 the International Circulation Managers' Promotion Award for the best promotion program in the United States.

CHAPTER 19

Promoting Circulation Through Salesmen

WHILE THE CARRIER ORGANIZATION is chiefly relied upon by most newspapers to sell subscriptions and keep circulation at a high standard, the publisher must not overlook the effectiveness with which salesmen may be used in handling tough selling situations. Most circulation managers have found the work of salesmen, employed either full time or for a limited period, to be a good supplement to all the selling that may be done by carrier-salesmen.

The promotion department, if it is alert, knows when selling assistance of this kind is needed. It knows also how to develop sales groups and institute sales methods that will really do the job. Circulation promotion through salesmen generally falls into four categories:

1. Solicitation by experienced salesmen operating on full or part time.
2. Working in special campaigns with a crew of salesmen to build up circulation in a definite area.
3. Selling by individuals or groups inspired by special premiums, prizes and other inducements.
4. Increasing sales of single copies.

EXPERIENCED SALESMEN BUILD PERMANENT CIRCULATION

Although personal solicitation is expensive because of the limited number of sales that may be made per hour, results are perhaps more permanent than from any other method of subscription selling, for subscribers are less likely to discontinue when they feel a sense of responsibility to the salesman.

[297]

Robert N. Weed, promotion director of the Minneapolis *Star* and *Tribune* (combined circulation 502,252, population 521,718), believes that few newspapers are taking advantage of the tremendous opportunities for face-to-face newspaper selling. "When it comes to selling newspapers," he says, "nothing matches personal salesmanship."

Advantages of Face-To-Face Selling

Hugh Patterson, circulation manager of the Waterloo, Iowa, *Courier* (circulation 49,013, population 65,198), has well demonstrated the effectiveness of this type of selling in the rural districts surrounding Waterloo, and points out these advantages:

1. It helps to stabilize mail circulation.
2. Most disgruntled readers can be appeased through proper handling by a qualified solicitor.
3. Public acceptance of the paper can be enhanced by the personality of a good solicitor.

"When given extra responsibilities and some authority, solicitors develop great pride in their work," Patterson adds. "The time spent in training and indoctrinating them pays dividends."

For soliciting work, the Waterloo *Courier* looks for a man of maturity with successful sales experience and some agricultural background. He must be somewhat of an extrovert, able to observe the fine points of promotion and public relations; be neat in appearance and above all have a good reputation in his community.

"We have an understanding with each solicitor that he has certain obligations to the *Courier* in addition to the obvious responsibility of maintaining mail circulation in his territory," Patterson says. "For example, he is charged with improving, wherever possible, public relations in his area. He is mail circulation's front line, and as opportunities arise he is expected to perform reasonable services which will enhance his and the *Courier's* reputation in our neighboring communities. He is expected to be a student of the newspaper he is selling and is encouraged to familiarize himself with competitive papers. He must inform our office of service errors, whether they are the result of mishandling in our mailing room or an error of the postal service. When he learns of a news story, he must contact the proper correspondent or our news room, and he is instructed to be on the alert for good feature material. Some of our better features have been initiated by our solicitors. He must make an honest effort to personally contact each reader in his territory whose subscription is due for expiration and he must remit for all business on which he is to receive commission."[1]

---

[1] *Editor & Publisher*, Sept. 5, 1953, p. 38.

An experienced solicitor will assemble information in advance of his calls, such as the correct names of prospects, their interests and their connections in the community, their ability to subscribe and perhaps their political leanings. Salesmen who work in a territory from month to month and year to year develop a close personal friendship with people of the area and through the proper approach win them as subscribers. Several calls over a rather long period of time may be required to sell the newspaper to some, but when won for the newspaper they usually remain on the subscription list.

The closer a salesman may come to his prospects, the greater success he will have in getting their names on the dotted line. George Williams, publisher of the Spencer, Iowa, *Reporter* (circulation 6,090, population 7,446), who has spent the greater part of his active newspaper life in circulation promotion, is a strong believer in personal salesmanship. When he worked in the circulation field, he stressed to the limit the personal touch. If a prospect was not at home when he called, he left a copy of the paper at the door, and on it he scribbled with a heavy pencil this personalized note:

"Dear Bill: I notice you're not taking the *Reporter*. We're trying to put out a good paper. Wish you'd take it, if you agree and think the price is right. George."

This little gesture of friendship was 50 per cent effective, and in one year it added over 200 subscribers.

The experienced salesman knows also the best seasons of the year, days of the week and hours of the day in which to make calls upon various classes of prospects. This is more important than most persons believe.

Temporary absences and summer vacation periods cause difficulty for solicitors in some areas. Holidays, curiously enough, are accompanied by a reaction that causes prospects to feel that if money is spent it should be for instant enjoyment. The weather, too, has its effect. Prospects do not react kindly to being held in rain, snow or cold to hear a solicitor explain the merits of his newspaper. On a bright, cheerful day people are in a better frame of mind and more readily listen even though they may be busier at their regular responsibilities. In some cases, outdoor interviews are more resultful than those conducted in offices or living rooms. Contrary to the usual thought that salesmen must get their feet inside the door, newspaper solicitors who work rural districts during summer months find that a sale is more easily made in the open than within the house.

Months immediately preceding a political election are not the best time for face-to-face solicitation. Most solicitors prefer to avoid those times because political news causes arguments and probably disagreement. Salesmen don't want to be put on the defensive.

Any day of the week except Saturday and Sunday is a good time for selling. Many families hie to the lakes or nearby resorts for recreational weekends. Prospects are more likely to be at home during morning hours. Then, too, at that time of day the temperature is more comfortable and prospects usually are in a more receptive mood.

A salesman determined to bring in a good report at the end of the day and earn for himself a substantial commission knows also the importance of having with him all the necessary material and equipment that may be needed in making sales. On his person should be: (1) a copy of the newspaper, (2) $20 in change, (3) a pad of receipts, (4) blank checks, (5) a short, sharpened pencil for writing receipts, (6) a fountain pen for writing checks, and (7) a notebook for memoranda or news items that may be picked up along the way.

Telephone Selling Also Successful

For some newspapers, voice-to-voice salesmanship has been almost as effective as face-to-face selling. Some of the large newspapers employ both men and women to spend from four to eight hours a day in selling by telephone. The New York *Times* (circulation 600,319, population 7,891,957) carries on a continuous campaign of telephone solicitation for home delivered circulation. On a typical evening there will be 25 or more specially trained solicitors calling up potential *Times* buyers.

Most full-time or part-time salesmen, doing house-to-house or telephone calling, work mainly on a commission basis. Some, however, are paid a small salary plus commission or are allowed an expense account. The usual commission is from 40 to 50 per cent for new subscriptions and from 20 to 50 per cent for renewals. The Waterloo, Iowa, *Courier* has ten full-time and three part-time solicitors who are compensated on a straight commission basis of 28 per cent for renewals and 50 per cent for new subscriptions.

CAMPAIGNS BRING QUICK RESULTS

Often publishers decide that they should extend their newspaper's circulation into new areas or at least increase the circulation in a certain town or part of the county where few homes are receiving the paper. To do this successfully, five steps are required:

1. A survey of the territory to find out just what homes need to be contacted.
2. Obtain some interesting news and features from the territory to indicate that the paper will contain material of special interest to those who live there.
3. Set up a system that will assure prompt delivery in the area.

4. Deliver the paper free for one week to each home in the territory not on the regular subscription list.

5. Develop a crew of experienced or trained salesmen to go into the territory at the end of the week of free delivery and obtain orders.

Local People Make Best Salesmen

It is highly important, of course, to have the salesmen well informed concerning the reading needs of the community and the newspaper's offerings. The territory should be carefully divided so that each salesman may quickly cover the section assigned to him and the campaign may be completed promptly.

Not every home owner will be persuaded to become a subscriber in the initial campaign, but a strong first step will have been taken. A few months later the procedure may be repeated and the number of subscribers in the area considerably increased.

Newspapers often have developed rural circulation by instituting an interesting and practical farm page or by introducing features that will interest the children of rural schools.

A representative of the Independence, Mo., *Examiner* (circulation 10,713, population 36,963) was invited to accompany the county superintendent of schools and the county farm agent on a tour of the county's rural schools, including stops at every school to make talks to the pupils. The *Examiner* reporter made a newsy and somewhat flattering writeup of each school with the names of the children and their teacher. He followed the publication of each story with a shower of marked sample copies in the school district and also made a special subscription rate to the teacher, asking her to place the newspaper on the schoolroom reading table for reference. The editor of the paper had agreed to conduct for the farm agent through the columns of the paper an agricultural question contest for school children in the county. The farm bureau gave a prize each month to the school giving the best answers and the newspaper announced the winners. Most teachers were glad to cooperate, and many schools erected mailboxes so the paper could be delivered right at the school house. This contest encouraged parents of many children who competed to order the *Examiner* sent to their homes.

This served a good community purpose by linking together the farm bureau and the rural schools in a program for the education and interest of rural youth, and at the same time aided in promoting the newspaper.

A booth at the county fair is another good promotion feature for a newspaper. The booth should display the features offered by the newspaper and explain its most important services. An attractive young woman with sales ability at the registration stand can obtain orders as well as develop a valuable list of prospects.

The San Jose, Calif., *Mercury* and *News* (combined circulation 116,006, population 127,564) gave to each person who registered at its fair booth a yellow sunbonnet with the name of the newspapers and telephone number printed in blue on both sides. Fair visitors were amused in looking over the immense crowds to see these bonnets dotting the area each day.

A prize drawing for a puppy, a bicycle, a pony or a vacation trip is another sure-fire crowd-puller. The Columbia *Missourian* (circulation 3,954, population 31,974) once offered a free 3-month subscription to every 100th person who registered at its booth during the county fair.

Professional Sales Groups Seldom Needed

Newspapers occasionally employ professional subscription-selling organizations to conduct campaigns, but this method is frowned upon by many publishers. These drives usually are in the nature of popularity contests, drawing into selling competition a group of young women to whom are given votes for subscriptions obtained.

Under the stress of a contest, the professional organization may be tempted to misrepresent the newspaper, and many of the subscriptions thus obtained will not be permanent, and the ill will engendered will prove costly in the long run.

Contests conducted by professionals also are expensive. A good weekly, in a town of 3,000, entered into a contract with a contest company, which of course "guaranteed results." The gross receipts from the contest were $6,000, but the contest company took 25 per cent, or $1,500, and costs for prizes and other items were $2,300, running the total expense up to $3,800. Of the $6,000 gross receipts, $4,200 was cash for subscriptions, $400 more than the contest cost. The other $1,800 received came from sale of credit slips for job work and advertising. Thus, the contest cost the publisher 63 per cent of the amount grossed, and on the basis of subscription receipts alone, it cost 90 per cent. During several months following the contest very little money came in from any source and the publisher was in trouble financially.

This, of course, is not the experience of all newspapers which have engaged professional companies. For a beginning newspaper, a contest may help to get off to a quick start with a substantial circulation. Some such companies operate on a sincere service basis but the results obtained usually are disappointing in the long run.

Seldom can an outside company do as well in selling subscriptions as a local sales group directed by the newspaper's own promotion department. Harry C. Purcell, publisher of the Broken Bow,

Nebr., *Custer County Chief* (circulation 5,713, population 3,396) personally plans and directs an annual subscription-selling campaign, which has all the attractive features that may be offered by a professional organization and at the same time is devoid of the mistakes that can occur when the contest is conducted by someone not personally known to local people and unfamiliar with local conditions.[2]

SELLING FOR PREMIUMS AND PRIZES

If a newspaper desires the assistance of persons outside the regular newspaper staff in building circulation, offering inducements to local individuals and groups usually will attract personable and enthusiastic salesmen (see Fig. 19.1).

The promotion department of the Columbus, Ohio, *Dispatch, Ohio State Journal* and *Star* (combined circulation 319,636, population 375,901) has boosted substantially the circulation of those newspapers by sponsoring airline trips to distant countries and around the world. When it offered a trip around the world, it obtained 20,233 subscriptions.[3] This contest enlisted many adults as well as young people, and those who did not win trips received commissions on all orders they obtained. When commissions as well as prizes are offered, entrants come from many walks of life. They may include widows and other housewives who appreciate a source of additional income, retired men, shopkeepers, handicapped persons and the general run of honest, everyday citizens who want to earn extra money.

Premiums also are effective for quick selling. A newspaper may make subscription salesmen out of many subscribers by offering seasonable items. An attractive low-priced premium for a small number of orders brings in a better response than an expensive premium given for a large number of orders. The Chicago *Tribune* (circulation 868,455, population 3,620,962) once offered an automatic electric deep fryer for four new home-delivery subscriptions. The Union City, N. J., *Hudson Dispatch* (circulation 60,309, population 55,537) offered a miniature hot-rod to anyone obtaining two new 26-week subscriptions. Both offers brought good returns.

Young people, however, are more easily interested than adults. When a good inducement is offered, youngsters usually are prompt to take part in subscription-selling contests. The Fair Oaks, Calif., *San Juan Record* (circulation 2,048, population 3,500) each year institutes a lively competition between boys and girls over ten years

---

[2] Frank W. Rucker, *Newspaper Circulation — What, Where and How,* Iowa State University Press, Ames, Iowa, 1958, p. 236.

[3] *Circulation Management Magazine,* July, 1953, p. 23.

KIDS

YOU CAN WIN THESE

PRIZES

FOR JUST CALLING
ON FOLKS YOU KNOW

MILKMAN MAILMAN

AUNT

UNCLE

YOUR FOLKS' FRIENDS   GRANDMA   GRANDPA

THE PLUMBER   THE MINISTER   SISTER'S BOY FRIEND

LADY NEXT DOOR

TEACHER   COUSINS   NEIGHBORS

THE DRUGGIST   DAD'S BOSS   BABY SITTER   GROCER   DOCTOR

IT'S EASY! IT'S QUICK!

Here's how you can do it.

1. Pick out your prospects from your friends, your folk's friends, the milkman, mailman, grandpa or grandma . . . (see the list above). You can probably think up a dozen more.

2. Call on them at their home; or see them when they make their rounds and tell them you can win a prize by selling JUST ONE ORDER . . . their order.

3. Tell them of the unusual FREE offer you can give them for a limited time.

YOU DON'T HAVE TO BE A NEWSPAPER CARRIER . . . anybody can win.

YOU DON'T HAVE TO DELIVER PAPERS (our regular carrier will)

YOU DON'T HAVE TO COLLECT ANY MONEY.

Start Now, Today

See the big list of prizes on the following pages . . .
Win at least one before the day is over.

Figs. 19.1 — Front page of a promotion folder put out to induce youngsters to sell subscriptions for premiums.

of age. Each participant is paid a commission on every order or renewal turned in, but only at half the normal rates. The other half of the commission is counted as a certain number of votes toward a major prize. The first prize one year was a bicycle, second prize a table-model radio, and third prize a choice of a nylon lariat rope or fishing tackle. The newspaper announced the contest with a large display advertisement, reprints of which were distributed to upper grades in all the local schools, and prizes were displayed in store windows.

The contest runs for five weeks. A week before the contest closes, the paper announces the standings of the contestants to help give it a push. Each year there have been more than a score of entries and at least 100 new subscribers turned in, plus a similar number of renewals.[4]

One of the most successful of the many special means employed by the La Porte, Ind., *Herald-Argus* (circulation 11,817, population 20,414) to gain assistance from persons outside those regularly employed, is a subscription-selling contest for high school seniors. The chief prize is a 5-day trip to Washington, D.C., and other points of historic interest near the national capital. During the first eleven years that it was offered, 607 seniors earned the trip. The *Herald-Argus* makes plain that this campaign is not sponsored by the school system but by the newspaper. "The offer is to seniors," the announcement says, "in order that they may achieve a more complete education and that they may have a fuller appreciation of our American heritage."

Awards are made on a point basis for mail and carrier subscriptions. Points for mail subscriptions are: 2 years, 75; 1 year, 32; 6 months, 12; 3 months, 3; college year, 24. Points for subscriptions delivered by carriers are: 1 year, 40; 6 months, 18; 3 months, 8. Each student who accumulates a total of 1,056 points is guaranteed the trip. Those who do not earn the trip are given credit on the basis of points earned, and may pay the balance of the trip cost and thus qualify. Those not meeting requirements for the trip are paid 10 per cent commission on all money they turn in.

INCREASING SALES OF SINGLE COPIES

In addition to building circulation through sales by carriers, full-time salesmen and persons induced by premiums and prizes, a newspaper may increase its grand total circulation by using street salesmen, newsstands, vending machines, newspaper racks and special features for the sale of single copies.

---

[4] *Circulation Management Magazine*, July, 1954, p. 14.

Wilbur Peterson, head of the Bureau of Media Service, State University of Iowa, made a special study of single-copy sales methods used by 269 weekly newspapers. He learned that while single-copy sales for some papers represented no more than one per cent of circulation, for some others they represented as much as 99 per cent. In the thickly populated East, single-copy sales account for a higher percentage of total than anywhere in the country. The second ranking section in per cent of total circulation is the South. Papers published in towns under 5,000 population in the East and South have larger volume of single-copy sales than papers in similar-sized towns of other sections.

Street Salesmen Boost Single-Copy Sales

"Extras," of course, do not have the appeal today that they had in pre-radio and pre-television days, but a high percentage of the circulation of metropolitan papers is on the single-copy basis, and even in small and medium-sized cities, street salesmen will sell hundreds of copies as they hawk them at street corners or diplomatically approach persons in restaurants, halls and corridors.

Some weekly newspapers serve many of their patrons through street salesmen, also. The Mount Holly, N.J., *Herald* (circulation 10,474, population 8,206), a weekly published within 19 miles of Philadelphia, handles a great portion of its circulation by spotting boys at many salient points to sell copies to the street trade. The Clinton, Tenn., *Courier-News* (circulation 3,628, population 3,712), another weekly, has 50 or more boys each week selling papers on the street.

"Silent Salesmen" Can Help

Surprising indeed is the great number of newspapers that may be sold through newspaper racks and vending machines. These "silent salesmen" are good feeders for home-delivery circulation, a convenience to regular subscribers who have need for extra copies and make buying easy for travelers and others who buy irregularly.

The most successful stands for single-copy sales are those in drugstores, grocery stores, newsstands, cigar stores, stationery stores, confectionery stores, newspaper offices, factories, hotels, bus depots, restaurants and taverns. Sales here may be greatly helped by promotion of newspaper features (see Fig. 19.2).

The Norristown, Pa., *Times Herald* (circulation 26,084, population 38,126) uses five automatic machines and 30 other self-service boxes strategically located in the circulation area. These sell more than 10,000 papers a month with a profit of approximately $200 a month, according to John T. McGuire, circulation manager.[5]

---
[5] *Editor & Publisher*, Nov. 10, 1956, p. 32.

Fig. 19.2 — Brilliantly colored promotion card placed by the Des Moines **Register** at newsstands to help sales of single copies.

"The use of these boxes and machines gives an opportunity for effective promotion of the newspaper," he points out. "You can list all the locations at which you sell papers from these devices. When you do this it helps the sale of papers generally and is a means toward obtaining more sales spots. The businessman in front of whose place you have the box or machine is pleased to see his name in the ad. Most times when you run this promotion you receive a couple of telephone calls from markets or gasoline stations, asking whether they may set papers in front of their places. This is an easy way to obtain additional outlets."

Some large city papers have set up dispensing racks in city buses and thus have served commuters eager to read the news as they go to and from work. The Milwaukee, Wis., *Sentinel* (circulation 184,302, population 637,392) established this service in 35 communities served by 21 bus lines. Within four months after starting this sales method, it disposed of 8,600 copies per month on the buses.

Racks for the *Sentinel* were placed at the rear of the coaches. Above each rack was a display card saying, "The Milwaukee Transport Company Suggests: Step Back to Today's *Sentinel.*" The card carried also some promotion of the *Sentinel*.

Transit officials hailed the sales on buses as an exceptional public service. It provided patrons with clean, dry copies of the morning newspaper, no matter what the weather. It was also a definite factor in getting passengers to the rear of the bus, particularly during the early morning rush hours.

The Pottstown, Pa., *Mercury* (circulation 22,132, population 22,589) made a similar arrangement with city bus lines for sale of newspapers to their patrons. Special wire racks were installed, each equipped with a coin box. The bus operators shared in the profits from sales. To get the newspaper sales off to a good start, the publisher attached to one newspaper in each bus a coupon worth one dollar.

Small newspapers, as well as large ones, have boosted circulation with vending machines and sales racks.

The Warsaw, Ind., *Times-Union* (circulation 9,068, population 6,965) has found vending machines of great value in providing improved service to rural subscribers whose papers, delivered by mail, would arrive a day late. It has stationed 15 machines in small towns within a 30-mile radius of Warsaw, and 20 vendors at various points within the city, where papers are available fresh from the press. Jack Kennedy, circulation manager, says that out-of-town vending-machine sales have grown from nothing to an average of 370 copies daily.

The *Times-Union* placed vending machines on fair grounds and sold from 600 to 800 copies a week while county fairs were in progress.

Puzzle Contests Whoop Sales

While discussing the promotion of single-copy sales, attention should be called to the use of the puzzle contest or "word game," in which prizes of $20, $25, $50 or perhaps $100 a week are offered on a cumulative basis. If no correct answer to the puzzle is sent in on one week, the amount of that prize is added to the prize for the next week's puzzle. At times the prize jumps to a very liberal amount. This creates great interest and boosts the sale of single copies. A contestant may send in as many as five solutions to each puzzle.

A "Cashword Puzzle" developed an 8,000 increase in circulation for the Des Moines, Iowa, Sunday *Register* (circulation 513,023, population 177,965). Prizes in this contest at times have run up into thousands of dollars. The contest rules as outlined in one issue were as follows:

CASHWORD CONTEST RULES

1. *The Des Moines Sunday Register* will pay $4,200 for the correct solution to this Sunday's CASHWORD PUZZLE — if more than one correct solution is received the $4,200 prize money will be divided equally among those submitting the correct solution. If NO correct solution is received to this Sunday's puzzle, the $4,200 prize money will be added to next week's $100 award making next week's prize $4,300.

2. *Solve The Clues As You Would* for any crossword puzzle. Determine from each clue the word that best fits the clue definition. Remember there is ONLY ONE answer that is the best word fitting the clue. Only answers exactly matching the prepared solution will be considered correct. This contest is based on skill. The decision of the judges will be final and all contestants taking part must agree to accept that decision as a condition of entry.

3. *After You Have Filled in the Puzzle* clip it along the dotted lines, paste or tape it, face up, to a postcard and mail it to: CASHWORD CAL, P.O. Box 853, Des Moines, Iowa. Your entry must be postmarked not later than Monday, Aug. 25, and reach the Des Moines Register and Tribune Company by 8 a.m., Aug. 28 to be considered in the judging. Or you may deliver your entry to the lobby of the Register and Tribune Building, 715 Locust St., Des Moines, Iowa, not later than midnight, Aug. 25.

4. *A Bonus of 10 Per Cent* will be paid any winner whose entry is pasted, taped or otherwise attached face-up to any type of postcard and not mailed in or on an envelope. Entries deposited at the Register and Tribune Building need not be attached to anything to qualify for the 10 per cent bonus.

5. *Do Not Erase or Write Over Entry.* Entries containing erasures or write-overs will not be judged. Print your answers clearly.

6. *The Contest Is Open to Residents* of Iowa and counties bordering on Iowa (including directly across the Missouri and Mississippi Rivers) and in other areas where home carrier delivery service is maintained — except employees of the Des Moines Register and Tribune Company, the Cowles Broadcasting Company, Cowles Magazines, Inc., and members of their immediate families. No more than five entries will be accepted from any one contestant for one puzzle. No entries submitted on mechanically reproduced or printed facsimiles of the puzzle will be judged (one-fourth inch graph

paper is all right — the vertical and horizontal lines only — but no other part may be produced mechanically).

7. *Winners, If Any, and the Correct Solution* to this Sunday's puzzle will be announced — and a new puzzle published — in the next Des Moines Sunday *Register.*

8. *It Is Not Necessary To Purchase* the Des Moines Sunday *Register* to enter CASHWORD. Reasonably accurate facsimilies of the puzzle form may be used. A copy of the Des Moines Sunday *Register* may be examined free of charge in the library of the Register and Tribune Building, 715 Locust St., and at many public libraries.

To further promote single-copy sales and increase regular sub-scriptions, the *Register* and *Tribune* made circulation salesmen out of some of the contestants when from time to time it offered a "jackpot bonus." For this a winner might receive double his share of the cash prize by sending in a new subscription to the daily *Register* or the daily *Tribune.*

While the word puzzle is effective in stimulating single-copy sales, it does not build a large, sustained circulation. Many copies are sold on the day the puzzle appears and public attention is heavily centered on the newspaper for a time, but when the contest feature is discontinued, interest in the newspaper falls.

Both silent and audible salesmen are effective in promoting newspaper circulation, and a newspaper's promotion department will determine what plans are best.

CHAPTER 20

100 Tested Ways
To Promote Circulation

NEWSPAPER SUBSCRIPTIONS ARE OBTAINED by various methods and appeals. Described here are 100 promotion schemes that have been put to the test and proved resultful in increasing newspaper circulation — over and above the numerous good examples already given in other chapters. Not all of these will meet the approval of all publishers and circulation managers but every method outlined has some supporters.

TO STIMULATE SALES BY CARRIERS

1. **Treasure Chest Hunt** — The St. Paul, Minn., *Dispatch* and *Pioneer Press* (combined circulation 210,007, population 311,349) conducts a King Boreas Treasure Chest Hunt each January in connection with a winter carnival. A treasure chest containing a certificate for $1,000 cash is hidden in the snow on public property within city limits. Poetic clues are given in front-page boxes for 10 days preceding the hunt. Extra copies are bought to receive the clues.

2. **12-Week Bicycle Contest** — The Elizabeth, N. J., *Journal* (circulation 50,331, population 112,817) in an intensive 12-week contest offered a bicycle to each carrier who obtained a certain number of subscribers. A total of 1,417 new subscribers was obtained.

3. **Trips as Prizes** — The Nashville *Banner* and *Tennessean* (combined circulation 220,617, population 174,307) realized an increase of 980 in circulation by offering to carriers who showed the greatest increases on their routes during a 6-week contest, trips to Daytona Beach and Mammoth Cave.

4. Jet Trip to London and Paris — The top prize in a carrier contest put on by the Oakland, Calif., *Tribune* (circulation 205,942, population 384,575) and *Parade Magazine* was a 10-day trip by jet plane to the British and French capitals.

5. Silver Seal Offer — Carriers of the Minneapolis *Star* and *Tribune* (combined circulation 502,252, population 521,718) were spurred to extra solicitation when each carrier who turned in four orders was given a mystery prize and a "silver seal" card which entitled parents to an award ranging from a knife set to a large refrigerator.

6. Turtle Offer — The Des Moines *Register* and *Tribune* (combined circulation 345,146, population 177,965) gave a baby racing turtle to each carrier who obtained two new orders in a solicitation campaign. Seven thousand turtles were distributed and 14,000 new subscribers obtained.

7. Bosses' Night — The Kansas City, Kans., *Kansan* (circulation 29,894, population 129,553) added 272 subscribers when it conducted a "Bosses' Night." Carriers were told that the *Kansan's* bosses would be with their district managers that evening and they would have a gift for each carrier checking back with one signed order.

8. Red Tag Sale — In a contest for 18 free air trips, carriers for the Champaign-Urbana, Ill., *News-Gazette* (circulation 28,903, population 62,397) wore red tags when making calls. New subscriptions were rated by points, and boys who did not earn enough points to win a trip were paid cash.

9. Trip to State Fair — The La Crosse, Wis., *Tribune* (circulation 32,514, population 47,535) each year puts on a subscription-selling campaign allowing carriers to earn a trip to the state fair.

10. Increased Commissions — The Dayton, Ohio, *Daily News* (circulation 144,687, population 243,872) has two major prize campaigns a year to stimulate subscription sales. These sales provide increased commissions for carriers and counselors.

11. Offered Thimble Drome Racers — As an incentive to carriers in obtaining new subscribers, the Champaign-Urbana, Ill., *Courier* (circulation 30,610, population 62,397) gave Thimble Drome Racers as prizes. These all-metal racers, only 10 inches long, attain a speed of 80 miles an hour.

12. Theater Tickets as Prizes — The Michigan City, Ind., *News-Dispatch* (circulation 14,110, population 28,395) makes arrangements with local theaters for tickets at a reasonable rate and gives them to carriers as prizes for obtaining new subscriptions.

13. Visit to Air Force — Each carrier for the Pittsburgh, Pa., *Press* (circulation 301,730, population 676,806) who took orders for 2 daily and Sunday subscriptions was taken to the Greater Pittsburgh Airport to visit the U.S. Air Force and inspect at close hand many of the newest Air Force jets.

14. "Forty-Niners' Club" — The Bloomington, Ill., *Pantagraph* (circulation 39,384, population 36,127) sponsored a Forty-Niners' Club with gold nuggets for new subscriptions and renewals. The main reward was a trip to the homes of Abraham Lincoln at New Salem and Springfield. Carriers who did not qualify for the trip were paid off at the rate of 5 cents a nugget.

15. Turkeys for Thanksgiving — Each carrier for the South Bend, Ind., *Tribune* (circulation 108,793, population 131,770) had the opportunity to earn a Thanksgiving turkey for his family. Over 400 10-pound birds were given away one year to carriers who had increased the number of customers on their routes.

16. Hayride for Carriers — The Moline, Ill., *Dispatch* (circulation 28,423, population 37,397) hit a popular note when it arranged an old-fashioned hayrack ride for carriers who had built up their routes in a given time.

17. "Beat the Heat" Offer — A 24-bottle case of soft drinks was offered during July to each carrier of the Battle Creek, Mich., *Enquirer-News* (circulation 37,170, population 48,666) who increased the number on his route by three.

18. "Cow Hands" in a Roundup — Carriers of the Grand Junction, Colo., *Sentinel* (circulation 15,709, population 14,504) became "cow hands" in a "Maverick Roundup" of new readers. Each carrier was given a "cow poke" handle to his name, and 634 new subscribers were steered into the corral.

19. "Beat the Clock" Contest — The Detroit, Mich., *News* (circulation 463,469, population 1,849,568) put out an attractive folder showing various merchandise prizes arranged in clockface style. For each hour there was a prize for the subscription obtained during that hour.

20. Balloon Race — The Minneapolis *Star* and *Tribune* conducted an interesting "balloon race" which created fun for its carriers, developed great public interest and produced new subscriptions. Whenever a carrier brought in an order during the contest he was allowed to release a balloon with a return card addressed to his home.

21. Tee Shirts as Prizes — For three new subscriptions the Niles, Mich., *Star* (circulation 7,763, population 13,145) gave a carrier a tee shirt attractively lettered *"Niles Daily Star."*

22. Value Chart — The Bloomington, Ill., *Pantagraph* presented to each carrier a chart showing to him the value of each customer. It revealed that a carrier would have to deposit in a bank $131.67 to draw the same amount of interest that his profit on a single subscriber amounted to.

23. Four Star Mystery Prizes — The Minneapolis *Star* and *Tribune* offered four mystery prizes to increase subscriptions for its Sunday issue: No. 1, worth $3, was for 3 Sunday orders; No. 2, worth $2, was for 2 Sunday orders; and Nos. 3 and 4, each worth $1.50, were for 1 Sunday order.

24. Christmas Candy Offer — In the period just preceding Christmas the Des Moines *Register* and *Tribune* gave a full pound box of Peggy Ann candy to each carrier who obtained two new 6-week orders.

25. Basketball Bonanza — Carriers for the Minneapolis *Star* and *Tribune* became hustling subscription salesmen at the beginning of the basketball season when they were offered a basketball for 3 orders, a basketball goal for 3 orders, basketball shoes for 5 orders, knee guards for 2 orders, and basketball socks for 1 order. Some carriers won the complete equipment.

26. Bonus Prize — As a recognition of superior salesmanship in a district contest the Detroit *Free Press* (circulation 456,117, population 1,849,568) gave a Cushman motor scooter as a bonus prize. This went to the carrier who turned in the most orders to bring to the district a total increase of 1,000.

27. Samples With Follow-up — Ten carriers for the Paso Robles, Calif., *Press* (circulation 3,088, population 6,148) were asked to get 5 signed orders from non-subscribers for 2 weeks free delivery. Then particular emphasis was placed on service to these sample recipients, and at the end of the 2-week period, follow-up solicitation calls were made. From the 50 persons to whom samples were delivered, 33 became subscribers.

28. Telephone Order Day — The Davenport, Iowa, *Democrat* and *Times* (combined circulation 51,327, population 74,549) added more than 400 new subscribers in one day when they set up for their carriers a Telephone Order Day. Carriers were to solicit orders and telephone them in to the newspaper office as soon as obtained. Special prizes were offered for subscriptions turned in during first hour, second hour, etc. An alarm clock was set to ring at a certain hour. Then a bicycle was given to the boy who turned in a subscription nearest to the time when the alarm went off.

29. "Increase Club" — The Champaign-Urbana, Ill., *Courier* formed an "Increase Club" and at a banquet awarded emblems to boys who had procured a specified increase each month of the year.

30. Sputnik Rocket — Carriers worked hard to obtain subscriptions when the Minneapolis *Star* and *Tribune* gave for a single 8-week order, a Sputnik Rocket that would shoot 100 feet into the air.

31. "World at Your Doorstep" — The San Francisco *Call-Bulletin* (circulation 140,207, population 775,357) issued an attractive booklet for carriers to leave on the doorsteps of prospective subscribers. This explained the many features to be found in the *Call-Bulletin*. Each page had plenty of action, pictures, a hand-lettered heading and some color. It was titled "The *Call-Bulletin* Puts the World at Your Doorstep — a Behind-the-Press View of Your Friendly Newspaper."

32. Vacation-Pak — The Birmingham, Ala., *News* and *Post-Herald* (combined circulation 279,782, population 362,037) keeps its circulation up during vacation periods by having carriers save papers for each customer on vacation and delivering them in a neat, clean bundle when the family returns.

33. Junior Olympics — The Topeka, Kans., *State Journal* (circulation 25,650, population 78,791) has a hot summer promotion which produces "cool" circulation messages. It is called the Junior Olympics and involves theater tickets, a first and second round of competition, followed by a trip.

34. "Two-Dollar Bill" Contest — The Reno *Gazette* and *Nevada State Journal* (combined circulation 31,261, population 44,795) obtained 196 new subscribers in a system of straight cash awards called the "Two-Dollar Bill Contest." To obtain a crisp, new $2 bill, a carrier accumulated credits for increases in his area. For example, 1 increase credit was 30¢, 3 increases $1, and 5 increases $2.

35. Costume Jewelry for Mother — The Honolulu *Star-Bulletin* (circulation 97,680, population 248,034) in an effective subscription-selling campaign offered as a prize to carriers, costume jewelry for Mother's Day gifts.

36. Outdoor Life Contest — The Portland *Oregon Journal* (circulation 182,956, population 373,628) offered camping, hunting and fishing equipment to carriers in an effective circulation-building campaign.

37. "Prize-A-Thon" — The Indianapolis, Ind., *News* (circulation 170,490, population 427,173) offered a host of attractive items and cash as prizes in a carriers' contest to obtain 13-week orders. This was called a "Prize-a-Thon" and was promoted extensively.

38. "Raciest Contest Yet" — The Rockford, Ill., *Star* and *Register-Republic* (combined circulation 83,973, population 105,438) designed a carrier contest around a dinner at a downtown hotel and a free bus trip to the local stock-car speedway with cut-price seats right down front. The buses returned the boys to the newspaper plant, where they were picked up by parents. This contest, called "The Raciest Contest Yet," produced a lot of speed in selling subscriptions and substantially increased circulation.

39. "C-B-F-E-C" — During December of one year the carriers for the Des Moines *Register* and *Tribune* were stormed with post cards, letters, broadsides and telegrams talking about a C-B-F-E-C promotion. The letters stood for "Columbia Bicycle for Every Carrier."

40. Work in Crews — The Worland, Wyo., *Northern Wyoming Daily News* (circulation 5,420, population 4,202) obtains better selling results from carriers when they work in crews rather than singly. Once or twice a week the best carrier salesmen, with members of the circulation staff, are assigned to a certain area. In this way they receive valuable training and meet with greater success.

41. "World Series" Contest — When the Florence, Ala., *Times* (circulation 10,186, population 27,465) couldn't send its carriers to the real World Series, it created a "World Series" of its own. The circulation manager divided his city carriers into five teams with ten boys on a team. The fictional baseball game was played between teams each week on a fixed schedule. Each route increase procured by a player scored a run for his team. The team that scored the most runs was declared the winner of that week. As a reward for their efforts, each member of the championship team received an inscribed Official League baseball, and the two top teams were guests at a special party.

42. "Hit Parade" Contest — The Passaic, N.J., *Herald-News* (circulation 65,713, population 51,702) stimulated great interest in a subscription-selling campaign when each carrier was offered a watch if his district hit a certain quota. Fifty-one watches were awarded and the campaign produced 723 orders.

43. Breakfast Selling — The Des Moines *Register* and *Tribune* organized a crew of six to ten carriers to do some concentrated selling between 8 and 9 A.M. on Saturday. Immediately after 9, the supervisor and boys went to a convenient restaurant for a big breakfast of pancakes with trimmings. This brought in from 15 to 25 orders each time it was tried.

44. Movie Ticket for 10 Calls — The circulation manager of the Monterey, Calif., *Peninsula Herald* (circulation 21,086, population 21,840) furnished each of his carriers a card with spaces for the names of 10 prospective customers upon whom he would call. There was space for the prospect's reasons for not subscribing, if that should be the case. The carrier-salesman was given a theater ticket for the card when filled out and returned to his district manager, and also 50¢ for each new subscriber he obtained.

45. Puppy Prizes — The Des Moines *Register* and *Tribune* had excellent success in subscription selling when they offered purebred puppies as prizes to carrier-salesmen. Some of the boys took females and went into a profitable small business of raising more puppies.

46. Easter Ham Prize — For six new 3-month subscriptions obtained by any one of its carriers, the Los Angeles, Calif., *Times* (circulation 476,746, population 2,243,901) gave an 11-pound canned ham for Easter.

47. Chocolates for Valentine's Day — The Redondo Beach, Calif., *South Bay Breeze* (circulation 22,477, population 41,723) offered a 1-pound, heart-shaped box of chocolates for two new subscriptions. Out of 125 carrier-salesmen, 45 received one or more boxes of chocolates.

48. Trumpet Contest — In a subscription-selling contest, the Detroit *Times* (circulation 391,295, population 1,849,568) gave a shiny trumpet with song book and lyre stand to each carrier who brought in eight subscriptions.

49. Prizes for District Managers — The Rock Island, Ill., *Argus* (circulation 25,612, population 49,461) provides special incentives for district managers as well as carriers whenever it puts on a subscription-selling campaign, and has found out that it pays off in a big way.

50. "Frosting on the Cake" — The Minneapolis *Star* and *Tribune* put life into a carrier contest by calling it "Frosting on the Cake" and adding the frosting with new stunts and prizes from time to time. This kept carriers interested and on the sales mark.

51. "Last Fling" Trip — To top a season of intensive selling by carriers, the Phoenix, Ariz., *Republic* (circulation 111,339, population 106,818) gave those ranking highest in all contests a vacation trip to Catalina Island early in September.

52. Championship Drive — The Cleveland *Plain Dealer* (circulation 309,267, population 914,808) instituted a "Championship Drive" for new subscribers at the beginning of the baseball season. "Every customer means a hit for you," it told its carriers, "and every hit boosts your batting average. Come up with the best batting average and you come up with the top prizes."

53. Autos as Prizes — The greatest prize offer ever given to carriers of the Des Moines *Register* and *Tribune* included six new automobiles. For each three copies of Sunday or daily increase, a carrier was entitled to one entry in the contest. There was no limit on the number of entries a carrier or route salesman might have. Parents of carriers had a part, too. They were asked to complete the sentence, "I like my son to be a *Register* and *Tribune* carrier, because . . . ."

54. "King for a Day" — The Los Angeles *Herald and Express* (circulation 348,351, population 2,243,901) adopted a "King for a Day" carrier sales promotion. The winning carrier was given a limousine and chauffeur, a tour of film and television studios, a dinner for his family and guests, and other prizes.

55. Ring the Bell for $33 — The Davenport, Iowa, *Democrat* and *Times* gave each carrier a unique order book that would be worth $33 for 30 new Sunday orders. The pay-off was on a graduated scale. Starting at three for $10, each succeeding group of three would be worth 50¢ more, up to a maximum of $6 for the last group. All orders over 30 paid $2 each. In addition, every sixth order was a bonus order providing the salesman with a chance on Thanksgiving turkeys and a portable TV set. Many carriers rang enough doorbells and sold enough subscriptions to win the $33 offered. New orders received in this contest produced a net increase of 4,642 in home-delivered Sunday circulation.

56. Twilight Contest — The Madison, Wis., *Capital Times* and *Wisconsin State Journal* (combined circulation 93,795, population 96,056) assembled all carriers in a district at 4 P.M. or as soon as school was out, and announced a contest to begin then and end at 7 P.M. Each carrier was given five order blanks and a sharpened pencil. The pay-off was cash plus prizes for top boys.

57. Freezer for District Manager — The Phoenix, Ariz., *Gazette* (circulation 66,583, population 128,841) developed exciting competition between district managers when it offered a freezer to the district manager whose carriers averaged the greatest number of sales during the contest. The carriers in the winning district turned in an average of 25 new subscriptions for their manager.

58. Ant Farms as Prizes — Carriers for the Pittsburgh, Pa., *Press* won ant farms as prizes in a carrier contest. With each ant farm was an "Ant Watcher's Manual," giving complete instructions for the care and feeding of ants and amusing sidelights on ant lore.

59. 1,000, No Less — The Hackensack, N. J., *Bergen Record* (circulation 81,574, population 29,219) conducts each year a campaign to add 1,000 subscribers. Fifty awards are offered, varying in value from a free show or television ticket to a $3 basketball, and a strong competition is fanned up between districts.

60. Sweetest Deal — The Audubon, Iowa, *News-Guide* (circulation 2,744, population 2,808) offered a 5-pound sack of sugar with a subscription, new or renewal. It was advertised as the "sweetest deal ever offered." The drive added 60 subscribers and grossed $2,900 in 30 days.

TO OBTAIN MAIL SUBSCRIBERS

61. Get-Acquainted Mail Offer — The Battle Creek, Mich., *Enquirer-News* added 760 mail subscribers when it sent out post cards offering a 6-weeks trial subscription for $1.

62. Fall Solicitation — The Newton, Iowa, *News* (circulation 7,333, population 13,572) has found that the best time of the year to obtain subscriptions from farmers is in the fall when the most of their year's work is done. It is a good time also to seek renewals.

63. Correspondents' Contest — The Woodbridge, N.J., *Independent-Leader* (circulation 5,893, population 17,000) arranged for its rural correspondents to conduct a telephone solicitation with every non-subscriber in their respective communities. Each correspondent was given a kit containing rules of the contest, instructions on telephone procedure, list of prizes offered and subscription forms to be turned in each week. The 12 correspondents turned in a total of 600 orders in a little more than a month.

64. Summer Bargain Offer — The Mattoon, Ill., *Journal-Gazette* (circulation 9,416, population 17,547) one year made a summer bargain offer of a $3 reduction on an order for an $8 subscription by mail. This was during a period when it was hard to sell to farmers.

65. Summertime Bonus — Those who renewed subscriptions or entered new subscriptions to the Overton, Tex., *Press* (circulation 1,725, population 2,001) during the last two weeks of July were offered a 5-month bonus. Thus they were paid up through the following year if they subscribed at that time, or were paid up for 17 months from the time the subscription expired. The plan brought in sizable revenue during a slow month.

66. A Look-in for Rural Prospects — The Philadelphia *Inquirer* (circulation 619,381, population 2,071,605) created and delivered to rural box holders an attractive and forceful 6-page folder. This told well the *Inquirer*'s story — what subscribers had to say about the paper; how during a deliverers' strike thousands came to the plant and stood in line for their papers; and what interesting features the paper contains.

67. An Appeal by Cartoonists — The Philadelphia *Inquirer* devised a clever letter to readers whose subscriptions were about to expire. It reproduced a page of cartoon personalities — Dick Tracy, Blondie, and others — saying, "We're going to miss you. If what the circulation manager says is true, we won't be seeing you anymore." This was followed with a strong sales talk. The letter carried signatures of all the cartoon characters.

68. Booths at Fairs — The Plainfield, N. J., *Courier-News* (circulation 36,661, population 42,366) operates information booths at fairs and ties in its organization on solicitation efforts with generous commissions on orders received at the booths.

69. Mailbox Reflectors — Light-reflecting name plates for rural mailboxes helped the Ottawa, Ill., *Republican Times* (circulation 13,222, population 16,957) to convert 70 per cent of its short-term subscriptions into 1-year payments.

70. Campaign in the Granges — The Utica, N. Y., *Observer-Dispatch* (circulation 45,002, population 101,531) conducted a satisfactory subscription campaign in the Granges, with prizes and commissions as inducements to farmer members.

71. Students' Subscriptions — The Centerville, Iowa, *Iowegian and Citizen* (circulation 4,990, population 7,625) appealed to parents to send the paper to their youngsters away at college. It compared the home paper to the city papers saying that a seed catalogue is big and has nice pictures in it, but most anyone would rather have a letter from home.

72. Quarterly Mail Offer — The Oil City, Pa., *Derrick* (circulation 13,250, population 19,581) four times a year makes a special offer of some sort for new subscriptions by mail. These offers overlap and yield about a 2 per cent return.

73. Mystery Farm Feature — The Ada, Minn., *Norman County Index* (circulation 2,696, population 2,121) added 200 subscribers in 15 weeks when it engaged a man to take, from the air, pictures of farms in the area and ran the pictures in the newspaper. A prize was offered to the person who first identified the farm.

74. Monthly Payment Plan — The La Crosse, Wis., *Tribune* has increased rural circulation by selling subscriptions on a monthly payment plan. The subscriber pays $1 when the order is given, then $1 a month until the full amount for a year is paid.

TO ENLIST NEWCOMERS

75. Made Friends of Newcomers — The Toronto, Ontario, *Telegram* (circulation 207,840, population 667,706) offered a free translation service to newcomers with language problems. Those in that category were encouraged to write letters to the editor in their own language. The aim was to establish the newspaper as an immediate friend.

76. Brochure Helped Carriers — The Kansas City, Kans., *Kansan* (circulation 28,485, population 129,553) helped carriers interest newcomers and prospective subscribers by issuing an 8-page brochure which listed regular features to be found in the newspaper, telling about services offered, and doing a thorough selling job.

77. New Development — To obtain subscribers in a new development on the outskirts of town, the Hammonton, N.J., *News* (circulation 3,438, population 8,411) sent a photographer into the area and took pictures of everything in sight — people, homes, children's pets, etc. It then ran a feature page about the new development, welcoming its residents to Hammonton. The next step was to sign up a correspondent in the area and to get someone to follow up for subscriptions.

78. Samples for a Week — The Bloomington, Ind., *Herald-Telephone* (circulation 13,373, population 28,163) obtains from public utilities offices, the names of families moving into the town and has the paper delivered to them for a week. Then carriers call at homes for subscription orders.

79. "Apples for the Teacher" — In an early fall subscription-selling campaign, the Bloomington, Ill., *Pantagraph* featured an "apple for the teacher" in the form of a year's subscription to the *Pantagraph*. The drive was directed toward new teachers in the public schools.

80. For Babies Only — With the headline "A Standing Offer" under a picture of a baby, the Lambertville, N. J., *Record* (circulation 678, population 4,477) periodically runs a message written in rhyme, offering a year's subscription to parents who report the birth of a child within a week of its birth. These free subscriptions are usually renewed at the regular price when the year is up.

81. Picture Pages — Publishers of the Ripon, Wis., *Commonwealth Press* (circulation 4,230, population 5,619) credit liberal use of local pictures for a circulation increase of 3,400 for their weekly paper.

82. Sampling Campaign — The Port Huron, Mich., *Times Herald* (circulation 31,203, population 35,725) conducted a sampling campaign that netted nearly 1,000 new subscribers. The program was based on getting carriers to list names of families along their routes who did not take the paper. Boys obtained 125 new orders while compiling their lists.

83. Wedding Present — Every time the King City, Mo., *Tri-County News* (circulation 1,859, population 1,031) publishes a wedding story the publisher sends a 6-month subscription to the bride and groom as a wedding present. Publisher Louis Bowmen says this results in almost 100 per cent renewals.

TO INCREASE SINGLE-COPY SALES

84. "Match the Stars" Contest — The Winnepeg, Manitoba, *Free Press* (circulation 117,157, population 255,093) increased single-copy sales substantially with a "Match the Stars" contest featuring 60 Hollywood stars. A first prize of $1,000, and 168 other cash prizes were offered.

85. "Who Am I?" Contest — The Los Angeles *Examiner* (circulation 356,000, population 2,243,901) promoted newsstand and street sales with a "Who Am I?" contest. The newspaper carried a series of pictures of movie, radio and TV stars and other famous persons with distorted faces as they would appear in the curved mirror of a fun house. Prizes worth $35,000, including a trip for two to Rio de Janeiro and an Oldsmobile car, were offered to readers for the best lists of correct identifications.

86. Sales at a Drive-in — Copies of the La Crosse, Wis., *Tribune* were distributed to the first 200 persons to arrive at a local drive-in theater during the theater's opening five days. After that, copies of the *Tribune* were placed on sale at the refreshment stand at the regular price so early arrivals might read the paper while waiting for the picture to start.

87. Roving News-mobile — The Allentown, Pa., *Call-Chronicle* (circulation 84,637, population 106,756) has a canopy-topped trailer labeled "Call-Chronicle News-mobile." This is attached to a car and is used on trips to distant carrier routes and potential vendor outlets.

88. Curb Service — Vending units with coin boxes were placed on curbs by the Philadelphia, Pa., *Bulletin* (circulation 695,960, population 2,071,605). Persons pulled up to the curb, put their money in coin boxes and obtained copies of the *Bulletin* without getting out of their cars.

SPECIAL OFFERS THAT APPEAL

89. Government Bond Contest — The Gary, Ind., *Post-Tribune* (circulation 54,517, population 168,884) offered government bonds of $25 to $100 in a 3-day selling of 13-week subscriptions. Competitors wore white buttons with this slogan: "I'm trying to win a Gary *Post-Tribune* Scholarship Bond."

90. Mop as Premium — The Olympia, Wash., *Olympian* (circulation 12,235, population 15,819) realized fair returns from a fringe area when it offered an O'Cedar sponge mop in a subscription renewal campaign.

91. Free Offer on TV — The Cincinnati, Ohio, *Enquirer* (circulation 203,960, population 503,998) used television to announce a free item with a subscription order and, in this way, obtained 2,500 starts.

92. Television Spots — The Des Moines *Register* and *Tribune* spends more than $100,000 annually on television and radio, using seven television and five radio stations, to promote circulation. This is considered a most effective way to reach non-readers and make personal solicitation easier.

93. "Match the Twins" Contest — The Indianapolis, Ind., *Times* carried individual pictures of twins, running one each day. Readers were asked to match the twins. The *Times* offered $10,000 in cash prizes for the 53 most accurate entries. This contest was a real factor in building circulation.

94. Incentive Plan for All Employees — The Long Beach, Calif., *Press-Telegram* (circulation 107,155, population 250,767) had an incentive plan whereby all members of the circulation department shared an increased income from increases in circulation. A base was established and each person's salary was predicated upon an increase of the circulation within his territory.

95. House as Top Prize — In a subscription-selling contest which lasted 2½ months, the Houston, Tex., *Chronicle* (circulation 192,062, population 596,163) offered a house worth $10,000 as the first prize. It was won by a non-employee.

96. Obtains Women Salesmen — To induce women to sell subscriptions to the Portland *Oregon Journal,* its circulation department gave a 102-piece dinnerware ensemble for 16 new 13-week orders. The ensemble consisted of 32 pieces of chinaware, 34 pieces of silverware, 18 pieces of glassware and a 28-piece accessory set.

97. Insurance With Subscription — The Plymouth, Ind., *Pilot-News* (circulation 7,406, population 7,334) sold insurance with subscriptions. Readers paid for the paper and insurance in combined monthly payments. This was helpful in building and maintaining home-delivered circulation.

98. Camera Premium — The Visalia, Calif., *Times-Delta* (circulation 9,186, population 14,521) obtained a nice circulation increase when it gave a camera to each reader who turned in a new 8-month subscription.

99. Charity Tie-up — The Detroit, Mich., *Free Press* conducted a charity tie-up telephone solicitation that lifted the circulation total quite a bit and yielded over $33,000 to a children's hospital. Before launching the campaign, the *Free Press* received approval for it from the community fund-raising authorities and the Better Business Bureau.

100. Family Picture as Premium — As an inducement to persons moving into a newly created suburb, the Elgin, Ill., *Courier-News* (circulation 22,565, population 47,565) gave with a 3-month subscription a picture of the family in front of their new home.

Promotion Through
Public Relations

CHAPTER 21

Promoting Morale
Within the
Newspaper Organization

THE PROMOTION OF GOOD WILL and cooperation within the newspaper's own plant is an important step in developing right relations with all elements of the community it serves. Organization morale, to a large extent, determines publishing success. It is important, therefore, for a publisher to give special attention to:

1. Recruitment of capable employees.
2. Definite information for all employees regarding the newspaper's aims and policies.
3. Training of employees for the special work to which they are assigned.
4. Cooperation of employees in creating a smooth working organization for the making of a well-balanced newspaper.
5. Interesting and wholesome social and recreational activities for employees.
6. Fringe benefits that contribute to financial security, health and general contentment of employees.

Recruitment Essential to Progress

In order to keep progress alive in the newspaper organization, employees must be kept in touch with modern ideas and methods, and new blood must be pumped into the staff from time to time. The recruiting of competent help has become a major project of many newspapers, and should be accepted by all as an important responsibility.

[325]

Press associations and other groups of newspapermen know that more bright young men and women are needed in the ranks of journalism. They are looking at this with the broad attitude that what may be done to draw capable young people into the general profession of journalism, will help to provide security and progress for every individual newspaper. Through liaison with schools and colleges, such organizations are conducting aggressive selling programs to interest potential personnel. A publisher may have no employment worries today, but he realizes that is no assurance for the future, so despite his immediate good fortune, he feels obligated to help less fortunate members of the profession and to brighten the outlook for all.

Sensing this situation and anxious to help solve employment problems, Sigma Delta Chi in 1946 ordered Pete Eiden of the San Diego, Calif., *Union* (circulation 88,646, population 494,201) to send a questionnaire to members of the National Newspaper Promotion Association to find out what was being done about training and recruitment of editorial personnel. From this it was learned that:

1. There is a lack of interest in newspapering as a career on the part of high school and college graduates.

2. There is a segment of educators and students who believe newspapering offers low pay, poor hours, limited self-expression and little opportunity for advancement.

3. There is a need among newspapers for planned, comprehensive training programs for personnel entering the field from college and high school.

4. There is a preference for college graduates on the part of larger newspapers and an acceptance of high school graduates by smaller newspapers.

5. There are many activities now sponsored by newspapers to encourage new personnel and then to train them.

6. Newspapermen consider a college education an excellent preparation for a newspaper career, but believe newspapering is better learned in the field of experience and, because of newspaper stylization, there is need for apprentice training.

Since this survey much concerted effort has been made to interest youth in journalism, with emphasis placed on the advantages and opportunities to be found in the profession. Valuable contacts have been made with high school teachers and students to interest youth in journalism education. Journalism schools have given valuable cooperation by inviting to their campuses groups of high school and college students for clinics and conferences. Newspapers have conducted tours of their plants, offered scholarships in journalism to high school graduates and have provided summer employment to students looking toward a career in journalism.

With advertisements in their columns promoting the University of Alabama School of Journalism, the Florence, Ala., *Times* (circulation 10,186, population 27,465) and the Sheffield, Ala., *Tri-Cities Daily* (circulation 9,194, population 10,767) encourage high school and college students to enter the field of journalism.

The Tucson, Ariz., *Citizen* (circulation 35,058, population 48,774) conducts a summertime "observer program" for high school students in which they accompany reporters at no charge and without pay; the students send their copy to the assistant manager for careful criticism.

The Eureka, Calif., *Humboldt Times* and *Humboldt Standard* (combined circulation 25,928, population 27,951) sponsor an annual Journalism Day at Humboldt State College. This includes round-table discussions, addresses on problems in specific fields and luncheon with an outstanding newspaper publisher.

The Indianapolis, Ind., *Star* and *News* (combined circulation 379,052, population 461,173) maintain a high school correspondent system and publish a weekly "Teen Star" section with a high school student staff.

The Salt Lake City, Utah, *Deseret News and Telegram* (circulation 85,105, population 182,121) distribute journalism career publications to schools, provide speakers and films to interested groups, maintain high school stringers to report school activities, and employ university journalism students for night information service and news assignments.

Many newspapers conduct annual interviews with seniors at university schools of journalism and usually employ several in order to keep new blood in their organizations.

Some newspapers have drawn young people of their communities into journalism by allowing them to come into their plants to gain knowledge and experience. During the Second World War, when the Nevada, Mo., *Mail* (circulation 4,651, population 8,009) was faced with a shortage of help, it used high school youngsters for many jobs in which skill was not particularly necessary. When a boy or girl showed aptitude in any department, he or she was placed under a training program, and the newspaper in this way gained several fine employees. One student later attended the University of Missouri School of Journalism and returned to the *Mail* to become its advertising manager.

The *Mail* sent four girls to the University of Missouri School of Journalism and two young GI's to the printing school at Pittsburg, Kans. The young men and two of the young women returned to take positions with the newspaper.

A girl who helped during her junior year in high school later went to college in Nevada and continued to give valuable help in the newspaper office by handling many assignments, writing a column and taking care of the newspaper's "morgue."

"She was worth every cent we paid her and through her we obtained the interest of both the high school and the college groups," says Ben Weir, publisher. "This kind of a contact helps to sell papers and also brings us new students all the time who want to get into our business."

Newspapers everywhere can help their profession greatly by introducing young people of their communities to the practices and advantages of journalism. This is promotion of the highest type.

Keep Employees Informed

Another important step in maintaining high morale within the newspaper organization is the continuous dissemination of information to employees regarding the newspaper's policies and plans. The more that employees may be taken into the confidence of the publisher, the more interested they will become in the welfare of the newspaper. When employees understand the general program of the organization and the responsibilities that rest upon them, they will perform better.

It is the custom with many large papers, and particularly with chain newspaper companies, to immediately acquaint a new employee with the general policies of the publishing company.

New Mexico Newspapers, Inc., use for this purpose a "General Policy Booklet" which carefully outlines the company's policies regarding the handling of news, advertising, circulation, accounting, mechanical operation and employee relations. It consists of 36 pages and the paragraphs under each subject heading are numbered so that attention may easily be drawn to any point needing to be emphasized.

The St. Louis, Mo., *Globe-Democrat* (circulation 332,823, population 856,796) has an illustrated booklet entitled "What Makes the St. Louis *Globe-Democrat* a Great Newspaper." This gives to new employees and also to plant visitors a clear picture of the newspaper's organizational setup, its history, equipment and personnel.

In the early 1900's the late William Randolph Hearst wrote in longhand on a stack of telegraph blanks his ideals of journalism and sent the copy to Victor Polachek, managing editor of the Chicago *Herald* and *Examiner*. Later, E. M. Carney, promotion supervisor, had this printed and sent to all publishers and managing editors of Hearst newspapers, and it hangs today on the walls of most newspapers in that organization.

Statements of policy such as these make clear to beginning newspaper men and women the high principles of the profession they are entering.

Supplementing creeds and statements of policies may be bulletins, house organs and employee newspapers, issued at intervals throughout the year. House organs generally are attuned to promoting staff pride, presenting human interest items and pictures of employees, news of employee activities, plant improvements and policy changes. They contribute materially to morale and loyalty.

"Cuff Stuff," company publication of the Oklahoma Publishing Company, goes to 1,500 employees of its two newspapers, farm magazine and three radio stations. In addition to personal items, it contains stories about plant expansion and employee benefits.

The Brush-Moore Newspapers, Inc., put out a magazine of 20 to 30 pages six times a year for their employees. Emphasis is on the employee, his job and his family, with an eye to better employer-employee relations and understanding.

"Usually we do not single out individual staffers for features unless they have done a particularly fine job on a large assignment or unless they have a hobby or interest that will make good reading," Arthur J. Keeney, promotion manager, explains.

Employees of the Vancouver, British Columbia, *Province* (circulation 112,210, population 365,844) put out every three months the *Province Parade,* a paper that is definitely their very own. Management has nothing to do with it, except to pay the bills. The first time the publisher knows what is in it is when he sees a copy, and he has yet to interfere in any way, according to Kay Cronin, assistant promotion manager.

Another attractive employee publication is *The Headliner,* put out by two members of the promotion department of the Atlanta, Ga., *Journal* and *Constitution* (combined circulation 447,028, population 331,314). Concerning this publication, Richard R. Slate, the editor, says: "We never use items that tend to ridicule anyone or subject them to undue embarrassment. Naturally we wouldn't use stories that could possibly put the company executive or department heads in a bad light. At the same time we don't apple-polish the company officers. All material of every issue is reviewed before publication, first by the head of the promotion department, and second by the vice-president and general manager of the company."

A company magazine, in which employees have an important part and over which there is capable direction, does much to maintain a high morale in the newspaper organization. The first requirement for the success of such a project, says Harrison M. Terrell in *Industrial Marketing,* is "the laying down of main objectives and sound planning. The next is to find the man or the agency to carry the message to Garcia. A company magazine is only as good as its editor."[1]

Training Is Important

In addition to understanding the aims and policies of the newspaper, employees need to be well trained for the responsibilities to

---

[1] *Industrial Marketing,* Dec., 1948, p. 50.

which they are assigned. Publishers may use the greatest care in selecting persons to serve in the various departments, but unless some special training is provided, new employees may have difficulty adjusting to new responsibilities. Even those who have been long on the payroll will benefit from periodic special training, for new methods, new ideas and new systems are continuously being devised, and a newspaper needs to keep its staff members in step with progress. Here again it is the obligation of the promotion department to sense needs and answer them.

There are always better ways to write a news story, to prepare advertising copy, to sell classified advertising, to meet the general public and to accomplish good for the community. Success in newspaper publishing depends greatly upon the attitude of those who make the paper. As Norman Isaacs, managing editor of the Louisville, Ky., *Times* (circulation 175,579, population 369,129) once said: "It is the people we hire — their ability, their drive and their character — who make the kind of newspapers America gets. A helpful attitude exists only when employees know how to perform well and are happy at their work."

Newspapers, like other business institutions, need to use care in holding good employees on their jobs. It is expensive business to have promising young men and women become dissatisfied and go elsewhere for employment. According to the American Management Association, the average cost of hiring, training and losing a salesman is $6,684, with many companies putting the figure at $10,000 or more. Efforts should be made to have employees step up through the ranks to executive positions.

With that very purpose in mind, the St. Petersburg, Fla., *Times* (circulation 90,014, population 96,738) designed a 26-week course of seminar lectures and on-the-job training for 18 men selected from the secondary management level. This course trained them in the rudiments of modern management techniques and made them potential executive candidates.

They spent three days of every two weeks in the newspaper's 18 different departments, learning by doing. Accountants changed ductors on the press, classified ad salesmen learned the mechanics of news writing and credit department personnel became acquainted with the problems of engraving. Each learned how those in other departments performed and became fully convinced of the importance of cooperation between departments all along the way.

As a supplement to on-the-job training, each trainee participated in a weekly 2-hour seminar. At each meeting, a member of the class presided. Topics for discussion ranged from the psychological basis of the supervisor's job to the fine points of advertising photography. There were lectures in accounting, advertising principles, executive management, classified advertising, newspaper history and newspaper production.

Free textbooks for the course were furnished to each student in the form of subscriptions to *Dun's Review and Modern Industry, Editor & Publisher, Printing Equipment Engineer* and the Sunday issue of a metropolitan newspaper.

A 2-hour examination covering the first 13-week period was given at "mid-term" and a second examination at completion of the course.

Other newspapers have developed training programs for reporters, copyreaders, advertising copy writers, classified advertising salesmen and district circulation managers in order to acquaint them with the newspaper's standards and system of operation. This is important because a newspaper succeeds by the efficiency of its executives and staff members.

To assist in maintaining high standards of efficiency in their news and advertising departments, the Gannett Newspapers conduct a 21-week training program for beginning reporters and retail advertising salesmen.[2] The course includes:

1. One day of orientation and explanation of basic newspaper goals and principles.

2. Three weeks of study and work in the circulation department, with a circulation executive directing the training in marketing area coverage, qualitative values, delivery systems and growth factors.

3. Two weeks in observing mechanical department operations, copy handling and copy flow (five days in the composing room, one in engraving, two in stereotype and two in the pressroom).

4. Twelve weeks in the department for which the trainee is being prepared. Newsmen spend this in working on every desk and every major beat, studying techniques and writing routine stories. Advertising trainees spend one week in classified, nine weeks in retail — accompanying regular salesmen in making calls and studying copy preparation and layout — and two weeks in general advertising.

5. Three weeks for ad men in the newsroom and newsmen in the advertising departments.

6. Eight days in the business office studying bookkeeping and accounting practices, newsprint accounting, statistical cost surveys, billing and budgeting.

No persons connected with a newspaper contact the public more often than the boys who deliver the papers and the girls who answer telephones. Each of these has the opportunity of building good will or ill will for the newspaper. Some persons judge a newspaper organization almost solely by the way the boy delivers the paper to the home or the way he greets the customer at the door when he calls to

---

[2] *Editor & Publisher*, Oct. 5, 1957, p. 13.

collect. A newspaper's reputation depends also upon the courtesy and consideration shown by those who answer telephones in the newspaper office. A pleasant telephone voice is worth much to a business institution; an unpleasant one is a liability. The importance of molding courtesy and pleasantness into the voice is emphasized in some newspaper plants by keeping constantly before telephone operators, reporters and secretaries a list of simple suggestions, such as:

1. Answer all calls promptly.
2. Identify yourself properly.
3. Always have paper, pad and pencil handy.
4. Obtain caller's name, address and telephone number as early in conversation as possible.
5. Repeat caller's name, address and telephone number for confirmation.
6. Repeat items as the caller gives them.
7. Use easily understood words and phrases.
8. Always thank the customer for calling.

A newspaper's promotion department must keep employees happy, courteous and efficient so the public will be pleased.

Employees' Suggestions Are Helpful

Another way to bolster the morale of employees is to invite them to express themselves regarding operations within the newspaper plant. When a publisher induces staff members to think about the newspaper business as if it were their very own, he develops a spirit of pride and cooperation that gives smoothness to the daily operation.

"Suggestion boxes" in many newspaper plants have drawn publishers and employees together in the solving of management problems and have produced hundreds of money-saving and efficiency-building ideas. In a so-called "Wipe Out Waste" campaign, the Minneapolis, Minn., *Star* and *Tribune* (combined circulation 502,252, population 521,718) received 1,266 suggestions from 517 of their 1,450 full-time employees. The newspapers paid $1,902.50 in cash awards for these suggestions but they were well worth the cost.

In the newsroom, a reporter suggested that all editors be notified of out-of-town reporter and photographer trips scheduled in advance so that additional pictures and stories might be picked up on these one-shot trips. In the composing room, a printer suggested that employees fill out their time cards at their machines rather than waste time going to the time clock and standing in line at overtime rates. A man in the pressroom diagrammed how an old press could be rebuilt at little cost to make it uniform with newer antifriction presses. A classified advertising salesman suggested that the last two weeks of the campaign be devoted to a special error-reduction effort in that department, with the result that for 15 days the classified department's street force and production men and women maintained a perfect record of no adjustments while handling 11,000 pieces of copy and 200,000 lines of advertising.

"I can't tell you how pleased we were to have *our own* people make these suggestions for more efficiency and less waste," said Otto Silha, business manager.

The promotion department of the Des Moines, Iowa, *Register* and *Tribune* (combined circulation 345,146, population 177,965) set up for employees a full year's program of suggestion giving. Employees were urged to think about ways to improve their own work and to see what could be done to make the newspaper plant a better, happier and more productive place in which to work. Cash awards were offered throughout the year for practical suggestions. The program as outlined, with a suggestion topic for each month, follows:

JANUARY — *Public Relations*: Plant tours, plant services, civic promotions, school promotions.

FEBRUARY — *Records* and *Reports*: How can some of the records and reports in your department be improved? Are there some that do not give sufficient information? Are there others that serve little purpose or are antiquated?

MARCH — *Circulation Ideas*: Carrier offers and contests, subscription offers, sales slogans for specific selling events or sales meetings.

APRIL — *Editorial Ideas*: What features or services do you think would be good additions to our newspapers or to the radio station? Are there any that you think should be eliminated? Give your reasons.

MAY — *Activities Club Suggestions*: What projects should the Activities Club undertake? Are there any other types of events you would like to see sponsored?

JUNE — *State Fair Exhibit*: Ideas for the main attraction must be of sufficient interest to draw over 100,000 persons during fair period.

JULY — *Improve Working Conditions*: If the ventilation or lighting is not right, what may be done to improve it? Are your relationships with persons in your department harmonious? Could the company or department morale be higher? How?

AUGUST — *Local Advertising Promotions*: Ideas that will sell more advertising, special merchandising days or weeks, cooperative advertising ideas, new plant and store opening ideas, tip-offs on new accounts and prospects.

SEPTEMBER — *National* and *Farm and Home Register Advertising*: Sales presentation ideas, sales helps, new account tip-offs, projects that result in additional advertising, such as Soil Conservation Field Days and Weed and Pest Control Clinics.

OCTOBER— *Classified Advertising Promotions*: Mail-order page advertisers, new classifications, new account tip-offs, improvement in counter service, improvement in weekly newspaper want ad service, improvement in phone room service, special promotion weeks.

NOVEMBER — *How To Save Materials and Supplies*: Wherever waste of supplies and materials is apparent, suggest how it may be eliminated.

DECEMBER — *Company-Employee Relations*: Ideas that would bring about more complete understanding, plans used by other companies that would be adaptable.

The Winston-Salem, N.C., *Journal* and *Twin City Sentinel* (combined circulation 102,931, population 87,811) goes farther than the use of a suggestion box in obtaining helpful ideas from employees. It has a Junior Management Board, composed of elected representatives from the various departments. This board confers with a Senior Management Board, composed of the publisher or general manager and department heads. Suggestions made by individual employees are considered by the two boards and those that receive a unanimous vote are submitted for consideration to heads of departments that would be affected.

"Almost all phases of the company's business have been subjected to the investigation of the Junior Board," says James A. Gray, Jr., general manager. "Job vacancies are now posted on the bulletin board, tours of the building have been improved, a closer watch is being kept on the use of our 'morgue,' the newsroom deadline of our afternoon paper has been changed, better housekeeping has been promoted, our group-insurance plans have been reviewed, new maps have been purchased for our newsroom, a mailbox has been installed in our composing room, a new metal pot has been purchased, and more. All of these have resulted from recommendations passed upon by the Junior Board."

Other newspapers that operate successful suggestion systems are the Oklahoma City *Oklahoman* and *Times* (combined circulation 259,311, population 243,504), Canton, Ohio, *Repository* (circulation 68,558, population 116,912), Lexington, Ky., *Herald* and *Leader* (combined circulation 65,607, population 55,534) and Bloomington, Ill., *Pantagraph* (circulation 39,384, population 36,127).

A survey of 83 daily newspapers in the 55,000-or-more circulation class revealed that only 17 had idea promotion plans, and most of these were not instituted or had failed because of: (1) indefinite objectives, (2) inadequate rewards, and (3) slipshod procedures for soliciting and processing suggestions.

Out of the experiences of those who have conducted successful suggestion systems comes the following checklist:

1. Make cash rewards, and make them realistic. If an idea leads to a money-saving or money-making operation, however indirect, pay for it. When possible to assess the gain, pay a specified amount for the idea and another amount as a percentage of the gain (10 per cent of the annual gain is reasonable).

2. Promote the system. Use the house organ, notes in the pay envelope, broadsides in the plant, reminders at company parties, department memos, notes of appreciation for every suggestion. Recognition is promotable and a key phase of the plan.

3. Carefully define "suggestion." But don't imply that ideas have to be barn burners to be money makers.

4. Use a definite system for processing ideas. Get it through the hopper quickly — from collection box to announcement of reward or rejection.

5. Don't consider scrapping the program if it doesn't show a big, tangible profit. The cost for even a big program is nominal.

"Most employees are looking for the opportunity to talk things over with the boss," says Robert D. Gray, director of Industrial Relations Section, California Institute of Technology. "This means the boss must listen."

Mr. Gray offers an 8-point program for within-the-plant relations, which may be applied in the newspaper plant as well as in any other type of industry: (1) give encouragement, (2) give credit when credit is due, (3) give praise — go out of your way to acknowledge good work, (4) accept suggestions, (5) be fair, (6) make periodic appraisals of performance, (7) assist in developing individuals through coaching on the job, and (8) listen.

Too much attention cannot be given to the building of a high morale within the newspaper organization.

Activity Program for Employees

Interesting and wholesome social and recreational activities for employees also help greatly in developing a spirit of satisfaction, comradeship and cooperation within the newspaper organization. This is a part of morale building that is better left to employees themselves. They can work out a program of activities for themselves better than management can do it for them. Management may assist by providing a place and the needed equipment, but it is well to let those who are to take part develop their own program. The promotion department should encourage in every way possible and assist when called upon, but other than that it should remain in the background. The more nearly the activities program comes out of the ideas and interests of participants the more successful it will be.

A good example of how an activities program should be developed and what it may accomplish is to be found within the ranks of employees of the Des Moines *Register* and *Tribune*. An Activities Club, composed entirely of employees, sets up a schedule of social and recreational events each year, and these are enjoyed to the limit by members of the newspaper's force and their families. Each department of the newspaper organization elects a representative on the club's board of directors, and this group elects officers and adopts an annual budget. A program of events is decided upon, and committees from the membership are appointed to take care of all activities. Among events are card parties, a golf tournament, roller skating party, bowling tournament, square dances, company picnic, swimming party, banquets and a variety of stunts for children.

The club has its own quarters, including table-and-chair groupings in the newspaper plant and a recreational area. This is "home" for members of the *Register* and *Tribune* family.

Other newspapers have provided recreational facilities and activities for their employees. Eugene C. Pulliam, publisher of the Phoenix *Gazette* and *Arizona Republic* (combined circulation 177,922, population 128,841) turned over a 23-acre recreational area to his employees there. Named the Lazy G and R Ranch, the area is a lush citrus grove at the foot of a mountain. It provides a 75 x 35-foot swimming pool, a 20 x 35-foot wading pool, a large pavilion, bath houses and a clubhouse.

For employees of his Indiana newspapers — the Indianapolis, Ind., *News* and *Star* — Mr. Pulliam has provided a 22-acre recreational area with a large swimming pool.

The Bloomington, Ill., *Pantagraph* maintains Pantagraph Cabin on Lake Bloomington for its employees and their families. Fishing and swimming are available on the grounds which surround the cabin.

Provisions such as these make the lives of employees more secure, comfortable and pleasurable, and in the long run this makes for a better newspaper.

Provide Future Security

Many publishers have gone still farther in making life pleasant and profitable for their employees. A common practice is to provide:

1. Health insurance.
2. Hospitalization.
3. Life insurance.
4. Salary dividends.
5. Stock ownership and profit sharing.
6. Retirement benefits.

Insurance in various forms is provided employees of many newspapers on a satisfactory share-the-cost plan. This may be (1) life insurance for the protection of the employee's family in the event of death from any cause, (2) sickness and accident insurance, (3) hospital expense insurance for employees and their dependents, (4) special hospital service insurance to help pay for anesthesia and other hospital charges, (5) physician's attendance insurance to help defray expense of physician's visits to hospital for other than surgical purposes, (6) surgical operation insurance to cover surgical costs up to a certain amount, and (7) maternity benefits for women employees and wives of employees to help pay bills in maternity cases.

All of the above types of insurance are provided by the Oklahoma City *Oklahoman* and *Times*. The management explains that it does this "because it wants every one of the company's men and women to be free from the worry and financial shock from the loss of time, hospital, surgical and medical emergencies; also because it wants all its employees to have the protection which life insurance provides."

When a person joins the staff of the *Oklahoman* and *Times* he is presented a booklet entitled "More Security for You and Your Dependents," in which all the insurance and other benefits made available by the company are explained. The company shares largely in the costs.

The American Newspaper Publishers Association one year made a survey to learn to what extent its members are providing special benefits for their employees. This survey revealed that 80 per cent of the group provided group life insurance, 70 per cent hospital insurance, 62 per cent surgical insurance, 40 per cent accident and sickness insurance and 37 per cent accidental death and dismemberment insurance. About two out of three plans were on a contributory basis. The ratio of contributory to noncontributory plans was higher on accidental death and dismemberment, accident and sickness, and group life insurance than on hospitalization and surgical insurance.

Another means used in some plants to express ownership's interest in the welfare of those who make the newspaper is a profit-sharing plan whereby employees receive financial benefits above regular salaries when the newspaper has profitable years.

The Hackensack, N.J., *Bergen Record* (circulation 81,574, population 29,219) in 1940 instituted in its plant a salary-dividend plan, which aroused the interest of publishers throughout the country and caused many similar plans to be started.

This plan is based on the distribution of net profits after taxes have been paid. Of this amount 6 per cent is set aside as a net return to the owners on capital investment. Then what is left is split two ways: half of it is plowed back into the business for expansion, and the other half is divided equally among the 188 year-round salaried employees. During most years this has been equal to 24 weeks of additional pay to each.

In addition to the above plan, the *Record* has a bonus plan, based on advertising linage. For every million lines added annually, each employee gets a full 10 per cent salary increase.

The full year's salary dividend is anticipated every June and half of it is paid out so that employees can use it for their vacations. The rest is disbursed at the end of the year. In each pay envelope is an accounting slip, showing the year's earnings and how the individual employee's share is estimated.

Although the *Record* maintains an open shop and has no guild unit, there have been no serious labor difficulties since the plan was inaugurated. Composition costs have been cut considerably with no slowdowns or mechanical delays. The men realize that the more efficiently they work, the more they earn.

Stock ownership, profit sharing, pension plans and retirement benefits are other important provisions made by newspaper publishers for their employees. In the early 1940's, many newspapers began sharing profits with their employees, establishing happier relations that have continued to be mutually profitable.

Employees are allowed stock ownership in some of the best American newspapers, including the Milwaukee, Wis., *Journal* (circulation 361,856, population 637,392) and the Kansas City, Mo., *Star* (circulation 334,518, population 456,662). A number of chain newspaper organizations also make this provision for employees who have served for a number of years.

John P. Harris and his associates, who own five newspapers in Kansas, have set up a trust whereby employees, after becoming 21 and serving six months, may share in profits of the company and invest their portion of profits in company stock.[3]

The Greenville, S.C., *News* and *Piedmont* (combined circulation 100,538, population 58,161) set up a profit-sharing trust with an initial deposit of $25,000. Within twelve years this grew to $622,375, and within that time paid out to employees $143,000. Payments are made (1) on retirement at the age of 60, (2) on death, either in a lump sum or installments to the beneficiary, (3) on total and permanent disability, and (4) on voluntarily leaving the company. The trust is administered by a local bank and invested chiefly in government bonds, savings-and-loan associations and first mortgages on real estate.

One of the chief purposes in establishing this employee-benefit program was to obtain a more stable labor force. The owners wanted each employee to be contented and to take an interest in the company, its affairs and advancement.

Such plans build morale within the newspaper organization and make more pleasant and successful all work that is done. "A good organization is what every newspaper manager wants," says Derek Dunn-Rankin of the Charlotte, N.C., *News* (circulation 65,508, population 134,042). "If he wants it, he can have it. It doesn't take fabulous salaries to build a top-flight organization. It does take leadership, clear policy and direction, good training, a progressive atmosphere in which an employee wants to work and keep on working, and the right kind of manpower to start with."[4]

The promotion department is largely responsible for initiating and maintaining these morale-building programs.

---

[3] Frank W. Rucker and Herbert Lee Williams, *Newspaper Organization and Management*, Iowa State University Press, Ames, Iowa, 1955, p. 486.

[4] *Publication Management*, Sept., 1958, p. 23.

CHAPTER 22

Promoting the Newspaper to Groups

A NEWSPAPER IS THE SERVANT of all the people. If it is to receive general approval, it must bend its efforts toward interesting and benefiting persons of various backgrounds, tastes, vocations and denominations. Every group within the community should receive its attention. Consequently, far-seeing publishers give special attention to community activities of every kind and see that their newspapers maintain close public relations with:

1. Service clubs.
2. Youth organizations.
3. School groups.
4. Women's organizations.
5. Trade groups.
6. Visiting delegations.

Establish Close Contact With Community Clubs

"A newspaper is more than just a business," says Virgil Fassio, former circulation manager of the Tarentum, Pa., *Valley News* (circulation 23,192, population 9,540). "It is a public servant with a million and one different ways in which it may become the heart of the community."

Certainly one of the primary responsibilities of a newspaper's promotion department is to see that a binding relationship exists between the newspaper and the community's most important service organizations. It is important for members of the newspaper's staff to be active in the Chamber of Commerce and in the various service clubs. Participation in community movements brings the newspaper into contact with important news sources and puts it at the very center of community progress.

"Become a leader in your community," Byron Vedder, general manager of the Champaign-Urbana, Ill., *Courier* (circulation 30,610, population 62,397) told members of the International Circulation Managers Association. "And be that leader not by virtue of your position, not because of the newspaper for which you work, but be that community leader on your own merit. In this day of radio and television, our newspapers must take nothing for granted. We must have good smart newspapermen contributing to community enterprise."

It is extremely important to have persons on the staff who can properly represent the newspaper, both in the shop and out among readers and advertisers of the community. The entire newspaper force, in fact, should be willing to get out and meet with people who make their jobs possible. No member of the community, no organization or club is too insignificant to deserve recognition from the newspaper and its staff.

Newspaper publishers like to have members of their force active in service clubs not only to provide leadership but to give newspaper support to existing leadership. Working with officers and committees of the Chamber of Commerce, the service clubs and other community groups in their efforts to improve the community is in many respects a better way for a newspaper to give impetus to progress than for it to set up campaigns itself and assume the leadership. It certainly is a better way to build good will for the newspaper and usually a more effective way to bring about permanent results. However, newspaper publishers and staff members should always be ready to assume leadership in any important movement when others entrusted with leadership are lagging. It is not the nature of newspaper people to see progress sacrificed or to see movements fail when they can be saved.

When the Community Chest in Dade County, Florida, failed to reach its goal by better than 59 per cent, James L. Knight, general manager of the Miami, Fla., *Herald* (circulation 270,573, population 259,035) and a few other key business leaders stepped in to reorganize it and put it back in business. John D. Pennekamp, another member of the *Herald* staff, was one of the leaders in a campaign for the establishment of the Everglades National Park after other groups had failed for years to get government action.

It often is necessary for a newspaper to create public favor and initiate action for community betterment. One week it may be raising funds for the Red Cross or the March of Dimes. Next week it may be clearing vacant lots or removing an eyesore in some area. The following week it could be an all-out effort to attract new industries. Closely knit into the fabric and pattern of good public relations for any newspaper is a cooperative relationship with community organizations and movements.

Newspaper executives and staffers, usually better informed than anyone else on matters of special interest and importance to the community, often are called upon to speak before service clubs and other groups. They should readily give this service. Some papers operate speakers' bureaus and set up speaking engagements for their editors and reporters. When asked to supply a speaker, the Minneapolis *Star* (circulation 287,425, population 521,718) sometimes sends out three or four of its staff members to comprise a discussion panel.

Eugene A. Simon, publisher, and George N. Scheid, advertising manager, of the Tarentum, Pa., *Valley News*, are greatly in demand as after-dinner speakers. Mr. Simon was one of the first newspapermen to enter Russia after the war, and when he spoke to groups throughout the newspaper's circulation area almost every night for six months on his experiences, he created inestimable good will for his newspaper.

The line, "in cooperation with the *Oakland Tribune*," has appeared in connection with almost every community event held within the circulation area of the Oakland, Calif., *Tribune* (circulation 205,942, population 384,575). This slogan has become synonymous with the success of these events and is a mark of distinction, assuring expanded activities, improved attendance and greater response, according to Walter A. Brown, public relations director.

In Mr. Brown's opinion, newspaper service can outdo that of any other media because it is the perfect instrument to do a public service job. It has the facilities to work with and just naturally carries the burden of the load of most any campaign, crusade or project that the community wants to sponsor.

"When you throw a newspaper's resources behind a community project," he says, "you prove the outstanding service that a newspaper performs."[1]

Public service is essential to the success of any newspaper's promotion program.

Work With Youth Groups

Newspapers must look to oncoming generations for reporters, advertising men and women, copyreaders, editors and newspaper mechanics, and from the youth of today also must come the readers and advertisers of tomorrow. There are 16,000,000 teen-agers in America, and the promotion directed toward them today will influence the number of them that enter the newspaper profession or become newspaper patrons.

---

[1] *Editor & Publisher*, Aug. 16, 1958, p. 36.

Any publisher who is not developing a close relationship with the youth groups of his community is hindering his success as a publisher and is weakening the influence of the press. An opportunity comes to every newspaper to be of great help to Boy Scout organizations, 4-H Clubs, Campfire Girls, Girl Scouts, Future Farmers of America, and various school and church groups. Members of the newspaper's staff should readily respond when requested to talk before such groups, to serve as members of examining boards or judging committees or to give publicity and financial aid in carrying out their programs.

The Florida Scholastic Press Association each year sponsors what it terms a Tournament-by-Mail, a kind of "journalistic track meet" in which staff members compete in ten or more contests five times a year by mail. Newspapers provide appropriate trophies, journalism books or other awards in recognition of superior work.

A Youth Forum, sponsored by the Dayton, Ohio, *Daily News* (circulation 144,687, population 243,872) and the Junior Service League of Dayton, gives young people the opportunity to express their ideas before schools and communities. This gives publicity to teen-age thinking on subjects of common interest to both young people and adults.

Charles Earnhart, promotion manager of the *News,* explains that the pivot group of the program is made up of eight young persons selected from the public and parochial schools of the area through painstaking screening process. Principals of area high schools each select their two outstanding students. This group then is screened by a battery of psychological tests and personal interviews. The finalists are outstanding in intelligence, character, poise, wide range of interests and ability to voice their opinions.

The finalists are divided into two teams which visit high schools in the area where they conduct forums for upperclassmen or in student assemblies. Reporters and photographers of the Dayton *News* cover each forum.

Typical of the questions currently discussed are: "Are Teen-Agers Misunderstood?" and "Do Teen-Agers Have Too Much Freedom?" Each student in the school being visited receives a discussion guide and a bibliography of suggested readings.

"Interest in this news program — the first of its kind in the United States — has been overwhelming," Earnhart reports. "School administrators, teachers, parents and the students themselves are eager for the opportunity of student self-expression which the *News* is offering."[2]

In 1956 the Louisville, Ky., *Courier-Journal* and *Times* (combined circulation 392,224, population 369,129) sponsored a Soil Conservation Essay Writing Contest open to Kentucky grade and high school students. Prizes, totaling $3,250 in U.S. Savings Bonds, included

---

[2] *Editor & Publisher,* Apr. 27, 1957, p. 66.

$100, $75 and $50 for winners in the state contest; in addition, these winners received an all-expense-paid trip to Louisville. A $25 U.S. Savings Bond was given to the first-prize winner in each of the 121 soil conservation districts, and a certificate of merit was given to the writer of the best essay in each school.

Contacts with youth groups to give them encouragement and assistance are an important part of a newspaper's promotion program. Dean Laurence R. Campbell of the Florida State University's School of Journalism expressed it well when he said: "A responsible press cannot continue to describe itself as a family necessity unless, day in and day out, it demonstrates that it serves the teen-agers as well as their parents."[3]

Meet Youth in Schools

A newspaper may make an effective contact with youth through the schools in its circulation area.

William T. Hageboeck, publisher of the Iowa City, Iowa, *Press-Citizen* (circulation 11,945, population 27,212) told members of the Inland Daily Press Association that working at the grass-roots level to interest young people in journalism is the kind of public relations that will pay off well in the long run. By "grass-roots level" he meant in the schools.

"First of all," he said, "visit your high school teacher or teachers and the faculty supervisor of the school newspaper. Offer to talk to the journalism classes at various times during the year concerning your work. Ask the teachers to give you a list of six or eight points to discuss or ask her to get three questions from each member of the class."

Other practical suggestions by Hageboeck are these:

1. Set up a day for the school paper's staff and the adviser and teacher to visit your plant and conclude a tour of the plant with a luncheon.
2. Set up some cash prizes for the best story of the month in the high school paper or the best story of the semester.
3. Give a similar reward for the best picture.
4. Award a college scholarship to the best senior student in journalism at the end of the high school year.
5. Lend engravings or mats to high school papers.
6. Sponsor an Annual High School Journalism Day for school paper staffs of schools in newspaper's territory.
7. Select an alert member of school paper's staff to serve as newspaper's correspondent.
8. Provide each high school a free subscription to newspaper for school library or reading room.
9. Represent the profession of journalism at high school "Career Days."

---

[3] *Editor & Publisher,* Apr. 27, 1957, p. 68.

The Minneapolis, Minn., *Star* and *Tribune* (combined circulation 502,252, population 521,718) developed a valuable relationship with high school students when it conducted a High School Journalism Clinic. This consisted of three sessions, arranged by Robert Weed, promotion director.

The first session included showing a newspaper film entitled "The Miracle at Your Door," an interview with Betty Leonard, staff writer, and a talk by Richard Kleeman, education reporter. In the second session, students divided into groups to consider certain phases of newspaper work, including sports coverage, news reporting, editorial direction, column writing, interviewing, photography and illustration, feature writing, advertising, headline writing, production and make-up. In the final session, school papers were analyzed and discussed.

In some communities, a current events program, sponsored by the local newspaper, has been a popular means of developing good will with high school youngsters. Pupils, teachers, school boards and outstanding citizens in all walks of life have praised it.

One of the most successful of such programs was conducted by the Dayton, Ohio, *News* with the assistance of the Dayton Educational Television Foundation, Miami Valley public and parochial schools, Dayton Council on World Affairs and a local television station. This feature was entitled "You and Your World." A list was prepared of study subjects which seemed most in need of understanding, and one of these subjects was presented each week during the school year through the newspaper, the television station and in the school classrooms. A typical week's program was:

MONDAY — Special article in the *News* with free reprints available to students whose parents were not subscribers.

THURSDAY — Questions and answers in the *News* — ten on the special article and ten on news events of the week in world affairs.

FRIDAY — Panel discussion by high school students over television.

In promoting this program, the *News* said: "Good citizens are made, not born. They are the product of their education. But education today is not found in books and classrooms alone. It comes to us through newspapers and periodicals — through radio and television — through discussion and comparison of our ideas with others."

Newspapers have actually become textbooks in many elementary and secondary schools of the nation. The Milwaukee, Wis., *Journal* (circulation 361,856, population 637,392) provides as a guide to its use in the classroom a book, "The Newspaper in the Classroom." This book shows how a good newspaper may be a valuable help in every part of the teaching curriculum. It gives specific recommendations for the development of a current affairs workshop in the larger school to facilitate the use not only of the newspaper, but of magazines, films, radio and television. It has similar practical suggestions to assist the teacher in a one-room school in using available facilities for the integration of the newspaper in classroom work.

The book then goes through the entire school curriculum, devoting a chapter to the use of the newspaper in many of the branches of classroom study, including such chapter titles as "In Teaching the Social Sciences at the Elementary School Level," "In Teaching Elementary School English," "Constructing Arithmetic Problems from Current Materials," and "Enrichment of the Science Curriculum." There are also chapters on the use of the newspaper in civics, economics, sociology, advanced English, home economics, music appreciation and the arts. Charts and illustrations are used to good advantage to implement the text, sample projects and study programs are outlined and suggested quiz material is listed.

Considerable space is given to the suitability of the newspaper for teaching character, education, health, safety and history. A general list is included of new and progressive textbooks available to the teacher interested in the better use of current educational materials.

Another newspaper that contributes liberally to the education of youth is the Miami, Fla., *Herald*. A News Institute is conducted each year by members of the *Herald* staff for selected journalism students from high schools of the county. This is a joint effort with the University of Miami. The *Herald* and its radio station WQAM one year provided free to schools of the state a film program on current world happenings. The film, a professional production of Warner Pathe News, was distributed through the Film Library of the General Extension Division of the University of Florida. Many schools incorporated the film into regular study courses.

All such efforts by newspapers through their promotion departments to establish helpful contacts with youth groups bring rich returns.

Implement Women's Group Activities

Women's organizations comprise another group with which the newspaper should develop close relationship. The publisher who makes all the services of his newspaper available to these groups establishes and maintains a firm footing in his community.

Daughters of the American Revolution, League of Women Voters, Business and Professional Women's Club, study clubs, church groups and other organizations of women are great sources of news and, when given attention, become great agencies of good will for the newspaper. The publisher and his department heads may assist them in planning interesting programs and in developing projects for community betterment.

Whatever may be done to draw these community forces together should not be disregarded for any assistance or distinction that may be given to women's groups brings rich returns to the newspaper.

When the Independence, Mo., *Examiner* (circulation 10,713, population 36,963) invited the local Business and Professional Women's Club to put out the *Examiner* on the national organization's birthday, there was ready acceptance. Women took over the various desks in the news and business offices, carried out news assignments, produced feature stories and special columns, and sold advertising to merchants. They produced a highly creditable issue and received the hearty approval of *Examiner* readers. It was a wonderful day and an experience the business and professional women of that community will never forget. They were drawn to their home-town newspaper with ties of friendship and good will that became permanent.

The Women's Institute of St. Paul, a project sponsored by the St. Paul, Minn., *Dispatch* and *Pioneer Press* (combined circulation 210,007, population 311,349), brings together each year 12,500 women for a week of programs featuring some of the world's most renowned speakers, musicians and entertainers (see Fig. 22.1). Appearing on the program one year were Eleanor Nash, Eleanor MacVickar, Andre Kostelanetz and orchestra, John Mason Brown, Henry Scott, Robert Anshen, James Melton in concert, Dr. Will Durant, Randolph Churchill, Gladys Miller, Tito Guizar and ensemble, David Seabury and Eleanor Steber.

The idea of the institute was conceived by B. H. Ridder, president of the St. Paul *Dispatch* and *Pioneer Press,* and his civic-minded wife. Their intention was to awaken the pride of the women in their city and to use the energy and enthusiasm of thousands of women in a service planned to increase buying power, improve the service of retail stores, and to interest women in improving and beautifying the shopping district of St. Paul. The programs by outstanding artists served to draw the women together, forming the basis for an active organization.

In this important undertaking they have been eminently successful. The institute has grown with the years and its scope has broadened until it is an integral part of every phase of St. Paul life.

Strengthen Relations With Trade Groups

Another important contact is with trade organizations and merchant associations. Here is presented the opportunity to explain the newspaper's advertising service as well as its efficiency in giving the news and providing features.

Some newspapers have had films made that show the operations within their plants, the results obtained by their advertisers or the home life of their employees. Others have conducted surveys and are prepared to present valuable facts concerning public reaction to the newspaper's services.

Fig. 22.1 — St. Paul **Dispatch-Pioneer Press** wins good will with its Women's Institute.

The Nashville *Banner* and *Tennessean* (combined circulation 220,617, population 174,307) prepared a study called "Let's Get the Picture Straight," showing the meager coverage by national magazines contrasted with the vast circulation of the Nashville newspapers in the local area. There were four important steps in this effective promotion:

1. They staged a luncheon presentation to all members of the Nashville Food Brokers Association and, of course, gave each of them a copy of the study. Most of those present told the sales promotion manager that they intended to contact their suppliers and insist on representation in locally edited newspapers rather than in national magazines.

2. The following week they made the same presentation to the local food wholesalers and executives of the large food chains. The results were immediate and gratifying. Five color advertisements were signed up for 26 weeks and one advertisement, also in full color, for 52 weeks.

3. They presented the findings to the retail furniture dealers of Nashville, and they all signed a round-robin letter to their principal suppliers demanding representation on a local basis rather than a national one.

4. Presentations were made to all the department stores. These were sold on the idea that the next time a salesman told them about the "wonderful backing" their product would get in national magazines, they were to show them this study and explain how much more important it was to get complete coverage at the local level.

As a result of these important contacts, the Nashville papers received advertising schedules they had been unable to touch before.

Promotion managers of newspapers may be of great assistance to each other by arranging with their Chambers of Commerce, service clubs or other groups to have visiting promotion managers speak at their luncheons. The visiting newspapermen can discuss with them the influence of the press in the local community perhaps better than the newspaper's editor, publisher or promotion manager could.

Welcome Visiting Groups

Visiting delegations comprise another class of persons with whom the newspaper should make friendly contacts. Whatever the publisher and his staff may do toward making the city's welcome to these visitors ring with genuine sincerity will be appreciated not only by the guest delegates but by the convention hosts.

The Independence, Mo., *Examiner,* alert to its promotion opportunities, with great regularity produced a welcome page whenever conventions came to town. Sometimes cordial verses of greeting touched up a page containing pictures of the hosts. On several occasions it produced special sections of the newspaper devoted to the organization in convention and to the assets and accomplishments of the host city.

The variety of ways in which a newspaper may promote itself and its community to groups is unlimited. Walter R. Humphrey, editor of the Fort Worth, Tex., *Press* (circulation 57,861, population 278,778) used fitting words when he told members of the Colorado Press Association: "We have sometimes been timid in selling our service reputation. It may be the biggest thing we have to sell and too often we have taken it for granted."

CHAPTER 23

Promoting
Community Progress

A NEWSPAPER CAN PROGRESS only as its community progresses, but it must not depend on the community to pull it along. The only sure way of getting ahead is for the newspaper to promote progress in every phase of community life. Newspapers, therefore, have found it profitable to conduct programs promoting:

1. Public improvements.
2. Better living.
3. Trade expansion.
4. Education and religion.
5. Safety and health.

Encourage Community Improvements

Certainly there is no better way for a publisher to put out a newspaper with perfect ease of conscience and with the respect of the community than through consistent initiation and sponsorship of needed community improvements. No one is in a better position than the publisher to sense important community needs or to lead in answering them and the extent to which he gains good will through worthwhile service determines largely the value of his newspaper as a going concern.

Thomas L. Robinson, publisher of the Charlotte, N.C., *News* (circulation 65,508, population 134,042), said in a bulletin issued by the Southern Newspaper Publishers Association: "To be worthy of the public's respect and acceptance, a newspaper must be honest, fearless, imaginative and enterprising. It must have absolute integrity and represent courage, in addition to scintillating qualities of resourcefulness, brightness and verve."

All these qualities are helpful to a newspaper in planning and carrying out a constructive community program, and have been evident in many areas where progressive newspapers are published.

In determining a year's program that would benefit the city, the St. Louis, Mo., *Globe-Democrat* (circulation 332,823, population 856,796) discovered that better transportation facilities were badly needed. It lamented the fact that St. Louis, eighth largest city in America, lagged badly in the matter of airline service. It published a series of articles and editorials, which resulted directly in competitive nonstop service from St. Louis to New York and to Washington, and similar service to San Francisco, Miami and New Orleans, as well as greatly improved service to Chicago, Minneapolis, Cincinnati and many other points.

The *Globe-Democrat* sensed also the need for a new bus terminal. Photographs and a series of news articles appearing in its columns were given credit by the Greyhound Company for its decision to build a new terminal in downtown St. Louis. For more than two years this newspaper has been campaigning to give people of the surrounding area at least one free bridge across the Mississippi River. This, too, undoubtedly will be realized as a result of effective promotion.

Smaller newspapers, as well as the large ones in great cities, expend themselves just as resultfully in promoting community progress. The persistent, aggressive attitude of the Farmington, N. Mex., *Times* (circulation 8,562, population 15,115) was largely instrumental in bringing to a prompt realization the Navajo Dam project in northwestern New Mexico. This project, along with other important projects which had been authorized by Congress, was threatened to be held up when funds previously set up for their construction were canceled in the spring of 1958.

Immediately the *Times* put its news and editorial staffs to work. Day-by-day coverage was given to all that took place in Washington, and close touch was kept with New Mexico senators and congressmen by telephone and telegraph. Resolutions for signatures were submitted to groups throughout the state.

In the face of such constructive information and statewide influence, together with mounting unemployment, funds for the Navajo Dam were restored to the budget and construction was resumed.

City playgrounds, stadiums, libraries and community auditoriums have been provided for many communities through newspaper influence and leadership. Better sewage disposal, greater water supply, more street paving, improved parking facilities, better schools and economical light and power service have been realized in the same way.

The Aspen, Colo., *Times* (circulation 1,750, population 916) was given a community service award at the University of Colorado's Newspaper Week in recognition of leadership in community development. The honor was based largely on a 10-article symposium on the goals of education, which included an honest appraisal and constructive criticism of the Aspen school situation.

C. E. Townsend, editor and publisher of the Granite City, Ill., *Press-Record* (circulation 15,391, population 34,189), was chosen "Illinois Editor of the Year" in recognition of a strong community service program conducted by his newspaper. It promoted a $2,200,000 school building bond issue, a $650,000 community hospital fund drive, a proposed referendum on city manager form of government, a 7,000-acre park and recreation area development, a master sewer and drainage plan for Granite City and two other nearby communities, and a campaign to add sodium fluoride to city water.

Other publishers of weekly and biweekly newspapers have been strong factors in community development and have found great satisfaction in it.

"To me the most rewarding part of running a newspaper is to look around town and see the many improvements that have come about by the leadership and influence my newspaper has given," says O. J. Lere, publisher of the Le Roy, Ill., *Journal* (circulation 1,161, population 1,820). "Offhand, I can think of all-weather blacktop streets all over town, modern street lights in and adjoining the business district, municipal iron removal and soft water plant, city zoning ordinance, new elementary school, vacant lots converted into a playground, city's water supply one of the best in the state to be fluorinated, kindergarten in our schools, city tax-financed garbage collection system and a well-equipped community fire protection system — all of which came about because the *Journal* sowed the seeds and nourished the projects editorially."[1]

The Smithfield, N.C., *Herald* (circulation 7,370, population 5,574) has been the leader in or has given its support to many projects of community importance. Among these have been movements for a community hospital, municipal recreation facilities, a public library, a bond issue for support of schools, local highway safety, expanded municipal services, paved streets, sewerage extensions, reorganization of Chamber of Commerce, scientific farming and better race relations.

The Patchogue, N.Y., *Advance* (circulation 6,560, population 8,288) carries on its editorial page two listings of projects, which it endorses. These are community needs in Brookhaven and Patchogue, two principal towns it serves. As soon as any one of the needs is met, a check mark is placed before the listing of that need to show what has been accomplished. In 1958 these listings were as follows:

---

[1] *Publishers' Auxiliary,* Apr. 5, 1958, p. 4.

Brookhaven Needs:

1. To further develop the town of Brookhaven's property on South Haven Avenue, Medford, part of which is now used for rifle range.
2. An increase in the minimum size of new houses.
3. More light and diversified industry.
4. A well-planned incinerator program.
5. The dredging of Swan Creek.
6. To preserve the Dare House, Revolutionary War landmark in Selden.
7. A traffic light at the intersection of Route 27 (Montauk Highway) and Hawlett Avenue for the protection of ambulances and private cars going to and returning from Brookhaven Memorial Hospital.
8. A Town Hall annex.

Patchogue Needs:

1. A new railroad station.
2. To extend its sewer lines.
3. A new bus terminal.
4. Proper drainage on East Main Street in front of the post office.
5. More access roads to provide easy ingress and egress without bottling up traffic on Main Street.

Special editorials appeared from time to time to emphasize further the needs presented in the *Advance*'s community service programs. This newspaper's editorial page has won honors in many contests.

The Bloomington, Minn., *Sun* (circulation 5,468, population 9,902) was the leader in a community-wide celebration when the city completed improvements of its main business street. The improvements included street widening, new curbs and gutters, sidewalks and fluorescent lights.

"We sent all merchants in the area two promotion pieces in advance of the celebration," says Ray Wallentine, co-publisher. "We also carried a progress report for the committees which were organizing and planning the program. A big part of the celebration's success undoubtedly was due to our two-pronged effort in informing the merchants."

The Marysville, Kans., *Advocate* (circulation 3,981, population 3,866), another enterprising weekly, goes all out for school activities, bond issues for school improvements, obtaining conventions and improving the airport. Byron E. Guise, the publisher, says: "Money should never be the controlling factor in what the newspaper promotes. A newspaper should always work for the best interests of the community and the individual."

Maurice Leckenby, editor of the Steamboat Springs, Colo., *Steamboat Pilot* (circulation 2,245, population 1,913) feels the same way. He says that "the rewards of accomplishing something for the community, the state, or even helping in a broader field, give an inner glow that beats getting rich."

A survey made by Adolph O. Goldsmith, assistant professor of journalism at Louisiana State University, reveals that most weekly publishers participate gladly in legitimate community projects and quite often as the motivating force. However, they generally prefer the assistance of other sponsors.[2]

In the volume of war contracts awarded during World War II, Louisville, Ky., became the eighteenth largest industrial area in the country. Determined that this area should maintain its industrial leadership following the war, the Louisville, Ky., *Courier-Journal* and *Times* (combined circulation 392,224, population 369,129) started immediately following V-J Day to make a survey and compile facts that would help toward making Louisville an even greater industrial center in the years to come.

There is much that a newspaper of wide vision and determination may do to keep its community constantly going forward.

Promote Better Living

While general progress is taking place in a community there are always good opportunities to promote better living — to point out to residents ways in which they may make home life more pleasant, comfortable, meaningful and economical. Here again community leadership becomes a potent factor.

The St. Louis *Globe-Democrat* conducted a Modern Living Show for five days in mammoth Kiel Auditorium with an attendance of more than 215,000 people. One hundred and fifty booths exhibiting modern equipment for the home, a cooking school, a fashion show, a baking contest, three modern home exhibitions and other features held the attention of thousands each day from noon until 10 o'clock at night. This show was a tremendous stimulus to business as well as a popular attraction. The newspaper received excellent cooperation from business firms and good will from the people of Greater St. Louis for sponsoring it.

Twice each year the *Globe-Democrat* conducts a fashion show to acquaint women of its circulation area with the newest styles and fashions and to focus attention on St. Louis as a prominent fashion center of the Midwest.

The Dayton, Ohio, *Daily News* (circulation 144,687, population 243,872), sponsor of many public service features, joined with the University of Dayton one year in promoting a course in family financial management entitled "Better Living for Your Money." Weekly discussion meetings were held at the university with special tie-in features published in the *News*. This constructive help was highly appreciated.

The Salt Lake City, Utah, *Tribune* and *Deseret News and Telegram* (combined circulation 184,434, population 182,121) each year

---

[2] *Publishers' Auxiliary,* June 21, 1958, p. 1.

focus the attention of youth on greater charm and modern styles. The *News* stages a teen-age fashion and charm clinic called "Seminar for Sallies." It is managed by Elaine Cannon, the paper's teen editor, and is part of a back-to-school promotion to help Salt Lake City merchants. The *Tribune* sponsors "Debbie's Coming Out Party," equally interesting to youth. Dan Valentine, a staff member, directs this school, and one year had three syndicated columnists, Ann Landers, Lydia Lane and Edan Wright, appear on the program.

Beauty shows have great appeal to women readers, and none perhaps has been more successful than the Philadelphia, Pa., *Inquirer's* "Beautyrama." The *Inquirer* (circulation 619,381, population 2,071,605) received the cooperation of 26 cosmetic manufacturers in staging this event, which drew more than 8,000 women during its 3-day run. On the day prior to opening the show, the *Inquirer* carried a supplement containing news of the event, editorial support for each individual exhibitor and a minimum of 500 lines of advertising from each cosmetic manufacturer. Beauty clinics were held each hour, one for adult women and another for teen-agers.

Cooking schools and home shows have been conducted with remarkable success by newspapers of all sizes. Food manufacturers, furniture dealers and appliance stores readily cooperate in staging such events. An experienced home economist uses many popular recipes in demonstrating various food items and cooking utensils. The newspaper usually employs the demonstrator and sells advertising to the firms whose goods are represented in the show. The revenue from advertising usually is not sufficient to cover all expenses, but the good will established with the women who attend is considered of sufficient value to warrant the deficit.

Style and good living in these days seem to be about as closely connected with automobiles as with clothing, household utensils and furnishings. Consequently, the annual auto show, in the success of which the newspaper plays an important part, is an exceptionally popular event. One newspaper put on an automobile show and transportation exhibit that produced a net profit of approximately $2,000. This amount was turned over to the treasury of the local automobile dealers association. The newspaper's direct benefit was from the great volume of advertising carried in its columns in the week preceding and during the exhibition.

But when it comes to sponsoring something that contributes to better living in an even more practical way, consider the Youth Talent Exhibit sponsored by the Lansing, Mich., *State Journal* (circulation 63,999, population 92,129), the Grand Rapids, Mich., *Herald* (circulation 52,239, population 176,515) and the Battle Creek, Mich., *Enquirer-News* (circulation 37,170, population 48,666). There is an interesting story behind this.

At a meeting of newspaper promotion men in Gary, Ind., a group of high school students complained that "the only time they get their names in the paper is when they do something wrong." This struck home to representatives of the three Michigan newspapers and they proceeded to tailor an event that would bring youth into their columns in a highly favorable light. They planned a Youth Talent Exhibit, which became an annual affair. The newspapers explained that the aim of the exhibit was "to give public recognition to young people, allowing many a youth his only chance for a day in the sun and inspiring others in the pursuit of worthwhile creative activities in the arts, crafts and sciences."

Newspaper stories were the main means of promoting the exhibit. Liberal space was given to feature stories that met every requirement of bona fide news value. Each paper followed a planned schedule for two months of two features each week, plus such daily breaks as events provided. During the last two or three weeks prior to the exhibit, this tempo was quickened to practically a story every day. On the "big days" the news staffs enthusiastically devoted large spreads to the opening of the show, announcement of winners and many interesting sidelights.

Some unusual editorial taboos, laid down for covering this event, were taken in good grace when the motive was made clear. The word "hobby" was never used; all emphasis was on creative talent, not just spare time amusement. The word "teen" was shunned because of its association with the "coke" bar and clothes-horse sort of concept, and also on the theory that the newspaper should appeal to youth as young adults rather than as members of a problem-child group in the community. Commercialism of any kind was eliminated, even to the extent of prohibiting advertisers from using the Youth Talent idea as the basis of a selling approach. Phrases such as "juvenile delinquency" or "character-building value" were never mentioned. It was felt that the positive value of the project was implicit; the newspapers did not want to be cast in the role of evangelists. In advance stories, prizes were played down, sometimes rating a spot in the deck but never in the head. Text matter on prizes was buried in the story in the spirit that prizes were arranged "to add zest to the event." All this treatment was a consideration in obtaining the support of educators. Such an event definitely refutes the charge that the press plays up to the misdemeanors of youth.

Foster Trade Expansion

When a newspaper promotes better living, it creates at the same time greater business within the community it serves. Trade expansion naturally becomes a major project for every progressive newspaper, and it must be done on an extensive as well as an intensive basis.

Widening the community's trade territory becomes as important as increasing business within the limited trade area. Here, too, a newspaper's promotion department plays an important role.

Newspapers have helped communities to expand trade areas by promoting (1) bridges across streams to shorten routes to town from important areas, (2) highway improvements, (3) larger and better airports, (4) better bus and train service, (5) improved parking facilities, (6) sites to interest tourists, (7) increased and improved hotel and tourist court services, (8) closer cooperation between merchants in developing trade, and (9) more consistent and more attractive advertising by firms that serve the area.

When business leaders of Kankakee, Ill., decided that a spirit of progress needed to be revived, the *Journal* (circulation 25,494, population, 27,908) was the chief moving factor in a drive that buried existing gloom and brought optimism and united energy and enthusiasm into community life. "Let's Go" was the slogan. While the Chamber of Commerce and service clubs staged for the public a mock trial of Mr. Gloom, convicted him to death and buried him deep down in his own mud and muck, the *Journal* ran articles calling attention to the city's many assets, the inherent strength of the community and the enthusiasm, good will and energy with which favorable factors were brought into existence. A 92-page "Let's Go" edition, loaded with encouraging facts and glowing with optimism, was delivered to every home in the Kankakee trade area. The *Journal,* in fact, organized all its facilities on an emergency basis and cooperated as the perennial home town exponent of civic progress.

The *Journal* in still other ways has been instrumental in developing greater trade in its area. It launched a campaign for a larger airport, and supported the idea with stories about what other communities had done. It explained how they had organized airport authorities in order to qualify for state and federal aid and how it was possible to do the same in Kankakee. "Let's stop building other people's airports and build an adequate one for ourselves," the newspaper admonished. When the question was brought to a vote, citizens responded and authorized greater acreage for a modern airport.

Traffic congestion is a baffling problem in many cities. Many downtown business areas are battling for their very lives. If they are to hold patronage they must provide convenient parking for cars or provide other convenient, economical transportation to their business centers. Of special interest to Chicagoans and suburbanites is the commuter railroad situation and impending transportation crises. In a series of timely articles, editorials and reports of reactions, all well illustrated with maps and pictures, the Chicago *Sun-Times* (circulation 534,063, population 3,620,962) explained how the trouble started and what might be done to prevent a traffic congestion that would strangle the Chicago downtown area.

To combat the competition provided by suburban business centers springing up all around them, the uptown merchants of Independence, Mo., arranged with the Independence *Examiner* (circulation 10,713, population 36,963) to carry a Christmas catalog section of 24 pages, advertising gift specials at their stores. The front page of this section said: "Shop from your easy chair in this big Uptown Christmas Catalog...Thousands of Gifts in wide variety for easy selection from your Uptown Merchants...For Bigger Values Every Day Shop the Uptown Independence Way." It was printed in two colors and carried appealing trade messages from 21 of the city's largest stores.

Such efforts on the part of newspapers are vital factors in solving trade problems and promoting community growth.

Tourist trade is important to areas where there are sites of scenic and historic interest. Newspapers may draw hundreds of visitors to their areas by pointing out tourist attractions and advertising available accommodations for tourists. "What's There For a Tourist to See?" was the title of a series of highly illustrated articles in the Lincoln, Nebr., *Star* and *Journal* (combined circulation 67,370, population 98,884). These articles called attention to the unique state capitol, planetarium, state museum, art gallery, city park with live buffalo, and state historical library.

Spring openings, fall festivals, dollar days, community sales days and many other similar trade-building events may be staged effectively in any community with newspaper cooperation.

Work for Higher Level of Culture and Morality

Newspapers may help to raise the standards of community thought and action by promoting projects relating to education and religion. Among such projects successfully sponsored are: (1) forum discussions on world peace, (2) community Lenten services, (3) schools for voters, (4) music festivals, (5) oratorical contests, (6) talent shows, (7) press conferences, (8) lecture series, (9) spelling contests, and (10) church news clinics.

In the early years of the United Nations, the Denison, Tex., *Herald* (circulation 12,252, population 17,504) sponsored an open forum in the Denison High School auditorium on the subject, "Is World Government a Solution?" In 20- to 30-minute talks, four prominent Texans discussed the historical parallel between the federation of the 18 American colonies and today's need for world unity, the religious aspects of proposed world government and the political problems in setting up world government. This program was offered by the *Herald* as a public service and as a means of celebrating its eighth anniversary under existing ownership.

Newspapers use various means to promote better government and to heighten interest in clean politics. In 1948 the Lincoln, Nebr., *Journal* (circulation 42,885, population 98,884) was awarded a Pulitzer Prize for sponsoring an all-star preferential primary. Through the newspaper's efforts, and before the nominating conventions were held, Nebraska voters were given the opportunity to vote for their choice of all known candidates of both parties. Behind-the-scenes political maneuvers also were described in full detail.

Cultural activities were encouraged in the Upper Midwest by the Gideon D. Seymour memorial lectures given at the University of Minnesota. These lectures established in memory of Gideon D. Seymour, executive editor of the Minneapolis *Star* and *Tribune* from 1944 to 1954, brought distinguished personalities to the university campus in a program symbolic of Mr. Seymour's great interest in the cultural advancement of the community his newspaper served.

The Minneapolis *Star* and *Tribune* (combined circulation 205,252, population 521,718) made another contribution to community education and culture when it sponsored a Press Conference for Minnesota club women in cooperation with the Minnesota Federation of Women's Clubs and other women's organizations of the state.

The National Tournament of Orators, with its various contests in many parts of the United States, is another public affair sponsored by newspapers which brings history and politics to the fore. Adults and young people both benefit greatly in communities where these contests are staged. Records on the 1956 tournament revealed that during five months of competition, 13,000 students in 60 colleges and 470 high schools in areas covered by sponsoring newspapers were contestants, and close to 100,000 other persons, including parents and teachers, attended the preliminary contests. The final contest was held in the Metropolitan Opera House in New York City before 4,800 people. This project, sponsored by the Hearst newspapers, is a valuable educational program for youth.

Many newspapers participate also in the National Spelling Bee, which drives thousands of boys and girls to their spelling books and into warm competition. The Minneapolis *Tribune* (circulation 214,827, population 521,718) sponsors annually a lively preliminary contest for students in the schools of Minnesota, North Dakota, South Dakota and western Wisconsin. Each school sends one representative to the Minneapolis contest. The *Tribune* champion then is awarded a five-day, all-expense-paid trip to Washington, D.C. to compete in the National Spelling Bee finals. One hundred and forty-four county and city champions chosen out of 100,000 grade school pupils in more than 25,000 schools of the Upper Midwest participated one year in the annual *Tribune*-sponsored contest at Minneapolis.

Newspapers also enjoy sponsoring music festivals for the cultural opportunities they provide the youth of their communities. Winners from 14 preliminary contests in 1957 competed in a National Musical Festival before an audience of 80,000 people at Soldiers' Field in

Chicago. Singers were accompanied by a 100-piece Festival Symphony Orchestra. Prominent singing stars of radio, television and the movies headlined a cast of 8,000 professional and amateur entertainers from 40 states and Canada.

Question and essay contests on the Bible, sponsored by newspapers, have received the endorsement of ministers and other church people. The Birmingham, Ala., *News* (circulation 184,893, population 326,037) received from persons in its circulation area interesting stories of how they had found spiritual help in times of need. These were the result of a contest, in which an award of $50 was offered for the best 250-word story, $15 for the second best, and $5 for the third best.

The Louisville, Ky., *Courier-Journal* and *Times* sponsored a state contest for 4-H Club achievements and community leadership in agriculture and home economics. Prizes to the amount of $325 were offered, and the money was used by the winners to further develop the project or projects they were engaged in. All Kentucky 4-H Club members 15 years of age or older, who had been in club work four years or longer, were eligible to compete.

Many opportunities to sponsor contests and programs of an educational or religious nature come to newspapers and such events are easily handled with a well-organized promotion department.

Sponsor Improved Health and Safety

Newspapers again have rendered important service to their readers and have won great good will by sponsoring programs and features pertaining to health and safety.

Free health forums are conducted each year in many cities by newspapers in cooperation with local doctors and hospitals. These make a strong contribution to healthful living.

The Lynchburg, Va., *News* and *Advance* (combined circulation 33,435, population 47,727) and the Lynchburg Academy of Medicine sponsored a series of health forums scheduled at 2-week intervals over a period of ten weeks. The Shreveport, La., *Times* (circulation 87,184, population 127,206) cooperated with the Shreveport Medical Society in conducting a similar program. Readers of the *Times* were urged to attend and submit questions they would like discussed, using blanks printed in the *Times*.

A health forum of four sessions, conducted by the Dayton, Ohio, *Daily News* in cooperation with the Montgomery County Medical Society, was a well-planned and well-supported event. Moderator, speakers and panel members were supplied by the medical society. Programs were rehearsed by the entire cast to assure a smooth performance. Questions to be answered were submitted in advance on coupons printed in newspaper ads. Nurses from the Dayton hospitals were volunteer ushers, wearing their uniforms for the occasion. The *News*

believed strongly in this project and promoted it extensively. It carried
five full-page ads, 24 1-column ads, several 3-inch ads and front page
stories on Sunday, Monday and Tuesday before each forum. It used
also 92 television spot announcements and 126 radio spots. As a con-
sequence, 6,000 persons attended the four sessions.

Newspapers have been instrumental also in enabling hospitals to
obtain highly expensive modern equipment. The St. Louis *Globe-
Democrat* became aware of the need for the most modern type
of heart-lung machine — one that would make difficult surgery possible
for hundreds of cases of congenital heart defects treated at St. Louis
hospitals. In a full-page editorial and an accompanying rotogravure
section, the newspaper asked: "How much are the lives of 300
children a year worth to you?" and in this way launched a campaign
for $65,000 starting with a $1,000 gift of its own. In twelve days,
$85,000 was subscribed and, even though the newspaper asked that
no further contributions be made, more than $102,000 was subscribed
in less than a month. The machine was built and dedicated in 1958,
and immediately went into full use.

Much news and editorial space has been devoted to safety as well
as to health, and newspapers have been credited with much of the
success achieved by the National Safety Council in promoting safe
driving on the highways.

The New Orleans, La., *States-Item* (circulation 162,805, population 570,445) caused many of its readers to do some constructive
thinking regarding safety measures, and to exchange their ideas when
it cooperated with the city's Department of Public Safety, the Automobile Dealers Association and the New Orleans Safety Council in
conducting a traffic safety essay contest. This lasted for four weeks
with a $25 government bond going to each week's winner. Then from
the four weekly winners, first and second prize winners were selected,
the former receiving $300 in cash and the latter $200. The essay consisted in completing the following sentence in 100 words or less: "I
suggest the following to improve traffic safety in the city of New
Orleans...."

The Atlanta, Ga., *Constitution* (circulation 193,558, population
331,314) conducted a vigorous highway safety campaign, which received the hearty endorsement of the Governor, other state officials
and safety leaders.

Newspapers have been more liberal with space for questions of
health and safety perhaps than for any other subjects pertaining to
public and individual welfare.

"The newspaper is a
dynamic institution,
reaching into
the very roots of
community culture
and happiness."

— STEWART HARRAL,
Director of
Public Relations Studies,
University of Oklahoma

CHAPTER 24

Providing Community Entertainment

THE AMERICAN NEWSPAPER has been a vital factor in community culture and entertainment, not only by what it gives to readers through its columns, but also through its sponsorship of entertaining and community-improvement events in which the people of its circulation area participate.

It is easy for a newspaper to foster helpful community events. The publisher knows what is considered appropriate entertainment for his readers and how such entertainment features may be obtained. He has in his newspaper the most effective medium that may be used to promote and advertise such events. He recognizes the good-will advantages centered in anything he may do to bring pleasure and culture to his readers, and readily grasps opportunities to provide entertainment and recreation.

Such newspaper-sponsored programs are of three general classes:

1. Participation events.
2. Spectator events.
3. Recognition events.

Participation Events Are Popular

Participation events are highly recommended by some publishers as good-will builders with their newspaper readers. The Santa Monica, Calif., *Outlook* (circulation 26,940, population 75,132) believes strongly in this type of promotion.

"Merchandising is not adequate promotion," says Mrs. Charlot Holzkamper, the *Outlook*'s community service director. "People are

[361]

rapidly turning to personal participation in home and community events as a means of fighting the impersonal aspects of urban life. This is a great challenge."[1]

That the *Outlook* has accepted the challenge is shown in the great number of interesting participation events it sponsors each year, and increasing participation attests the public interest in each event. A Holiday Workshop held in cooperation with the city's Parent-Teacher Association Council drew 1,500 women. A bicycle Roadeo conducted in cooperation with the police department brought 500 youngsters to a local school ground for field tests.

The Nashville *Tennessean* (circulation 120,824, population 174,307) feels just as the Santa Monica newspaper feels about providing heart-warming events for the people of its circulation area. Its East High School talent contest held annually and its summer park concerts illustrate the warm relations between this newspaper and its public. Several years ago, the winner of the East High contest was Pat Boone. He went from there to the big-time talent shows in New York and the *Tennessean* has gone with him every step of the way to his present stardom.

In summarizing the reaction to such contacts between the newspaper and its readers, editor Coleman A. Harwell says: "Participants in our events come to feel a fellowship with various individuals of our newspaper; most importantly, with the newspaper itself as an individual. Although the number of people affected in any one event or in any one period of time may be small, the accumulative effect of such appearances is tremendous. The friendship it creates is beyond reckoning."[2]

Other newspapers have staged events of equal importance and popularity. Usually they are kept on the amateur basis in order to induce greater participation. However, careful planning and extensive publicity, as only a newspaper can give, are required to assure their success. In participation and spectator appeal, they range from that of a mutt dog parade to that of a boat regatta or an amateur golf tournament.

The St. Paul, Minn., *Dispatch* and *Pioneer Press* (combined circulation 210,007, population 311,349) looked beyond mutt dogs to plug horses, giving the latter their day in the sun by sponsoring for 6 continuous years, the Plug Horse Derby at the Minnesota State Fair (see Fig. 24.1).

"You'll CHEER — you'll CHUCKLE — you'll HOWL when those strapping big work horses come thundering down the track," said the *Dispatch* and *Pioneer Press* one year in promoting this event. "Every

---

[1] *Editor & Publisher*, Nov. 23, 1957, p. 46.
[2] *The Quill*, Sept., 1958, p. 23.

YOU'LL HAVE **FUN**

WATCHING THE

ST. PAUL
DISPATCH-PIONEER PRESS

PLUG HORSE DERBY

LABOR DAY
AFTERNOON

at the

MINNESOTA
STATE FAIR

What's more fun than a barrel full of monkeys? A track full of burly, fleet-footed work horses, galloping to a thundering finish in the thrill-filled Dispatch-Pioneer Press Plug Horse Derby!

And you'll see not just one such race ... but FOUR ... on Labor Day afternoon at the Minnesota State Fair! Starting at 2 p. m., there'll be three preliminary heats of six county fair champions each, racing it out for a crack at the final championship event. The first and second place winners in each of the three heats will then battle it out for the Plug Horse crown in the six-horse title event at 4 p. m., right after the auto races!

Every one of the 18 steeds you'll see racing on Labor Day is a Minnesota or Wisconsin county fair champion ... the cream of the work horse crop ... so don't miss this action-packed fairtime event!

Notice!

If you can't possibly be in the Grandstand for the 1956 Plug Horse Derby, turn your radio dial to 830—WCCO—at 4 p. m., for a special on-the-spot broadcast of the final championship race!

Fig. 24.1 — The St. Paul **Dispatch** and **Pioneer Press** sponsored popular Plug Horse Derby at the state fair.

one of the burly steeds is a Minnesota or Wisconsin county fair champion — the cream of the work-horse crop — racing to dramatic finish in the dizziest, daffiest horse race you'll ever see."

This was a popular annual event until 1957 when, with tractors replacing horses on the farm, it became difficult to obtain entries. The newspaper was forced to discontinue it and in its place sponsored the Kids' Bicycle Derby, which was conducted on the same plan as the Plug Horse Derby. This was equally well promoted, drew a great number of entries and, like its predecessor, became a popular attraction at the fair.

Some years ago the Independence, Mo., *Examiner* (circulation 10,713, population 36,963) and the local Kiwanis Club launched a mutt dog parade, which drew a great number of youngsters and their pets into competition for prizes offered to dogs with longest ears, shortest ears, longest nose, shortest nose, shortest tail, longest tail, smallest dog, largest dog, youngest dog, oldest dog, best trick dog and the like. The mayor rode at the head of the parade as chairman of the judging committee and the high school band furnished music. There were as many dogs running loose through the crowd as were seen in the parade. It was a great day for kids, their pets and their parents — so successful an event that it has since been conducted annually with no subsidence whatever of interest and participation.

The Dubuque, Iowa, *Telegraph-Herald* (circulation 39,033, population 51,223) sponsors an annual amateur golf tournament which has always drawn a large number of participants and spectators. As a way of showing appreciation for long-time accounts, the newspaper buys $1,200 worth of merchandise prizes from its regular advertisers. When entry fees exceed expenses, proceeds from the tournament are turned over to the City Recreation Department for promotion of its junior golf program.

Boat racing and bowling are other important participation sports easily and effectively promoted by sports-minded publishers. The Charleston, W. Va., *Gazette* (circulation 70,592, population 73,501) cooperates with the Charleston Boat Club in sponsoring the annual West Virginia Boat Racing Championships, for which there is heated competition and great spectator interest. Competition in the various classifications for hydroplanes and outboards is stimulated by substantial prizes.

The Milwaukee, Wis., *Sentinel* (circulation 184,302, population 637,392) gives a roaring promotion to its annual Winnebagoland Outboard Marathon. One year it drew 272 entries for the race and 70,000 spectators to the shores of the lakes and rivers traversed by the contestants. The *Sentinel*'s promotion department prepared an elaborate press book of the marathon, giving some interesting facts concerning the contestants. It described the chap who carried a fuel tank on his lap, the 14-year-old girl who raced against 199 men, the art student who built his own boat and all the Tom Sawyers and Huck Finns of the outboard motor world who came to the marathon.

Another boating event of great beauty and interest is the annual Regatta on Lake Michigan sponsored by the Chicago *News* (circulation 547,796, population 3,620,962). This has grown since the 1920's to become the world's largest inland regatta in participation and attendance. More than 300 sailing youths compete annually in 32 races. Champion water skiers displaying their strength and skill, a power boat parade, a thrilling air-sea rescue demonstration, and fireworks at night on the lake front are other highlights of this spectacular event.

The great interest taken by boys and girls in fishing is demonstrated at the annual Fishing Derby sponsored by the Barre, Mass., *Gazette* (circulation 1,500, population 3,406). Nearly 500 youngsters take part in this event sponsored by a weekly newspaper that knows how to build good will in its community.

The Corning, Iowa, *Adams County Free Press* (circulation 3,200, population 2,104) offers annually six trophies to reading and spelling contest winners, five plaques to winners in a summer baseball league and, during a county fair, gives a $25 bond to the winner in a 4-H Club letter-writing contest.

Much fun for younger children is provided by the annual Easter Egg Hunt sponsored by the Dallas, Tex., *Times Herald* (circulation 178,848, population 434,462). Each year more than 100,000 colored eggs are distributed for the hunt in twenty-one of the city's parks.

Events of much promotion value to the New York *Journal-American* (circulation 563,792, population 7,891,957) are the men's and women's Bowling Classics, which attract thousands of entries and pour $50,000 into the pockets of the bowlers. The event for men has been the largest of its kind in the country. It became so popular that the *Journal-American* was compelled to limit the entries to a startling total of 3,150 teams. Interest in the women's event has been growing from year to year, and Al Lattin, former president of the American Bowling Congress, gives this newspaper credit for introducing bowling to women and bringing them out to the alleys in important numbers. "The *Journal-American*'s promotion of women's bowling tournaments," he said, "proved a turning point in our business and changed the entire concept. Only a newspaper could have achieved it."

In addition to promoting many events to provide recreation, play and competition, a newspaper may give valuable cooperation to those who are responsible for providing wholesome community recreation. The Omaha, Nebr., *World-Herald* (combined circulation 247,478, population 256,588) one season issued a 16-page booklet entitled

Playtime in Omaha, which was distributed to 37,000 public and parochial school children just before the beginning of summer vacation. This booklet told exactly what public recreation facilities were available in Omaha and commented on youth centers, libraries, neighborhood houses and camps.

The Winner, S.D., *Advocate* (circulation 3,248, population 3,252) and the Dallas, Tex., *News* (circulation 207,156, population 434,462) each brings the Yuletide touch to the residence section of its community by sponoring a Christmas-tree lighting contest (see Fig. 24.2).

Give Pleasure to Spectators

While the newspaper-sponsored events previously described are designed to provide competition, they also provide excellent entertainment for spectators. Persons privileged to sit in comfortable seats and enjoy programs of high class entertainment at the expense of newspapers do not easily forget the favor accorded them, thus bringing the sponsors into the good graces of a wide group.

Each year the promotion department of the Des Moines, Iowa, *Register* and *Tribune* (combined circulation 345,146, population 177,965) is joint sponsor with manufacturers and jobbers of Des Moines in a Fall Fellowship Day for all Iowa retailers. The program of the day includes a tour of the newspaper's modern plant and a full evening of entertainment in the city's largest theater. Humorists, jugglers, comedians and dancing girls — the best from Hollywood and elsewhere — provide a scintillating, 2-hour program. Free tickets are passed out to retailers and their families by 100 local manufacturers and jobbers. Each year many letters are received by the Des Moines newspapers and business firms who were hosts on Fellowship Day, expressing appreciation for the cordial welcome and fine entertainment provided.

In the same manner that retailers are ingratiated by the Des Moines newspapers through hospitality and entertainment provided them, so are American golfers courted for favor by the Washington, D. C., *Post* and *Times Herald* (circulation 390,104, population 802,178) through the annual National Celebrities Golf Tournament, sponsored by the newspaper and WTOP, its radio station. The effectiveness of this tournament as an event for spectators is indicated by the attendance, which usually runs up to 15,000, and by the receipts, which generally top $30,000. The nation's greatest golfers participate and are great factors in drawing immense crowds. The newspaper's editorial, advertising and promotion departments go all out to make this annual event a marked success. Profits derived from this great outdoor show go to the support of some worthy cause. Organizations benefited have been the Metropolitan Police Boys Clubs,

Last week to enter...

THE 1959 DALLAS NEWS

Christmas Lighting Contest

$3,680 in Cash Prizes

Deadline: Entries must be in Dallas News building by midnight, Dec. 7

CONTEST DATES: December 15 through 31

Let's make Dallas County the brightest in the Nation this Christmas!

Here's All You Have To Do To Enter:

If you plan to decorate the outside front of your residence this Christmas, just clip and mail the coupon below. The deadline for entering the contest is Dec. 7, but decorations do not have to be up and lighted on your residence until Dec. 15. Judging will start Dec. 15 and continue through Dec. 23. Winners will be announced Dec. 25.

- Decorations on the front of the house and/or yard should be up by Dec. 15 and remain through Dec. 31.

- Decoration lights should be on from 6 p.m. 'til 10:30 p.m. during the above dates.

- All residences in Dallas County are eligible.

MAIL COUPON TODAY. You may fill in your neighborhood Garden Club or any Garden Club as a sponsor. It is NOT necessary to enter the name of a Garden Club to qualify.

The Dallas Morning News
TEXAS' LEADING NEWSPAPER

- The County has been divided into four areas. The following cash prizes will be awarded in EACH of the four areas.

CASH PRIZES

AWARDED IN EACH OF THE FOUR AREAS

FIRST PLACE $200.00	SECOND PLACE $100.00
THIRD PLACE $50.00	FOURTH PLACE $30.00
FIFTH PLACE $20.00	SIXTH PLACE $10.00

Plus: Additional $200.00 for County GRAND PRIZE Winner

(DUPLICATE PRIZES TO SPONSORING GARDEN CLUBS)

Please Mail to:

CHRISTMAS LIGHTING
CONTEST EDITOR
The Dallas Morning News
Dallas 22, Texas

NAME_____

ADDRESS_____

CITY_____PHONE_____

My entry is sponsored by

_____Garden Club

Fig. 24.2 — The Dallas, Tex., **News** adds brightness to the holiday season by sponsoring a Christmas Lighting Contest.

the Merrick Boys Club summer camp, the Salvation Army's camps for boys and girls and the Barney Neighborhood House.

A great annual event for the entertainment of people residing in and near Minneapolis is the city's Aquatennial, which carries through the day and into the night with colorful parades, demonstrations and other festivities. The Minneapolis *Star* and *Tribune* (combined circulation 502,252, population 521,718) is a moving factor in this spectacular event, giving pages of advance publicity and the full support of its promotion department.

Entertainment of high cultural quality often is provided communities by their newspapers. The Cape Girardeau, Mo., *Southeast Missourian* (circulation 15,263, population 21,578) has staged for its people some of the greatest theatrical and musical attractions, including the play *Green Pastures,* the Dennishawn Dancers, U.S. Marine Band, Minneapolis Symphony Orchestra and St. Louis Symphony Orchestra.

The Smithfield, N.C., *Herald* (circulation 7,370, population 5,574) sponsors annual concerts by the North Carolina Symphony Orchestra for adults and children of its community. *Herald* editor L. J. Lassiter is president of the Symphony Chapter.

The Michigan City, Ind., *News-Dispatch* (circulation 14,110, population 28,395) sponsors a Gala Summer Festival, which one year included a mammoth street parade, a concert by the Navy Training Station Band, a beauty contest to select "Miss Indiana," a Venetian Nights boat parade, a mock landing of the U.S. Marine Corps and a fireworks display staged at the lake front.

A unique and effective promotion for San Diego, Calif., as a city truly alive and growing, was a display of photographs taken by staff photographers of the San Diego *Union* and *Tribune* (combined circulation 207,064, population 494,201). These were put together in a "City Alive" exhibit by Patrick T. Malone, director of the art center at La Jolla, Calif. After the local showing, they were sent to Tokyo where they were seen by almost a million people at the International Trade Fair. Concerning the exhibit, T. S. Irvin wrote in *Editor & Publisher*: "As with all newspaper-sponsored community promotions, this becomes a terrific promotion for the sponsoring newspapers themselves. Inevitably they bask brightly in the reflection of a young, growing, zestful community — the kind of community that attracts advertisers."[3]

Recognition Events Win Deep Regard

Events in recognition of outstanding services by individuals or special groups within a community win deep and abiding gratitude for the newspaper which sponsors such events.

---

[3] *Editor & Publisher*, Aug. 31, 1957, p. 51.

One of the most successful affairs ever conducted by the Birmingham, Ala., *Post-Herald* and *News* (combined circulation 279,782, population 326,037) was a party for Alabama's golden wedding couples. Honeymooners of a half-century ago relived memories, met old friends, talked over early days and sang old-time favorite songs. The Municipal Auditorium was thronged. Some of the anniversary couples came in wheel chairs, some on crutches, and many were escorted by sons, daughters and grandchildren. A highlight of the occasion was the appearance of 80-year-old Joe Howard, popular composer and singer of earlier years. Guests joined with him in singing "Bicycle Built For Two," "Let Me Call You Sweetheart," "Take Me Out to the Ball Game," "Goodbye My Lady Love," "Good Old Summertime" and many other ballads recalling sweet memories.

Old friends are a newspaper's best friends. No organization realizes this better than the Memphis, Tenn., *Commercial Appeal* (circulation 205,710, population 396,000), which has established an Old Friends Club. This organization, which has developed into an important public relations project, springs from an article entitled "Old Friends of Old Reliable," which appeared in the issue of Sunday, January 26, 1958. "Old Reliable" is what many readers call the *Commercial Appeal*. George Sisler, editorial promotion director, felt that something should be done to make firm this friendship between the newspaper and its long-time friends. Membership cards were issued to all who desired to affiliate.

"The response to this idea was terrific," says Mr. Sisler. "So successful that we want to pass it along for possible use by other newspapers with as much to brag about as we have. Our editor, Frank R. Ahlgren, seldom goes overboard on any promotion, but this one truly sent him overboard."[4]

The Washington, Iowa, *Journal* (circulation 4,197, population 5,902) follows much the same idea with its Three-Quarters Century Club. Each year it invites persons 75 years old and older as guests at a dinner at the Country Club, and usually 150 or more attend.

Baby shows are just as popular as Old Folks Days and many newspapers sponsor them, providing parents the opportunity to have their darlings' pictures published. Such recognition events hold the interest of grandparents, uncles, aunts, brothers and sisters as well as baby's parents. Thus, a newspaper may win warm good will through several generations.

And those of an age between babies and grandparents also appreciate recognition when it is given to them. Public school teachers, family doctors, outstanding farmers, courteous police officers and veterans are often given hearty back pats by friendly newspapers.

---

[4] *Editor & Publisher*, Feb. 8, 1958, p. 36.

The Birmingham, Ala., *Post-Herald* (circulation 94,889, population 326,037) annually conducts a Favorite Teacher contest, based on merit rather than popularity. Nominations are received from all schools in the Birmingham area for candidates who must be leaders in church and community as well as in the classroom.

And who is more deserving of gratitude and applause than the family doctor ready to answer calls at any hour of the day or night? The Dallas, Tex., *Times Herald* cooperates annually with the Dallas County Medical Society in selecting and honoring the Family Doctor of the Year. This is an event in which newspaper readers delight to have a part.

The Lincoln, Nebr., *Journal* and *Star* (combined circulation 67,370, population 98,884), with their wide distribution to farmers, honors the Farm Family of the Year. Selection is made from nominations sent in by readers throughout the state. Members of the winning family are guests of the newspaper at a luncheon, where they are lauded for their achievements and good example and are given $500 in a ceremony presided over by the publisher and managing editor.

Farmers who have been outstanding in soil conservation are honored each year at a recognition dinner given by the Sidney, Nebr., *Telegraph* (circulation 4,687, population 4,912). Nebraska newspapers appreciate the contributions to community progress made by farmers of their communities and are quick to recognize their accomplishments.

The courage and sacrifice of veterans in behalf of their country is a story that newspapers can never allow to be forgotten. One year more than 3,000 disabled veterans were guests of Minnesota sportsmen and the Minneapolis *Star* and *Tribune* at a pheasant dinner, served at 4 hospitals with special programs at each. Huntsmen from 70 counties contributed 2,200 ring-necks for the meal.

Those who lead in community activities, too, are often brought to the footlights and to the newspaper's columns for special recognition. The Blackwell, Okla., *Journal-Tribune* (circulation 6,072, population 9,199) sponsors an annual dinner for officers of the Parent-Teacher units in its circulation area.

Such events always warm the hearts of those honored and their friends and relatives. They also provide pleasing entertainment for many more. When a newspaper helps a community to express gratitude to local benefactors, it builds an abundance of good will for itself.

"There is a paramount
need for the
newspaper to present
a graphic picture
of itself to
the community."

— HAROLD C. FILDEY,
Director of
Public Relations,
Lansing, Mich.,
State Journal

CHAPTER 25

100 Ways To Build
Community Good Will

BRIEFLY DESCRIBED below are 100 ideas for community service that have been tested by American newspapers, both large and small, and found effective for building good will. From this list any publisher may devise a year's program of events that will draw his newspaper nearer to its public.

GIVE HONOR WHEN DUE

1. **Thanks to Community** — The Columbia, Mo., *Missourian* (circulation 3,954, population 31,974), a daily community newspaper put out by faculty and students of the University of Missouri School of Journalism, presented a series of advertisements containing letters from alumni and former students expressing appreciation for kindnesses shown them by Columbia townspeople while the writers were students in the School of Journalism.

2. **Fireman of the Year Award** — The Dallas, Tex., *Times Herald* (circulation 178,848, population 434,462) gives every year a $250 cash award to the city fireman who, in the opinion of his superiors, contributes the most civic service to his community.

3. **Golden Deeds Award** — The Baton Rouge, La., *State Times* and *Advocate* (combined circulation 66,993, population 125,629) each year provides an annual award and citation to the Baton Rougean most outstanding in civic performance during the previous year. Selected by a committee of the Inter-Club Council from public nominations, the recipient is given a tray and plaque suitably inscribed.

4. **Country Cousin Contest** — The Sherman, Tex., *Democrat* (circulation 13,921, population 20,150) one year sponsored a "Country Cousin" contest. Residents of Sherman were invited to submit lists

of their cousins in Grayson, Fannin and Collin counties, and prizes were awarded to the three contestants with the largest number of cousins in the area.

5. Community Art Exhibit — The New Bedford, Mass., *Standard-Times* (circulation 61,527, population 109,189) sponsored an art show which drew more than 500 entries from artists, all in Greater New Bedford. The best entries were displayed in the public library for two weeks.

6. Women of Achievement — For three successive years the St. Louis, Mo., *Globe-Democrat* (circulation 332,823, population 856,796) selected ten outstanding women of Greater St. Louis to be honored as Women of Achievement in various categories. The honorees were presented with engraved silver plates at a large community luncheon.

7. Old Newsboys Club — The Pittsburgh, Pa., *Press* (circulation 301,730, population 676,806) organized an "Old Newsboys Club," composed of Pittsburgh men who in their earlier days sold newspapers on the street or handled a carrier route. This organization one year raised $75,000 for the Crippled Children's Hospital in Pittsburgh.

8. Kiwanians Became Editors — The Independence, Mo., *Examiner* (circulation 10,713, population 36,963) invited members of the Kiwanis Club to put out an issue, which they did in grand style. It contained everything from advice to the lovelorn to a financial column, and the Kiwanians felt they had been honored by being made editors for a day.

9. "You Should Know" — The Columbia *Missourian* ran daily under the heading "You Should Know," the picture of a prominent business or professional man and some brief facts about his career, connections and hobbies.

10. "Old Faithful" Contest — The Atlanta, Ga., *Journal* (circulation 253,470, population 331,314) gave a dinner and theater party for persons who had been readers of the *Journal* for more than 50 years.

11. Amateur Snapshot Contest — The Memphis, Tenn., *Commercial Appeal* (circulation 205,710, population 396,000) conducts a 14-week amateur snapshot contest that attracts 3,000 or more contestants.

12. Bouquet of the Week — The Pottsville, Pa., *Republican* (circulation 26,721, population 23,640) conducts a "Bouquet of the Week" column, which features a local resident who has done something worthy of recognition, then sends the honored person a bouquet of flowers.

13. Most Courteous Hunter — The Klamath Falls, Ore., *Herald and News* (circulation 14,091, population 15,875) offered a $25 cash prize to the most courteous hunter of the season, the winner being chosen by the Sportsmen's Association.

14. Farm Woman of the Month — The Paris, Tex., *News* (circulation 10,418, population 21,643) featured a "Farm Woman of the Month." The person to be honored was selected by local, state and national farm organizations.

15. Businessmen as Columnists — During August, when the editor of the Independence, Mo., *Examiner* was on vacation, the editorial page was written by local businessmen who discussed community problems. They appreciated this recognition of their ability to write about local affairs.

16. Women's Press Party — The Gary, Ind., *Post-Tribune* (circulation 54,517, population 168,884) invited publicity chairmen and officers of women's organizations to a "press party" sponsored by the newspaper's Women's Page.

17. F.F.A. Boy of the Week — The Columbia, Mo., *Missourian* featured each week on its Farm Page an outstanding member of the Future Farmers of America. The boy's activities and accomplishments were outlined in the news columns and merchants congratulated him in the advertising columns.

18. Remembers Centenarians — When a long-time subscriber celebrates his 100th birthday, the Jackson, Mich., *Citizen Patriot* (circulation 36,617, population 51,088) sends a bouquet of roses.

19. Handsomest Policeman Contest — The Forest Park, Ill., *Review* (circulation 3,706, population 14,969) sponsored a Handsomest Policeman contest. It ran pictures of all city policemen and asked readers to vote.

OBSERVE SPECIAL DAYS

20. Free Phone Call to GI Overseas — The Tulsa, Okla., *Tribune* (circulation 75,732, population 182,740) offered as a Christmas present a free telephone call to some overseas GI. Those wanting to be considered for the gift call were asked to submit certain information on or before November 9, and from these applications, one was selected. The *Tribune* made all arrangements, giving everyone in the immediate family an opportunity to talk with the relative, and made a tape recording of the conversation for the person putting in the call.

21. Free Coffee on Christmas Eve — Free coffee was served at several restaurants and drug stores in Anadarko, Okla., on Christmas Eve, with the compliments and best wishes of the Anadarko *News* (circulation 3,919, population 6,184).

22. Christmas Song Festival — The San Francisco *Examiner* (circulation 257,251, population 775,357) filled the San Francisco Opera House with an audience of 4,000 for a Song Festival staged in conjunction with the Salvation Army. Concert pianists and radio stars had parts in the program.

23. Tricks or Treats for Orphans — The Duluth, Minn., *News-Tribune* and *Herald* (combined circulation 79,902, population 104,411) observed Halloween by sponsoring "Tricks or Treats for Korean Orphans." Children collected clothing instead of treats and more than four tons of clothing were received for shipment overseas.

24. Toycrafter Fair — The Nashville, *Tennessean* (circulation 120,824, population 174,307) sponsored a Toycrafter Fair during the Christmas season. Prizes were offered for toys made by children under 16. After the event, toys were given to children in an orphans' home.

25. Doll Dressing Contest — The Detroit, Mich., *Times* (circulation 391,295, population 1,849,568) conducted a doll dressing contest. The newspaper furnished dolls which the children dressed. At Christmas the dolls were given to underprivileged children.

26. Halloween Party — The Alliance, Ohio, *Review* (circulation 14,886, population 26,161) sponsors an annual Halloween celebration for children of the community.

27. Lenten Guidepost — The Birmingham, Ala., *News* (circulation 220,915, population 326,037) in several Sunday issues preceding Easter printed a series of "Lenten Guideposts," autobiographical sketches, telling how various well-known persons had found spiritual help at times of need. A contest conducted in connection with the series offered an award of $50 for the best 250-word story of a similar nature by a *News* reader, with $15 for the second and $5 for the third best stories.

PROMOTE HEALTH, RELIEF AND SAFETY

28. Health Forum — The Lynchburg, Va., *News* and *Advance* (combined circulation 33,435, population 47,747) were co-sponsors with the Lynchburg Academy of Medicine in a series of health forums. Question forms printed in the *News* and *Advance* were used by readers to submit questions which were discussed at succeeding health sessions.

29. Traffic Safety Contest — The New Orleans, La., *States-Item* (circulation 162,805, population 570,445) was co-sponsor with the city's department of public safety, Automobile Dealers Association and Safety Council, in a 4-week contest for essays on traffic safety. A $25 defense bond went to each week's winner, and from these four essays, first and second winners were selected for prizes of $300 and $200.

30. Starts a Storm Fund — The Nashville, Tenn., *Banner* (circulation 99,793, population 174,307) made a gift of $1,000 to inaugurate a storm fund to be administered by the Red Cross in the rehabilitation of a tornado-stricken community within the newspaper's circulation area. Publicity through the *Banner* brought numerous contributions from readers.

31. Ice Show — The Chicago *Sun Times* (circulation 534,063, population 3,620,962) staged an Ice Show as a benefit for hospitalized war veterans. A crowd of 20,000 paid admission prices up to $3.60.

32. Junior Police Force — The Columbus, Ohio, *Dispatch* (circulation 181,410, population 375,901) organized a Junior Police Force as a deterrent to juvenile delinquency. Units were formed in the schools and they were addressed by members of the police force on care of property, rules of safety and good conduct. Each member was fitted with a Sam Browne belt and an attractive badge for identification.

33. Fund for Hospital — The Omaha, Nebr., *World-Herald* (circulation 125,805, population 251,117) launched a campaign to raise funds for a Christian's Memorial Hospital, where children of all races and religions might receive treatment.

34. Purchased Baby Elephant — The Toledo, Ohio, *Blade* (circulation 183,143, population 303,616) purchased a baby elephant to be used as a mascot in a safety campaign. School children, who participated in the campaign, named the elephant Amber, which means "caution."

35. Cotton Auction — The El Centro, Calif., *Imperial Valley Press* and *Post* (combined circulation 8,191, population 12,590) conducted a cotton auction in front of the newspaper office to boost the Imperial Valley Fund for polio patients.

36. Grade A Milk Campaign — The Steamboat Springs, Colo., *Steamboat Pilot* (circulation 2,245, population 1,913) promoted a campaign which placed Grade A milk from county herds in local chain stores.

37. Water Fluoridation Drive — The Laramie, Wyo., *Boomerang* (circulation 4,829, population 15,581) staged an intensive campaign which resulted in fluoridation of city water.

ENCOURAGE CLEAN SPORTS

38. Sports and Vacation Show — The Dallas, Tex., *News* (circulation 207,156, population 434,462) sponsored a Southwestern Sports and Vacation Show for the entertainment and information of sports lovers. Profits from the show were contributed to the Dallas Park Board for encouragement of outdoor recreation.

39. Special Events Program — The Oklahoma City *Oklahoman* and *Times* (combined circulation 259,311, population 243,504) one year booked a total of seventeen special entertainment and sports events, in addition to other minor activities of community-wide interest.

40. Football Jamborees — The Baton Rouge, La., *State Times* and *Advocate* (combined circulation 66,993, population 125,629) sponsor high school and grammar school football jamborees each fall with 6 teams playing 1-period games. Proceeds from the high school event go to the competing schools for athletic programs. Proceeds from the grammar school games go to the Goodfellows Christmas Fund for needy children.

41. Bowling Tournament — The Oklahoma City *Oklahoman* and *Times* sponsor an annual bowling tournament for men and women. It is conducted along regular bowling tournament rules and a number of prizes are offered.

42. Baseball Clinic for Women — A baseball clinic for women was launched by the Milwaukee, Wis., *Sentinel* (circulation 184,302, population 637,392). A panel, composed of the home team manager and players and *Sentinel* sports writers, answered questions and instructed the women on technicalities that would help them to understand and enjoy the game.

43. Learn-To-Swim Campaign — The Omaha *World-Herald* is cosponsor with the Red Cross in an annual Learn-To-Swim campaign. More than 5,000 children are taught to swim in five city pools each year.

44. Free Ski School — The Traverse City, Mich., *Record-Eagle* (circulation 12,821, population 16,974) located in a region of abundant snowfall, sponsors an annual free Ski School for youngsters 7 to 14 years old.

45. Ping-Pong Tournament — The Fremont, Ohio, *News-Messenger* (circulation 13,888, population 16,537) conducted a ping-pong tournament in which many young people of the community competed for prizes.

46. Hole-in-One Golf Tournament — The St. Louis, Mo., *Globe-Democrat* sponsored annually a Hole-in-One golf tournament with attractive prizes. This developed great interest among golfers.

47. Apple Bowl Football Game — The Nebraska City, Nebr., *News-Press* (circulation 5,542, population 6,872), published in the heart of the Nebraska orchard country, cooperates with the American Legion and the high schools in sponsoring an annual Apple Bowl football game.

48. Water Carnival — The Chicago *American* (circulation 467,557, population 3,620,962) conducted a free swim carnival featuring a medley of races, water ballets and other water events. The show was concluded with a series of races for boys and girls who had graduated from the *American*'s "Learn to Swim" classes and who, seven weeks previously, could not swim at all.

49. Baseball School — The Modesto, Calif., *Bee* (circulation 34,432, population 17,389) put on a baseball school in which 160 boys learned the fine points of the game from local professionals. Each boy who attended received a big league ball and glove from the newspaper and a membership in the Knothole Club, which admitted them to all games in August.

50. Tennis Clinic — For tennis enthusiasts the Dallas, Tex., *Times Herald* sponsored a free clinic where two professionals demonstrated techniques of the game.

51. Grade School Field and Track Meet — The Gary, Ind., *Post-Tribune* sponsored a 2-day field and track meet for grade school youngsters. The newspaper awarded medals or chevrons to first, second and third place winners in each event.

PRESENT THE UNUSUAL

52. Old Car Parade — The Rochester, N.Y., *Times-Union* (circulation 122,540, population 332,488) hit a vein of considerable interest with an Old Car Parade which was open to all cars over 25 years old. Prizes were awarded on the basis of the car's age and the driver's authentic costume of the time when the car was manufactured.

53. Atomic Energy Exhibit — The nation's most complete atomic energy exhibit was made available to 40,000 Minnesotans in four areas of the state through a joint program sponsored by the University of Minnesota and the Minneapolis *Star* and *Tribune* (combined circulation 502,252, population 521,718).

54. Aqua Jesters — One hundred business and professional men make clowning a year-long civic enterprise through the Minneapolis *Star* and *Tribune* Aqua Jesters. Under *Star* and *Tribune* sponsorship, the Jesters perform at water fetes, parades, in hospitals and for shut-ins, reaching half a million people annually.

55. National Folk Song Festival — The St. Louis, Mo., *Globe-Democrat* sponsors annually a Folk Song Festival for singing groups of its circulation area.

56. Puppy of the Week — The Nashville *Tennessean* used a unique plan to help the Humane Association find homes for orphan puppies. Each week a puppy was given as a prize to a child, age 6 to 12, who wrote the best essay on announced subjects.

57. Picture of the Week — To encourage an interest in art, the Mexico, Mo., *Ledger* (circulation 8,426, population 11,623) sponsored a Picture of the Week display at the city library to acquaint the public with paintings by great artists.

58. Children's Puppet Shows — The Minneapolis *Star* and *Tribune* sponsored free outdoor puppet shows in Minneapolis parks.

59. "Horse Sense" Riding Tournament — The Nashville *Tennessean* conducted a riding tournament for young riders. Professionals gave pointers on improving riding skills. It was a great public attraction.

60. Fishing Contest — The St. Paul, Minn., *Dispatch* and *Pioneer Press* (combined circulation 210,007, population 311,349) awarded weekly prizes in five classifications during a 17-week, state-wide fishing contest, May through September.

61. Pet Parade — An outstanding promotion feature of the Memphis, Tenn., *Commercial Appeal* is its annual Pet Parade. Entries range from goldfish to ponies and from snakes to parrots.

62. Cherry Pie Baking Contest — The Muscatine, Iowa, *Journal* (circulation 9,799, population 19,041) sponsored a pie baking contest for 4-H girls in order to select a winner to represent Iowa in the National Cherry Pie Baking Contest.

63. Square Dance Jamboree — The Salt Lake City *Tribune* (circulation 99,349, population 182,121) provided entertainment for 4,000 participants and 8,000 spectators when it sponsored a square dance in a large city parking lot.

64. Sing Trophy — The Minneapolis *Star* and *Tribune* offered a Sing Trophy for which 90,000 singing enthusiasts competed.

65. Foreign Newspapers Display — The Monroe, Mich., *News* (circulation 18,679, population 21,467) exhibited at a county fair newspapers from more than 60 countries. Youngsters particularly were interested in comics appearing in the foreign press.

66. Kitten Naming Contest — The Washington, N.J., *Star* (circulation 5,691, population 4,802) asked school children to name the kittens born to a stray cat in the pressroom. Many names were submitted and youngsters who submitted the selected names, received prizes.

67. Sewing Contest — The Tulsa, Okla., *Tribune* conducted a sewing contest with attractive prizes preliminary to a national contest in New York. Entry blanks were printed in the *Tribune,* and winners were selected by prominent local seamstresses.

INTEREST CHILDREN AND YOUTH

68. 4-H Club Leadership Program — One hundred Georgia 4-H Club boys and girls shared in a state-wide junior leadership program sponsored by the Atlanta, Ga., *Constitution* (circulation 193,558, population 331,314). Participants were selected by county and home demonstration agents and prizes for outstanding leadership were offered, including leadership pins, trips to 4-H Club Congress and trophies.

69. Annual Journalism Contest — Each year the Dallas, Tex., *Times Herald* awards plaques in seven divisions for the best school newspapers published during the current year in the Dallas County schools. The entries are judged on journalistic contents alone, the methods of mechanical reproduction not being considered.

70. High School Art Competition — The Dallas *Times Herald* also sponsored a Greater Dallas High School Art Competition. Winners at each school received awards, and their original work was exhibited for some time at the art museum.

71. High School Awards — Each year the Minneapolis *Star* and *Tribune* award $10 in cash and a Certificate of Honor to the outstanding senior from each of the city's public and parochial high schools. The award is based on outstanding qualities of leadership, scholarship and service.

72. Photography Clinic and Contest — The Miami, Fla., *Herald* (circulation 302,264, population 249,276) conducted a 2-day clinic and fair for amateur photographers. This was followed by a 4-week contest, which gave photographers the opportunity to show what they had learned at the clinic.

73. Interviews for "Keen-Teeners" — The Chicago *Daily News* (circulation 547,796, population 3,620,962) arranged for high school editors a series of interviews with colorful and prominent leaders, including the President of the United States. It was a rewarding experience for keen teen-agers interested in journalism.

74. School Teacher-Newspaper Institute — The Binghampton, N.Y., *Press* (circulation 66,978, population 80,674) conducted a School Teacher-Newspaper Institute which explained to the teachers the aims of the newspaper and pointed out how the newspaper and the school may combine their efforts in making a better community.

75. "All-Out Americans" Club — The Gary, Ind., *Post-Tribune* organized a junior citizens club composed of 12,000 children from 33 public and parochial schools, which proved a definite contribution to the newspaper's campaign against juvenile delinquency. The name "All-Out Americans" was selected by members. The club functioned under the supervision of civic and school leaders.

76. Scouters' Institute — An institute to train scoutmasters was set up by the Rochester, N.Y., *Times-Union*. Sessions included demonstrations, dramatizations and discussions pertaining to boy leadership, troop finances, the patrol method, safety programs and indoor activities.

77. Painting Tours — The Akron, Ohio, *Beacon Journal* (circulation 163,191, population 274,605), in cooperation with a local art institute, sponsored a series of 6 painting trips for young people interested in art. The Art Institute and the University of Akron furnished instructors.

78. Easter Egg Hunt — The Dallas, Tex., *Times Herald* staged an Easter Egg Hunt in 21 of the city's parks. More than 100,000 eggs were gathered in by children from all sections of the city.

79. Outdoor Art Fair — The Washington, D.C., *Post* and *Times Herald* (circulation 390,104, population 802,178) sponsored an Art Fair held outdoors. Students in art schools and in high school art classes competed for prizes totaling $2,000. Several of the art schools gave scholarships to high school students showing unusual ability.

80. Bird House Building — The Detroit, Mich., *News* (circulation 463,469, population 1,849,568) conducted a bird house building contest in connection with the city's annual Flower Show. Suitable prizes were offered, and a great number of novel bird houses were displayed.

81. Bicycle Light Brigade — The Cleveland, Ohio, *Plain Dealer* (circulation 309,267, population 914,808) organized units of boys who owned bicycles into what was called the Bicycle Light Brigade. The boys were taught traffic regulations and rules of safety and competed in drills.

82. "Cradle Roll" and "Toddlers Club" — The Cleveland, Ohio, *Press and News* (circulation 385,000, population 914,808) registers babies born during the year in a "Cradle Roll" and transfers their names to the "Toddlers Club" on their first birthdays.

83. Sightseeing for Graduates — The Louisville, Ky., *Courier-Journal* (circulation 216,645, population 369,129) provided for 300 high school graduates in communities near Louisville a sight-seeing tour of the city. Included, of course, was a visit to the newspaper plant.

84. Lake and Lodge for Scouts — The Michigan City, Ind., *News-Dispatch* (circulation 14,110, population 28,396) led in building an artificial lake for the Boy Scouts, and a $10,000 lodge for the Girl Scouts of Michigan City.

85. Young Editors' Day — The Lansing, Mich., *State Journal* (circulation 63,999, population 92,129) observed "Young Editors' Day" during National Newspaper Week by having talented journalism class members from all high schools within 20 miles of Lansing serve as reporters.

86. Junior Good Citizen Contest — The Lincoln, Ill., *Courier* (circulation 7,289, population 14,362) conducts an annual Junior Good Citizen Contest for high school seniors. Trophies are given to winners during the county fair.

87. Science Fair — The Providence, R.I., *Journal-Bulletin* (circulation 57,908, population 248,674) directs a committee of science teachers in putting on an annual exhibit of scientific projects carried on by students.

88. Annual Spelling Bee — The Kansas City, Kans., *Kansan* (circulation 28,485, population 129,553) conducts an annual spelling contest, in which 10,000 school children participate.

89. Essay-Writing Contest — Seniors of the La Porte, Ind., high schools compete annually in an essay-writing contest sponsored by the *Herald-Argus* (circulation 11,817, population 17,882). The winner one year received a trip to Washington and runners-up received savings bonds.

90. 4-H Club Contest — The Louisville, Ky., *Courier-Journal* and *Times* (combined circulation 392,224, population 369,129) sponsor an annual state contest in agriculture and home economics for 4-H Club boys and girls. Substantial prizes are offered in several categories.

PROMOTE COMMUNITY BETTERMENT

91. Plant-To-Prosper Program — The Memphis, Tenn., *Commercial Appeal,* working with county agents throughout the area, each year enrolls 100,000 families in a diversified crop, soil conservation and self-dependence program. When the farm season is over, each family submits a report of its operations and profits. Prizes are awarded to winners in each county and state, and there is a grand prize for the family outstanding in the contest.

92. Forestry Award — The Louisville, Ky., *Courier-Journal* and *Times* gave $400 in prizes to farmers for forestry development. A grand prize of $200 was given for a complete forestry program, a $100 prize for protection, management and utilization of established wooded area, and a $100 prize for planting young trees.

93. County Tours — The Columbia, Mo., *Missourian* mapped seven tours which led to points of historic and scenic interest in the county. The roads were marked so that citizens had no difficulty in following the routes.

94. Soils Day Show — The Bloomington, Ill., *Pantagraph* (circulation 39,384, population 36,127) sponsored a Soils Day show for farmers and others interested in improved farming methods. This attracted more than 10,000 spectators.

95. Better Rooms Competition — The Chicago *Tribune* (circulation 868,455, population 3,620,962) conducted a "Better Rooms for Better Living" competition, offering 161 cash prizes ranging from $100 to $1,000 each. The awards were for the best ideas for furnishing and decorating each of seven rooms: living room, combination living and dining room, dining room, master bedroom, juvenile or infant's bedroom, kitchen, and recreation room. Competition was open to both professionals and amateurs.

96. Name The Area Contest — The Minneapolis *Star* and *Tribune* wanted a better name than "The Northwest" for the territory they served. Readers took time to think about the potentials of the area in which they lived and sent in 9,000 entries for prizes totaling $500. The two names selected were "The Upper Midwest" and "Top of the Nation."

97. Speakers' Bureau — The Columbus, Ohio, *Dispatch* sends its staff members to speak on cooking, homemaking, politics, history and sports. Speakers are allowed 6 cents a mile for travel and are paid $5 for daytime talks, $7.50 for night.

98. Name-Your-Farm Contest — The Paris, Tex., *News* awarded prizes to owners of farms most appropriately named. Hundreds of farmers in the area named their farms and erected signs in order to compete.

99. Industrial Tour — To acquaint merchants with industrial development, the Port Huron, Mich., *Times Herald* (circulation 31,203, population 35,725) took 150 merchants on a tour of the city's most important manufacturing area. The newspaper chartered buses for the trip and entertained the merchants at lunch.

100. Community Affairs Clinic — The publisher of the Lakeview, Ore., *Lake County Examiner-Tribune* (circulation 2,110, population 2,831) was host at a dinner to discuss community affairs. The 19 citizens who were guests represented all major interests of the community.

"Newspapers promote many
weeks, from National
Garter Week to
National Orange Week,
but too few of them
support National
Newspaper Week."

— Joseph Costa,
Chief Photographer,
King Features

CHAPTER 26

Observing National Newspaper Week

D RAWING ATTENTION TO THE MERITS and many services of newspapers, National Newspaper Week has been observed annually for twenty years. It was proposed in 1940 by John Long, general manager of the California Newspaper Publishers Association, as a means of emphasizing the important services performed by newspapers. Despite some original scoffing at the idea by publishers and some reluctance on their part to enter heartily into the plan, it has grown in scope and emphasis each year, finally becoming one of the more significant of the many special weeks observed annually in this age of extensive promotion and public relations.

Pressed for assistance in the promotion of so many weeks set up to benefit other fields of business and society in general, newspaper publishers were not too enthusiastic at first about promoting a week for themselves. Some continue to feel that way but a majority now see the opportunity it provides to bring their newspapers into closer relationships with their public. In an editorial during the 1958 National Newspaper Week, the Eugene, Ore., *Register-Guard* (circulation 33,987, population 35,879) well explained this original reluctance and final conversion:

"They are faced with an embarrassing dilemma," it said, "like a bunch of boys with new sling shots and pockets full of rocks but who have just recited the Cub Scout promise. Their first impulse is to dash off a trite piece, bury it somewhere deep inside the next edition and go to more important things. A lot of them follow that impulse. But some wrestle with their conflicting attitudes and decide

[383]

that, after all, Newspaper Week is one of those special observances
in which the public has an interest. Why? Because, in a sense, a
newspaper is everybody's business."

True enough, the community newspaper is everybody's business to
those who live in the community, and National Newspaper Week is
accepted as a justifiable means of acquainting them with the newspaper's important services. The enthusiastic response of the public
to the efforts of publishers who wholeheartedly observe the week is
causing many formerly indifferent publishers to finally join in
this national movement to promote newspaper service.

Much of the credit for this change of attitude must be given to
Newspaper Association Managers, Inc., a national organization of
state, regional and national press association managers, which sponsors National Newspaper Week and sets up each year the special
theme, upon which publishers are requested to center their promotion. In 1957 the theme was "Your Newspaper Serves," in 1958 it
was "Your Newspaper Guards Your Freedoms," and in 1959 it was
"The Newspaper — Freedom's Textbook." Thus, observance of the
week is kept on a high plane. In addition to telling their own stories, newspapers in 1958 reminded all Americans of the advantages
derived from living in "a land with a FREE press — that freedom
thrives only in an informed nation — that a FREE press is its voice."

BENEFITS FROM NEWSPAPER WEEK

Both the press and the public derive definite benefits from National Newspaper Week. Chief among these are:

1. A clearer understanding by publishers of their responsibilities
   toward the making of a better life in their respective communities.
2. A better understanding by the public of the services provided
   for them by the newspaper.
3. A clearer view of the relationship between good government
   and the freedom of the press.
4. An insight into the problems faced by publishers in carrying
   the news and advertising to the public.
5. A closer relationship between the newspaper and its patrons.

When newspaper publishers throughout the nation think together
for one week on the problems that face them and the dependence
they must place upon the public in helping to solve them, they come
to a higher appreciation of the communities they serve and a better
understanding of their responsibilities toward them. National Newspaper Week becomes, first of all, a period of introspection, of publisher self-analysis. The newspaper manager, editor and staff ask
themselves many pointed questions and most likely find answers.

They sense their personal responsibilities toward the making of a better life in the communities their newspapers serve, and this is pre-eminently good for both the newspaper and the public.

Unless some special effort is made to enlighten them, readers know little about the many steps taken and many hands applied in gathering and authenticating the news, writing it, heading it up and presenting it to them in attractive and convenient form. And they know even less about the efforts required by the advertising department to bring to them facts about the best offerings in seasonable and reliable merchandise. Readers can profit from the information about what newspaper personnel do in their various capacities to bring about better living conditions and greater cooperation between all elements that may contribute to community progress. A week of consistent hammering on all these points establishes with the public many facts they ought to know.

National Newspaper Week presents an opportunity also to point out the vital relationship between good government and freedom of the press. In a free country such as ours, the people have a right to know how those elected to represent them in office fulfill the responsibilities entrusted to them. The newspaper battles relentlessly to defend the people's right to know. Through its access to sources of information and its close watch upon the acts of public officials it serves to discourage inefficiency and to inhibit purposeful wrongdoing. Revealment of the truth enables people to demand what is right and good. The best policeman in the world is publicity.

"Here the newspaper performs its greatest service," says Buford Boone, publisher of the Tuscaloosa, Ala., *News* (circulation 17,205, population 46,396). "It is the eyes, ears and conscience of a community. It jealously guards the many rights of people while giving them the facts and information necessary to be good citizens. For only when we know the truth can we support what is good or condemn what is bad."

An insight into problems faced by publishers in carrying the news and advertising to the public is another appropriate part of National Newspaper Week. Difficulties often are faced in digging out facts for stories the public should have. There are contact problems that every news editor and reporter must face. Advertisers sometimes make unreasonable requests and unjustly criticize. Economic questions confront publishers. Labor problems come up and newsprint supply is not always abundant. But many of these misunderstandings and hindrances may be cleared away by acquainting the public with the problems and the methods used to overcome them. Tours of the plant and conferences with community groups are worth all the time, effort and expense they require.

"We have always had a fairly extensive and intensive program of promotion during National Newspaper Week," says Bob Turner, promotion manager of the Columbus, Ga., *Ledger* and *Enquirer* (combined circulation 52,221, population 79,611). "Not that we believe our virtues should be sold only once a year, but because the occasion provides us a vehicle with which we are able to 'shock' readers and advertisers out of a complacency developed quite normally in connection with anything so commonplace as the daily newspaper. We believe that once a year is not too often to let people know — in a sugar coated manner, of course — what our plant and equipment investment is, how many people figure in the production of their daily fare, and how concerned we are with the public welfare."

Certainly, once a year is not too often to make this approach and, even though great evidence of increased good will and cooperation may not be apparent immediately, there are possibilities of remarkable accumulation through the years to come. That a special week of friendly educational contact with the public develops a closer relationship between the newspaper and its patrons is the experience of those who make the most of National Newspaper Week.

OUTSTANDING NEWSPAPER WEEK PROGRAMS

The many ways in which a newspaper may establish important contacts and promote its services during National Newspaper Week are revealed in programs that have been carried out by newspapers of all sizes in various parts of the nation.

Cooperation From All Departments

The Columbus, Ga., *Ledger* and *Enquirer* used the week to publicize the newspaper and its role in public affairs, and as an employee-relations tool in promoting the various departmental activities. Churches, schools and service clubs cooperated with all departments of the staff in the week-long observance.

Preparations were made early, beginning on September 1 and continued through October 8, as follows:

Monday, September 1 — Mimeographed copies of National Newspaper Week plans were distributed to department heads requesting departmental cooperation and participation.

Sunday, September 14 — Champion Carrier Contest was started, allowing readers to nominate and vote for their favorite carriers; work was begun on radio and television scripts; first promotion ad appeared in newspaper.

Friday, September 26 — Letters were mailed to local ministers, requesting their cooperation in observance of Religion and Press Day; billboard advertisement went up at Traffic Circle.

JUNIOR PRESSMEN!

PULL OUT THIS PAGE!

(and adjoining one)

Be sure to pull out this entire sheet, don't tear. Then fold it so that you have a double newspaper page of full page size.

And, here's a challenge to your hat-making ability. When you make your hat, try and see if you can make the Junior Pressman sign at upper left appear on the front of your hat.

You can see how it's done tonite on television.

Watch
Colonel Chick's Show
TONITE AT 6
on WRBL-TV Channel 4
He'll show you how!

DIRECTIONS ARE
ON PAGE 35

COLUMBUS LEDGER The Columbus Enquirer

Fig. 26.1 — The Columbus, Ga., **Ledger** and **Enquirer** make much of Junior Pressman Day in their promotion of National Newspaper Week.

Sunday, September 28 — Special National Newspaper Week section appeared; special classified ad rate, 7 insertions for the price of 4, was announced in display advertisement.

Monday, September 29 — Outside promotion of Newspaper Week was begun; banners were placed across front of newspaper building; special newsstand cards were placed in racks; posters went up on circulation trucks; counter cards were placed announcing special classified rate; *Ledger* began contest for oldest copy of *Ledger* with $25 prize offer; releases began appearing in civic club bulletins and advertisements in 4 local high school papers.

Tuesday, September 30 — Classified promotion ad appeared; bumper strips and lapel tags were passed out to employees; correspondence desk began using rubber stamp on mail; promotion spots began on local and state radio and television stations; displays of photoengraving and mechanical department were erected in lobby; retail advertising display was set up in Fourth National Bank.

Wednesday, October 1 — High school journalism students edited the *Ledger* and began special work outlined for them in production departments; "famous deadline" front pages were framed and placed in 10 downtown store windows; large posters were placed in lobby and on outside photo board; switchboard operator began answering phone calls with "This is National Newspaper Week"; filler ads began appearing in the *Enquirer;* series of 6-column promotion ads were started; 4-column promotion ads on classified began appearing; Mayor's Proclamation was published; 2-column ad entitled "Newspaper Facts" appeared.

Thursday, October 2 — Rural correspondents were brought in for tour of buildings, round-table discussions, lunch and afternoon at movies; "aggressor" soldier, carrying sign emphasizing freedom of American press, picketed newspaper building; pictures of soldier were sent out on Wirephoto; promotion ads were run featuring "Better Understanding," "Newspaper Facts" and "Junior Pressmen."

Friday, October 3 — Forty high school students toured the newspaper plant and received fact sheets, booklets and tablets; Champion Carrier was selected, and he and district winners were feted at banquet; Champion Carrier appeared on radio; Junior Pressmen were featured in 10-column advertisement; instructions issued for making Pressman's Hat (see Figs. 26.1 and 26.2) and invitation to wear it on visiting plant (see Fig. 26.3) to see press run, when visitors would receive balloons, tablets and movie passes; advertisements were run featuring "Better Understanding," "Newspaper Facts" and a salute to newsboys.

Saturday, October 4 — Full-page advertisement was run, featuring Newspaperboy Day; carriers were interviewed on local radio stations; Junior Pressmen's Day was observed; youngsters saw press run.

Fun For All!
See the Giant Presses Run!
Free Tickets to the Fair!

Make Your Own
PRESSMAN'S HAT

Wear it to the Ledger-Enquirer
Tomorrow at 12:00 Noon

FREE GIFTS

- A FREE Gate Pass to the Chatta-hoochee Valley Exposition to the first 250 Junior Pressmen! Enjoy the art, farm, livestock and other ex-hibits free!
- Free Balloons!
- Free Tablets!
- A Free Copy of the Paper You'll See Being Printed!

If you can make the PRESSMAN'S HAT by following the directions below, you're in for a fine time tomorrow. You'll be the guest of the Ledger-Enquirer to watch the giant presses roll out the day's edition, and receive souvenir gifts, too! So get Dad to help; call in the gang; but put together a pressman's hat and come on down to the Ledger-Enquirer building tomorrow at 12:00 noon.

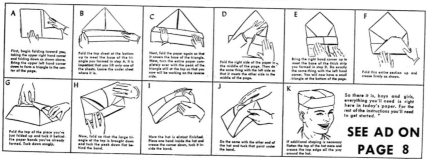

Fig. 26.2 — Making a Pressman's Hat is a big part of the preparations of the younger groups for their annual visits to the **Ledger** and **Enquirer** plant.

Fig. 26.3 — Successful completion of the Pressmen's Hats is evident as the enthusiastic Junior Pressmen visit the **Ledger** and **Enquirer** during National Newspaper Week.

Sunday, October 5 — Journalism scholarship was announced; sermons were given in churches on "Religion and the Press"; three promotion ads appeared in Sunday issue.

Monday, October 6 — Leo Aikman of the Atlanta, Ga., *Constitution* (circulation 193,558, population 331,314) addressed Muscogee Lions Club; 15 high school students toured plant; more promotion ads appeared in newspaper.

Tuesday, October 7 — Jess Gorkin, editor of *Parade Magazine,* addressed Kiwanis Club and Lions Club; more promotion ads appeared.

Wednesday, October 8 — Jess Gorkin spoke to Junior High School assembly and Rotary Club; 15 Central High School students toured plant and received fact sheets, booklets and tablets; more promotion ads appeared.

At the conclusion of this program all members of the Columbus newspaper staff had a better understanding of their responsibilities and all citizens of the community came to a higher appreciation of the newspaper that serves them.

Promotion Directed to Specific Groups

The San Diego, Calif., *Union* and *Tribune* (combined circulation 207,064, population 494,201), it seems, leaves nothing undone to make its observance of National Newspaper Week a smashing success. One year it used newspaper promotion, spots on local radio, house organs of civic clubs, windshield stickers, bumper strips, billboards (see Fig. 26.4), window cards and posters (see Fig. 26.4). The brief-cases of its advertising salesmen carried National Newspaper Week stickers. The theme of the week was imprinted on the newspaper's report blanks, stationery and bank checks. All outgoing mail during the week had a postage meter stamp bearing National Newspaper Week identification, dates and theme. All newspaper personnel wore chrysanthemum corsages with the week's slogan imprinted on ribbons. When representatives of the newspapers attended club meetings they wore lapel buttons imprinted with the Newspaper Week slogan. Special events took place also to feature the press and its many services.

In addition to this broad approach to the mass market, a special effort was made to reach specific publics, such as adults and children, employers and employees, the civilian and the military, students and teachers (see Fig. 26.6), men's and women's clubs, civic leaders and advertisers. News releases concerning the week were sent to all school papers, the military base paper and the Chamber of Commerce newspaper. Particularly striking was the great number of stories carried in the *Union* and *Tribune* to direct attention to the week and its meaning. Among these were:

1. Article by Norman E. Wollitz, principal of Longfellow School, pointing out the use of newspapers in the classroom.
2. Letter from the executive secretary of the Downtown Young Men's Christian Association, thanking the *Union* and *Tribune* for "generous and outstanding service to the community."
3. Feature article on the remarkable variety of circumstances confronted by newspaper reporters as they pursue their beats.
4. Story and art on visit by newspaperboys and their fathers to the Marine Corps Depot.
5. Story on reporter's problem in getting story ready for publication.
6. Story by Sue Seay of the Women's Department staff entitled "Women's Page Writers Are Human — Almost."
7. Story on Lloyd Taylor, winner of California Newspaper Foundation Award.
8. United Press International story about President Eisenhower's salute to newspaperboys.
9. Editorial entitled "Newspaperboy, the Vital Link."

Fig. 26.4 — Outdoor advertising is used with good effect to promote the San Diego, Calif., **Union** during National Newspaper Week.

10. Story about Secretary of the Interior Fred A. Seaton's tribute at Columbia, Mo., to the nation's working newspapermen.
11. Story about speed, accuracy and fairness demonstrated by Associated Press and United Press International.
12. Journalist's Creed by Walter Williams featured in story entitled "Journalist's Creed Expresses Spirit of Newspaper Week."
13. Statement by Governor Knight entitled "Press Stands for Freedom."
14. Stories about clubs participating in National Newspaper Week.
15. Special section entitled "Sputnik, Year One," devoted to activities of the week.
16. Editorial entitled "An Agent For the People."

The campaign was planned and directed by Paula Kent, promotion director, and won first place in the 1958 National Newspaper Week contest for daily newspapers.

Introduced Their New Buildings

Newspapers that had completed new buildings during the year centered their observance of National Newspaper Week on acquainting the public with their new and improved facilities.

The Jackson, Tenn., *Sun* (circulation 15,071, population 30,207), which completed and moved into a handsome new plant in June, conducted tours for civic clubs, women's organizations, school groups and youth organizations. From each of these groups the publishers afterward received letters of congratulations and appreciation and reproduced them in the newspaper (see Fig. 26.7).

A great volume of promotion material was carried in the newspaper during the week (see Fig. 26.8) and in spot announcements and newscasts on radio. Copies of a 54-page brochure on selling opportunities in the counties served by the newspaper were delivered to business firms. Bound copies of a 160-page "New Home Edition," put out when the newspaper's new plant was completed, and copies on hand of a 216-page "Anniversary Edition," issued in 1948, were delivered to all school libraries in the area.

Members of the newspaper staff carried the Newspaper Week message to various schools and organizations. Col. Albert A. Stone, vice-president and general manager, spoke at Union University and the Jackson High School. Gen. A. Lacy Price, assistant vice-president and advertising director, made talks at Lane College, North Side High School, West Tennessee Business College, Tigrett Junior High School and over Radio Station WJAK. Robert P. Mahon, associate editor, appeared before students at Merry High School, Jackson Junior High School, Lambuth College and South Side High School and before the Jackson Kiwanis Club and the Tennessee State Teachers Association.

Fig. 26.5 — Posters and displays helped promote the San Diego **Union** and **Tribune** during National Newspaper Week.

Fig. 26.6 — Members of a girls' club are fascinated by meeting the staff cartoonist and examining his original drawings at one of the many displays arranged by the San Diego **Union** and **Tribune**.

The San Bernardino, Calif., *Sun* and *Telegram* (combined circulation 60,514, population 83,145) featured the opening of their new building and the installation of a new press with appropriate ceremonies during Newspaper Week. Special programs were conducted before community organizations, inviting them to visit the plant, and later receptions were held at the newspaper building to give the public an opportunity to meet Frank Adams, cartoonist; Dr. Paul Popenoe, author of the feature, "Your Family and You"; Joseph J. Littlefield, creator of another feature, "Romance of the Flowers" and Earl E. Buie, columnist.

A booklet entitled "The San Bernardino *Sun* and *Telegram* Story" was given as a souvenir to each visitor at the plant. It introduced the staff and the building and contained other facts regarding the newspapers and their general policies. A 12-page tabloid section, put out with a regular issue of the Sunday *Sun-Telegram* to open Newspaper Week, explained how the newspapers expand as San Bernardino County grows (see Fig. 26.9). More than 2,000 persons attended the receptions and tours put on by the *Sun* and *Telegram* during the week.

The Dunsmuir, Calif., *News* (circulation 1,761, population 2,256) conducted an open house during National Newspaper Week to acquaint its readers with its new plant. To each visitor was given a free classified advertisement (15 words or less), and new subscriptions were offered at a special price. To make clear to visitors the capacity and the value of each piece of equipment, Chapman Wentworth, the publisher, had signs attached to them. The sign on the Heidelberg press explained that it "can print 5,000 copies per hour" and the one over the Intertype composing machine said: "To replace this machine would cost $20,000."

During this week the newspaper carried pictures of the new building and the staff and much interesting information regarding the newspaper operation. It related how many miles, pounds and hours go into a weekly newspaper, and carried the Walter Williams "Journalist's Creed" over the signatures of all members of the newspaper force.

Gave Inside Stories

The newspaper's inside story was a common theme of National Newspaper Week in 1958. The Eugene, Ore., *Register-Guard* presented its story in 6 full-page promotion ads. With words and pictures it revealed operations in the news, advertising, circulation and mechanical departments. Two additional pages were devoted to the newspaper's "junior dealers" and its rural correspondents. Steve Belko, University of Oregon basketball coach, spoke at a banquet honoring the news-

National Newspaper Week
Your Newspaper Guards Your Freedom

MR. STEWART

The Young Men's Christian Association
Jackson, Tennessee
October 2, 1958

Mr. Albert Stone
The Jackson Sun
Jackson, Tennessee
Dear Sir:

May we offer our congratulations on the observance of National Newspaper Week.

The Young Men's Christian Association appreciates the support and interest shown to our organization. Most of all we appreciate the individuals who make up the personnel of the Jackson Sun. The wonderful civic interest in our city exemplified by staff members is most encouraging.

We would express a word of personal thanks to Bob Mahon, J. M. Parish, Jack Hilliard and others who have cooperated so wonderfully with our effort to help in building character in our young people. Then Frank Procter, with your affiliate W.T.J.S. Radio, is most helpful in many ways.

We would just like to take this occasion to say, Thanks!

Sincerely,
Virgil Stewart
General Secretary

National Newspaper Week
Your Newspaper Guards Your Freedom

MISS CARAWAY

West Tennessee Hearing and Speech Center
Jackson, Tennessee
October 3, 1958

Mr. R. P. Mahon
The Jackson Sun
Jackson, Tennessee
Dear Mr. Mahon:

The observance National Newspaper Week affords us an excellent opportunity to thank you and The Jackson Sun staff for the splendid publicity which you have given to the West Tennessee Hearing and Speech Center.

Your articles and pictures have informed the peole of this area about the services available at the center, and in many instances parents have informed us they first heard about the center through an article in The Jackson Sun. You came to our assistance when we were trying to publicize the need for expansion of our program and a building.

Your personal interest has been appreciated and we are looking forward to working with you in the future.

Yours truly,
(Miss) Betty J. Caraway,
Director West Tennessee Speech and Hearing Center

Fig. 26.7 — Typical letters of appreciation received by the Jackson, Tenn., **Sun** are published as features of National Newspaper Week promotion.

paper's 250 carrier-salesmen, and Edwin M. Baker, business manager of the *Register-Guard,* addressed the Advertising Club on "Truth in Advertising."

Wide Observance by Weeklies

National Newspaper Week was widely observed in 1958 by weekly as well as daily newspapers. In various ways they publicized the services they offered and promoted progress within their communities.

The Dalton, Ga., *Citizen* and *News,* issued on Wednesday and Friday (combined circulation 12,564, population 15,968), presented 3 full-page 2-color promotions. One entitled "Looking to Brighter Horizons" explaind the newspaper's community service. Another entitled "Your Key to the Dalton Market" featured for advertisers the many homes in the area. The other promotion was devoted to the newspaper's departments and personnel. Its slogan was "On all points — news, pictures, advertising — your weekly news-papers serve you best."

Several smaller ads appeared during the week. Features, editori-als and pictures outlined the services rendered by the newspaper. Letters of appreciation from the Red Cross, the Young Men's Chris-tian Association and school children were published.

The Chester, Ill., *Herald-Tribune* (circulation 5,400, population 5,389) used the week to develop in the youth of the community a greater interest in journalism. Twenty members of the Chester High School *Buzz* staff, which prepares a weekly department of high school news for the *Herald-Tribune,* were brought to the news-paper office and given news assignments. They spent 2 hours in the morning and 2 in the afternoon conducting interviews and writ-ing stories and editorials. Representatives of the *Buzz* staff appeared also on radio in a panel discussion with editors of the area. The big event of the week, however, was a banquet at the Elks Club with the *Buzz* staff as guests and Dr. Howard R. Long, chairman of the Department of Journalism at Southern Illinois University, as speaker. For this occasion the newspaper put out a miniature banquet edition and tag cards.

In a letter to the newspaper, the *Buzz* staff said: "Thanks to you for making it possible for us to have such a memorable and en-joyable experience as reporters for last week's issue. Even though our careers were short lived, for some of us they may extend to a lifelong occupation in the field of journalism. Our interest cer-tainly has been awakened by this experience. Thanks for giving us a peek into the newspaper world."

Even very small newspapers found Newspaper Week a good time in which to develop a closer contact with the people of their areas. The Greenville, Ga., *Meriwether-Vindicator* (circulation 856, population 733) carried out an extensive program, including:

1. Letters to all civic organizations in the area, announcing plans for observing the week.
2. A contest at Greenville High School, in which all seniors were invited to write a paper on "What My Newspaper Means to My Community."
3. Obtained Leo Aikman of the Atlanta *Constitution* to address the Greenville Kiwanis Club.
4. Made posters explaining the services offered by the newspaper and placed them in store windows throughout the business district.
5. Wrote letters of gratitude to 19 families who had been readers of the papers for 50 years or more.
6. Wrote letters of appreciation to all advertisers.
7. Invited pastors to speak in their churches on themes appropriate to the week.

SUGGESTIONS FOR OBSERVING THE WEEK

Many other ideas for the observance of National Newspaper Week are used by newspapers large and small. Some of these are original with the publishers, while others are suggested by Newspaper Association Managers, Inc. Among the most valuable of all presented are the following:

News and Editorial

1. Run a series of articles on "How My Newspaper Serves."
2. Request editorials from leading citizens on the theme of National Newspaper Week.
3. List the various community activities of the year in which the newspaper played an important part.
4. Describe the variety and amount of information each issue of the newspaper contains.
5. Write a feature story on "How To Read the Newspaper."
6. Invite letters from readers on "How My Newspaper Helps Me."
7. Write a feature on how the newspaper, merchants and residents of the community may cooperate to promote progress.
8. Explain in an editorial how a newspaper develops its editorial policy.
9. Explain "freedom of the press" as a right belonging to the public.
10. Explain in detail the responsibilities of all those who work in the news and editorial departments.

There's Gold in Jackson And Madison County

IF WE'LL ONLY

DIG

FOR IT!

•

To "Turn up" More Customers

LET

𝕿𝖍𝖊 𝕵𝖆𝖈𝖐𝖘𝖔𝖓 𝕾𝖚𝖓

Do Your "Spade Work"

An Economical Advertising Program Is the Most Effective Way of "Digging Out" Your Share of the More Than Our 83 Million Dollar Annual Buying Income* in Jackson and Madison County

KEEP OUR 62,200* MADISON COUNTIANS INFORMED OF YOUR MERCHANDISE, PRODUCTS AND SERVICES.

Let's Call a Spade a Spade"

Everybody has a "shovel" available here; it's The Jackson Sun. Use It For Results.

ADVERTISING IN THE SUN "RINGS THE BELL" ON YOUR CASH REGISTER. *From Standard Rate & Data Service, 1958.*

Fig. 26.8 — The Jackson, **Sun** uses National Newspaper Week to promote its own advertising department.

11. Write an editorial urging young people to consider journalism as a career.
12. Write an article explaining the courses offered at an accredited school of journalism.
13. Have editors of local high school papers help in getting out an issue of your newspaper during National Newspaper Week.
14. Use direct mail, window displays, radio, television and other media to tell the story of the newspaper and its importance to readers.
15. Run some highlight facts about your newspaper's history.
16. Count the number of names appearing in a typical issue and write a story about how the newspaper is interested in the activities of all its readers.
17. Write a "Thanks for Cooperation" editorial and mention persons who have been most helpful in obtaining news, developing editorials or assisting in community campaigns.
18. Develop new ways and ideas for emphasizing the closeness of readers and the newspaper.
19. With assistance of carriers, conduct a survey of newspaper readers' likes and dislikes.
20. Stage a "Voice of the People" dinner, honoring those persons who have had letters to the editor published during the year.
21. Run pictures and comments by some long-time readers.
22. Tell in a feature story how the different employees of the newspaper assist in various community activities.
23. Write a review of recent changes in newspaper equipment and operation to give readers the best production and service.
24. Prepare a story on the paper, ink, equipment, supplies, personnel, etc., necessary to produce your newspaper.
25. Run a page of pictures used during the year and emphasize the importance of pictures in reporting the news.

Circulation

26. Explain how employees in the circulation department serve readers, accenting the importance of deadlines, timing and attention to details.
27. Review changes in equipment for handling newspapers as they come from the press and go into the hands of carriers.
28. Write a story, comparing the growth in newspaper circulation with the growth of the community in population.
29. Explain the problems faced by the circulation department in providing prompt delivery for readers in all areas.
30. Write a story on how vendors and vending machines serve.

31. Explain the importance of and reliance on "little merchant" carriers.
32. Plan special recognition for carriers on National Newspaperboy Day.
33. Consider some plan of awards for outstanding newspaperboys at a luncheon or banquet with parents and leading local citizens present.
34. Run "then and now" pictures of former newspaperboys who are now successful businessmen with comments from each on how newspaperboy training helped toward success.
35. Interview parents of newspaperboys and write feature stories containing their comments.
36. Write and print a series of advertisements on the value of newspaperboy training.
37. Carry pictures of circulation department personnel, including carriers.
38. Dramatize the newspaper as a necessity in every home.
39. Offer special subscription rate during Newspaper Week.
40. Review methods of newspaper delivery and explain how operation is designed to serve readers.

Local Advertising

41. Hold a dinner or luncheon for your regular advertisers and prospective advertisers.
42. Prepare a story or photo feature on how your newspaper serves merchants and readers through its advertising columns, citing the newspaper as the best source of buying information.
43. Obtain statements from readers on the advantages they have derived from patronizing advertisers in your newspaper.
44. Obtain testimonials and result stories from regular advertisers and publish them during National Newspaper Week.
45. Conduct a letter-writing contest on "Why I Like To Read Ads in My Newspaper."
46. Write a story on the amount of advertising refused because of standards set by the newspaper to protect the public.
47. Explain the various services provided advertisers by the newspaper, including merchandising, marketing, surveys, community data, dealer route lists, etc.
48. Arrange for civic club talks on the value of local newspaper advertising.
49. Run an editorial on "How Advertising Serves."
50. Run pictures and brief sketches of advertising department personnel.
51. List local business firms that advertise in your newspaper.

★   ★   ★   ★

THE SUN-TELEGRAM
EXPANDS
As San Bernardino County
GROWS

RICHARD DITTMER
The Sun-Telegram Carrier-Salesman

Fig. 26.9 — The San Bernardino, Calif., Sunday **Sun-Telegram** issues a special supplement for National Newspaper Week, featuring parallel expansion of both community and newspapers.

Classified Advertising

52. Run a feature story or promotion advertisement explaining how to use classified advertising.
53. Offer a special trial rate on classified ads placed during National Newspaper Week.
54. Plan a "Kids' Want Ad Day" with a special rate or a free offer.
55. To encourage advertising of unwanted items around the home, conduct a "Classified Cleanup Sale" for subscribers only.
56. Solicit comments from readers on the value of classified advertising and how it serves readers.
57. Highlight the human interest side of classified advertising.
58. Run a series of promotion ads, featuring the various classifications represented in the classified section.

National Advertising

59. Explain what national advertising is and how it benefits readers.
60. List all national advertisers in a promotion advertisement.
61. Explain how tie-in and cooperative advertising assist in acquainting readers with well-established products.
62. Explain the value of advertising in introducing new products.
63. Stress the importance of the newspaper in building sales to serve readers and national advertisers.
64. Entertain sales representatives of manufacturing companies at dinner and discuss with them the newspaper's policy of cooperation with national advertisers.
65. Explain to readers the services provided by advertising agencies.

Legal Advertising

66. Explain to readers the value of legal advertising.
67. Define the various types of legal advertising and explain their importance.
68. Feature the "right to know" angle of legal advertising, and point out that it is important information for all taxpayers.
69. Write an editorial on "How Legal Advertising Serves," explaining that it is more important today than ever before because of increased population, greater demand for public service and increased taxes.
70. Emphasize the importance of advertising for bids on public construction in order to obtain the most for the money and to decrease or eliminate collusion and graft.

CHAPTER 27

Promoting Through Special Editions

VALUABLE PROMOTION MATERIAL to benefit a community as well as the newspaper may be presented in special editions or sections. Advertising by merchants of the community in these issues will add valuable revenue for the newspaper. It is not unusual, therefore, for newspapers to produce several such issues in the course of a year.

Some regular advertisers may not look upon special editions with the same favor they do upon regular issues of the newspaper as conveyors of store news to their customers. Consequently, they do not so readily buy space in special editions. The ones more likely to advertise in specials are those firms for whom the theme of the special edition may have unusual appeal and who are thus glad to help promote a worthy cause or institution. Other firms who have not been regular advertisers may feel that an ad in a special edition is at least a small recognition of the newspaper's efforts to build a better community.

Special editions are expensive. They usually require additional salesmen and writers and considerable overtime work in all departments of the newspaper. A large volume of news and feature material is required to fill them, and many column inches of advertising to support them. Therefore, good planning is required to carry through a successful special edition. Every detail should be watched to assure favorable reaction from readers and advertisers alike when the finished edition is presented for public consumption.

Domenic E. Didoardo, retail advertising manager of the Plainfield, N.J., *Courier-News* (circulation 36,661, population 42,366), says: "We at the *Courier-News* study every special edition proposal that comes to our attention and we ask ourselves a few questions: Will a strong reader interest result? Can the news department handle the required editorial material in stride? Will the advertisers use extra linage without cutting regular advertising? Will the flow of copy to the composing room be sufficiently steady to keep mechanical cost to a minimum?"[1]

These are all-important questions, and only when they may be answered in the affirmative should such a project be attempted. Most publishers believe there is an important place for special editions in the production program of a good newspaper; that when the publisher keeps in mind the readers' best interests and the community's progress, these editions perform a valuable service by promoting both the community and the newspaper.

The Bowling Green, Ohio, *Sentinel-Tribune* (circulation 8,697, population 12,005) one year produced 5 special editions or sections with satisfactory results — a Traffic Courtesy issue, a Cook Book section containing recipes by local housewives, a Home and Garden edition, a County Fair edition and a High School Graduation issue. The Peoria, Ill., *Journal Star* (combined morning and evening circulation 97,785, population 111,856) also issued 5 specials in a single year — a section devoted to a new subdivision, a Home Improvement edition consisting of 2 tabloid sections, a colored Sunday section on Home Fashions and Furnishings, and a section on Men's Fashions. The Saratoga Springs, N.Y., *Saratogian* (circulation 11,657, population 15,473) also put out 5 successful editions within a year.

"Special sections are definitely a part of the newspaper business," says Edwin J. Lanfear, advertising manager of the *Saratogian*, "and as such should be used to the very best advantage of all concerned — the reader, the advertiser and the newspaper."[2]

PROMOTE VARIETY OF EVENTS AND SUBJECTS

Special editions of newspapers have been helpful in promoting a wide variety of events and institutions. Usually they revolve around such subjects as:

1. Anniversaries.

2. Fall, Winter, Spring and Summer Openings.

3. New Buildings and Other Improvements.

4. Community Progress.

5. Civic Programs and Achievements.

6. Special Days, Weeks or Seasons.

---

[1] *Editor & Publisher,* June 21, 1958, p. 20.

Unusual Anniversary Editions

Birthdays seem to be as important to newspapers and other organizations as they do to individuals. When an institution has existed for 10, 15, 25, 50 or 100 years, its members feel that it has developed a record worthy of recognition and is capable of producing still greater growth and service. Among various types of special editions, those that commemorate an anniversary are perhaps most common.

Newspapers consider anniversaries good opportunities to show how they and their communities have grown along together. Those that have served 50 or 100 years or even more become valuable community histories. More often the contents of these special editions are almost entirely historical, but occasionally they discuss freely the outlook for future development and advancement.

When the Detroit, Mich., *Free Press* (circulation 456,117, population 1,849,568) completed its 125th year, its publishers decided that the occasion was worthy of special distinction and its readers were deserving of an issue extraordinary. They determined that the slogan for the issue should be "Michigan Tomorrow," a theme that would cover all activities and fields touching the lives of readers in terms of the future and tune in the past for background and supplementary stories.

To further distinguish the *Free Press* anniversary observance from those of many other newspapers, Frank Angelo, managing editor, and his staff developed four special rotogravure anniversary sections with full-color covers; these were distributed with regular issues of the paper on successive Saturdays in August and September. This they felt was better than combining the several sections into one large issue. It staggered the work load for editorial and mechanical personnel, gave advertising more selling points and helped in promotion efforts to build interest over a period of time.

Every detail concerning the anniversary sections was carefully planned and executed. On the actual birthday, May 5, readers were alerted to the fact that the newspaper was gathering for them the best material possible on the future of science and industry, religion and education, housing, labor, the cities of Michigan, suburban development and other features.

Assignments were drawn up by major classifications. For the section on Detroit, for example, there were stories on "The Heart of Detroit — Today and Tomorrow," "Our Leaders Look Ahead," "Will We Have Monorails, Subways or Nonstop Buses?" as well as reports from educators, labor leaders, churchmen, home builders, utility companies and fashion and beauty experts. With due dates for assign-

---

[2] *Editor & Publisher,* June 21, 1958, p. 20.

ments staggered from mid-May to early June, there was a steady flow of copy which avoided any jam for those who had to gather and write the material and those who had to process it.

All stories were handled by the city desk and written by staff members. As far as possible, specialists handled the assignments in their fields. The overflow was handled by general assignment, beat and rewrite men and departmental reporters. Practically every *Free Press* staffer received an anniversary memo with assignment attached.

Production was handled on a week-to-week basis. The advertising staff supplied dummies as early as feasible, and copy was moved section by section to the composing room. Photographs and other illustrations were processed as the layouts arrived and the sections were made up in the 3 days preceding publication night. Promotion within the newspaper's own columns, direct mail, newsstand placards and radio and television spots informed all who could read or hear about the "Michigan Tomorrow" edition. A heavy flow of orders and happy reader acceptance were the rewards for a job well performed.

Under the heading "100 Years of Headline Building for Tomorrow" the Davenport, Iowa, *Democrat* (circulation 22,043, population 74,549) divided its history into decades and presented it in 10 daily editions. Each decade had a theme:

1855–1865 — Years of Prosperity, Panic, War
1865–1875 — Boats, Bandits and Bustles
1875–1885 — Elegant Age of Easier Living
1885–1895 — The Gaudy, Naughty Nineties
1895–1905 — Fight, Flames and Flight
1905–1915 — Flickers, Flivers and Gibson Girls
1915–1925 — War and Peace, Gin and Jazz
1925–1935 — Revels, Rackets, Boom and Bust
1935–1945 — Blood, Sweat and Tears
1945–1955 — The Atomic Age — What Next?

This method of featuring the newspaper's centennial increased readership, general interest and advertising linage.

When the Racine, Wis., *Journal-Times* (circulation 31,262, population 71,193) and its Sunday issue, the *Bulletin* (circulation 30,852) celebrated their centennial, they produced their anniversary sections serially rather than combined in one edition. Seven attractive sections were distributed on successive Sundays from October 7 through November 18. These were then bound with a souvenir cover and an introductory page carrying letters from the Wisconsin governor and the newspapers' publishers, Harry R. LePoidevin and J. D. McMurray.

A similar plan was carried out by the Paducah, Ky., *Sun-Democrat* (circulation 25,185, population 32,828) in observing its 100th anniversary. Ten issues, containing 342 pages of editorial matter, pictures and advertising, were published on ten successive days.

The Winona, Minn., *News* (circulation 21,018, population 25,031) issued a 324-page, 16-section Centennial Edition, one of the largest full-page-sized editions ever published in Minnesota. A century of continuous newspaper service in one community was worthy of elaborate promotion.

MAY HAVE GREAT EDUCATIONAL VALUE

In producing a special edition to commemorate a newspaper's anniversary, a publisher is not required to confine contents to the happenings of the past and the accomplishments of the present; he may as well reflect the prospects for years ahead. Some newspapers in following this pattern have produced editions of an extremely high order from an educational and cultural standpoint.

Outstanding among editions of this kind was the Fiftieth Anniversary Edition of the *Christian Science Monitor* — 104 pages in 6 important sections dealing with the strivings for freedom and peace in the world, the development of relations between nations, the explorations and discoveries in space, and the influence of all these on all phases of life and in all parts of creation.

In Section One, which was entitled "Man and Space: Freedom of the Universe," Erwin D. Canham, editor, explained that for the contents of this edition, the *Monitor* "...turned not inward on itself nor backward on its history, but outward to the stars and forward to man's future. And, indeed, it looks poignantly into the lives of humble people everywhere." The challenge of distant planets was brilliantly explained.

The wakening of peoples who have lived in oppression and ignorance and their yearnings for self-government were described in Section Two, while the remarkable advances being made toward freedom from material limitations were discussed in Section Three. Atomic energy, electronics and technological advancement were all treated from the standpoint of science, economics, politics and morals.

Man's relation to man and the freedom that has come to him for spiritual unfoldment were presented graphically and forcefully in Section Four. Some of the headlines for stories in this section revealed its wide scope: "Education Pushes on to the Golden Ideal of Equal Opportunity for All," "The Growth of Moral Sensitivity in Man's Thinking," "Christian Unity Marches Forward" and "Literature Imprints Era of Experiment."

Section Five dealt with the relations of nations, pointing out how the United Nations focuses public opinion on world controversies and problems and how moral power provides a solid foundation for world peace.

The final section of this great issue was the regular news section, dealing with current happenings throughout the world and editorial discussion of current problems.

Extensive research, authentic information, brilliant writing, modern typography and color printing combined to make this an exceptional issue, a perfect illustration of the educational service that may be given in an anniversary edition.

Another exceptional anniversary edition was one put out by the Houghton-Calumet, Mich., *Mining Gazette* (circulation 10,599, population 5,085) in 1958 to commemorate its centennial. This was different from many special editions in that it contained little advertising. It consisted of 32 pages but only six of these pages carried advertising. Twenty-six solid pages were devoted to the history of the newspaper and the community it served and to their prospects for a vigorous tomorrow.

WEEKLIES, TOO, STAR IN THIS ROLE

Weekly newspapers can produce attractive anniversary editions as readily as daily papers. The Birmingham, Mich., *Eccentric* (circulation 12,489, population 15,467), in fact, produced one of the most comprehensive editions ever put out by any publication to celebrate its 75th anniversary. In addition to the regular news section, it contained twelve 16-page tabloid sections pertaining to the anniversary — 252 pages in all. The anniversary sections carried 215 individual advertisements totaling 9,510 column inches, plus 896 column inches of 4-color advertisements in a special section and 3,900 column inches of advertising in the regular news section — a grand total of 14,246 column inches of advertising. Total revenue from the anniversary edition was about $27,000.[3]

Work was begun on this special edition eight months before date of issue. A definite plan was formulated well in advance for the whole edition and for the contents of each section, and assignments had to be completed within a certain period of time. The material appearing in the edition was carried under 17 main headings. The outline of assignments as designed by George R. Averill, editor and publisher, and George William Averill, managing editor, is a good pattern for any newspaper to follow in developing an anniversary edition:

I. FOUNDING AND HISTORY OF TOWN

A. Front page dedication to those who founded the town.
B. Story of first settlers.
C. Pictures of all parts of town at various periods in history.
D. Story and pictures of first houses.

II. HISTORY OF TOWN GOVERNMENT

A. Pictures of Municipal Building — past and present.
B. Chronological story of town government, including prominent figures who held public office.
C. Story of tax growth from time all farmers paid $2 per year taxes.

---

[3] *American Press*, July, 1953, p. 12.

III. HISTORY OF MUNICIPAL DEPARTMENTS

A. Growth of fire department — with pictures of old and new equipment.
B. Post Office — with pictures of past and present.
C. Growth of police force — with pictures.
D. History of library — with pictures.
E. Origin of local park.
F. Work of recreation board.
G. History of cemetery.

IV. HISTORY OF LOCAL EDUCATION

A. Start of county school system.
B. Story and pictures of original schools.
C. History of education from time principal received a yearly salary of $800.
D. Formation of school districts.
E. Story of PTA.

V. HISTORY OF NEWSPAPER

A. Story by publisher on his experiences in building paper.
B. Chronological history of newspaper — change of owners, etc.
C. List of prizes won by newspaper.
D. Story by business manager on growth of job printing.
E. Full-size pictures of first issue of newspaper.
F. Pictures of all of newspaper and printing staffs.
G. Pictures of equipment.

VI. HISTORY OF TRANSPORTATION

A. Story of first railroad — pictures of train, station, etc.
B. Story of road building in the county.
C. Story and pictures of first local automobiles.
D. Story of bus transportation.
E. Establishment of first airport.

VII. HISTORY OF UTILITIES

A. Establishment of electric company and story of first lighting.
B. Phone service — history of, with pictures of first exchange and present exchange.
C. History of local water system.
D. History of gas service.

VIII. HISTORY AND GROWTH OF LOCAL BUSINESS

A. Pictures and stories of first store.
B. Story on establishment of local mills.
C. Establishment of first movie house — and story about the pictures shown.
D. History of local stores and business enterprises.

IX. HISTORY AND GROWTH OF NEIGHBORING COMMUNITIES

A. Pertinent facts concerning the founding, development and existing condition of each community.

X. WOMEN'S CLUBS AND SOCIAL ORGANIZATIONS

A. Complete stories on the establishment, growth and influence of: Women's Club, League of Women Voters, Community House, Rotary Ann Club, Business Women's Club, WCTU, Farm and Garden Association, Newcomers Club, DAR, Music Guild, Village Players, Moms of America, Inc., Dramatic Guild, Community Association, Exchange Club, Altrusa International, Auto Club, Democratic Club, Country Clubs.
B. Pictures of past and present meeting places of clubs.

XI. MEN'S CLUBS AND ORGANIZATIONS

A. Complete stories of establishment and growth of local chapters of all organizations, including: Masons, Kiwanis, Rotary, American Legion, Veterans of Foreign Wars, Chamber of Commerce, Junior Chamber of Commerce, Dad's Club, Odd Fellows, Lions, Male Chorus, Metropolitan Club of America, Stamp Club, Expectant Fathers Club.

XII. CHURCHES

A. Story of town's first church — with pictures.
B. History of each present church.
C. Pictures of past and present churches.
D. Organization of Council of Churches.
E. Stories about church societies and organizations.

XIII. CHARITABLE ORGANIZATIONS

A. Story of local Red Cross chapter and its services during emergencies.
B. History of Junior League.
C. History of Needlework Guild.
D. Stories of fund-raising drives.

XIV. CHILDREN'S ACTIVITIES

A. Story of 4-H Club.
B. History of local Girl Scouts, Boy Scouts, YMCA.
C. Celebrations of Halloween and the Fourth of July.

XV. SPORTS

A. Establishment of Gun Club, and history of hunting in the area.
B. Establishment of Fishing Club, and history of fishing in the area.
C. Establishment of Hunt Club.
D. Story of Baseball League.

XVI. NEWS HIGHLIGHTS

A. Stories and pictures of memorable fires, floods, etc.
B. "I Remember" columns written by old-timers. These were scattered throughout the newspaper.
C. Women's Suffrage Crusade.
D. Human interest shorts from back issues.

XVII. CONGRATULATORY MESSAGES

A. Reproductions of congratulatory letters from the Governor, Congressmen, local officials, etc.
B. Congratulatory messages in paid advertising.

NEWSPAPERS PROMOTE CITY CENTENNIALS

Newspapers deem it advantageous and proper to observe the centennials of cities, counties and states as well as to honor their own records of many years.

The Tell City, Ind., *News* (circulation 4,569, population 6,516), progressive weekly, issued a tabloid edition of 118 pages in celebration of the city's 100th anniversary. This issue, printed on bright book paper with a cover in color, told how the city was planned and how it doubled its population the first year of its existence, how it fought and overcame the flood waters of the Ohio River and made the river an important factor in its growth and development. It paid tribute to early citizens and gave the history of important industries, some of which were as old as the city. The movement for a community hospital, the coming of the first railroad, the love of the Swiss inhabitants for good music as revealed in the various bands and singing groups, the city park development, the growth of churches and schools, the financial development through banks and savings institutions, the community's military record, its Chamber of Commerce and other civic clubs — all these were fully described and illustrated.

Three pages of the edition were used to outline an interesting historical tour. A map of the city showed 68 historic spots of interest to citizens and tourists. The issue was truly a great advertisement for the community and the newspaper.

Season's Styles Are Featured

Most newspapers issue three or four special sections or editions during the year, featuring seasonal styles and offerings at local stores.

Spring brings forth a Spring Opening Edition and probably an Easter Section, revealing the newest in spring wear for men, women and children. Fall features heavier clothing for cooler days.

Summer brings bathing suits and vacation apparel to the show windows and to advertising columns. A section devoted to comfortable seaside and hiking garb makes interesting and valuable reading and stimulates business for home town merchants.

Style-conscious readers appreciate also a section devoted to winter styles — the latest in sweaters and furs and snappy apparel for skiing and other winter sports.

Stores usually cooperate in a communitywide opening display of all that's new at the beginning of each season. Home furnishings as well as apparel go on display. The Williston, N. Dak., *Williston Plains Reporter* (circulation 3,740, population 10,886), an enterprising weekly, issued one fall both a "Fashion Section" and a "Home Edition." The latter consisted of 36 pages filled with news and revamped ideas for making the home beautiful.

To Dedicate New Buildings

Another time in which special editions prove their value is when newspapers and other institutions within the newspapers' areas erect new buildings and open them to the public. An explanation is needed of the improved facilities offered, and a special section or issue of the newspaper is the best means of providing it.

A 44-page tabloid section, attractively illustrated and printed in color, was produced when the Chicago *Sun-Times* (circulation 534,063, population 3,620,962) entered its handsome new 9-story building in the heart of the great city. Pictures and stories explained how every inch of its more than 700,000 square feet of floor space is utilized to produce quickly and efficiently a daily newspaper of many pages and wide circulation.

On the cover was shown the commodious building with lights gleaming from its hundreds of windows. The American flag, floating proudly above the building, helped to symbolize the brightest possession of a free world — "the people's right to know."

Shown seated at his desk with a copy of his newspaper opened before him, Marshall Field, Jr., editor and publisher, states: "In dedicating this building, we have dedicated ourselves to the task of applying its resources and facilities to the making of a great newspaper."

The section takes the reader from department to department, to observe the convenient arrangement of desks and other equipment, the attention given to art, comfort, health and efficiency, and the mechanical operation and automation that add power to all the manual thought and labor going into the newspaper. In no better way could be explained the improved service the *Sun-Times* would be able to bring to its readers and advertisers.

The great number of new newspaper plants erected within the past decade have brought forth an abundance of attractive editions explaining important improvements and drawing the papers closer to their readers. They provide a valuable study in plant architecture and arrangement, a service to other newspapers planning to build, as well as adding to the interest and information of the newspaper's immediate constituency.

Progress Editions Are Plentiful

Anything that pertains to the progress of a newspaper, its community or any institution within the community is good material for a newspaper, and much of it is gathered and presented in Progress Editions of great variety.

TO SHOW CITY'S PROGRESS

The rapid advancement made by the town of Littlefield, Tex., inspired the local businessmen to publicize these facts in promoting still greater progress. They had no difficulty in obtaining the whole-hearted support of the town's rapidly growing weekly newspaper, the *County Wide News* (circulation 3,891, population 6,540).

The merchants and the publishers decided on a Progress Edition with the slogan, "Industry Makes Its Mark in Littlefield," to show all that had been accomplished in the brief period of two years. Readily produced was an issue of 150 pages, which told the fascinating story of how a small group of men with foresight were able to organize formidable leadership, inspire enthusiasm among the citizens and sell Littlefield as an ideal industrial center.

"To these men who proved the power of faith and hard work, we dedicate this issue, one of the largest ever produced in a city of this size in the Southwest," declared Sam L. Williams, publisher, in a front-page editorial. Of the 210 advertisements from local business institutions, 58 were full-page size and only 29 were less than 3 columns wide.

With an attractive 72-page tabloid section, printed in color, the

Pittsburgh, Pa., *Sun-Telegraph* (circulation 181,106, population 676,806) gave to itself a "New Look" and prescribed for its readers a new view of the opportunities surrounding them as citizens of Pittsburgh.

"We pledge our newspaper and our staff to further the progress we have made," said Alan G. Nicholas, the publisher, "to serve your every need in keeping the freedoms we have enjoyed available for our children, grandchildren, great grandchildren and their children to come."

All departments and the services they performed were presented. Editors rolled up their sleeves to do a thorough job of giving the news, ace lensmen went speedily to get prize pictures, feature writers brightened the pages with stories of human interest, the drama critic watched the passing scene, and expert copywriters and salesmen designed and sold ads that pulled business. Readers were given a quick glance at the *Sun-Telegraph*'s gigantic production in the composing room, the stereotyping department and the pressroom. Furthermore, the many community projects promoted by the newspaper revealed its activity in community progress.

Other outstanding examples of successful Progress Editions are a 388-page New Era Edition of the Painesville, Ohio, *Telegraph* (circulation 18,672, population 14,432) , a Year-End Edition of the Middletown, Ohio, *Journal* (circulation 21,449, population 33,695) which was devoted to business development within the newspaper's circulation area, and a 5-section Progress Edition put out by the weekly Rock Springs, Wyo., *Miner,* (circulation 5,713, population 10,857) .

TO PROMOTE CIVIC PROGRESS

In order that taxpayers may fully know how their tax money is being spent in conducting the city's business and in improving the community, many city administrations have departed from the old custom of publishing a brief statement in small type to merely meet legal requirements. Instead the city council authorizes the city clerk to arrange with the local newspaper for an entire section of news and information concerning the city's accomplishments of the preceding year. Here is a good example, as related by James G. Ward, Jr., general manager of the Escanaba, Mich., *Press* (circulation 10,301, population 15,170) to a group of fellow publishers at a meeting of the Inland Daily Press Association:

"For many years the city of Escanaba customarily spent from $700 to $1,000 to publish a dull annual report in mimeograph form. It was 25 pages of statistical information that few people would bother to read. A thousand copies of this report were made available at the city library, the three banks in the city and at the treasurer's window in the city hall.

"The mayor and council became convinced that the report as

presented and distributed had little consumption. They decided the report would be more readable and interesting and would receive more attention if it were published in attractive form in the *Press*. The cost would be about half that of the mimeographed report, and 95 per cent of the people of Escanaba would see it, to say nothing of a large percentage of the 35,000 other people in the trading area outside the city.

"The report was written mainly in news style with striking headlines and illustrations and consumed an entire 8-page tabloid section. It was prepared from formal departmental reports and illustrated with appropriate pictures from the newspaper and city files. The *Press* advertising staff supervised the layout, and the entire section was paid for by the city at the newspaper's regular local display contract rate."

A newspaper's promotion department knows what is required to sell an idea, and its advertising department can formulate an effective presentation of a city's needs and plans for achieving them. Here's how the Bloomington, Ill., *Pantagraph* (circulation 39,384, population 36,127) worked with a planning commission to promote the city's central business district:

Fifteen tabloid sections were prepared and run in the *Pantagraph*, one each Tuesday from March 6 to June 12, inclusive. These were paid for by local merchants, manufacturers and other citizens, who looked upon the publicity in this form not as advertising but as a long-range investment in the solidity of the community. The amounts contributed toward this project ranged from $10 to $500, a surprising number being in the higher amount. All sponsors' names were listed on the back of each tabloid section and were given equal prominence regardless of the amount they contributed.

When the last tabloid had been published, the newspaper ran 1,150 extra sets of the entire series and made them up in bound form. Of these bound volumes, 550 were donated to local schools and colleges and to members of the planning commission. Six hundred were retained to be sold at the *Pantagraph* office at $1 each.

The results obtained were highly satisfactory and the newspaper was considered an indispensable agent in an important community project.

TO PROMOTE LOCAL INSTITUTIONS

Newspapers often are asked by business institutions to produce for them special editions or sections to commemorate an anniversary, or to call attention to plant improvements or important changes of business policy.

Usually each such section contains chiefly a history of the business institution and a description of improvements instituted, together with an abundance of ads from fellow merchants congratulating the celebrator upon his achievements. This, however, is not always the case.

Worthy of special attention is an anniversary section issued by the Bloomington, Ill., *Pantagraph* for a large insurance company operating in that city.

In addition to observing its anniversary, the company wished to celebrate the issuing of its five millionth policy. The company is highly regarded by the business concerns of Bloomington, and merchants were anxious to express their good will in an effective way. They approached the newspaper with the proposition that they would contribute the cost of 12 pages in a 20-page section if the newspaper would provide the remaining eight pages. Instead of using individual ads to extend congratulations, the merchants would contribute as they desired to a fund to cover the cost of publication, and use only one page to say who the sponsors were without mentioning the amount each contributed.

"This was a good deal for them and for us," says Loring Merwin, publisher, "and we readily agreed."

Special Editions on Other Themes

Many other opportunities are presented for producing special editions in the course of a year. Special days, weeks and months come along in rapid order.

The Warren, Pa., *Times-Mirror* (circulation 8,504, population 14,849) in 1958 issued a 38-page "Honeymoon Special" keyed to a month-long "June Wedding" community-wide sales promotion. To clear up any confusion that might result from the use of the "Wedding Days" theme, it was pointed out that the wedding referred to was among the merchants of the city who were "taking the vows" to promote Warren as a first-class shopping center and to furnish service and satisfaction to all customers. The project was sponsored by the retail division of the Greater Warren Chamber of Commerce with the newspaper giving full publicity and providing part of the entertainment.

At Colville, Wash., which is the center of one of the country's largest herds of whitetail deer, the *Statesman-Examiner* (circulation 3,925, population 3,033) put out a special "Hunting Edition." This contained hunting laws, the dates of seasons on all game in the area and many other features of interest to hunters. Extra copies were distributed to motels, hotels and gas stations to be given to hunters coming into the territory.

An important annual event in Williston, N. Dak., is "Band Day," when the Chamber of Commerce invites bands from surrounding high schools to come to town and compete for honors and be entertained. The *Williston Plains Reporter* took advantage of this to produce a 36-page "Band Edition." Appearing in it were the pictures of 33 bands, 13 majorettes and two band leaders. It was an issue of great interest to readers, and readily won good will for the newspaper.

A more unusual edition was one put out by the Monett, Mo., *Times* (circulation 3,997, population 4,771) to celebrate "Chicken Eatin' Week." Poultry raising is a major industry in the Monett area. A feature of the week was an Annual Poultry Improvement Day sponsored by the Chamber of Commerce. The Lions Club conducted a barbecue, and chicken was on the lunch menu at public schools for four straight days. The *Times'* edition of 24 pages contained chicken recipes and advertisements from 47 merchants, each ad featuring chicken.

EVALUATION OF ADVANTAGES

If a newspaper should decide to put out a special edition in observance of every special day fostered by various industries and interests, it would produce one every week and perhaps more often — too often, in fact, to obtain sufficient advertising support and too frequently to maintain reader interest in the routine news of the day.

Some publishers issue many specials, others only a limited number, while still others seem to avoid them entirely. Good reasons both for and against them have been advanced. It is easy to point out their disadvantages as well as their advantages. Principally they are:

Advantages

1. Provides opportunity to give readers extra pages of reading material.
2. Enables newspaper to obtain additional advertising.
3. Is a good means of promoting worthwhile events and movements.
4. Provides means of interesting non-advertising merchants in using space.
5. Is a good promotion of community's progress.
6. Presents the newspaper as an instrument of enterprise and progress.

Disadvantages

1. Usually too bulky to receive thorough reading by regular subscribers.
2. May cause overselling of advertising and thereby reduce space in regular issues.
3. May cause advertisers to think that the primary purpose is to "bait" them for useless advertising.
4. Costly to produce because of overtime hours of labor.
5. Consumes newsprint that may be needed for regular issues.
6. Extra time required for special issues causes neglect of regular issues.

AMERICAN ASSOCIATION FOR STATE AND LOCAL HISTORY
First Award Of Merit, 1958

AUDRAIN COUNTY COUNCIL OF CHURCHES
"For Outstanding Public Services To The Churches Of Audrain County, 1952"

MEXICO CHAMBER OF COMMERCE
OUTSTANDING ACHIEVEMENT AWARD, 1952
For "Bringing Honor and Distinction To Our Community"

Mexico Evening Ledger

A. B. C. | LEDGER NEWSPAPERS, INC. | A. P. — U. P. I.

PHONE JU 1-1111

L. M. WHITE,
R. M. WHITE, II,
Co-Editors and Publishers

WILLIAM HAAS, Business Manager
JAMES E. STERNER, Managing Editor
VERNON DUFFY, Circulation Manager

Mexico, Missouri

SIGMA DELTA CHI
DISTINGUISHED SERVICE AWARD
For Editorials, 1952

•

NATIONAL BETTER NEWSPAPERS CONTEST (NEA)
COMMUNITY SERVICE
First Place, 1949
BEST EDITORIAL
Third Place, 1959
Third Place, 1957
Second Place, 1949
Second Place, 1948
HERRICK EDITORIAL AWARD
Honorable Mention, 1956
Third Place, 1949
GENERAL EXCELLENCE
Honorable Mention, 1954
Honorable Mention, 1946
TYPOGRAPHICAL EXCELLENCE
Honorable Mention, 1958
Honorable Mention, 1956
Honorable Mention, 1954
Honorable Mention, 1946

•

N. W. AYER & SON
(F. WAYLAND AYER CUP)
TYPOGRAPHICAL EXCELLENCE
Finalist, 1950

•

FREEDOMS FOUNDATION
EDITORIAL DIVISION
Award, 1949

•

NATIONAL SAFETY COUNCIL
Public Interest Award, 1949

•

NATIONAL COUNCIL OF FARMER COOPERATIVES CONTEST
SPECIAL EDITION
Second Place, 1947

•

INLAND DAILY PRESS ASS'N
WILLIAM ALLEN WHITE AWARD
PUBLIC RELATIONS
First Place, 1953
First Place, 1952
First Place, 1950
TYPOGRAPHICAL EXCELLENCE
Third Place, 1955
Honorable Mention, 1949
Second Place, 1947
LOCAL NEWS COVERAGE
First Place, 1958
Third Place, 1956
Third Place, 1955
First Place, 1953
First Place, 1951
Third Place, 1950
Third Place, 1948
FEATURE PICTURES
Honorable Mention, 1951
Second Place, 1951

•

MISSOURI PRESS ASS'N
GENERAL EXCELLENCE
Honorable Mention, 1959
First Place, 1958
Honorable Mention, 1957
Honorable Mention, 1956
First Place, 1953
Third Place, 1951
First Place, 1950
Honorable Mention, 1949
BEST EDITORIAL WRITER, 1952
BEST FRONT PAGE
First Place, 1952
TYPOGRAPHICAL IMPROVEMENT
First Place, 1954
BEST FARM COVERAGE
Honorable Mention, 1957
First Place, 1956
Honorable Mention, 1954
BEST EDITORIALS
Honorable Mention, 1959
Second Place, 1958
Second Place, 1957
Second Place, 1956
Second Place, 1954
BEST LOCAL PICTURES
Honorable Mention (2), 1955
Honorable Mention, 1954
SPORTS PICTURE
Second Place, 1951

•

MISSOURI AP
BEST FEATURE STORY
Honorable Mention, 1951

March 19, 1959

Mr. Frank W. Rucker
School of Journalism
University of Missouri
Columbia, Missouri

Dear Frank,

Enclosed is a picture of most of our awards, a picture of the front, and a blue promotion piece reproducing the "Believe It or Not" illustration of our front. In the blue promotion piece, please notice the quote from Printing News, London, England, at the bottom of Page 2.

If we can be of any further help, please let us know.

With warmest personal regards, I am

Sincerely,

Robert M. White II

RMW/bd
ENC/3

P.S. The list of awards on this letterhead is up to date. When we receive an award -- for example typography -- we do a front page piece about the honor to the Ledger and Mexico, and specifically list by name those staff members who participated.

THE SADDLE HORSE AND FIRE CLAY CENTER OF THE WORLD

Fig. 28.1 — The Mexico, Mo., **Ledger** lists on its letterhead its many awards for publishing excellence.

CHAPTER 28

Recognition Through Contest Awards

MANY AWARDS ARE OFFERED to newspapers and newspapermen by press associations, foundations, educational institutions and business and eleemosynary organizations to stimulate greater efficiency in journalistic work and to broaden newspaper service. This form of promotion is carried on extensively and gains wide participation.

The awards take various forms. They may be no more than a handsomely printed or engraved certificate of merit or as much as several thousand dollars. No matter whether the token of appreciation is large or small, it brings recognition to the recipient and establishes him as above average in successfully meeting competition or in serving his community and his profession.

Press Associations Conduct Contests

Many national, area and state associations of editors and publishers conduct friendly competition between member newspapers in maintaining high standards of excellence in their various departments and services.

Trophies, plaques, certificates of merit or cash awards are given annually by press associations for good local stories, excellent news coverage, intelligent use of correspondents' material, outstanding community service, attractive typographical makeup and effective advertising copy — in fact, for all the features and services connected with a first-class newspaper. As a press association secretary explains, "The awards are set up to encourage individual aspects of newspapering which, when put together, come close to making a newspaperman's newspaper."

Fig. 28.2 — The Mexico, Mo., **Ledger** displays its many certificates of contest awards on office walls where they are in constant view of employees and customers.

Such contests in many instances have caused publishers to analyze more carefully the service they are giving and to widen its scope. One press association credits its annual competitions with tripling, within that state, the number of editors that write their own columns and the number of newspapers that have full-fledged editorial pages. Staff members as well as publishers are brought to a higher appreciation of their newspapers and a greater sense of responsibility. Each wants the newspaper for whom he works to be a winner. When special attention is given to making the newspaper continuously better, a publisher may win top honors in many contests.

Publishers Proudly Display Winnings

Many offices of editors and publishers are decorated with certificates of merit, trophy cups, ribbons and other tokens their newspapers have won. The Mexico, Mo., *Evening Ledger* (circulation 8,426, population 11,623) lists contest winnings — 58 in all — on the newspaper's letterhead (see Fig. 28.1) so that all persons receiving correspondence from staff members know that they are producing a prize-winning newspaper. This is promotion of a high order. The *Ledger* also has one wall of its newspaper plant entirely covered with tokens of its winnings (see Fig. 28.2). They are in plain view of all persons who enter the office to do business and are constantly before employees. This creates in all of them a sense of pride in the newspaper that represents their community.

"When he dims his lights, I'll dim mine."

P.S. Both claimed a victory — Death claimed their lives.

Fig. 28.3 — The Oklahoma Natural Gas Company cooperates with the Oklahoma Press Association in sponsoring an editorial-writing contest.

McCLELLAN VAN DER VEER
Editor of The Birmingham News

Freedoms Foundation Honors

McClellan Van Der Veer, Editor of The Birmingham News

for the most outstanding newspaper editorial on the subject of FREEDOM in 1958.

The Birmingham News congratulates Mr. Van Der Veer on winning Freedoms Foundation's top national award for editorial w r i t i n g. We proudly reprint e x c e r p t s from his July 4th editorial.

Not only on July 4th, but day in and day out, The Birmingham News strives, in its news and editorial columns and in every other way, to strengthen American freedoms.

Mr. Van Der Veer exemplifies many of the finest ideals of his own newspaper colleagues and American newspaper people everywhere.

"How Well Are We As A People Meeting the Demands of Freedom?"

"For a nation or an individual a declaration of independence can be a basically important act, but freedom is never a fixed and completely achieved reality for men. It is something that must be constantly guarded and achieved over and over again. It is an ever rising goal. No human being is wholly free . . .

"We have many great liberties—political, social, religious, economic—in this fortunate country. We are free from tyranny. We are free from many practices and conditions that have limited men in other times, that now limit them in other lands. But as individuals we are not free from human weaknesses of many sorts, weaknesses often causing us to fall short of the standards of conduct and achievement we would like to exemplify constantly.

"How free are we from the domination of: Self-seeking that limits our growth in freedom? Apathy and indifference as to the fundamentals of justice and integrity upon which freedom must depend? Cynicism that testifies to grave lack of faith in men essential to democracy, to real liberty? The fears, hatreds, intolerance that . . . undermine the freedom of a nation as well as the freedom of an individual?"

The Birmingham News   Birmingham Post-Herald

MORNING • EVENING • SUNDAY

KELLY-SMITH NATIONAL REPRESENTATIVES

Fig. 28.4 — Freedoms Foundation honors are basis of promotion by Birmingham, Ala., **News** and **Post-Herald** in **Editor & Publisher.**

"When we receive an award," says Robert M. White II, co-publisher, "we do a front-page piece about the honor to the *Ledger* and to Mexico, and specifically list by name those staff members who participated. In the case of typography, it would list the advertising manager for drawing up the page dummies, the managing editor for completing the page dummies to include the news makeup and picture and feature layout, the punch operators, monitors, straight-matter operators, ad machine people, etc., throughout the mechanical department — citing the role played by each. Obviously, our target is to show the community and each member their individual importance to the paper.

"I believe strongly that awards have something to do with staff morale," White adds. "I also think they offer a test for a monopoly newspaper, a test it cannot receive in any other way. I say this in full recognition of the varying opinions of varying judges at varying times. And then, of course, there is the obvious prestige that comes to the community when its newspaper wins awards. While I list this last, I consider it nevertheless an important asset."

What Constitutes General Excellence?

Occasionally an editor "blows his top" because he didn't win an award he thought he deserved. Again, some newspapers that win a prize in editorial writing, news coverage or even for general excellence may prove later to be financial failures.

Elmer E. White, manager of the Michigan Press Association, believes that no general excellence award should be given unless the newspaper submits a profit and loss statement. "For what doth it profit a publisher," he adds, "if he winneth all possible contests and loseth his newspaper for lack of making sound business decisions?"

William M. Long, manager of the Colorado Press Association, says that his officers and board members have observed that contests not sponsored by the press association have a little more of the aspect of spontaneity and for this reason may be a little more significant. "In other words," he adds, "there is no aspect of appearing that we are banded together to honor ourselves or each other."

The Colorado Press Association, however, sponsors contests in many categories and Colorado publishers compete heartily.

Awards for Special Writing

Business institutions often collaborate with press associations in granting awards (see Fig. 28.3). Professional organizations and eleemosynary groups that foster services contributing particularly to better health, greater safety on the highways, better understanding of civil rights and more friendly relations between nations also believe that newspapers and newspapermen who give valid service to such worthy causes are deserving of recognition and reward.

Important in this category are the awards made by the National Safety Council and the American Trucking Association for news coverage and editorial comment that may lessen the increasing loss of life on highways; the Albert Lasker Medical Journalism Award for outstanding reporting on medical research and public health; the Howard W. Blakeslee Award offered by the American Heart Association for distinguished reporting of advances in the field of heart and blood vessel disorders; the English-speaking Union Awards in recognition of continuing effort to achieve better understanding between the people of the United States and those of the British Commonwealth of Nations; the National Conference of Christians and Jews Award for helping to develop greater understanding among all Americans in order to offset hate and prejudice; the William the Silent Award for furthering Dutch-United States understanding; and the Maria Cabot Awards for advancement of international friendship in the Americas.

Foundation Awards Have Strong Appeal

Some of the most coveted newspaper awards are not offered by press associations or business organizations, but by foundations established to encourage excellence in journalism. The award usually is of greater value, draws competition from a wider area and requires of the winner greater knowledge and ability. Consequently, considerable distinction is accorded the newspaper or the newspaperman who is honored.

The most outstanding of these awards are the Pulitzer Prizes, which honor the late Joseph Pulitzer. Administered annually through Columbia University, they recognize meritorious public service, distinguished editorial writing, correspondence, cartooning, photography and reporting.

Other prominent awards in this category are the Ayer Cup Awards, sponsored by N. W. Ayer & Son, Inc., to spotlight fine work in newspaper typography, makeup and printing, and to stimulate interest in improving the appearance and readability of newspapers; the Sigma Delta Chi Awards, which give recognition to outstanding service in all branches of carrying the news to the public; the *Editor & Publisher* Awards for excellence in newspaper promotion; the Raymond Clapper Memorial Award created to inspire Washington newspapermen to emulate the high ideals exemplified by Clapper in his profession; the Heywood Broun Memorial Award by the American Newspaper Guild; the Ernie Pyle Prize given by the Scripps-Howard Ernie Pyle Foundation for gentleness and understanding in feature stories about people; Freedoms Foundation Awards for a better un-

*five first-place
awards won by
The Miami News...
the largest number of
firsts ever won by
any Florida newspaper*

*The awards won by members of The Miami News
staff included first in "Human Interest
Stories"; first in "Feature Stories"; first
in "Sports Pictures"; first in "Feature
Pictures"; first in "Sports Features".*

*Never before in the history of the annual
awards granted by The Associated Press of
Florida and The Florida Daily Newspaper
Association has one newspaper won so many
first prizes.*

*Far more important than pride in this achievement
is the satisfaction of results obtained from constant
appraisal and a flexibility of mind that permits
swift changes to bring a freshness and a new
readability to an already good newspaper.
To the dimensions of length, breadth and
thickness, we add and emphasize the
dimensions of quality.*

THE MIAMI NEWS
"The Best Newspaper Under The Sun"

COX NEWSPAPERS

THE MIAMI NEWS • THE ATLANTA JOURNAL • THE ATLANTA CONSTITUTION • DAYTON DAILY NEWS • DAYTON JOURNAL HERALD • SPRINGFIELD DAILY NEWS & THE SUN

Fig. 28.5 — Five first place awards won by Miami, Fla., **News** are featured in promotion
advertisement in **Editor & Publisher**.

Take A Good Look
at the

New UTICA!

Fig. 28.6 — The Pulitzer medal for Meritorious Public Service is basis of promotion advertisement for Utica, N.Y., **Press** and **Observer-Dispatch** in **Editor & Publisher.**

derstanding of the American way of life (see Fig. 28.4); and the Overseas Press Club Awards for outstanding reporting from abroad.

Still other awards provide for special study in order that talented young people may be more fully trained for the responsibilities of journalism. Prominent among these are the Nieman Fellowships, the Julius Ochs Adler Memorial Scholarship, and the Gilbert M. Hitchcock Scholarship.

Journalism Schools Recognize Achievement

An interest in newspaper improvements and higher professional standards is further stimulated through contests and special awards sponsored by schools and departments of journalism.

Most schools of journalism cooperate with their state press associations in the setting up of contests and in judging the entries. In many instances they provide trophies. It is the custom of some schools to give annual recognition to men and women of the profession and newspapers whose services have been exceptionally worthy.

ANNUAL NEWSPAPER AWARDS

A vast number of awards are offered annually to men and women of the press and their newspapers in recognition of general excellence within the profession. Winners of these awards find them to be excellent basic material for effective promotion (see Figs. 28.5 and 28.6). New awards are being offered each year in every journalistic endeavor. So even greater opportunities exist than can be indicated by the more than 500 diversified offers listed on the following pages.

It is possible for a good entry to win more than one award. Classification has been arranged to aid in finding all awards for which an entry may be eligible, with addresses to which the entry is to be mailed. Awards listed on pages 428 to 437 are open to any newspaper published in the United States; pages 438 and 439 list awards available only to members of the Inland Daily Press Association; pages 439 to 466 list awards available only to newspapers within each state and Canada. Fellowships and scholarships are listed on page 467.

OPEN COMPETITION

ADVERTISING AND PROMOTION

Name	Classification	Award	Address
ABC Promotion Awards	Best promotion advertisement submitted by a publisher in each of its five member groups	*Plaques*	Audit Bureau of Circulation, 123 N. Wacker Drive, Chicago 6, Ill.
	Best entries in special promotion (brochures, pamphlets, presentation, etc.)	*Plaques*	
Arthur Kudner Awards	Excellence in creative writing for institutional advertising	*Bronze medal and $500*	Arthur Kudner Foundation, 575 Madison Ave., New York 22, N. Y.
Editor & Publisher Awards	Outstanding promotion in (1) National advertising promotion (2) Retail advertising promotion (3) Circulation promotion (4) Classified advertising promotion (5) Public relations (6) Research	*Plaques and certificates*	Editor & Publisher, 1700 Times Tower, 1475 Broadway, New York 36, N. Y.
National Editorial Association Awards	Best advertising idea or promotion	*Plaque*	National Editorial Association, 1025 Connecticut Ave., NW, Washington 6, D.C.
	Best classified advertising sections (1) Newspapers with circulation over 4,000 (2) Newspapers with circulation of 4,000 and less	*Plaques*	
	Most comprehensive promotion program	*Plaque*	

CARTOONING

Name	Classification	Award	Address
Freedoms Foundation Awards	Best cartoons promoting understanding of the American way of life	*$1,000, $50, and George Washington Honor medal*	Freedoms Foundation, Valley Forge, Pa.
National Safety Council Award	Newspaper cartoonist creating cartoon most effective in curbing the Christmas holiday traffic accident toll	*$300 to cartoonist and plaque to newspaper*	National Safety Council, 425 N. Michigan Ave., Chicago 11, Ill.
Pulitzer Award	Distinguished example of a cartoonist's work published in American newspaper during the year; determining qualities being that the cartoon shall embody an idea made clearly apparent, shall show good drawing and striking pictorial effect, and shall be intended to be helpful to some commendable cause of public importance—due account being taken of the whole volume of the artist's newspaper work during the year	*$1,000*	Advisory Board on Pulitzer Prizes, Columbia University, New York 27, N. Y.
Sigma Delta Chi Award	Excellence in editorial cartooning	*Medallion*	Sigma Delta Chi, 35 E. Wacker Drive, Chicago 1, Ill.

COLUMN WRITING

Name	Classification	Award	Address
National Editorial Association Awards	Excellence in column writing (1) On single topic (2) On variety of topics	*Plaques*	National Editorial Association, 1025 Connecticut Ave., NW, Washington 6, D. C.
National Headliners' Award	Outstanding newspaper column	*Silver medallion*	Mall Dodson, Exec. Secy., National Headliners' Club, Convention Hall, Atlantic City, N. J.

COMMERCIAL PRINTING

National Editorial Association Award	Best job printing exhibit	*Plaque*	National Editorial Association, 1025 Connecticut Ave., NW, Washington 6, D. C.

EDITORIAL WRITING

ABC Promotion Award	Best promotion editorial submitted by publisher	*Plaque*	Audit Bureau of Circulations, 123 N. Wacker Drive, Chicago 6, Ill.
American Trucking Association Safety Awards	Best editorials on safety	*$500, $300, and $100*	American Trucking Association, Inc., 1424 16th St., NW, Washington 6, D. C.
Freedoms Foundation Awards	Outstanding editorial on freedom	*$1,000, $50, and George Washington Honor medal*	Freedoms Foundation, Valley Forge, Pa.
Herrick Editorial Award	Newspaper with best editorials	*Plaque*	National Editorial Association, 1025 Connecticut Ave., NW, Washington 6, D. C.
National Editorial Association Award	Best editorial Open to American weeklies	*Plaque*	
Pulitzer Award	Distinguished editorial writing during the year, limited to the editorial page; test of excellence being clearness of style, moral purpose, sound reasoning, and power to influence public opinion in what the writer conceives to be the right direction—due account being taken of the whole volume of the writer's editorial work during the year	*$1,000*	Advisory Board on Pulitzer Prizes, Columbia University, New York 27, N. Y.

FEATURE WRITING

Name	Classification	Award	Address
National Editorial Association Awards	Best feature story (1) Newspapers with circulation of 2,000 and over (2) Newspapers with circulation of less than 2,000	*Plaques*	National Editorial Association, 1025 Connecticut Ave., NW, Washington 6, D. C.
National Headliners' Awards	Outstanding feature series	*Silver medallion*	Mall Dodson, Exec. Secy., National Headliners'
	Generally excellent feature writing by an individual with newspaper or syndicate	*Silver medallion*	Club, Convention Hall, Atlantic City, N. J.
	Reporter-photographer for general excellence in feature writing and photography	*Silver medallion*	

NEWSPAPER EXCELLENCE

National Editorial Association Awards	General excellence (1) Weeklies with circulation less than 1,000 (2) Weeklies with circulation from 1,000 to 2,500 (3) Weeklies with circulation from 2,500 to 6,000 (4) Weeklies with circulation over 6,000 (5) Daily newspapers	*Plaques*	National Editorial Association, 1025 Connecticut Ave., NW, Washington 6, D. C.

PHOTOGRAPHY

Associated Press Awards	Excellence in photography (1) Newspapers published in cities above 200,000 population (2) Newspapers published in cities of 200,000 population or less	*Cash prizes for both photographers and newspapers*	Associated Press Bureaus of each area
Cigar Institute Awards	Best published photos in which man is shown smoking a cigar with enjoyment and relaxation	*$500, $250, $100, and $25*	Cigar Institute of America, 1270 6th Ave., New York 20, N. Y.
Freedoms Foundation Awards	Best photographs promoting understanding of the American way of life	*$1,000, $50, and George Washington Honor medal*	Freedoms Foundation, Valley Forge, Pa.
Jimmy Hare Awards Sponsored by University of Missouri School of Journalism, Encyclopedia Britannica and National Press Photographers Association	Best newspaper portfolio and other categories in International Picture Competition and Exhibition	*Prizes and certificates*	School of Journalism, University of Missouri, Columbia, Mo.

Name	Classification	Award	Address
Look Magazine Awards	Press photographer for quality photography and reporting in the field of sports	*$250 and $100*	Look Magazine, 488 Madison Ave., New York 22, N. Y.
National Editorial Association Awards	Best feature picture	*Plaque*	National Editorial Association, 1025 Connecticut Ave., NW, Washington 6, D. C.
	Best news picture	*Plaque*	
	Best use of photographs (1) Newspapers with circulation over 2,000 (2) Newspapers with circulation of 2,000 and under	*Plaques*	
National Headliners' Awards	Outstanding feature picture	*Silver medallion*	Mall Dodson, Exec. Secy., National Headliners' Club, Convention Hall, Atlantic City, N. J
	Best sports action picture	*Silver medallion*	
	Best spot-news picture	*Silver medallion*	
Newspaper Picture of the Year Award Sponsored by National Press Photographers Association, Encyclopedia Britannica and University of Missouri School of Journalism	Best picture of the year	*$500*	Encyclopedia Britannica, 425 N. Michigan Ave., Chicago 11, Ill.
Overseas Press Association Award	Outstanding photographic reporting from abroad	*Citation*	Overseas Press Club, Inc., 35 E. 39th St., New York 16, N. Y.
Pulitzer Award	Outstanding example of news photography in daily newspaper. Open to amateurs and photographers regularly employed by newspapers, press associations or syndicates	*$7,000*	Advisory Board on Pulitzer Prizes, Columbia University, New York 27, N. Y.
Robert Capra Award	Photography requiring exceptional courage and enterprise abroad	*Plaque and gold medal*	Overseas Press Club, Inc., 35 E. 39th St., New York 16, N. Y.
Sigma Delta Chi Award	Outstanding news picture	*Medallion*	Sigma Delta Chi, 35 East Wacker Dr., Chicago 1, Ill.
Trans World Airline Awards	Best pictures pertaining to transworld air travel (1) Newspapers with circulation over 75,000 (2) Newspapers with circulation of 75,000 or less (3) Sunday newspapers and magazines	*$100 and plaque*	Trans World Airlines, Inc., 380 Madison Ave., New York 17, N. Y.
	Best travel photo	*$100 and plaque*	

PUBLIC SERVICE

Name	Classification	Award	Address
Maria Moors Cabot Awards	Advancement of international friendship in the Americas	*Gold medal to writer, plaque to newspaper*	Graduate School of Journalism, Columbia University, New York 27, N. Y.
National Editorial Association Awards	Outstanding service to agriculture (1) Newspapers with circulation over 2,000 (2) Newspapers with circulation of 2,000 or less	*Plaques*	National Editorial Association, 1025 Connecticut Ave., NW, Washington 6, D.C.
	Newspaper giving outstanding community service	*Plaque*	
	Best service to small newspaper industry	*Plaque*	
National Headliners' Award	Outstanding public service	*Silver medallion*	Mall Dodson, Exec. Secy., National Headliners' Club, Convention Hall, Atlantic City, N. J.
Pulitzer Award	Most distinguished and meritorious service rendered by an American newspaper during the year	*Gold medal*	Advisory Board on Pulitzer Prizes, Columbia University, New York 27, N. Y.
Sigma Delta Chi Awards	Newspaper for important public service in which exceptional courage or initiative is displayed	*Plaque*	Sigma Delta Chi, 35 E. Wacker Dr., Chicago 1, Ill.
	Outstanding public service	*Medallion*	

REPORTING

Name	Classification	Award	Address
Agricultural Writers Awards	Outstanding reporting on agriculture	*$1,000, $500, $250, $100, Silver plaques, and scrolls*	United Farm Agency, Inc., 2825 Main St., Kansas City, Mo.
Albert Lasker Medical Journalism Awards	Outstanding reporting on medical research and public health	*$2,500, scroll, and statuette of Winged Victory of Samothrace*	Albert and Mary Lasker Foundation, Chrysler Bldg., New York 17, N. Y.
George Polk Memorial Award	Best reporting requiring exceptional courage and enterprise abroad	*$500 and plaque*	Overseas Press Club of America, Inc., 35 E. 39th St., New York 16, N. Y.
Heywood Broun Memorial Award	Outstanding news reporting	*$500*	American Newspaper Guild, Philip Murray Bldg., 1126 16th St., NW, Washington 6, D. C.

Name	Classification	Award	Address
National Editorial Association Awards	Best news story (1) Newspapers with circulation over 2,000 (2) Newspapers with circulation of 2,000 or under	*Plaques*	National Editorial Association, 1025 Connecticut Ave., NW, Washington 6, D. C.
National Headliners' Award	Newspapers for consistently comprehensive coverage of local, national and foreign affairs	*Trophy*	Mall Dodson, Exec. Secy., National Headliners' Club, Convention Hall, Atlantic City, N. J.
Overseas Press Club Award	Outstanding press reporting from abroad	*Citation*	Overseas Press Club of America, Inc., 35 East 39th St., New York 16, N. Y.
Pulitzer Awards	Distinguished example of newspaper reporting	*$1,000*	Graduate School of Journalism, Columbia University, New York 27, N. Y.
Sigma Delta Chi Award	Excellence in general reporting	*Medallion*	Sigma Delta Chi, 35 East Wacker Dr., Chicago 1, Ill.

SPECIAL ISSUE, PAGE OR SECTION

Name	Classification	Award	Address
National Editorial Association Awards	Best special issue (1) Newspapers with circulation under 2,000 (2) Newspapers with circulation of 2,000 or more	*Plaques*	National Editorial Association, 1025 Connecticut Ave., NW, Washington 6, D. C.
National Real Estate Editors Awards	Best realty page or section	*$50*	National Association of Real Estate Editors, 1420 E. 9th St., Cleveland 14, Ohio
	Best home page or section	*$50*	

SPECIAL WRITING

Name	Classification	Award	Address
Albert Lasker Awards	Best article or series of articles dealing with the improvement of public health and medical research	*$2,500, silver statuette of Winged Victory of Samothrace, and scroll*	Albert and Mary Lasker Foundation, Chrysler Bldg., New York 17, N. Y.
ASTA Awards	In recognition of outstanding farm and garden writers	*Trophies*	American Seed Trade Association, 30 N. La Salle St., Chicago, Ill.

Special Writing *(Continued)*

Name	Classification	Award	Address
Catherine L. O'Brien Awards	Outstanding achievement in women's interests reporting	*$1,000, $300, and $200*	Catherine L. O'Brien Awards, Room 800, 130 E. 59th St., New York 32, N. Y.
Community Facility Newspaper Awards	Outstanding articles on community problems	*$1,000 and $500*	National Association of Home Builders, 140 S. Dearborn St., Chicago, Ill.
Cradle of America Tour Awards	Top two published articles which seek to encourage travel to Washington, D.C., and adjacent historic area	*Plaques*	J. W. Marriott Awards Committee, 1917 Eye St., NW, Washington 6, D. C.
Education Writers Awards	Outstanding education reporting	*Bronze plaques and certificates*	Education Writers Association, 525 West 120th St., New York 27, N. Y.
Empire State Awards	Excellence in medical reporting in newspapers published 5 or more times a week	*$500 and certificate*	Medical Society of the State of New York, 386 4th Ave., New York, N. Y.
English-Speaking Union Awards	In recognition of sincere and continuing effort to achieve better understanding between the people of the United States and those of the British Commonwealth of Nations	*Awards and citations*	English-Speaking Union of the United States, 16 E. 69th St., New York 21, N. Y.
Ernie Pyle Memorial Awards	Young men whose writing and reporting are judged "most nearly exemplifying the style and craftsmanship" of Ernie Pyle, World War II reporter and human interest columnist noted for his gentleness and understanding	*$1,000 and bronze plaque*	Scripps-Howard Newspapers, 230 Park Ave., New York, N. Y.
Howard L. Blakeslee Awards	Distinguished reporting of advances in the field of heart and blood vessel disorders	*$500 honorariums*	American Heart Association, 44 E. 23rd St., New York, N. Y.
Highway Safety Award	Special writing for encouragement of safety on highways	*$100*	National Foundation for Highway Safety, 425 N. Michigan Ave., Chicago 11, Ill.
Institute of Architects Awards	Outstanding news stories on architecture	*$500, $250, and certificates*	American Institute of Architects, 115 E. 40th St., New York, N. Y.
James J. Strebig Memorial Award	Outstanding reporting in the field of aviation	*Bronze plaque*	Aviation Writers Association, 600 York Rd. Jenkintown, Pa.

Name	Classification	Award	Address
James O. Supple Awards	Excellence in reporting the news of religion in the secular press	*$100 and certificate*	Religious Newswriters Association, c/o Richard Philbrock, Religious Editor, Chicago *Tribune*, 435 N. Michigan Ave., Chicago 11, Ill.
James T. Grady Awards	Important contribution to the American public's knowledge of chemical progress	*Gold medal and certificate*	American Chemical Society, 1155 16th St., NW, Washington 6, D. C.
Loeb Awards	Outstanding financial reporting and column writing	*$1,000 and bronze plaque*	Loeb Awards Advisory Board, University of Connecticut, Storrs, Conn.
Maria Moors Cabot Awards	Given annually to journalists for achievement "in advancement of international friendship in the Americas"	*Gold medal*	Graduate School of Journalism, Columbia University, New York 27, N. Y.
National Conference of Christians and Jews Award	In recognition of contributions to public service by helping to develop greater understanding among all Americans to offset hate and prejudice	*Plaque*	National Conference of Christians and and Jews, 43 W. 57th St., New York, N. Y.
National Real Estate Editors Award	Best realty news feature	*$50*	National Association of Real Estate Editors, 1420 E. 9th St., Cleveland 14, Ohio
National Safety Council Award	Exceptional service to safety	*Plaque*	National Safety Council, 425 N. Michigan Ave., Chicago 11, Ill.
Osteopathic Association Award	Outstanding news story pertaining to osteopathy	*$100*	American Osteopathic Association, 212 E. Ohio St., Chicago 11, Ill.
Overseas Press Club Award	Best interpretation of foreign affairs	*$500*	Overseas Press Club of America, Inc., 35 E. 39th St., New York 16, N. Y.
Russell L. Cecil Award	Excellence in science writing in the field of rheumatic diseases	*$500 honorarium*	Arthritis and Rheumatism Foundation, 10 Columbus Circle, New York 19, N. Y.

Special Writing *(continued)*

Name	Classification	Award	Address
Safety Story Awards	Best series of stories on safety	*$500, $300, $100*	American Trucking Association, Inc., 1424 16th St., NW, Washington 6, D.C
	Best single story on safety	*$500, $300, $100*	
Sidney Hillman Foundation Awards	Work on themes relating to civil liberties, representing government, trade union development and similar issues	*$500*	Sidney Hillman Foundation, 15 Union Square West, New York 3, N. Y.
Strebig-Dobbin Memorial Awards	Person or publication whose story or series of stories has contributed most to public understanding of commercial aviation	*$250, plaque, and a trophy which rotates among annual winners*	Trans World Airlines, Inc., 380 Madison Ave., New York 17, N. Y.
Ted V. Rogers Award	Article that contributes most to the improvement of American highways and their use	*$500 to school of journalism designated by winner*	American Trucking Association, Inc., 1424 16th St., NW, Washington 6, D.C.
Trans World Airlines Awards	Best news story dealing with commercial aviation or air travel	*$100 and trophy*	Trans World Airlines, Inc., 380 Madison Ave., New York 17, N. Y.

SPORTS WRITING

Name	Classification	Award	Address
Dutton Awards	Best news coverage of sports	*$250*	E. P. Dutton Co., 300 4th Ave., New York 10, N. Y.
	Best sports feature story	*$250*	
	Best sports column	*$250*	
Grantland Rice Memorial Award	Outstanding example of sports reporting in the Rice tradition	*Plaque*	Sportsmanship Brotherhood, 119 E. 19th St., New York, N. Y.

TYPOGRAPHY

Name	Classification	Award	Address
National Editorial Association Awards	Excellence in typography (1) Weeklies with circulation under 2,000 (2) Weeklies with circulation from 2,000 to 6,000 (3) Weeklies with circulation over 6,000 (4) Dailies	*Plaques*	National Editorial Association, 1025 Connecticut Ave., NW, Washington 6, D.C.

Name	Classification	Award	Address
N. W. Ayer & Son, Inc., Awards	Excellence in typography, makeup and printing (1) All newspapers (2) Newspapers with more than 50,000 circulation (3) Newspapers with circulation from 10,000 to 50,000 (4) Newspapers with less than 10,000 circulation (5) Tabloid newspapers	*Ayer Cup to winner in class 1, Honorable Mention certificates to winners in other classes*	N. W. Ayer & Son, Inc., 30 Rockefeller Plaza, New York 20, N. Y.

WRITING BY CORRESPONDENTS

Name	Classification	Award	Address
National Headliners' Award	Outstanding coverage of a major foreign news story	*Silver medallion*	Mall Dodson, Exec. Secy., National Headliners' Club, Convention Hall, Atlantic City, N.J.
Pulitzer Award	Distinguished correspondence, test being clearness and terseness of style, well-balanced and well-informed interpretative writing which shall make clear the subject covered in the correspondence or which shall promote international understanding and appreciation	*$500*	Advisory Board on Pulitzer Prizes, Columbia University, New York 27, N. Y.
Raymond Clapper Memorial Awards	To inspire Washington correspondents to emulate the high ideals exemplified by Clapper	*Scroll and $500*	Raymond Clapper Memorial Association, c/o Philip L. Graham, Pres., Washington *Post*, 1515 L St., Washington 5, D. C.
Sigma Delta Chi Awards	Distinguished example of foreign correspondent's work	*Citation*	Sigma Delta Chi, 35 E. Wacker Dr., Chicago 1, Ill.
	Distinguished example of Washington correspondent's work	*Citation*	
William the Silent Award by Prince Bernhard of the Netherlands	Correspondent judged to have done the most to further Dutch-United States understanding	*Trophy*	William the Silent Award, 50 Rockefeller Plaza, New York 20, N. Y.

RESTRICTED COMPETITION

OPEN ONLY TO MEMBERS OF THE
INLAND DAILY PRESS ASSOCIATION
(as noted by each heading)

The Inland Daily Press Association is an organization of newspapers in twenty or more states located generally in central United States. Five schools of journalism in this territory are co-sponsors with IDPA in granting six awards. In each case the school sets up the rules governing the contest, provides the awards, and does the judging. Any member of the association is eligible for an award, regardless of the location of the school sponsoring the award.

Name	Classification	Award	Address
Community Service Award	Newspaper for outstanding service to community	*Trophy*	School of Journalism, University of Missouri, Columbia, Mo.
Distinguished Service Awards	Newspaper editor for notable service to his community, state and nation	*Bronze medal and a certificate*	School of Journalism, University of Minnesota, Minneapolis, Minn.
Local Government News Awards	Newspaper for thoroughness and variety in local reporting of governmental affairs, including city, county and federal activities (1) Newspapers with circulation up to 5,000 (2) Newspapers with circulation from 5,000 to 10,000 (3) Newspapers with circulation from 10,000 to 25,000 (4) Newspapers with circulation from 25,000 to 75,000 (5) Newspapers with circulation over 75,000	*Certificates*	School of Journalism, University of Wisconsin, Madison, Wis.
News Picture Awards	Best color prints or transparencies	*Trophy*	Medill School of Journalism, Northwestern University, Evanston, Ill.
	Best feature photograph (1) Staff photographers on newspapers with 50,000 circulation or more (2) Staff photographers on newspapers with circulation less than 50,000 (3) Reporter-photographers or photographer-engravers whose photographic work is combined with other work on the newspaper	*Trophy and engraved certificates*	
	Best picture series Same classes as above	*Trophy and engraved certificates*	
	Best spot-news photographs Same classes as above	*Trophy and engraved certificates*	
	Best sports photographs Same classes as above	*Trophy and engraved certificates*	

Name	Classification	Award	Address
Public Relations Awards	Newspaper which has done the best public relations work in its own behalf	*Certificate*	William Allen White School of Journalism and Public Information, University of Kansas, Lawrence, Kans.
Typography Award	Outstanding newspaper typography (1) Newspapers printed on flat-bed press (2) Newspapers with circulation less than 10,000 and printed on rotary press (3) Newspapers with circulation from 10,000 to 25,000 (4) Newspapers with circulation from 25,000 to 75,000 (5) Newspapers with circulation over 75,000	*Plaques*	Medill School of Journalism, Northwestern University, Evanston, Ill.

Open Only to
NEWSPAPERS PUBLISHED WITHIN EACH STATE

ALABAMA

Alabama Press Association Awards	Best original column (1) Newspapers in cities over 3,500 population (2) Newspapers in cities 3,500 or less	*Plaques and certificates*	Alabama Press Association, P. O. Box 2008, University, Ala.
	Best editorials Same classes as above	*Plaques and certificates*	
	General excellence of newspaper Same classes as above	*Plaques and certificates*	
	Best use of illustrative material	*Plaque*	
	Best spot-news or sports photo	*Plaque*	
	Promoting and encouraging worthwhile community projects	*Plaque*	
	Best typography and makeup (1) Weeklies in cities over 3,500 population (2) Weeklies in towns 3,500 or less	*Plaques and certificates*	
University of Alabama Awards	Best news story (1) Newspapers in cities over 3,500 population (2) Newspapers in cities 3,500 or less	*Plaques and certificates*	"
	Greatest contribution in news and editorial content to promote general betterment in education Same classes as above	*Plaques and certificates*	

ARKANSAS

Name	Classification	Award	Address
Arkansas Press Association Awards	Best editorial aimed at promoting employment of handicapped	*$50 and $25*	Arkansas Press Association, 110 Stephens Bldg., Little Rock, Ark.
	General excellence in makeup and typography	*$600 in cash prizes, trophies and certificates*	
Bell Industrial Awards Sponsored by Southwest Bell Telephone Company and Arkansas Press Association	Excellence in promotion of area industry (1) Dailies (2) Weeklies	*Trophies*	"
Help the Physically Handicapped Award Sponsored by Employment Security Division, Little Rock Civitan Club and Arkansas Press Association	Best editorial aimed to aid in employment of physically handicapped	*$150*	"

CALIFORNIA

Name	Classification	Award	Address
California Newspaper Publishers Association Awards	Best newspaper promotion (1) Weeklies of 3,000 circulation or over (2) Weeklies under 3,000 circulation (3) Dailies over 100,000 circulation (4) Dailies of 10,000 to 100,000 circulation (5) Dailies under 10,000 circulation	*Trophies*	California Newspaper Publishers Association, 435 Holbrook Bldg., 58 Sutter St., San Francisco, Calif.
	Member newspapers with best editorial pages (1) Weeklies (2) Dailies	*Trophies and certificates*	
	General excellence of newspaper (1) Dailies with 7,000 circulation or over (2) Dailies with circulation under 7,000 (3) Weeklies with circulation of 3,000 or over (4) Weeklies with circulation under 3,000	*Trophies*	
	Best spot-news feature (1) Weeklies (2) Dailies	*Trophies*	
	Best travel page or section	*Trophy*	
	Best agricultural page, section, or coverage (1) Dailies (2) Weeklies	*Trophies*	

Name	Classification	Award	Address
	Best special edition (1) Dailies of 7,500 circulation or over (2) Dailies under 7,500 circulation (3) Weeklies of 3,000 circulation or over (4) Weeklies under 3,000 circulation	*Trophies*	
	Daily with best industrial or business page	*Trophy*	
	Best coverage of women's interests and activities (1) Dailies (2) Weeklies	*Trophies*	
	Best sports page or coverage (1) Dailies (2) Weeklies	*Trophies*	
	Best typography (1) Dailies with 7,500 circulation or more (2) Dailies with less than 7,500 circulation (3) Weeklies with circulation of 3,000 or more (4) Weeklies with circulation less than 3,000	*Trophies*	
	Outstanding community service	*Trophy and certificate*	California Newspaper Publishers Association, 809 Pacific Electric Bldg., Los Angeles 14, Calif.
Red Apple Awards	Meritorious service in California journalism Meritorious service in American journalism	*Membership in Order of the Red Apple and picture in the Gallery of Honor*	Department of Journalism, San Jose State College, San Jose, Calif.

CALIFORNIA - NEVADA

Name	Classification	Award	Address
California-Nevada Associated Press Awards	Outstanding feature story (1) Newspapers published in cities with population over 200,000 (2) Newspapers published in cities with population of 200,000 or less	*$50, $15, and $10*	Associated Press, Rincon Annex, P. O. Box 3554, San Francisco 19, Calif.
	Outstanding spot-news picture Same classes as above	*$50, $15, and $10*	
	Outstanding picture feature Same classes as above	*$50, $15, and $10*	
	Outstanding sports picture Same classes as above	*$50, $15, and $10*	
	Outstanding spot-news reporting Same classes as above	*$50, $15, and $10*	
	Excellence in sports writing Same classes as above	*$50, $15, and $10*	

CANADA

Name	Classification	Award	Address
Bowater Awards Sponsored by Bowater News- print Organiza- tion of Canada	Outstanding endeavors in research and writing to inspire high level of Canadian journalism (1) Social (2) Economic (3) International affairs	*$100 each*	Parliamentary Press Gallery, Ottawa, Ontario
	Excellence in economic and business reporting (1) On social, political and cultural subjects (2) On international and commonwealth affairs	*$1,000 in each class*	
Canadian National Newspaper Awards	Excellence in editorial writing	*$400 and certificate*	Toronto Men's Press Club, Box 309,
	Outstanding feature series	*$400 and certificate*	Postal Station A, Toronto, Ontario
	Excellence in feature photography	*$400 and certificate*	
	Excellence in spot-news photography	*$400 and certificate*	
	Outstanding spot-news reporting	*$400 and certificate*	
Canadian Weekly Newspapers Association Awards	Weekly with best editorial page	*Trophy*	Canadian Weekly Newspapers Association, 34 Front St., W. Toronto 1, Ontario
	Weekly with best local spot-news feature	*Trophy*	
	Weekly giving outstanding service to community	*Trophy*	
Charles Clark Award	Best all-round weekly with circulation between 1,000 and 2,000	*Cup*	"
Charters Award	Weekly with best Christmas edition	*Certificate*	"
David Bean Memorial Award	Weekly showing excellence in original or creative commercial printing	*Trophy*	"
David Williams Trophy	Best editorial page in weekly with circula- tion over 3,000	*Trophy*	"
George Legge Memorial Award	Weekly with general printing excellence	*Trophy*	"
Gertrude A. Dunning Memorial Award	Best all-round weekly with circulation of between 2,000 and 3,000	*Trophy*	"
John W. Eedy Memorial Award	Best editorial page in weekly with circula- tion of 1,000 or less	*Trophy*	"
Malcolm Macbeth Memorial Award	Best editorial page in weekly with circulation from 1,001 to 2,000	*Shield*	"

Name	Classification	Award	Address
Mason Award	Best all-round weekly with circulation over 3,000	*Trophy*	"
P. George Pierce Memorial Award	Best editorial page in weekly	*Trophy*	"
R. C. Smith Memorial Award	Best promotion campaign by weekly	*Trophy*	"
Walter Ashfield Memorial Award	Best all-round weekly with circulation of 10,000 or less	*Trophy*	"

COLORADO

Name	Classification	Award	Address
Adams State College Award	Colorado editor for outstanding service to education	*Certificate*	Journalism Department, Adams State College, Alimosa, Colo.
Colorado Press Association Awards	General newspaper excellence (1) Weeklies with circulation under 1,100 (2) Weeklies with circulation of 1,100 or over (3) Dailies with circulation under 4,000 (4) Dailies with circulation of 4,000 or over	*Trophies*	Colorado Press Association, 1445 Court Place, Denver 2, Colo.
	Excellence in photography (1) Weeklies and dailies with circulation under 30,000 without separate photography departments (2) Dailies with circulation of 30,000 and over, and where photography is by a special staff of photographers	*Trophies*	
	Outstanding service to agriculture (1) Weeklies with less than 1,000 circulation (2) Weeklies with circulation of 1,000 or over (3) Dailies with circulation under 4,000 (4) Dailies with circulation of 4,000 or over	*Citations*	
Crossman Award	Excellence in editorial writing	*Trophy*	School of Journalism, University of Colorado, Boulder, Colo.
Heinsohn Awards	Excellence in typography and presswork (1) Weeklies with circulation under 1,100 (2) Weeklies with circulation of 1,100 or over (3) Dailies with circulation under 4,000 (4) Dailies with circulation of 4,000 or more	*Trophy and certificates*	Colorado Press Association, 1445 Court Place, Denver 2, Colo.
University of Colorado Awards	Editorial excellence of newspaper	*Plaque*	School of Journalism, University of Colorado, Boulder, Colo.
	Outstanding Colorado editor	*Plaque*	
	Outstanding service to community (1) Weeklies (2) Dailies	*Certificates of merit*	

FLORIDA

Name	Classification	Award	Address
Florida Press Association Awards	Best advertising promotion	*Plaque*	Florida Press Association, 337 Stadium, University of Florida, Gainesville, Fla.
	Best original column	*Plaque*	
	Best editorial on any subject	*Oscar*	
	Best safety editorial	*Plaque*	
	Best feature story	*Trophy*	
	General excellence (1) Weeklies with circulation over 3,000 (2) Weeklies with circulation from 2,000 to 3,000 (3) Weeklies with circulation from 1,500 to 2,000 (4) Weeklies with circulation under 1,500 (5) Semiweeklies and triweeklies	*Plaques*	
	Best newspaper printed by offset process	*Trophy*	
	Best feature picture	*Plaque*	
	Best sports picture	*Plaque*	
	Best use of illustrative material	*Merchandise*	
	Best news photo (1) Weeklies with circulation over 3,000 (2) Weeklies with circulation from 2,000 to 3,000 (3) Weeklies with circulation from 1,500 to 2,000 (4) Weeklies with circulation under 1,500 (5) Semiweeklies and triweeklies	*Plaques*	
	Daily newspaper performing greatest public service	*Cash prize*	
	Daily or weekly for outstanding community service	*Plaque*	
	Best news story	*Plaque*	
	Use of news, pictures and editorials in presenting material pertaining to farm life	*Plaque*	
	Best typography and makeup (1) Weeklies with circulation of 3,000 or over (2) Weeklies with circulation from 2,000 to 3,000 (3) Weeklies with circulation from 1,500 to 2,000 (4) Weeklies with circulation under 1,500 (5) Semiweeklies and triweeklies	*Plaques*	
University of Miami Award through Florida Press Association	Best use of illustrations by newspapers	*Bronze plaque*	Journalism Department, University of Miami, Miami, Fla.

GEORGIA

Name	Classification	Award	Address
Georgia Press Association Awards	Editorial page excellence	*Trophy and certificates*	Georgia Press Association, 24 Ivy St., SE, Atlanta 3, Ga.
	General excellence (1) Weeklies with circulation 2,000 or more (2) Weeklies with less than 2,000 circulation (3) Dailies with circulation of 20,000 or more (4) Dailies with circulation less than 20,000	*Plaques*	
	Newspapers ranking highest in local pictures (1) Weeklies (2) Dailies	*Trophies*	
	Weekly for best use of feature material	*Trophy*	
H. H. Dean Award	Newspaper for best editorial	*Trophy*	"
Hal M. Stanley Award	Weekly presenting most attractive typographical appearance	*Trophy*	"
National Conference of Christians and Jews Award	Best editorial on cooperative understanding among Protestants, Catholics and Jews	*$50*	"
Otis Brumby Awards	Best editorial column on variety of subjects (1) Weeklies with circulation more than 2,000 (2) Weeklies with circulation 2,000 or less (3) Dailies with circulation more than 20,000 (4) Dailies with circulation 20,000 or less	*Trophy*	"
Salvation Army Awards	Best religious editorial (1) Dailies (2) Weeklies	*$50*	"
Sam W. Wilkes Awards	Best display advertising (1) Weekly (2) Daily	*Trophies*	"
Theron S. Shope Awards	Most fearless editorial (1) Dailies (2) Weeklies	*Trophies*	"
W. G. Sutlive Awards	Newspaper for outstanding community service (1) Weeklies (2) Dailies	*Trophy*	"
W. Trox Bankston Awards	Best local news coverage (1) Weekly judged best in local news coverage (2) Weekly giving best coverage of society (3) Weekly giving best coverage of sports	*Trophies*	"

ILLINOIS

Name	Classification	Award	Address
Edward Scott Beck Memorial Awards	Members of Chicago *Tribune* staff for outstanding work	*$500 each*	Chicago *Tribune*, 435 N. Michigan Ave., Chicago 11, Ill.
Elijah Parrish Lovejoy Award	Recognition of courage in weekly journalism	*Plaque*	Department of Journalism, Southern Illinois University, Carbondale, Ill.
Illinois Press Association Awards	Best advertising idea	*Plaque*	Illinois Press Association, 119 Gregory Hall, Urbana, Ill.
	Best original column (1) Newspapers with circulation under 3,500 (2) Newspapers with circulation 3,500 or over	*Plaques*	
	Best local editorials Same classes as above	*Plaques*	
	Best feature story Same classes as above	*Plaques*	
	General excellence (1) Weeklies and semiweeklies with circulation under 2,000 (2) Weeklies and semiweeklies with circulation from 2,000 to 5,000 (3) Weeklies and semiweeklies with circulation over 5,000 (4) Dailies with circulation under 15,000 (5) Dailies with circulation of 15,000 or over	*Plaques*	
	Best use of illustrative material (1) Newspapers with circulation under 3,500 (2) Newspapers with circulation 3,500 or more	*Plaques*	
	Excellence in news photography (1) News, feature or sports photographs (2) Human interest photographs	*Plaques*	
	Newspaper for outstanding service to community	*Plaque*	
	Best news story (1) Newspapers with circulation under 3,500 (2) Newspapers with circulation 3,500 or over	*Trophies*	
	Best typography and makeup Same classes as above	*Plaques*	
Illinois Press Association Editor-of-the-Year Award	Editor or publisher for outstanding achievements and distinguished service to the community	*Trophy*	"
Will Loomis Memorial Award	Most outstanding Illinois weekly or semiweekly	*Plaque*	"

IOWA

Name	Classification	Award	Address
Alpha Delta Sigma Awards	Iowa weekly and semiweekly for excellence in advertising layout and design	*Certificates*	School of Journalism, State University of Iowa, Iowa City, Iowa
Iowa Press Association Awards	Best advertising idea	*Plaque*	Iowa Press Association, 511 Shops Bldg., Des Moines 9, Iowa
	General excellence (1) All weeklies and semiweeklies (2) Weeklies in cities with population from 1,400 to 3,000 (3) Weeklies in towns with population between 800 and 1,400 (4) Weeklies in towns with population less than 800	*Trophies*	
	Best news picture	*Prize by Graflex*	
	Master Editor-Publishers	*Plaques*	
Kippa Tau Alpha Award	Outstanding alumnus of State University of Iowa	*Picture in Hall of Fame*	School of Journalism, State University of Iowa, Iowa City, Iowa
Sigma Delta Chi Awards	Outstanding service to agriculture	*Plaque*	Department of Technical Journalism, Iowa State University, Ames, Iowa
	Outstanding community service	*Plaque*	
	Excellence in column writing (1) Dailies (2) Weeklies	*Certificates*	School of Journalism, State University of Iowa, Iowa City, Iowa
	Editorial excellence (1) Weeklies (2) Dailies	*Certificates*	
State University of Iowa Awards	Best use of illustrative material	*Certificate*	"
	General excellence in typography (1) Weeklies (2) Semiweeklies	*Certificates*	
	Greatest general improvement in typography	*Certificate*	
Theta Sigma Phi Awards	Best coverage of women's news (1) Dailies (2) Weeklies	*Certificates*	"

KANSAS

Name	Classification	Award	Address
Kansas Press Association Awards	Best advertising campaign (1) Weeklies with circulation less than 1,000 (2) Weeklies with circulation between 1,000 and 2,000 (3) Weeklies with circulation over 2,000 (4) Dailies with circulation less than 4,000 (5) Dailies with circulation between 4,000 and 10,000 (6) Dailies with circulation over 10,000	*Plaques*	Kansas Press Association, 701 Jackson St., Topeka, Kans.
	Best classified advertising section (1) Dailies with circulation less than 4,000 (2) Dailies with circulation between 4,000 and 10,000 (3) Dailies with circulation over 10,000	*$100 scholarship and plaques*	
	Excellence in column writing (1) Weeklies with less than 1,000 circulation (2) Weeklies with circulation from 1,000 to 2,000 (3) Weeklies with circulation over 2,000 (4) Dailies with less than 4,000 circulation (5) Dailies with circulation from 4,000 to 10,000 (6) Dailies with circulation more than 10,000	*$100 scholarship and plaques*	
	Best editorial Same classes as above	*$100 scholarship and plaques*	
	General excellence (1) Weeklies with circulation less than 1,000 (2) Weeklies with circulation from 1,000 to 3,000 (3) Weeklies with circulation over 3,000 (4) Dailies with circulation less than 4,000 (5) Dailies with circulation from 4,000 to 10,000 (6) Dailies with more than 10,000 circulation	*$100 scholarship and plaques*	
	Best news and feature pictures (1) Weeklies with circulation less than 1,000 (2) Weeklies with circulation from 1,000 to 2,000 (3) Weeklies with circulation over 2,000 (4) Dailies with circulation less than 4,000 (5) Dailies with circulation from 4,000 to 10,000 (6) Dailies with circulation over 10,000	*$100 scholarship and plaques*	
	Best presentation of farm interests and activities in news, editorials, pictures and features (1) Weeklies with circulation less than 1,000 (2) Weeklies with circulation from 1,000 to 2,000 (3) Weeklies with circulation more than 2,000	*$100 scholarship and trophies*	

Name	Classification	Award	Address
	Excellence in special writing, including features, women's page and sports page (1) Dailies with circulation less than 4,000 (2) Dailies with circulation from 4,000 to 10,000 (3) Dailies with circulation more than 10,000	*$100 scholarships and plaques*	
	Excellence in presswork, typography and makeup (1) Weeklies with circulation less than 1,000 (2) Weeklies with circulation from 1,000 to 2,000 (3) Weeklies with circulation over 2,000 (4) Dailies with circulation less than 4,000 (5) Dailies with circulation from 4,000 to 10,000 (6) Dailies with circulation over 10,000	*Trophies*	
	Newsworthiness of country correspondence (1) Weeklies with circulation less than 1,000 (2) Weeklies with circulation between 1,000 and 2,000 (3) Weeklies with circulation of 2,000 or more	*$100 scholarship and plaque*	
	Outstanding service to journalism and community	*Certificate*	

KENTUCKY

Name	Classification	Award	Address
Enoch Graham Memorial Award	Member of Kentucky Press Association for editorial excellence	*Plaque*	School of Journalism, University of Kentucky, Lexington, Ky.

LOUISIANA

Name	Classification	Award	Address
Louisiana State University Award	Winning newspaper in Louisiana Community Service Contest	*Plaque*	Sigma Delta Chi Chapter, Journalism Department, Louisiana State University, Baton Rouge, La.

MARYLAND

Name	Classification	Award	Address
Maryland Press Association Awards	Best editorial (1) Weeklies with less than 5,000 circulation (2) Weeklies with circulation of 5,000 or more (3) Dailies	*Plaques and certificates*	Maryland Press Association, Journalism Bldg., University of Maryland, College Park, Md.
	General excellence (1) Weeklies with less than 3,000 circulation (2) Weeklies with 3,000 circulation or more (3) Dailies	*Trophy and certificates*	
	Best news pictures (1) Weeklies with circulation less than 5,000 (2) Weeklies with circulation of 5,000 or more (3) Dailies	*Certificates*	
	Outstanding community service Same classes as above	*Plaques and certificates*	
	Excellency in typography Same classes as above	*Plaques and certificates*	

MICHIGAN

Name	Classification	Award	Address
Michigan Press Association Awards	To advertising manager of daily who presents ad idea most easily used by other newspapers	*Plaque*	Michigan Press Association, 257 Michigan Ave., East Lansing, Mich.
	Michigan weekly for general excellence	*Certificate*	

	Outstanding photography
	(1) Dailies with circulation above 75,000
	(2) Dailies with circulation from 25,000 to 75,000
	(3) Dailies with circulation up to 25,000
	(4) Weeklies with full-time photographers
	(5) Weeklies with part-time photographers:
	  1. Picture portfolio
	  2. Spot-news picture
	  3. General news picture
	  4. Feature picture story
	  5. News picture story
	  6. Feature picture
	  7. Sports picture
	  8. Pictorial
	  9. Portrait and personality
	  10. Family interest picture
	  11. Colored picture
	  12. Picture sequence
		Certificates	

MISSISSIPPI

Name	Classification	Award	Address
Mississippi Press Association Awards	Most effective and ingenious promotion of (1) Daily (2) Weekly	*Plaques*	Mississippi Press Association, 316 E. Pearl St., Jackson, Miss.
	Outstanding editorial pages (1) Weeklies (2) Dailies	*Plaques and certificates*	
	General excellence (1) Dailies in cities with more than 25,000 population (2) Dailies in cities of 25,000 or less (3) Weeklies in towns of 3,500 population or more (4) Weeklies in cities with population from 2,000 to 3,500 (5) Weeklies in towns with less than 2,000 population	*Plaques and certificates*	
	Newspapers showing greatest over-all improvement (1) Weekly (2) Daily	*Plaques*	
	Outstanding community service	*Plaque and certificate*	
	Best special issue (1) Weeklies in cities with 3,500 population or more (2) Weeklies in cities with population of 2,000 to 3,500 (3) Weeklies in towns with population less than 2,000 (4) Dailies published in cities of more than 25,000 (5) Dailies published in cities of 25,000 or less	*Plaques and certificates*	

MISSOURI

Name	Classification	Award	Address
Lincoln University Awards	Significant contribution to better human relations	*Illuminated scroll*	Department of Journalism, Lincoln University, Jefferson City, Mo.
	Individual for outstanding performance in journalism	*Certificate of merit*	
Missouri Press Association Awards	Best personal column (1) Weeklies (2) Dailies	*Plaques*	Missouri Press Association, 115 Walter Williams Hall, Columbia, Mo.
	Best editorials Same classes as above	*Plaques*	
	General excellence (1) Weeklies with circulation of 2,000 or more (2) Weeklies with circulation less than 2,000 (3) Dailies	*Plaques*	
	Best local photograph	*Plaque*	
	Best use of local pictures	*Plaque*	
	Outstanding service to community (1) Weeklies (2) Dailies	*Plaques*	
	Best coverage of agriculture Same classes as above	*Plaques*	
	Best news story Same classes as above	*Plaques*	
	Excellence in typography Same classes as above	*Plaques*	
Poindexter Awards	Best advertisement sold to independent merchant in town with population less than 25,000	*Plaque and $40*	"
Soil Fertility and Plant Nutrition Council Award	Outstanding reporting and coverage of improved soil fertility and conservation practices	*Plaque*	"
University of Missouri Awards	Distinguished service in journalism (four to ten awards annually)	*Medals*	School of Journalism, University of Missouri, Columbia, Mo.

NEBRASKA

Name	Classification	Award	Address
Knights of Ak-Sar-Ben Awards	Member of Nebraska Press Association for outstanding service to agriculture	$100 and plaque	Nebraska Press Association, 129 N. 9th St., Lincoln, Nebr.
	Member of Nebraska Press Association for outstanding community service	$200 and plaque	
Nebraska Newspaper Promotion Award	Best newspaper promotion	Trophy	Nebraska Advertising Managers Association, 129 N. 9th St., Lincoln, Nebr.
Nebraska Press Association Awards	Editorial excellence	Certificate	Nebraska Press Association, 129 N. 9th St., Lincoln, Nebr.
	General excellence	$200 and plaque	
	Outstanding service to agriculture	Citation	
	Outstanding service to community	Citation	

NEVADA (See also California - Nevada)

Name	Classification	Award	Address
Nevada State Bar Association Awards	Editorial, story or series of presentations which best promote public understanding of the administration of justice	$100	Nevada Press Association, 633 Donner Drive, Reno, Nev.
Nevada State Press Association Awards	Best column	Certificate	"
	Best feature story	Certificate	
	Best news picture	Certificate	
	Outstanding community service (1) Dailies (2) Weeklies	Plaques	
	Best news or feature story by a woman reporter or regular correspondent for Nevada weekly or daily	Certificate	
	Excellence in typography (1) Dailies (2) Weeklies	Certificates	
Sigma Delta Chi Award	Best editorial on a Nevada subject	Plaque	"

NEW JERSEY

Name	Classification	Award	Address
Rutgers University Award	Outstanding service to state and university	Bronze medal	School of Journalism, Rutgers University, New Brunswick, N.J.

NEW MEXICO

Name	Classification	Award	Address
E. H. Shaffer Awards	Outstanding example of distinguished editorial writing	*$50 and certificate*	New Mexico Press Association, P. O. Box 1068, Carlsbad, N. M.
	Outstanding feature story	*$50 and certificate*	
	Outstanding sample of straight news story	*$50 and certificate*	
New Mexico Press Association Awards	Best display advertisements in dailies and weeklies	*Cups and cash prizes of $25, $15, and $10*	"
	Best feature picture	*$25 and certificate*	
	Best news picture	*$25 and certificate*	
	Best picture story	*$25 and certificate*	
	Best sports picture	*$25 and certificate*	
	Greatest service to community or state	*$50 and certificate*	
	Excellence in typography	*Trophy*	

NEW YORK

Name	Classification	Award	Address
George Polk Memorial Awards	Outstanding community service	*Plaque*	Long Island University, 385 Flatbush Ave., Brooklyn 1, N. Y.
	Outstanding news photography	*Plaque*	
	Distinguished local reporting	*Plaque*	
	Distinguished national reporting	*Plaque*	
	Foreign reporting	*Plaque*	
New York Press Association Awards	Outstanding newspaper promotion	*Trophy*	New York Press Association, Journalism Center, Syracuse University, Syracuse 10, N. Y.
	Advertising excellence	*Trophy*	
	Outstanding classified advertising	*Trophy*	
	Best column	*Trophy*	

Name	Classification	Award	Address
	Excellence in commercial printing (1) Letterhead and envelope (2) Booklet or brochure	Trophies	
	Best editorial page	Trophy	
	Excellence in editorial writing	Trophy	
	Best single editorial	Trophy	
	Best feature story	Trophy	
	Best use of feature material	Trophy	
	General excellence (1) Newspapers with less than 1,500 circulation (2) Newspapers with circulation between 1,500 and 3,000 (3) Newspapers with circulation over 3,000 (4) Tabloids	Trophies	
	Best feature picture	Trophy	
	Best original, creative photograph idea	Trophy	
	Best spot-news picture	Trophy	
	Best use of pictures	Trophy	
	Best picture layout	Trophy	
	Best news story	Trophy	
	Best special edition	Plaque	
	Champion country correspondent	Trophy	
	Outstanding community service	Trophy	
New York State Bar Awards	Constructive contributions to the administration of justice	$250 and bronze plaque	New York State Bar Association, 99 Washington Ave., Albany 10, N. Y.
Saint Bonaventure University Award	Outstanding member of press in western New York State	Citation	Department of Journalism, St. Bonaventure University, St. Bonaventure, N. Y.
Syracuse University Award	Outstanding service in the field of journalism	Medal	School of Journalism, Syracuse University, Syracuse 10, N. Y.

NORTH CAROLINA

Name	Classification	Award	Address
Associated Dailies Awards	General excellence in editorials	*$200 in cash prizes*	North Carolina Press Association, Box 1050, Chapel Hill, N. C.
North Carolina Press Association Awards	Excellence in editorial writing (1) Weeklies (2) Semiweeklies (3) Dailies	*$200 in cash prizes*	"
	Excellence in feature writing Same classes as above	*$200 in cash prizes*	
	Daily for outstanding service to local community	*Plaque*	
	Excellence in spot reporting (1) Dailies (2) Weeklies (3) Semiweeklies	*$200 in cash prizes*	
	Dailies for general excellence in covering sports	*$200 in cash prizes*	
William T. Polk Memorial Award	Excellence in reporting industrial and business news	*Trophy*	"

OHIO

Name	Classification	Award	Address
Bowling Green State University Award	Publisher or editor in weekly area who has given thirty or more years of public service in the newspaper industry	*Certificate of merit*	Journalism Dept., Bowling Green State University, Bowling Green, Ohio
Hooper Memorial Award	Weekly for outstanding community service	*Silver plaque*	School of Journalism, Ohio State University, Columbus, Ohio
Kent State University Awards	Northeastern Ohio newspaper for best use of pictures	*Certificate*	School of Journalism, Kent State University, Kent, Ohio
	Press photographers who have contributed significantly to the field on a national scale	*Citations*	
Ohio State University Award	Distinguished service by editors and publishers	*Election to Ohio journalism Hall of Fame, and citation*	School of Journalism, Ohio State University, Columbus, Ohio

OKLAHOMA

Name	Classification	Award	Address
Oklahoma Press Association Awards	Best classified page or section (1) Dailies published on rotary or stereotype press (2) Dailies published on flat-bed press	*Cash, ribbons, and certificates*	Oklahoma Press Association, Biltmore Hotel, Oklahoma City, Okla.
	Best advertising sold by newspaper (1) Dailies printed on rotary or stereotype press (2) Dailies printed on flat-bed press (3) Weeklies published in towns of 3,501 population or more (4) Weeklies published in towns of 1,501 to 3,500 population (5) Weeklies published in towns of 1,500 population or less	*Cash, ribbons, and certificates*	
	Excellence in column writing Same classes as above	*Cash, ribbons, and certificates*	
	Newspapers that excel in editorial writing Same classes as above	*$15*	
	Best news features in dailies (1) Papers printed on rotary or stereotype press (2) Papers printed on flat-bed press	*Cash, ribbons, and plaques*	
	General excellence (1) Dailies printed on rotary or stereotype press (2) Dailies printed on flat-bed press (3) Weeklies published in towns of more than 3,500 population (4) Weeklies published in towns with populations from 1,501 to 3,500 (5) Weeklies published in towns of 1,500 or less	*Cash, ribbons, and certificates*	
	General excellence in news and feature pictures Same classes as above	*$50 savings bonds*	
	Best coverage of farm news (1) Weeklies published in towns with population of 3,500 or more (2) Weeklies published in towns with population between 1,500 and 3,500 (3) Weeklies published in towns of 1,500 or less	*Cash, ribbons, and certificates*	

OKLAHOMA, Continued

Name	Classification	Award	Address
Oklahoma Press Association Awards	Excellence in presswork, typography and makeup (1) Weeklies printed on rotary or stereotype press (2) Weeklies printed on flat-bed press (3) Dailies published in towns of 3,501 population or more (4) Weeklies published in towns with population from 1,501 to 3,500 (5) Weeklies published in towns of 1,500 population or less	*Cash, ribbons, and certificates*	Oklahoma Press Association, Biltmore Hotel, Oklahoma City, Okla.
	Excellence in country correspondence (1) Weeklies published in towns of 3,501 or more (2) Weeklies published in towns of 1,501 to 3,500 population (3) Weeklies published in towns of 1,500 or less population	*Cash, ribbons, and certificates*	

OREGON

Name	Classification	Award	Address
Amos E. Voorhies Award	Newspaperman for outstanding journalistic achievement in public interest or in the interest of the welfare and honor of the journalistic profession	*Plaque*	Oregon Newspaper Publishers Association, Journalism Bldg., Eugene, Ore.

PENNSYLVANIA

Name	Classification	Award	Address
Pennsylvania State University Awards	Publishers for long and distinguished service	*Parchment scrolls*	Department of Journalism, Pennsylvania State University, University Park, Pa.
Pennsylvania Women's Press Association Awards	Member for best local column	*Engraved certificate*	Pennsylvania Women's Press Association, 252 W. 4th St., Williamsport, Pa.
	Member for outstanding community service feature	*Engraved certificate*	
	Member writing best editorial	*Engraved certificate*	
	Member for best feature story	*Engraved certificate*	
	Member for best photographic feature produced	*Engraved certificate*	
	Member for best general news story	*Engraved certificate*	
	Member for best coverage of social events	*Engraved certificate*	
	Newswoman of the year	*$100 U. S. savings bond*	
Temple University Award	Newspaper whose work during the year has been distinguished for its educational values	*Citation*	Department of Journalism and Communications, Temple University, Philadelphia, Pa.

TENNESSEE

Name	Classification	Award	Address
Edward J. Meeman Awards	Five weeklies that rank highest in all annual contests	*$100 each*	Tennessee Press Association, P. O. Box 8123, Knoxville, Tenn.
Tennessee Press Association Awards	Newspaper using the most original idea or local campaign in its advertising columns	*Trophy*	"
	Newspaper that publishes most distinguished editorials (1) Weeklies with circulation of 2,000 or less (2) Weeklies with circulation of 2,001 or more (3) Dailies with circulation of 25,000 or less	*$100*	
	Best single editorial (1) Weeklies and semiweeklies (2) Dailies	*Certificates*	
	Excellence in locally prepared feature material (1) Weeklies with circulation of 2,000 or less (2) Weeklies with circulation of 2,001 or more (3) Dailies with circulation of 25,000 and less	*Plaques*	
	Newspaper showing greatest improvement in news coverage, writing, makeup, editorial vigor and business enterprise	*Plaque*	
	Best local picture (1) Weeklies and semiweeklies with circulation of 2,000 or less (2) Weeklies and semiweeklies with circulation of 2,001 or more (3) Dailies with circulation of 25,000 or less	*Plaques and certificates*	
	Newspaper that has accomplished most in promoting welfare in its community (1) Weeklies with circulation of 2,000 or less (2) Weeklies with circulation of more than 2,000 (3) Dailies with circulation of 25,000 or less	*Plaques*	
	Best society section, open to all weeklies, semiweeklies and triweeklies	*Plaque*	
	Newspapers showing excellence in makeup, typography and general appearance (1) Weeklies with circulation of 2,000 or less (2) Weeklies with circulation of 2,001 or more (3) Dailies with circulation of 25,000 or less	*Plaques*	

TEXAS

Name	Classification	Award	Address
Panhandle Press Association Awards	Best column	*Plaque and certificate*	Panhandle Press Association, Box 518, Canadian, Tex.
	Excellence in commercial printing	*Plaque and certificates*	
	Best editorial published in newspapers of Texas Panhandle	*Plaque and certificates*	
	Excellence in presswork and typography	*Plaque and certificate*	
	Best special edition	*Plaque and certificate*	
Texas Gulf Coast Press Association Awards	Excellence in advertising copy and layout	*Plaque*	Texas Gulf Coast Press Association, c/o Houston Post, Houston, Tex.
	Best promotion of agriculture through news coverage and editorials	*Plaque*	
	Best column	*Plaque*	
	Best editorial page	*Plaque*	
	Best all-round newspaper	*Plaque*	
	Best news picture	*Plaque*	
	Newspaper sponsoring outstanding community project during the year	*Plaque*	
Texas Press Association Awards	Best column (1) Dailies with tubular or rotary press (2) All other dailies (3) Semiweeklies (4) Weeklies published in towns of 6,001 population or more (5) Weeklies published in towns of 3,501 to 6,000 population (6) Weeklies published in towns of 2,001 to 3,500 population (7) Weeklies published in towns of 2,000 population or less	*Plaques and certificates*	Texas Press Association, 1716 San Antonio St., Austin, Tex.
	Excellence in editorial writing Same classes as above	*Plaques and certificates*	
	Excellence in news writing Same classes as above	*Plaques and certificates*	
	Excellence in news pictures Same classes as above	*Plaques, trophies, and certificates*	
	Readability, originality, typography and general makeup Same classes as above	*Trophies*	

UTAH

Name	Classification	Award	Address
Utah State Agricultural Awards	Weekly for outstanding community leadership	*Plaque and certificate*	Utah State Agricultural College, Logan, Utah

VIRGINIA

Name	Classification	Award	Address
Copeland Memorial Award	Daily or weekly newspaper for outstanding community service	*Plaque*	Virginia Press Association, 510–514 Virginia Bldg., Richmond 19, Va.
Virginia Press Association Awards	Excellence in handling display advertising (1) Dailies with circulation up to 10,000 (2) Dailies with circulation between 10,000 and 25,000 (3) Dailies with circulation above 25,000 (4) Weeklies with circulation up to 2,000 (5) Weeklies with circulation between 2,000 and 3,000 (6) Weeklies with circulation above 3,000	*Plaques and certificates*	"
	Best local column (1) Dailies (2) Weeklies	*$25 savings bonds and certificates*	
	Best editorial (1) Dailies (2) Weeklies	*$25 savings bonds and certificates*	
	Best feature story (1) Dailies (2) Weeklies	*Plaques and certificates*	
	Best news photo	*Plaque*	
	Best feature photo	*Plaque*	
	Best sports photo	*Plaque*	
	Best news stories (1) Dailies (2) Weeklies	*Plaques*	
	Best news service staff writing	*Plaque*	
	Best combination news and picture story	*Plaque and certificate*	
	Best series of articles (1) Dailies (2) Weeklies	*Plaques and certificates*	

VIRGINIA, Continued

Name	Classification	Award	Address

Virginia Press Association Awards	Excellence in general makeup
	  (1) Dailies with circulation up to 10,000
	  (2) Dailies with circulation from 10,000 to 25,000
	  (3) Dailies with circulation above 25,000
	  (4) Weeklies with circulation up to 2,000
	  (5) Weeklies with circulation from 2,000 to 3,000
	  (6) Weeklies with circulation above 3,000
		Plaques and certificates	Virginia Press Association, 510–514 Virginia Bldg., Richmond 19, Va.

	Excellence in presswork Same classes as above	*Plaques and certificates*	

	Best sports writing
	  (1) Dailies
	  (2) Weeklies
		Plaques	

WEST VIRGINIA

Name	Classification	Award	Address

Press Club of Charleston Awards	Best news writing
	  (1) Dailies with circulation over 10,000
	  (2) Dailies with circulation of 10,000 and under
	  (3) Weeklies with circulation over 2,000
	  (4) Weeklies with circulation of 2,000 and under
		Plaques	West Virginia Press Association, Martin Bldg., Morgantown, W.Va.

West Virginia Education Award	News writer for best news or feature story of a teacher or teaching situation	*Plaque*	"

West Virginia Press Association Awards	Best advertising layout
	  (1) Dailies with circulation over 10,000
	  (2) Dailies with circulation of 10,000 or under
	  (3) Weeklies with circulation over 2,000
	  (4) Weeklies with circulation of 2,000 or less
		Plaques	"

	Best local column Same classes as above	*Certificates*	

Name	Classification	Award	Address
	Best editorial based on general excellence in writing and handling subject matter Same classes as above	*Plaques and merit awards*	West Virginia Press Association, Martin Bldg., Morgantown, W.Va.
	Best feature writing Same classes as above	*Plaques*	
	Newspaper photographer for best news feature or sports photograph	*Plaque*	
	Best photograph, women's page	*Plaque*	
	Best photographs (1) Dailies with circulation over 10,000 (2) Dailies with circulation of 10,000 and under (3) Weeklies with circulation over 2,000 (4) Weeklies with circulation of 2,000 or under	*Certificate*	
	Greatest contribution to community service Same classes as above	*Plaques*	
	Best example of court news reporting Same classes as above	*Certificate*	
	Best story or series of stories presenting West Virginia as an ideal location for new and expanding industry Same classes as above	*$50*	
	Best sports column Same classes as above	*Plaques*	
	Sports writer for best sports writing Same classes as above	*Certificates*	
	Best wire news coverage	*Plaque*	
West Virginia Sportsmen Unlimited Award	News writer for best story dealing with conservation or wildlife in West Virginia	*Plaque*	``
Women's Club of Charleston Awards	West Virginia woman writer for best local column	*Plaque*	`
	Woman writer for best feature story appearing in women's section	*Plaque*	

WISCONSIN

Name	Classification	Award	Address
Wisconsin Press Association Awards	Excellence in advertising typography (1) Weeklies with circulation more than 2,500 (2) Weeklies with 2,500 circulation or less (3) Weeklies with less than 1,000 circulation	*$25, $15, and $10*	Wisconsin Press Association, 235 Washington Bldg., Madison 3, Wis.
	Best local column	*Bronze plaque*	
	Best editorial (1) Weeklies with more than 2,000 circulation (2) Weeklies with circulation or 2,000 or less	*Bronze plaques*	
	Best editorial page Same 2 classes as above	*Bronze plaques*	
	Best farm editorial	*Bronze plaque*	
	Best farm feature story	*Plaque*	
	General excellence (1) Weeklies with more than 2,500 circulation (2) Weeklies with circulation from 1,000 to 2,500 (3) Weeklies with less than 1,000 circulation	*Plaques*	
	Newspaper showing greatest improvement	*Bronze plaque*	
	Best sports action photo	*Bronze plaque*	
	Excellence in photography	*$25, $15, and $10*	
	Best news story covering governmental affairs	*Bronze plaque*	
	Best newspaper typography	*$25, $15, and $10*	

WYOMING

Name	Classification	Award	Address
Hanway Award	Weekly for outstanding community service	*Ribbon and certificate*	Wyoming Press Association, 318 S. 11th St., Laramie, Wyo.
Heinsohn Awards	Dailies for typographical and printing excellence	*Ribbons and certificates*	"
Railroads of Wyoming Award	Newspaper contributing most toward bringing new industry into state	*Plaque*	"
Supplymen's Awards	Weeklies for typographical and printing excellence	*Ribbon and certificate*	"
University of Wyoming Award	Editorial leadership Alternates annually between weeklies and dailies	*Plaque*	Department of Journalism, University of Wyoming, Laramie, Wyo.
Wayne Winters Award	Excellence in local news and feature photography	*Trophy*	Wyoming Press Association, 318 S. 11th St., Laramie, Wyo.
Wyoming Trucking Association Award	Newspaper contributing most to highway safety	*Trophy*	"
Wyoming Press Association Awards	Best two-color advertisement	*Ribbon and certificate*	"
	Best newspaper promotion	*Ribbon and certificate*	
	Best full-page ad with local picture	*Ribbon and certificate*	
	Best community-type advertisement (multiple sponsored for a community project)	*Ribbon and certificate*	
	Best classified advertising page	*Ribbon and certificate*	
	Best change-of-pace ad	*Ribbon and certificate*	
	Best local column	*Ribbon and certificate*	
	Best teen-age column	*Ribbon and certificate*	
	Best local editorial	*Ribbon and certificate*	
	Best change-of-pace editorial	*Ribbon and certificate*	
	Best illustrated feature	*Ribbon and certificate*	

WYOMING, Continued

Name	Classification	Award	Address
Wyoming Press Association Awards	Best illustrated feature series	*Ribbon and certificate*	Wyoming Press Association, 318 S. 11th St., Laramie, Wyo.
	General excellence in feature photography	*Ribbon and certificate*	
	Best feature story	*Ribbon and certificate*	
	Daily for outstanding community service	*Ribbon and certificate*	
	Best women's page	*Ribbon and certificate*	
	Best sports page	*Ribbon and certificate*	
	Best sports column	*Ribbon and certificate*	
	Best use of correspondent's material	*Ribbon and certificate*	

FELLOWSHIPS and SCHOLARSHIPS

Name	Classification	Award	Address
Advanced Science Writing Fellowships	Representatives of newspapers, wire services, radio, television, magazines and industry	*Tuition, fees, additional funds for travel and living*	Graduate School of Journalism, Columbia University, New York 27, N. Y.
Clapp and Poliak Fellowships and Scholarships	Specialized training in economic writing and reporting	*$1,000 and $1,500*	Clapp and Poliak Foundation, Inc., 341 Madison Ave., New York, N. Y.
E. S. Fentress Graduate Fellowship	Graduate students in public affairs reporting in School of Journalism, University of Texas	*$1,200 annually*	Newspapers, Inc., Waco, Tex.
George A. Hough Memorial Scholarship	Advanced education in journalism	*$500*	Graduate School of Journalism, Columbia University, New York 27, N. Y.
Gilbert M. Hitchcock Scholarship	Advanced study in journalism	*$1,000*	"
Grantland Rice Fellowship Award	Exceptional sports reporting	*$1,500*	"
Julius Ochs Adler Memorial Scholarship	Advanced education in journalism	*$1,000 annually*	New York *Times*, New York, N. Y.
Louis Stark Fellowship	Excellence in labor reporting	*Fellowship*	Harvard University, Cambridge, Mass.
Newspaper Fund Fellowships	High school teachers to improve professional knowledge of journalism	*$1,000*	Newspaper Fund, Inc., 48 Wall St., New York 5, N. Y.
Nieman Fellowships	To promote and elevate standards of journalism in the United States, and to educate especially qualified journalists	*Fellowships*	Harvard University, Cambridge, Mass.
Pulitzer Traveling Fellowships	Students in Graduate School of Journalism, Columbia University, for study abroad	*$1,500*	Graduate School of Journalism, Columbia University, New York 27, N. Y.
U. S. Steel Graduate Fellowship	Two years of graduate study in journalism at the University of Missouri	*$3,000 to $4,200*	School of Journalism, University of Missouri, Columbia, Mo.
Walter Williams Memorial Fellowship	Two years of study in international press problems by graduate student proceeding toward Doctor of Philosophy degree	*$1,000*	"

Bibliography

Abel, Clarence Wallace, *Employee Profit Sharing and Stock Ownership in the Community Newspaper,* Master's thesis, University of Missouri, 1949.

Advertising Research Foundation of the Bureau of Advertising, *Continuing Study of Newspaper Reading,* American Newspaper Publishers Association, New York.

Albig, William, *Public Opinion,* McGraw-Hill, New York, 1939.

Allen, Charles L., *Free Circulation,* Louisiana State University Press, Baton Rouge, 1940.

Barnhart, Thomas F., *Newspaper Sales Promotion,* Burgess Publishing Co., Minneapolis, 1939.

———, *Weekly Newspaper Management,* Appleton-Century-Crofts, New York, 1952.

———, *Weekly Newspaper Writing and Editing,* Dryden Press, New York, 1949.

Baus, Herbert M., *Public Relations at Work,* Harper & Brothers, New York, 1948.

———, *Publicity in Action.* Harper & Brothers, New York, 1954.

Bedell, Clyde, *How To Write Advertising That Sells,* second ed., McGraw-Hill, New York, 1952.

Bellows, Roger Marion, *Psychology of Personnel in Business and Industry,* second ed., Prentice-Hall, New York, 1954.

Bernays, Edward L., *Propaganda,* Liveright Publishing Corp., New York, 1928.

———, *Public Relations,* University of Oklahoma Press, Norman, 1957.

Bridge, Don, *Men and Methods of Newspaper Advertising,* Arco Publishing Co., New York, 1947.

Broughton, Averell, *Careers in Public Relations,* E. P. Dutton and Company, New York, 1943.

Brown, Everett Martin, *A Study of Publicity Releases in Missouri Weekly Papers,* Master's thesis, University of Missouri, 1950.

Burnett, Verne, *You and Your Public,* Harper & Brothers, New York, 1943.

Center, Allen H., editor, *Public Relations Ideas in Action,* McGraw-Hill, New York, 1957.

Cheng, Hung-sheng, *Newspaper Personnel Relations Management,* Master's thesis, University of Missouri, 1949.

Childs, Harwood L., *An Introduction to Public Opinion,* John Wiley & Sons, Inc., New York, 1940.

Clary, Robert S., *71 Ways To Build Up Your Newspaper,* published by author, Los Angeles, 1951.

Conley, Chace, *Publicity and Its Relation to Selling,* Know-How Publishing Co., New York, 1954.

Cooper, Alfred M., *How To Supervise People,* third ed., McGraw-Hill, New York, 1952.

Cutlip, Scott M., and Center, Allen H., *Effective Public Relations,* second ed., Prentice-Hall, Englewood Cliffs, N.J., 1952.

Davenport, John Scott, *Newspaper Circulation — Backbone of the Industry,* Wm. C. Brown Co., Dubuque, Iowa, 1949.

Dyar, Ralph E., *Newspaper Promotion and Research,* Harper & Brothers, New York, 1942.

Eisen, Max, *How To Increase Daily Newspaper Circulation,* Columbia University Bookstore, New York, 1949.

Fader, Bob, *Role of National Advertising in Weekly Newspapers,* Montana State University School of Journalism, Missoula, 1951.

Feng, Hsi-liang, *Public Relations for Newspapers,* Master's thesis, University of Missouri, 1948.

Fitzgerald, Stephen E., *Communicating Ideas to the Public,* Funk & Wagnalls, New York, 1950.

Forsee, Joseph B., *A Study of 52 Former Newspaperboys To Determine Effects of Carrying Papers,* Master's thesis, University of Missouri, 1950.

Freese, Louise Julian, *Public Relations Departments of Certain Dailies,* Master's thesis, University of Missouri, 1953.

Ghiselli, Edwin Ernest, and Brown, Clarence, *Personnel and Industrial Psychology,* second ed., McGraw-Hill, New York, 1956.

Gill, Leslie Ernest, *Advertising and Psychology,* Longmans, New York, 1954.

Given, William B., *Bottom-up Management: People Working Together,* Harper & Brothers, New York, 1949.

Harlan, Gene, and Scott, Alan, *Contemporary Public Relations,* Prentice-Hall, New York, 1955.

Harlow, Rex F., and Black, Marvin M., *Practical Public Relations,* revised ed., Harper & Brothers, New York, 1952.

Harral, Stewart, *Patterns of Publicity Copy,* University of Oklahoma Press, Norman, 1950.

————, *Profitable Public Relations for Newspapers,* Edwards Brothers, Inc., Ann Arbor, Mich., 1957.

Hepner, Harry Walker, *Effective Advertising,* second ed., McGraw-Hill, New York, 1949.

Heron, Alexander, R., *Sharing Information with Employees,* Stanford University Press, Stanford, Calif., 1942.

Jefferson, C. K., *Carrier Leadership,* C. K. Jefferson Publications, Des Moines, Iowa, 1956.

Kleppner, Otto, *Advertising Procedure,* fourth ed., Prentice-Hall, New York, 1950.

Lee, Alfred McClung, *How To Understand Propaganda,* Rinehart, New York, 1952.

————, *The Daily Newspaper in America,* Macmillan, New York, 1937.

Lesly, Philip, editor, *Public Relations Handbook,* Prentice-Hall, New York, 1950.

Lund, John V., *Newspaper Advertising,* Prentice-Hall, New York, 1947.

McClure, Leslie W., *Newspaper Advertising and Promotion,* Macmillan, New York, 1950.

McDonald, Morton J., editor, *Principles and Practices of Classified Advertising,* Association for Newspaper Classified Advertising Managers, Inc., Murray and Gee, Culver City, Calif., 1952.

MacDougall, Curtis Daniel, *Understanding Public Opinion,* Macmillan, New York, 1952.

Maney, Richard, *Fanfare, the Confessions of a Press Agent,* Harper & Brothers, New York, 1957.

Michael, L. B., *Wage and Salary Fundamentals and Procedures,* McGraw-Hill, New York, 1950.

Moore, Herbert, *Psychology for Business and Industry,* second ed., McGraw-Hill, New York, 1942.

Mott, Frank Luther, *American Journalism,* revised ed., Macmillan, New York, 1950.

Nafziger, Ralph O., editor, *Journalism Research,* Louisiana State University Press, Baton Rouge, 1949.

National Newspaper Promotion Association, *Newspaper Promotion Primer,* Olsen Publishing Co., Milwaukee, 1955.

Newcomb, Robert, and Sammons, Marg, *Speak Up, Management,* Funk & Wagnalls, New York, 1951.

Parten, M. B., *Surveys, Polls and Samples: Practical Procedures,* Harper & Brothers, New York, 1950.

Pollard, James E., *Principles of Newspaper Management,* McGraw-Hill, New York, 1937.

Ramsberger, Jack F., *How To Make Publicity Work,* Reynal & Co., New York, 1948.

Reschke, Fitzpatrick, and Conrad, *The Newspaper in the Classroom,* North American Press and Milwaukee Journal, 1951.

Rucker, Frank W., *Newspaper Circulation — What, Where and How,* Iowa State University Press, Ames, 1958.

————, and Williams, Herbert Lee, *Newspaper Organization and Management,* Iowa State University Press, Ames, 1955.

Samstag, Nicholas, *Persuasion for Profit,* University of Oklahoma Press, Norman, 1957.

Sidey, Hugh, and Fox, Rodney, *1,000 Ideas for Better News Pictures,* Iowa State University Press, Ames, 1956.

Smith, Lloyd, *The Paper Route,* Burton Publishing Co., Kansas City, Mo.

Spriegel, W. R., and Lansburgh, Richard H., *Industrial Management,* fifth ed., John Wiley & Sons, New York, 1955.

Stephenson, Howard, and Pratzner, Wesley Fiske, *Publicity for Prestige and Profit,* McGraw-Hill, New York, 1953.

Texas Circulation Managers Association, *Newspaper Circulation,* Steck Company, Austin, 1948.

Texas Daily Newspaper Association, *Local News Coverage,* Austin, 1925.

Thayer, Frank, *Newspaper Business Management,* Prentice-Hall, Engelwood Cliffs, N.J., 1954.

Tredgold, Roger Francis, *Human Relations in Modern Industry,* International Universities Press, New York, 1950.

Winslow, Douglas Kenelm, *Editorial Publicity,* Pitman, London, 1954.

Wood, Donald J., *Newspaper Circulation Management, A Profession,* Newspaper Research Bureau, Oakland, Calif., 1952.

————, *Newspaper Personnel Relations,* Newspaper Research Bureau, Oakland, Calif., 1952.

Index

(Entries are by subject matter. Separate newspaper index begins on page 507)

Index of Newspapers,
by States